PALMISTRY
THE UNIVERSAL GUIDE

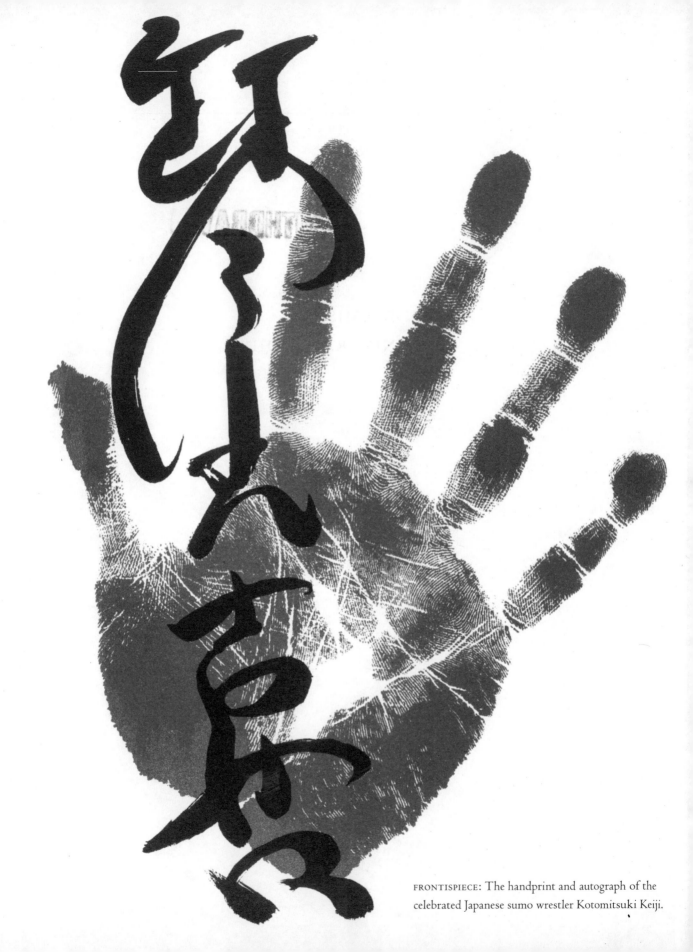

FRONTISPIECE: The handprint and autograph of the celebrated Japanese sumo wrestler Kotomitsuki Keiji.

# Palmistry

## THE UNIVERSAL GUIDE

Nathaniel Altman

STERLING

New York / London
www.sterlingpublishing.com

STERLING and the distinctive Sterling logo are registered trademarks of
STERLING PUBLISHING CO., INC.

**Library of Congress Cataloging-in-Publication Data**
Altman, Nathaniel, 1948-
  Palmistry : the universal guide / Nathaniel Altman.
      p. cm.
  Includes bibliographical references and index.
  ISBN 978-1-4027-4885-1 (hc-trade cloth : alk. paper)  I.  Palmistry.  I. Title.
  BF921.A465 2009
  133.6--dc22

                                                                    2009009736

10   9   8   7   6   5   4   3   2   1

Published by Sterling Publishing Co., Inc.
387 Park Avenue South, New York, NY 10016
© 2009 by Nathaniel Altman
Distributed in Canada by Sterling Publishing
C/o Canadian Manda Group, 165 Dufferin Street
Toronto, Ontario, Canada M6K 3H6
Distributed in the United Kingdom by GMC Distribution Services
Castle Place, 166 High Street, Lewes, East Sussex, England BN7 1XU
Distributed in Australia by Capricorn Link (Australia) Pty. Ltd.
P.O. Box 704, Windsor, NSW 2756, Australia

Book Design by Tamara Connolly
Art by Linda James, Igor V. Zevin, and Nathaniel Altman

STERLING ISBN 978-1-4027-4885-1

For information about custom editions, special sales, premium and
corporate purchases, please contact Sterling Special Sales
Department at 800-805-5489 or specialsales@sterlingpublishing.com.

# CONTENTS

# PREFACE

*Palmistry: The Universal Guide* is a comprehensive, authoritative, yet easy-to-read introduction to the fascinating art and science of hand analysis, popularly known as palmistry.

Though still widely viewed as a form of gypsy fortune-telling, hand analysis is gradually shedding its old sideshow image. Scientists at a number of major research centers, including the Galton Laboratory at University College in London and the Emory University School of Medicine in Atlanta, have investigated the medical and psychological meanings of the lines and skin ridge patterns of the hand, known as dermatoglyphics. In addition, a growing number of articles have been published about the medical and psychological significance of hand analysis in reputable peer-reviewed journals such as the *American Journal of Cardiology, Nature,* and *Gastroenterology.*

An increasing number of psychotherapists are viewing the hand as an important tool for self-knowing. They've discovered that the shape, contours, lines, nails, and skin ridge patterns of the hand enable them to better understand the character traits, health, and innate talents of their clients. In addition to revealing detailed information about an individual's personality, talents, health, career, relationships, and spirituality, the hands reflect present trends and future possibilities. By making lifestyle changes and adopting new perspectives, a person can actually make his or her hand lines change over time.

I first became interested in palmistry in 1968, while studying political science in South America. A friend was going to visit her cousin, who read hands, and invited me to join her. During the visit, her cousin read my hands, and I was deeply impressed by her insight and accuracy. After the reading, she mentioned that I might also become a good hand reader if I wanted to invest the time and effort. She recommended several books for me to read and offered to give me some basic instruction before I returned to the United States. By the time I left South America several months later, I had read the hands of more than a hundred people and had begun to collect handprints to observe whether any changes would occur in hands over time. Although there is certainly a predictive side to palmistry, I have always been interested primarily in the psychological aspects of hand analysis. In one minute, the hands can reveal personality traits that can take a trained psychotherapist months to uncover.

Over the years, my fascination with hands has continued to grow. In a sense, my study of palmistry—a discipline that I am still learning to this day—has been an amazing journey into understanding human nature as well as learning more about my own inner landscape.

This book is the product of almost forty years of research and experience. Focusing primarily on the Western palmistry tradition, *Palmistry: The Universal Guide* is based on five of my earlier published books on palmistry, including a collaborative project with the Australian palmist Andrew Fitzherbert and another with the late Eugene Scheimann, MD, a pioneer in the use of palmistry for medical diagnosis and health maintenance. Much new material has been added for this volume as well.

*Palmistry: The Universal Guide* is divided into six basic parts. The first section provides a thorough grounding in the essentials of hand analysis. The chapters that make up the first part focus on the meaning of hand shape and consistency and of the fingers, mounts, lines, and skin ridge patterns. The second part concentrates on the psychological aspects of hand reading and how they relate to our inner worlds of intelligence and character analysis. The third section focuses on love, sex, and relationships, while the fourth highlights medical palmistry. The fifth part is devoted to palmistry, life task, and spiritual fulfillment. The final section offers practical guidance on how to read hands, the taking of handprints, and organizing data. A detailed bibliography offers opportunities for further study.

# PART I PALMISTRY ESSENTIALS

# THE HAND AS HOLOGRAM

A HOLOGRAM OFFERS A THREE-DIMENSIONAL VIEW of reality. Taken together, the seemingly diverse aspects of the human hand create a type of living hologram that offers a multidimensional view of human nature and life potential.

When you look at your hands, what do you see? The most obvious characteristics are the fingers, the palm (along with the raised areas of the hand, such as the thumb ball), the color and texture of the skin, and at least three major lines, known in palmistry as the life line, the head line, and the heart line. If you look more closely, you can also notice the forms of your fingers, including their relative length, thickness, and flexibility and the way they bend toward or away from each other. If you have good eyesight (or use a magnifying glass), you can examine your fingerprints, the ever-changing network of smaller lines on the palm and fingers, and other patterns on the palm's surface, such as loops and whorls.

The human hand created our entire civilization and culture. It has ensured our survival through the years by fashioning implements for hunting, fishing, and farming. It has created every tool from a simple hammer to the most sophisticated electron microscope. With the aid of the hand, great ideas have been recorded that otherwise would have been lost to posterity. Exploration of outer space, as well as discoveries in microbiology, would not have been possible without the development of the hand-polished lens.

Through the harmonious cooperation of twenty-seven bones, dozens of muscles, and four major nerves, the human hand is a marvel of design and operation. The hands of a weight lifter can press hundreds of pounds, and the hands of karate masters can smash bricks and break a table in two. Yet the hand can perform the most delicate brain surgery, is capable of creating the finest needlepoint design, and can play as many as 960 notes per minute on a concert piano. Our hands express our love, our needs, and our desire to communicate. From the first moments of life, our hands are our basic link to the world and help us to learn and experience life.

## THE HAND IN HISTORY

The hand has fascinated us for thousands of years. Studies of the human hand—both as a tool for creative expression and as a mirror of our inner selves—go back more than five thousand years. It is believed that the ancient Chinese began studying the hand as early as 3000 BCE. Due to its unique composition, the palm has always been viewed as an important form of personal identification, as seen in Figure I.I, a legal document that gives the permission of a Taiwanese aboriginal chief to develop uncultivated land.

In India at the same time, Aryan sages developed a study of hand analysis called *hast samudrika shastra* as part of a larger science that interprets and forecasts human nature and destiny by scrutinizing the forehead, face, hands, chest, and feet. Writings related to the study of the human hand can be found in Indian literature dating back to 2000 BCE, while the earliest references to palmistry itself can be found in the ancient Vedic text *The Laws of Manu* (vi:50): "Neither by [explaining] prodigies and omens, nor by skill in astrology and palmistry, nor by giving advice and by the exposition [of the *shastras*], let him ever seek to obtain alms."

Although no written records remain, it is known that the ancient Chaldeans, Tibetans, and Babylonians studied the science of hand analysis, as did

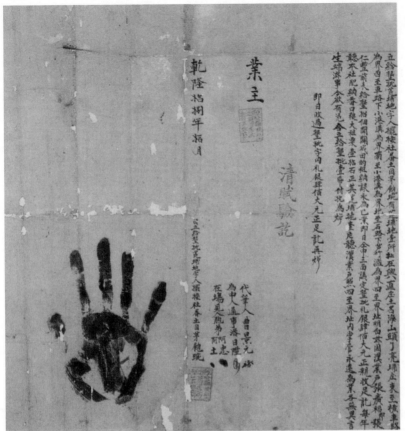

FIGURE 1.1. A permit to develop uncultivated land issued by Maobaowan of Patchieh to Chang Kuang-fu, 1753.

- Thumb: Keep the feast of Ramadan

- Index finger: Accomplish the pilgrimage to Mecca

- Middle finger: Give alms to the poor

- Ring finger: Perform all necessary ablutions

- Little finger: Oppose all infidels

Among the early Jews, hand reading (called *chochmat ha-yad*) was spoken of in the Zohar, the ancient compendium of kabbalistic wisdom. Among kabbalists, palmistry is the study of the secret codes within the lines on the palms of the hands. They believe that the Creator impressed spiritual mysteries on the palm and fingers of a person, and that every line and feature within a person's body and soul is a reflection of the Divine. According to volume 10, section 11, verse 136 of the Zohar,

*The lines of the hands are among the supernal mysteries, along with the fingers from the inside, that is, not on the side of the nails, but on the side of the flesh. In the hands, there are large lines and small, thin upper lines in the right. In the little finger on the right, there are thin impressions. This finger is fixed permanently on acts by the Other Side.*

A thirteenth-century drawing of an open hand with rabbinical notes relating to palmistry is reproduced in Figure 1.2.

The ancient Greeks, who were enthusiastic students of hand symbology and hand analysis, coined the term *chirosophy* (from *xier*, which means hand, and *sophia*, which means wisdom). Aristotle was

the early Egyptians and Persians. Throughout the Arab world today, hand reading, known as *ilm-ul-kaff*, remains a respected study and avocation.

Among modern Muslims, the hand is also considered important from a religious standpoint. It is seen as a sign of protection, and tiny models of hands often grace the sun visors of buses and automobiles in Arab countries. In the Muslim religion, the five fingers of the hand represent the different members of the holy family. The thumb symbolizes Muhammad, while the index finger represents the Lady Fatima. The middle finger stands for her husband, Ali, while the ring and little fingers symbolize Hassan and Hussein, respectively. The fingers of the hand also represent the five principal commandments of the Islamic faith:

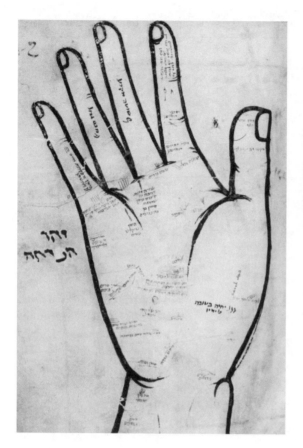

FIGURE 1.2. An open hand, with notes relating to palmistry, from a thirteenth-century French rabbinical manuscript.

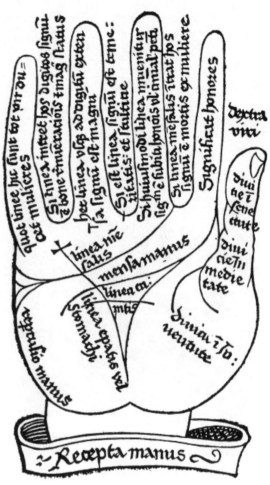

FIGURE 1.3. A page from *Chiromantia*, attributed to Aristotle. The edition in which this illustration appears was printed in Ulm in 1490.

supposed to have found an ancient Arabic document about chirosophy on an altar to Hermes. He is credited with having authored several specialized treatises on hands, including one written especially for Alexander the Great. Aristotle was particularly interested in the markings of the hand and the significance they have in our lives. In *De caelo* (On the heavens), he wrote, "The lines are not written into the human hands without reason; they come from heavenly influences and man's own individuality." A drawing of a hand from a translation of the book *Chiromantia*, attributed to Aristotle, can be seen in Figure 1.3.

Claudius Galen, Anaxagoras, Hippocrates, Artemidoros of Ephesus, and Claudius Ptolemaeus (commonly known as Ptolemy) were also serious students of both medical and psychological chirosophy as well as chiromancy, the art and science of foretelling the future by the lines of the hand.

The Holy Bible offers a wealth of references to the human hand and its significance. We find specific references to palmistry in Job 37:7 ("He sealeth up the hand of every man; that all men may know his work") and in Proverbs 3:16 ("Length of days is in her right hand; and in her left hand riches and honor"). Exodus 7:5 speaks of the hand as signifying God's presence and power, Ezra 7:9

as a sign of his benevolence, and Isaiah 8:11 as a conveyor of God's thoughts and wishes: "For the Lord spake thus to me with a strong hand, and instructed me that I should not walk in the way of this people."

The early Catholics saw a special meaning in the fingers of the hand. The thumb signified the chief person of the Godhead, while the index finger represented the Holy Ghost. The middle finger was seen as the Christ, while the ring and little fingers revealed his double nature—divine and human, respectively. Even today it is customary for a priest to bless his parishioners with the thumb, index finger, and middle finger raised, symbolizing the Father, the Son, and the Holy Ghost.

The hand has also enjoyed special religious significance in nearly every early world culture, including those of the Hindus, Buddhists, Egyptians, and Native Americans (Figure I.4). Prayer postures, including raising the hands and arms, holding the hands above the head, folding the hands, and clasping the hands, can be found in many of the sacred practices in the world's major religions. Mudras, or hand gestures, are essential to the performances of sacred dances in India and Bali. The symbolic hand movements of sorcerers, magicians, mystics, and priests in blessings, invocations, baptisms, and purification rituals have been known throughout the world.

FIGURE I.5. Healing light radiating from the hands of the Virgin Mary.

FIGURE I.4. Two open hands reaching for each other is the sign of peace among the Sioux.

Since the time of Jesus, the hand has also been considered important in the role of healing. As a bridge from the psychic to the somatic (physical) sphere, the hand is seen as a power center transmitting energy from one person to another.

The practice of laying on of hands has been a primary element in such diverse disciplines as shamanistic medicine in Nepal, Africa, North America, and Brazil and the healing ceremonies of the Roman Catholic Church. Among Roman Catholics, the hand has been seen as symbolizing the passion of Christ, and his hands (like those of Mary) have often been portrayed with healing light radiating from the palm and fingers (Figure I.5). The modern "therapeutic touch" techniques offered at the New York University School of Nursing and other institutions to doctors, nurses, and other health professionals are but the latest "hands-on" modalities of healing.

## HANDS: INFORMATION AND EXPRESSION

From our first days, the hands' tactile role in perceiving and recognizing surfaces is essential to our growth and psychological development. Children use touch to experience the people, objects, and spaces around them because hands are extremely sensitive to pressure, vibration, temperature, pain, and movement. In addition to being able to distinguish one substance or material from another (such as wool from polyester or cotton), the hands can tell—in an instant—whether a surface is hot, cold, wet, dry, sticky, oily, or moist.

Our sense of touch is essential for developing relationships with others. A simple handshake can provide volumes of information about another person; it can tell us whether he or she is warm, hostile, strong, friendly, supportive, or weak, all within a fraction of a second. Because our hands express our inner feelings toward one another, they can offer support, protection, comfort, and affection. The sensation of being touched by someone who loves us and cares about us can be among the most satisfying of experiences. Without the hands, human relationships would be limited and incomplete.

As a working tool, the hand is a magnificent piece of equipment. Because we have opposable thumbs, unlike some apes, we can hold objects, touch them on all sides at once, and use them as extensions of our hands. According to Professor John Napier, author of *Hands*:

> The movement of the thumb underlies all the skilled procedures of which the hand is capable. . . . Without the thumb, the hand is put back sixty million years in evolutionary terms to a stage when the thumb had no independent movement and was just another digit.[1]

Whether used for surgery, sports, massage, or calligraphy, the human hand is vital for its ability—in conjunction with the brain—to express who we are. Psychologists say that by the time we are twelve to fourteen months old, our hands have begun to express feelings of need, joy, sorrow, anger, surprise, and caring. They serve as vital components in everyday speech and enable us to express our deepest emotions to others.

The concept that our hands express who we are forms the foundation of chirology, or hand analysis (which is more psychologically oriented than predictive palmistry, or chiromancy). Although our manner of walking, facial expressions, and posture all express our inner being to some extent, the hands are far more expressive and specific and can reflect the essence of our lives with greater depth and accuracy than any other part of the body. This fact impressed the noted Swiss psychiatrist Carl Jung to such a degree that he decided to study psychochirology himself. In the introduction he prepared for *The Hands of Children* by Julius Spier, Jung wrote:

> Hands, whose shape and functioning are so intimately connected with the psyche, might provide revealing, and therefore interpretable expressions of psychological peculiarity, that is, of human character.[2]

Why is this?" As our basic instrument of touch, the hand plays a leading role in conditioning the brain, body, and emotions to develop certain responses to the world around us. In addition to being a mirror of our inherent genetic makeup, the hands can also reveal changing patterns of health, emotional stability, the development of talents, and major events that have been determined by the way we respond to our life experience. Since the lines of the hand have the ability to change, they offer us a special opportunity to monitor our life path and see into the past, the present, and the future.

Though thousands of years old, hand analysis is still a developing science. We do not know conclusively why and how the hands reveal what they do. Yet a complex system has evolved over the centuries that can show—through the study of the hand's shape, texture, contours, and lines—important information about our lives that can serve as a guidepost for self-understanding and personal fulfillment.

# ORIENTATION *chapter* 2

$W$HEN PEOPLE VISIT A HAND READER FOR A consultation, many questions often come to mind:

- How long will I live?

- When will I get married?

- Will I remain healthy?

- How many children will I have?

- Am I going to make lots of money?

Since the human hand can identify both present trends and future possibilities regarding health, career, personality, and relationships, many hand readers happily respond to these questions by making predictions about the future: "You will live to be sixty-five years old." "You will divorce by the time you are forty." "You will have three children." "You will make tons of money."

## TWO RULES

While it is always gratifying to receive specific answers to our questions, many hand readers may actually perform a disservice to their clients by making predictions. In addition to the possibility of being mistaken (which happens more often than many would care to admit), they forget two essential rules in palmistry:

1. The hand reveals tendencies, not always definite facts.

2. The lines in the hand can change over time.

Although obvious changes in the lines of the hand can be usually noticed over a one- or two-year period, I have seen major changes show up on a person's hand in as little as six weeks.

## WHAT CAN THE HAND REVEAL?

Like a hologram revealing several dimensions of reality, the hand can reveal our life situation in several basic ways.

First and foremost, it offers us a view of the genetic makeup we inherited from our parents, which reflects our ancestral gene pool. We can observe genetic traits not only through the size and shape of the hand, but by analyzing the fingers, nails, fingerprints, and other skin ridge patterns on the palm itself. Most of these characteristics cannot be changed, although some people can change the shape of their hands, reduce or increase the number of lines, and alter the strength and flexibility of their hands through heavy manual labor, working with chemicals, or weight lifting, especially if these activities are performed without gloves. A good hand reader will take these factors into consideration during a consultation.

Although we come into the world with a unique collection of lines, hand flexibility, nail form and color, and mounts on the palm (scientifically known as thenar elevations), these aspects of the hand can change over time as a result of environmental influences, including childhood experiences at home or in school, but also have to do with diet, exercise, stress management, and other lifestyle issues. As a result of these influences, lines may lengthen or become shorter, appear or disappear, break or mend. Mounts may become larger or smaller, and the nails may change in color and texture. Fingers may bend with time (whether due to personality changes or diseases such as arthritis), the color of the palm may become pale or reddish, and the hand itself may become more flexible. In some people, these features can change quite dramatically and are due to major life events or major changes in attitude, thinking, or lifestyle. They may or may not be due to a change in work habits, such as moving from an office job to one involving heavy physical labor.

By distinguishing between what is apparently "set in stone" and what can be changed over time, a reader can offer his or her client a balanced and genuinely useful hand analysis.

## A MATTER OF PERSPECTIVE

The way we interpret a line or other hand markings can make all the difference. For example, if a life line reveals a period of illness—such as heart disease, cancer, or food allergies—the hand reader can deal with this sign in one of two ways. He or she can say, "Your hand shows that you are going to have a heart attack when you are fifty years old," and leave it at that. If the reader happens to have made accurate statements regarding personality and work, the client will probably believe that a heart attack is inevitable. In addition to reacting to this unfortunate news with worry and despair (which can lead to stress-related diseases such as hypertension), the client may develop the belief that he does not have long to live and plan his life accordingly. This may lead him to decide not to take care of himself ("I'm going to die at fifty, so what's the use?") or not to become involved in a relationship ("What's the point in getting married, since I won't be around to see my children grow up?"), or he may decide to seek temporary employment as opposed to pursuing a fulfilling career.

Aware of the ever-changing nature of the human hand, a wiser hand consultant can observe the same problem in the hand and say instead, "If you don't take care of your health, I see a potential heart attack when you are fifty years old." This determination may be based on a broken life line, a broken heart line, or even genetic signs such as "watch-glass nails" or a highly placed axial triradius skin ridge pattern in the palm, which I discuss in Part IV.

However, a good reader understands that, like a doctor's findings in blood pressure or cholesterol levels, the hand reveals potential that *can be changed*. A low-fat, high-fiber diet, a healthy exercise regime, abstaining from smoking and excessive drinking, stress management, and other lifestyle changes can substantially reduce the potential for an early heart attack or other health problem.

By the same token, instead of saying "You will get divorced," a palmist can say, "If you don't work on this marriage, I can see a possible divorce." Rather than predict, "You will not have a good career," a reader can say, "You need to pay attention to your long-term career plans or I see problems ahead." Instead of "You'll become a drug abuser," a reader can advise, "You have to be especially careful of drugs, alcohol, and medications, since they can affect you more strongly than most people." By affirming that the hand shows potential and trends, the palmist empowers clients and assists them in taking charge of their own destinies. Instead of creating a future scenario of disease or marital disappointment, the reader offers insight and encouragement, knowing that each of us can take charge of the future through self-knowledge and a sincere desire to transform our life.

In some cases, lines may not change. Again, this is not to be interpreted as a wholly negative phenomenon. In many cases, a weak, broken, or islanded line can serve as a reminder to help us focus on a particular area of weakness. For example, if a person's career line remains weak or deficient over time, it does not necessarily mean that the person will have a problem in his or her work life: it can also be a sign that the person is not easily satisfied with work and constantly needs to focus on improving his or her career possibilities. If a union or relationship line is weak or broken, it does not always mean divorce: the weak line may also serve as a sign that the person must never take the relationship for granted, and should do whatever possible to improve it.

While a broken, islanded, or weak line may call our attention to a potential problem, it should not be interpreted as necessarily "bad." Very often we are confronted with challenges, choices, and difficulties in order to learn important lessons, which can be extremely valuable for us during the course of our lives. For this reason, it is important not to judge a feature of the hand, such as a broken line or curving finger, as a negative sign.

## PALMISTRY:
## A TOOL FOR SELF-KNOWING

Hand analysis helps people develop self-recognition on a deep level. It can indicate strengths and weaknesses, point out lessons we need to learn, and reveal major issues we need to resolve. By offering a deeper, yet more expansive, view of our personality and life tasks, palmistry can help us understand that conflict has a benign purpose in life and helps us develop wisdom, patience, courage, and experience.

Hand reading can offer a perspective that is both objective and real. It goes beyond our limited ego patterns and projections and gives us an idea of where we are in life and where we are going. It shows how our basic psychological nature can affect our health, career, and relationships and can indicate what we need to achieve a greater sense of harmony in our lives.

Because palmistry often confirms our basic insights and inner feelings, it can bring us a greater degree of self-confidence and self-reliance. This enables us to look at our lives with a deeper sense of ease and helps us work through challenges and obstacles with optimism and purpose. Hand analysis also enables a person to determine the types of activities that will bring the greatest amount of pleasure, interest, and self-fulfillment.

Hand analysis can reveal how our experiences fit into an overall pattern of events that constitute our basic life structure or life plan. It helps us see life in terms of an adventure to be experienced rather than an endless series of problems, obstacles, frustrations, and punishments.

Palmistry helps those we counsel to get in touch with their deeper essence, which goes beyond the ego-consciousness level. It allows them to draw from this wellspring of strength and inner wisdom so that they can move more confidently through periods of difficulty.

In addition to helping the person whose hand we are reading, palmistry can help the reader achieve a deeper level of inner attunement with the client. It helps us understand a person's real needs and arrive at an appropriate recommendation for therapy or care. For those who are serious about developing their knowledge of palmistry to serve others, hand analysis, like other intuitive arts, helps us get more in touch with our own inner selves and leads us to rely on intuition and inner wisdom in our work.

Finally, hand analysis affirms the uniqueness and specialness of every single human being. Each us has a hand like no one else's. In a culture that encourages sameness and conformity, palmistry reveals that each individual is a unique combination of personality traits, talents, and aspirations. Each of us has a special task in life and a unique combination of qualities to offer, and palmistry can help us both to understand our most important goals and to find ways to attain them.

# HAND TYPES

OVER THE YEARS, HAND READERS HAVE SOUGHT to classify the hands into distinct categories. While no system is perfect, classifying the hands gives us a general framework on which we can base a thorough hand analysis. Two of the most popular systems are presented in this chapter. Some hand readers tend to focus on one of them when they analyze a person's hands. In my own readings, I tend to use elements of both.

## RECEPTIVE AND REALISTIC

Essentially, there are two types of hands, receptive and realistic.

The *receptive hand* is often fragile and delicate in appearance and is usually long and conic in shape. Its owners tend to be sensitive, with many emotional currents affecting their lives. A rich line pattern, signifying many interests and paths of expression, is common.

The *realistic hand* is characterized by its more assertive, outgoing features. This type of hand is generally square and broad, giving an impression of being energetic, impatient, and well grounded in three-dimensional reality. Its owners tend to be robust, active, and determined.

## THE FOUR ELEMENTS SYSTEM

The noted British palmist Fred Gettings developed the four elements classification system in the 1960s. He based his system on ancient alchemical writings that correspond with the four elements: earth, air, fire, and water. His popular method of classification can easily be applied to the great majority of hands. Gettings's system encompasses both realistic and receptive hands.

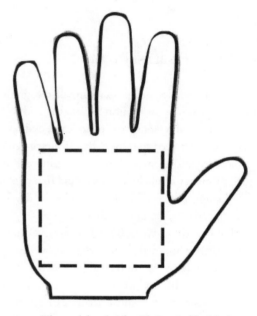

*The Earth Hand*

FIGURE 3.1. The earth hand. After *The Love Deck* by Marion Gale (Toronto: HandsUp, Inc., 2001)

Earth hands (Figure 3.1) feature broad palms with short, stubby fingers. The skin texture tends to be coarse, and the skin ridges are generally thick and well defined. There are only a few basic lines on the palm, but they tend to be strong and broad.

Owners of earth hands tend to be practical, reliable, and self-sufficient. They like being in nature and are often found living in the country. They also often gravitate toward physical work such as farming and working with machinery. Earth-handed people tend to be emotionally stable. They dislike change, are not rushed when making important decisions, and like to concentrate on one activity at a time.

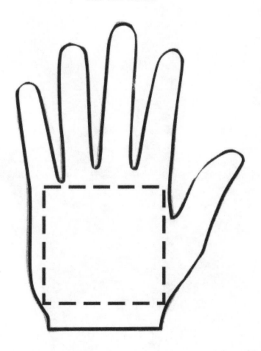

*The Air Hand*

FIGURE 3.2. The air hand. After *The Love Deck* by Marion Gale (Toronto: HandsUp, Inc., 2001)

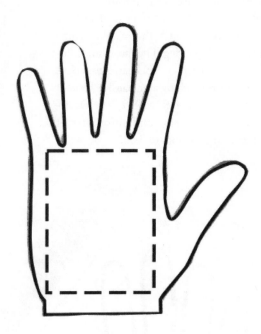

*The Fire Hand*

FIGURE 3.3. The fire hand. After *The Love Deck* by Marion Gale (Toronto: HandsUp, Inc., 2001)

The typical air hand features a squarish palm with long fingers, as seen in Figure 3.2. Skin ridges tend to be fine but clearly defined, and skin texture is fine. Both the main lines and the accessory lines are clear and well defined.

People with air hands tend to be intellectual and curious. Air-handed people are considered companionable, calm, and easy to get along with. They tend to be good communicators and are often drawn to professions like writing, broadcasting, and teaching.

You can recognize a fire hand (Figure 3.3) by its long palm and comparatively short fingers. The skin ridges are clear, and the palm contains a multitude of sharply defined and energetic lines.

People with fire hands are known for their boundless energy. They enjoy the challenge of new ventures and tend to abhor routine. They tend to be excitable and like being in charge. Of all the four hand types, fire-handed people are best at dealing with stress.

## The Water Hand

The typical water hand features long palms with long fingers (Figure 3.4). The main lines on the palm are clearly defined and are often accompanied by a sensitive mesh of fine accessory lines.

People with water hands tend to be refined, sensitive, and emotional. They often are known for their excellent taste in art, music, and fashion. They enjoy reading and thinking. They are easily influenced by what they see, hear, and feel. A good example of a water hand is that of Mary Pickford (1892–1979), the Oscar-winning movie star and cofounder of United Artists (Figure 3.5).

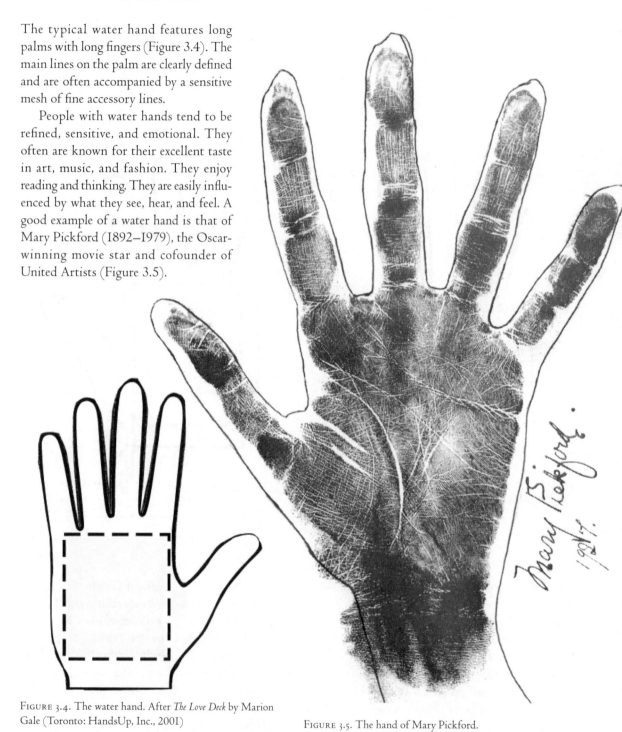

FIGURE 3.4. The water hand. After *The Love Deck* by Marion Gale (Toronto: HandsUp, Inc., 2001)

FIGURE 3.5. The hand of Mary Pickford.

## THE SIX-HAND-TYPE CLASSIFICATION

Another system is based on the different basic shapes of the hand, such as square, spatulate, and conic. Developed by the French palmist Captain Casimir Stanislas d'Arpentigny, it was first introduced in his book *La chirognamie*, published in Paris in 1843. It was later translated as *The Science of the Hand* by Edward Heron-Allen and was published in London and New York in 1886.

Captain d'Arpentigny believed that there are six types of hands: elementary, spatulate, square, knotty, conic, and pointed, or psychic. He later added a seventh category for "mixed" hands.

### The Elementary Hand: Reflecting Earth Energy

The first category is known as the elementary hand (Figure 3.6). Strongly realistic, the purely elementary hand contains only a few lines and roughly corresponds to the earth hand described earlier.

- Elementary hands are stiff and hard to the touch and feel heavy and thick in consistency.

- The palm tends to be broad and squarish.

- The fingers tend to be short and stubby.

- The thumb is short, thick, and stiff; it will not bend backward.

- The palm tends to be fleshy and usually contains very few lines; the three or four lines that appear tend to be strong and deep.

- The arch and loop types of fingerprints often predominate.

- The skin texture is coarse.

The vast majority of people with elementary hands are male. They are often realistic, are

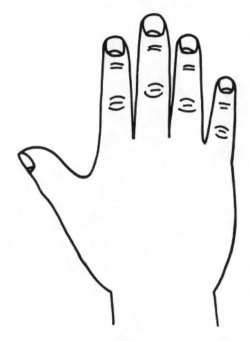

FIGURE 3.6. The elementary hand.

grounded in three-dimensional reality, and have the ability to function well in the material world. They tend to be deliberate, slow, and practical and prefer to see things in a simple, uncomplicated way. This is not an indicator of low intelligence, but rather a particular approach to viewing the world.

For the most part, the owner of the elementary hand dislikes change and prefers a stable and predictable work environment with few, if any, surprises. Careers in agriculture (such as farming), mining, work with heavy machinery, and similar activities involving strong physical labor are popular among individuals with this hand type.

Elementary-handed people tend to be attuned to nature, so they prefer to live and work in the country rather than in cities or towns. They work especially well with animals and plants. If you know someone with the proverbial green thumb, chances are good that he or she has an elementary hand.

People with elementary hands have a tough physical constitution and are often very strong. They can also be conservative and set in their ways. People

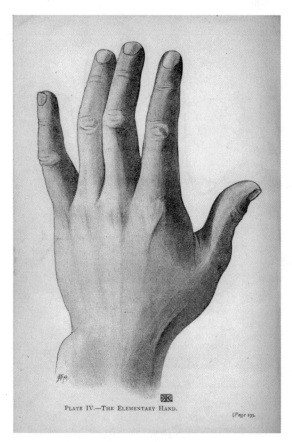

Figure 3.7. A higher elementary hand, as seen in the book *The Science of the Hand* (Ed. Heron Allen; London: Ward, Lock and Co., 1886), by Casimir Stanislas d'Arpentigny.

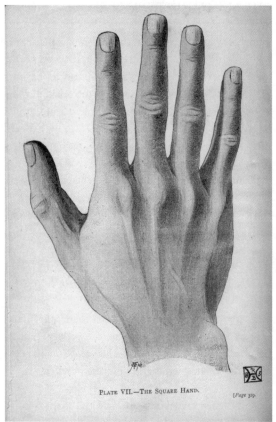

FIGURE 3.8. The square hand. From *The Science of the Hand* (Ed. Heron Allen; London: Ward, Lock and Co., 1886)

with these hands are steady and reliable. They like to be independent, and their values are often material ones. When threatened, they can be very violent.

The purely elementary type is primitive, basic, crude, and unrefined. Intellectual analysis and abstract understanding are often lacking. People with elementary hands are often slow to react and are not likely to easily reveal their feelings, especially those of vulnerability and affection.

A higher elementary type may still have the characteristic shape of the elementary hand, but the consistency of the hand is more elastic and the skin may have a finer texture. This indicates a more sensitive and flexible person who is more receptive to new ideas and feelings. Although Captain d'Arpentigny describes only one kind of elementary hand, like the one depicted in his book (Figure 3.7), this drawing more closely resembles an elementary hand of a higher type.

### The Square Hand: Practical and Levelheaded

The second category in the realistic classification is the square hand type (Figure 3.8). Recognized by its squareness in form as well as its squared-off fingertips, it is the hand of the organizer and planner. The square hand often corresponds to the air hand of the four elements classification.

- The hand is squarish in shape, with the palm and the fingers approximately the same length.

- The fingertips are often squarish in form.

- The nails are square, and slightly longer than they are wide.

- The fingers and thumb are firm and do not easily bend outward.

- The hand has a firm consistency.

Owners of this hand love order, method, and stability. Common sense rules their emotions, and they have a steady, systematic approach to life. They don't like confusion and often have difficulty adapting to new circumstances and situations, especially when the hand or thumb, or both, is rigid. They are often thorough, competent, and careful with money.

Often lacking in spontaneity, people with squarish hands prefer rules, methods, and structures. They like the tried and true and prefer to follow a fixed routine; they do not easily change, unless the hand is flexible.

People with squarish hands tend to be formal in their approach and are usually polite and reserved when dealing with others. They make excellent engineers, doctors, and bureaucrats. Square hands also give their owners an inordinate ability to persevere and to cope with difficult situations.

### The Spatulate Hand: Action!

Spatulate hands (Figure 3.9) also fall into the realistic category. Owners of spatulate hands are often original and inventive. They are known for their restless and exploring personality. This type of hand roughly corresponds to the fire hand of the four elements classification, although the fire hand does not necessarily have spatulate fingertips.

- Spatulate hands are often broad and strong, with slightly knotted fingers.

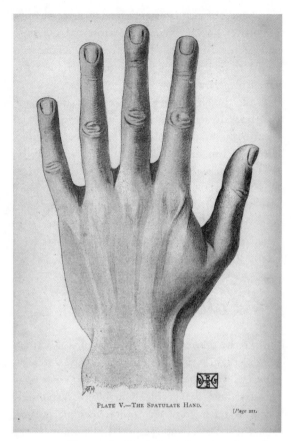

PLATE V.—THE SPATULATE HAND.                    [Page 221.

FIGURE 3.9. The spatulate hand. From *The Science of the Hand* (Ed. Heron Allen; London: Ward, Lock and Co., 1886)

- The fingertips fan out in the form of a spatula. The fingertip is often wider than the first phalange (the section from the base to the first knuckle).

- Broad nails are common.

- The palm is wider at the knuckles than at the wrist.

The best word to describe this hand is *action*. People with spatulate hands are energetic, tenacious, innovative, and self-confident. They are also independent, self-reliant, and curious about new ideas and unusual experiences. Like those with square hands, they are often practical and grounded in day-to-day reality.

Owners of spatulate hands tend to be creative and impulsive. They are generally extroverted, dynamic, and exciting to be with. They often have an uncanny ability to take advantage of a situation and use it to practical advantage.

Like the elementary hand, the spatulate hand is primarily sensate, and its owner favors activities on the material plane. Commerce, banking, construction, and entrepreneurship are popular areas of career interest for those with spatulate hands. People with spatulate hands are also good inventors and athletes. When flexible and pliable, however, a spatulate hand indicates an interest in sensual pleasures at the expense of work and other responsibilities.

### The Conic Hand: Lover of Beauty

Unlike the previous hand types, conic, or artistic, hands (Figure 3.10) are of the receptive category. They are the hands of people who are emotional, intuitive, and changeable. Roughly corresponding to the water hand of the four elements classification, this type of hand is especially common among women.

- Conic hands tend to be slightly tapered at the base of the palm and at the tips of the fingers.

- The skin texture is usually fine, denoting sensitivity and a love of beauty.

- The hand has a soft yet springy consistency as well as a flexible thumb and fingers.

- In addition to the four major lines on the hand, there are usually a great number of fine lines, including many vertical lines.

People with conic hands are governed by impulse and first impressions. Unlike those with squarish hands, who are ruled by reason, conic-handed people are sentimental, intuitive, impulsive, capricious, and romantic.

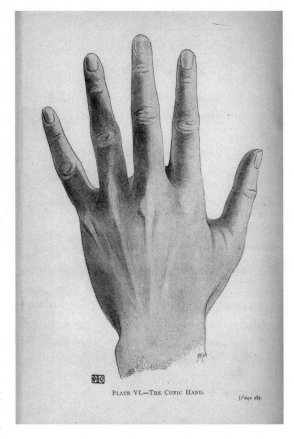

PLATE VI.—THE CONIC HAND.

FIGURE 3.10. The conic hand. From *The Science of the Hand* (Ed. Heron Allen; London: Ward, Lock and Co., 1886)

Inconsistency is said to be a major problem with those who possess conic hands. They often begin a project with great enthusiasm, and then leave it for someone else to complete, especially if the hands are flexible. Although conic-handed people tend to support the efforts of others, they shift loyalties often and have difficulty with commitment.

Creativity is high in owners of this hand. If the hand is firm and the lines well formed, creative energies are channeled toward mostly intellectual pursuits. When the hand is bland and fat, there is a strong sensuous nature. Rich foods, money, abundant sex, and comfortable surroundings are counted among the primary needs of individuals with this hand type.

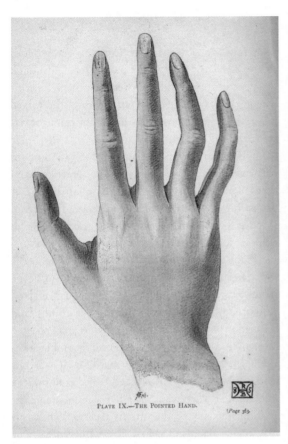

PLATE IX.—THE POINTED HAND.

(Page 363)

FIGURE 3.11. The psychic hand. From *The Science of the Hand* (Ed. Heron Allen; London: Ward, Lock and Co., 1886)

## The Psychic Hand: Painfully Idealistic

The psychic, or intuitive, hand (Figure 3.11) is relatively rare but quite distinctive. It is essentially an extreme version of the conic hand.

- The hand is beautifully formed and features long, graceful fingers with pointed tips.

- The hand's consistency is soft and yielding.

- The hand has a flexible thumb and fingers.

- The skin texture is very fine, with many lines on the palm.

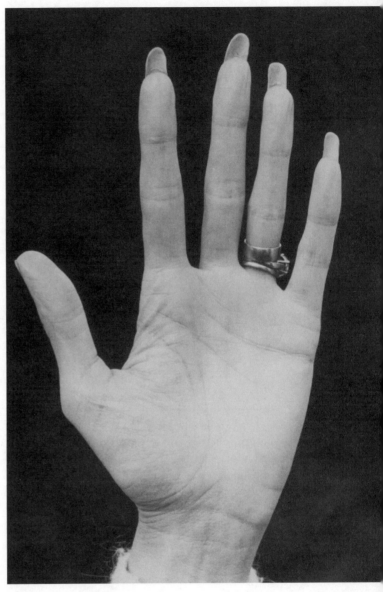

FIGURE 3.12. The hand of Faith Brown, as it appears in a photograph published in the *Sunday Mirror*.

- The nails tend to be oval, narrow, and quite long; when the hand is viewed from the back, a considerable amount of skin is visible along the borders of the nails.

Like people with conic hands, owners of psychic hands are very sensitive and have a strong interest in

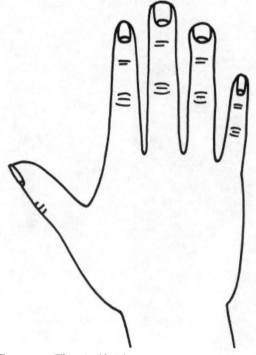

FIGURE 3.13. The mixed hand.

Very few hands actually conform in every detail to any one hand type in its purest form, although one type may predominate over the others. For this reason, we have a fifth classification—the mixed hand, which can provide an important frame of reference for an accurate hand analysis.

By definition, the mixed hand (Figure 3.13) contains characteristics of two or more of the previous hand types. The hand may be primarily squarish, yet one or two fingers may be spatulate in shape. The overall shape of the hand may be conic, yet it also may contain elements found in the more practical square hand.

The basic shape of the hand should serve as the foundation of a careful hand analysis. The fingers, mounts, and lines, as well as modifiers such as hand consistency and size, skin texture, flexibility, and skin ridge patterns, can often provide more specific information regarding character analysis and individual life expression.

For these reasons, we need to take *all* factors into account when we study a hand and evaluate the relationships among the various aspects. While this may appear daunting at first, you will eventually be able to achieve a thorough, balanced reading by cultivating intuition and patience. After some practice you will be able to recognize the basic gestalt of a hand after a few minutes of careful observation.

beauty. There is also a tendency to be high-strung and impressionable, and many people with this type of hand have strong psychic ability.

People with psychic hands are motivated by their deepest feelings. They are highly creative and possess a strong imagination. Common sense is not one of their primary attributes, and they often have trouble dealing with the nuts and bolts of life. A good example of a psychic hand is that of the iconic English actress, comedienne, and impressionist Faith Brown (Figure 3.12).

It is important for people with psychic hands to be grounded in the material world. While they need to deepen their love of beauty and their innate interest in spiritual matters, they also need to learn how to function in the everyday world. For that reason, they need strong and steady friends to help them deal with life's practical matters.

# CONSISTENCY, SIZE, AND SKIN TEXTURE

WHEN MOST PEOPLE LOOK AT HANDS, THEY GO straight to the lines. However, other aspects of the hand provide important background information on a person's energy, strength, and character. Before you look at the lines of the hand, take a few moments to learn about hand consistency and flexibility, hand size, and the texture of your client's skin.

## CONSISTENCY

Consistency of the hands is determined by gauging their hardness or softness under pressure. Understanding the basic consistency of the hand helps us to determine both a person's energy level and how it is expressed in daily life. By taking your client's hands in yours and gently squeezing them, you can gain an accurate idea about their consistency.

You can identify a flabby hand by the fact that the flesh easily crushes together when you squeeze gently. Such a hand betrays low physical energy, and as a result the individual has difficulty manifesting both feelings and concrete plans in the material world. In many cases, flabby hands are an indication of an idle, sensitive dreamer who dislikes both physical and emotional exertion.

When the hands are flabby and thick, the sensate aspects of the personality are more pronounced. Overindulgence in food, sex, drugs, and alcohol is common; unless the thumb is strong, willpower is often absent. When the hands are thin and weak, the individual's energy level tends to be extremely low. People with such hands find it difficult to sustain any long-term activity.

Soft hands do not feel bony under pressure. Although soft hands can reveal a deficient energy level, people with this hand type have far more potential for movement than do people with flabby hands. When the hands are soft and thick, overindulgence in food, sex, drugs, and alcohol is also common.

Elastic hands cannot be "crushed" easily by your grasp and tend to spring back under pressure. They show vitality, adaptability, and movement. When the hands are elastic, the qualities revealed by the mounts, fingers, lines, and skin ridge patterns are strengthened. Elastic hands are found on people who like to invent and create. These individuals have an ability to respond easily to new ideas and adapt to unexpected circumstances.

Firm hands are slightly elastic and yield to moderate pressure. They reveal an energetic, active, and strong individual who is both stable and responsible. While not as able to adapt to new ideas and unexpected circumstances as those with elastic hands, people with firm hands are able to take account of reality and adjust themselves to it accordingly, even though such an effort may take time.

Hard hands show no sign of yielding under pressure. Found mostly on men, these hands show no elasticity and are often coarse in texture. People with hard, rigid hands tend to be set in their ways. They lack mental flexibility and don't like change. In addition, they are often prone to hold in their energy, which can result in sudden outbursts of temper and stress-related diseases.

## FLEXIBILITY

A hand's flexibility can be determined by the ease with which it bends backward. William G. Benham, in his classic text *The Laws of Scientific Hand Reading*, wrote that the flexibility of the hand reveals "the degree of flexibility in the mind and nature, and the readiness with which this mind has power to unfold itself and 'see around the corner' of things."[1]

A very flexible hand can bend back to nearly a ninety-degree angle with a minimum of pressure. It reveals a person who is highly impressionable and easily ordered about by others, and who has difficulty being committed to one activity at a time. Such an individual frequently spends money faster than it is earned and can be very unpredictable with feelings and actions. If the thumb bends back easily as well, the person is generous to an extreme and can easily be taken advantage of by others.

A moderately flexible hand (Figure 4.1) bends back in a graceful arc. The owner of this type of hand can easily adapt to new and unforeseen circumstances. This person's mind is versatile, intuitive, and impressionable. While it may be easy for this person to express his or her feelings, to think

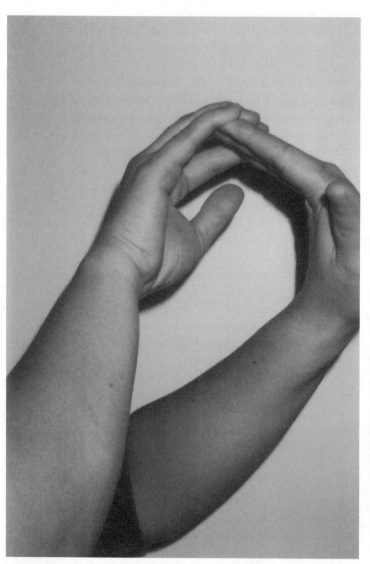

FIGURE 4.1. The moderately flexible hand.

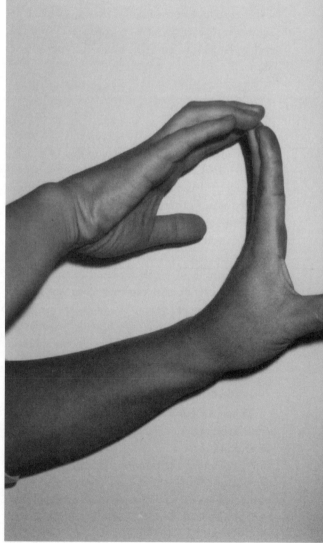

FIGURE 4.2. The stiff hand.

clearly, and to act readily, there is nevertheless the danger that he or she will become involved in too many activities or projects at the same time without committing to any one of them.

A firm hand hardly bends back at all under pressure. Although such a hand reveals an abundance of energy, there is a marked tendency to be careful with feelings, which are often kept hidden. While people with firm hands are open to new ideas, they are rarely impulsive and adapt to new circumstances and unfamiliar surroundings with difficulty.

A stiff hand (Figure 4.2) is extremely rigid and may actually turn inward in its natural state. While this hand reveals a person who is extremely cautious, highly responsible, and dedicated to hard work, stiff hands also betray a rigid character structure. Their owners tend to be stubborn and set in their ways and have difficulty dealing with new ideas and unexpected situations. People with stiff hands are often secretive and have difficulty sharing their personal problems or feelings with others.

## SIZE

The size of a person's hand is another indication of character. It can be interpreted in the context of a client's overall size, including height, weight, and bone structure. Generally speaking, small hands reveal an individual who views life on a grand scale. While harboring a basic aversion to details and minutiae (unless their fingers are knotted), people with small hands tend to perceive the totality of what interests them, be it a flower, a creative project, or a scientific theory.

By contrast, people with large hands appear to gravitate toward small things. Whereas a woman with small hands would admire a large building in its entirety, her large-handed companion would probably focus her attention on the brass plaque by the main entrance. Large hands are often found on watchmakers, mathematicians, computer programmers, and others who are drawn to detail work.

## WIDTH

Unlike the apparently counterintuitive meanings of a person's hand size, the width of a person's hands usually corresponds to his or her personality.

Narrow hands reveal a narrow, restricted way of looking at life, which is accentuated if the hands are also stiff and hard. Conversely, broad hands are generally found on people who are broad-minded, tolerant, and interested in new concepts and trends.

## SKIN TEXTURE

Aspects of skin texture also correspond to their emotional counterparts. The softer and finer the skin, the greater the degree of physical and emotional sensitivity. People with fine skin (Figure 4.3) are sensitive to their surroundings and require an environment that is conducive to peace and harmony. Coarse skin texture (Figure 4.4) reveals a more rough-and-tumble individual who is not strongly influenced by his or her emotional or physical surroundings.

I am often asked whether the work one does determines one's skin texture. It may be true that certain types of physical activity (such as lifting weights, gardening, and gymnastics) can produce calluses and may tend to coarsen an otherwise fine-textured hand. Yet I (and many other hand readers) have known people with coarse-textured hands whose most strenuous task was typing a letter on a computer keyboard, while owners of fine-textured hands can be found hard at work pouring molten steel and operating heavy road-building equipment.

## RIGHT OR LEFT?

Traditional Chinese palmists believe that we should focus on the right hand of men and the left hand of women. Some Western hand readers follow this rule. While I believe that it is important to study both hands, I also believe that we should focus primarily

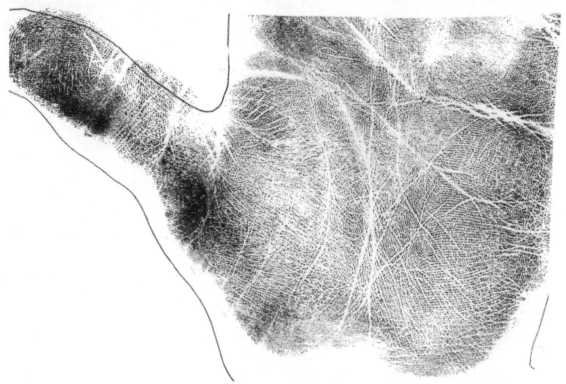

FIGURE 4.3. Fine skin texture.

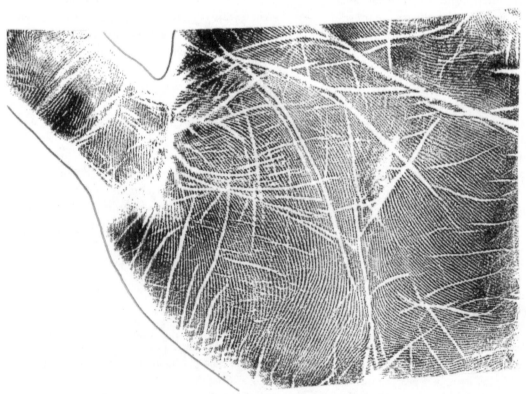

FIGURE 4.4. Coarse skin texture.

on a person's active, or dominant, hand, because this hand reveals the most valuable information about both present reality and future trends.

The nondominant, or passive, hand reflects our past and our innate potential, while the dominant hand shows primarily what we are doing with our lives at the moment. Very often the hands reveal marked differences between our innate potential and the degree to which it is being fulfilled.

To use the analogy of banking, the passive hand is like stocks, bonds, certificates of deposit, and other nonliquid holdings, while the active hand represents short-term investments and money market and checking accounts. Both can change over time. Like savings and checking accounts, the active hand appears to reflect changes in our lives more rapidly than the passive hand.

For example, let's say that a woman is right-handed. The life line on her left hand is strong and clear, while the life line on her right hand is weak and broken. This would mean that her heath potential is far greater than her present health reality. Even though it's not necessarily happy news, this information is useful because it forms the basis of a wake-up call. The woman can ask herself, "What am I doing that's good for my health and what am I doing that's unhelpful?" Because lines in the hand can change over time, lifestyle choices such as a better diet, becoming tobacco free, and managing stress will have a positive impact, which will likely be reflected in the right hand as an improved life line.

Sometimes an individual begins life with little promise. Poverty, the early death of a parent, living in civil strife, or childhood illness may have contributed to the probability of a bleak future. People in these circumstances might have a passive hand with a broken or missing fate line, while a strong and clear fate line appears in the active hand. This shows that the individual overcame tremendous odds to improve his or her life.

Generally speaking, the dominant hand is the one we write with. In the rare instances in which an individual is ambidextrous and writes with both hands, we need to observe both hands together. When the hands are different, we should ask questions as we proceed with the reading in order to discover which of the two hands is dominant.

# MOUNTS AND VALLEYS

*chapter*

*5*

Tʜᴇ ᴛᴏᴘᴏɢʀᴀᴘʜʏ ᴏꜰ ᴛʜᴇ ʜᴀɴᴅ ᴄᴀɴ ʙᴇ ᴄᴏᴍᴘᴀʀᴇᴅ to the mountains, valleys, and plains of the earth. Like the general shape of the hand, its regions and mounts have much to tell us about our personality traits, innate talents, and energy level.

The hand is divided into six primary zones and then into eight mounts (known scientifically as thenar elevations), very much like the division of a geographic region into counties and towns. While the six zones provide a general orientation regarding latent capacities and outward expression, the eight mounts reveal the far more specialized information we need for a thorough character analysis.

## THE LONGITUDINAL ZONES

The three longitudinal zones are formed by drawing an imaginary vertical line from a point between the index and middle fingers downward toward the wrist, and by drawing a second such line from a point between the middle and ring fingers, as shown in Figure 5.I.

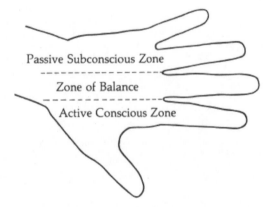

Passive Subconscious Zone

Zone of Balance

Active Conscious Zone

Fɪɢᴜʀᴇ 5.ɪ. The longitudinal zones of the hand.

The first division forms the active conscious zone, which represents the energy we consciously apply in our dealings with the material world. It relates to the assertion of the ego in daily life, on both an intellectual and a concrete level. It is the region of practical knowledge, outward movement, and the application of principles in our work, study, and relationships.

The zone located on the opposite third of the hand represents our hidden energy reserve, or the passive subconscious. It relates to our innate creativity, emotional awareness, and instinctual capacity.

The middle zone, or zone of balance, serves as a meeting place where these different energies can blend. This is an area where we often find the line of Saturn, or line of life task, which moves up from the base of the palm toward the middle finger. It speaks of career, movement in life, and the degree to which we have found our niche in the world.

## THE LATITUDINAL ZONES

The three latitudinal zones (Figure 5.2) are formed by drawing a horizontal line from the tip of the thumb across to a point below the base of the fingers, and another from just above the thumb ball directly across the palm.

The first division, the emotional/conscious zone, represents our active link with the world around us. Depending on the mounts that lie within this area, it is the zone of emotional expression, the application of power, inspiration, ambition, artistic creation, and business acumen. According to Walter Sorell, author of *The Story of the Human Hand*, it is the area of the hand that has kept the keenest sense of touch and holds the strongest power of connection with objects and people.

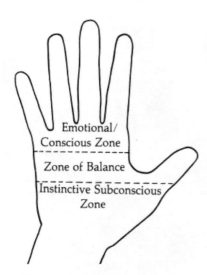

FIGURE 5.2. The latitudinal zones of the hand.

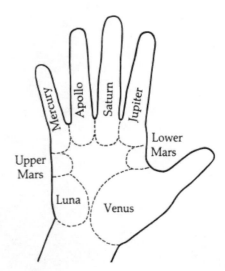

FIGURE 5.3. The mounts of the hand.

The lower region, the instinctive subconscious zone, is the zone of the Freudian id and our primary motivating forces. This zone relates to intuition, imagination, libido, and our deepest, most hidden desires.

The middle horizontal zone is the practical zone of balance. It is the region of logic, common sense, and reason, it represents the blending of thought and feeling. It is the area that filters and absorbs our subconscious drives and helps guide them toward concrete expression. It integrates our aspirations and intellectual abilities with our physical and instinctual drives.

## THE MOUNTS

Each of the mounts (Figure 5.3) has a name, and each one characterizes the type of energy that is channeled through that part of the hand. The mounts are named after planets, which are, in turn, named after Greek and Roman gods and goddesses. They represent aspects of our character that are symbolized by those mythological beings.

The strength of a particular mount depends on its relative size when compared with the other mounts of the hand. The more directly the mount is centered under its corresponding finger, the greater its strength and influence on the personality. You can determine the displacement of the mount by locating its apex. The apex of the mount is found where the ridges of the skin meet to form a pattern, as seen in Figure 5.4. If the apex of the Saturn mount, for example, leans toward the mount of Apollo, it will take on some of the characteristics of the Apollo mount.

Remember that other aspects of the hand, including the strength and shape of the corresponding finger as well as the clarity and strength of major and minor lines, can modify the strength of a particular mount.

### The Mount of Jupiter

The mount of Jupiter is located beneath the index finger, and is named after Jupiter, or Zeus, the king of the gods. The essential qualities of this mount reflect the outgoing aspects of life: generosity, gregariousness, charisma, inspiration, and magnanimity. The mount of Jupiter also reveals our degree of self-confidence, leadership ability, executive skills, ambition, and religious inspiration.

When the Jupiter mount is in harmonious balance with the other mounts, it represents the positive

FIGURE 5.4. The apices on the mounts of Jupiter, Saturn, and Mercury.

aspects of Jupiter: healthy self-assertion, a positive outlook, idealism, and the desire to help others.

If the mount is unusually strong and prominent, ambition plays a major role in its owner's life. Egotism, vanity, and pride are strong aspects of the personality, along with a tendency to be domineering and overbearing. If the fingers and lines complement the essential qualities of this mount, strong leadership and executive skills are indicated.

When modified by other aspects of the hand, positive Jupiterian traits can be distorted and can lead to a potential for greed, selfishness, arrogance, and lust for power and control.

If this mount is deficient or flat, the individual is likely to have a poor self-image. Unless this tendency is modified by other aspects, he or she may lack ambition and the drive to succeed. Such a person often feels awkward socially and has difficulty taking advantage of new opportunities.

## The Mount of Saturn

The mount of Saturn is named after the god Saturn, the judge, and is found under the middle finger. Whereas Jupiter represents the outgoing aspects of a person's character, Saturn is representative of the inward, self-directed side of the personality. When viewed in its positive light, the mount of Saturn symbolizes introspection, responsibility, study, healthy self-preservation, and the search for inner truth. As a balancing force, it enables us to sift through life's often conflicting currents, influences, and desires so that we can deal with them in a rational way.

A normal mount of Saturn reveals a person who is a lover of independence and solitude, one who is able to balance the desire to be alone with the need to share the company of others. Fidelity, constancy, self-awareness, prudence, and emotional balance are favored by a medium-size mount of Saturn, along with the ability to study and explore new ideas.

A highly developed Saturn mount often accentuates and distorts Saturn's essential qualities, especially if modified by other factors in the hands. Prudence can yield to fearful withdrawal, and healthy introspection can be overtaken by a tendency to be overly analytical and self-absorbed. A strong mount can be found on many people who are rigid, taciturn, and defensive by nature.

## The Mount of Apollo

Apollo is the god of power and self-expression, and his mount is located under the ring finger. While Western hand readers relate this mount to all forms of creativity, especially in the fields of art and music, Hindu palmists call this mount the *vidja sthana*, ruling education and scholarship.

A medium-size mount of Apollo reveals a deep love of beauty and a strong creative ability. This creative ability need not be restricted to art or music but can include cooking, acting, writing, and design. If a person has an attractive home or dresses well, chances are that he or she has a well-developed mount of Apollo.

As with the mounts of Jupiter and Saturn, a very large mount of Apollo can both strengthen and distort its basic qualities. A prominent Apollo mount often reveals a preoccupation with pleasure, wealth, or fame. A strong love of beauty can become a devotion to superficial values. Vanity and self-indulgence can replace the natural desire to look good.

When this mount is weak, it indicates a lack of the essential Apollonian qualities. Instead of being exciting and filled with beauty, a person with a weak Apollo mount could be living a life that is ascetic, boring, and flat. Deficiency in this mount can also indicate low physical energy.

## The Mount of Mercury

Mercury was the messenger of the gods. For this reason, the mount of Mercury, located under the little finger, rules communication and the objectification of life principles into spoken and written words. It is the mount of commerce, writing, healing, mathematics, and diplomacy. Mercury also governs sagacity and the ability to judge human nature.

A well-developed mount of Mercury—especially when accompanied by a long Mercury finger—points toward commercial talent and oratorical skill. Actors, diplomats, salespeople, and public speakers almost always possess a strong mount of Mercury.

A very prominent mount has no negative aspects by itself, although a poorly formed Mercury finger can modify its positive qualities. A small, flat mount of Mercury—especially if accompanied by a short or weak finger—reveals a lack of commercial and scientific ability. Communication with others on a one-to-one basis may also be a problem, especially in the context of an emotional relationship.

## The Mounts of Mars

There are two mounts of Mars on the hand. Both reflect the qualities of Mars, the god of war. The mounts of Mars represent the dynamic, egotistical, and separative, self-centered aspects of the personality. These mounts speak of the desire to survive, to move forward, and to overcome obstacles and difficulties.

The upper mount of Mars, also known as Mars negative, is located just under the mount of Mercury and symbolizes determination and resistance. When well formed and hard to the touch, it reflects a person who is both courageous and stubborn and resists being used or manipulated by others.

A small or soft mount reveals a lack of valor and resistance. When found on a soft and flexible hand, it indicates a person who is easily pushed around and has difficulty standing up for his or her rights. When the mount is extremely large and hard, violence and brutality are major components of its owner's character.

Unlike the upper mount of Mars, which symbolizes passive resistance, the lower mount of Mars, also known as Mars positive, reveals the more active and outgoing Martian qualities. Found between the mounts of Jupiter and Venus, it often appears as a small, yet distinct elevated pad located just inside the thumb joint.

A well-developed mount indicates strong self-assertion and the courage to face life's challenges and overcome them. For this reason, it is often found on the hands of people working in law enforcement, the military, and other careers that require courage, such as hospital emergency room personnel and social workers who work in dangerous neighborhoods.

When this mount is large, hard, and reddish, the person has a strong temper. When a large mount of Venus accompanies this large mount, there is also an abundance of sexual passion.

A small or deficient mount indicates a quiet, passive, and introverted individual who rarely gets angry with others.

## The Mount of Venus

Named after the goddess of love, the mount of Venus is an indicator of both our aesthetic nature and our ability to love.

Ideally, the mount of Venus comprises the thumb ball and is outlined by a widely sweeping life line. On most people, this mount takes up approximately one-third of the palm and should be neither too hard, nor too bland, nor too heavily lined. A good Venus mount should be smooth and firm to the touch, higher than the other mounts in elevation, and slightly pink.

A normal-size mount of Venus reveals warmth, vitality, and energy. It shows joie de vivre and the ability to love and be loved. A well-formed Venus mount also strengthens the life line and reveals a strong capacity to resist disease.

When the mount is excessively large in relation to the other mounts, there is an abundance of physical passion, with a large appetite for sex, food, and drink. The Venus mount shown in Figure 5.5 would be considered large when compared to the other mounts of the hand.

When the mount is also hard, this passion can easily spill over into aggression and brutality,

especially if the mount is reddish in color and the texture of the skin is coarse.

A small, flat, or weak Venus mount reveals a lack of vital energy and physical passion. The personality tends to be somewhat lymphatic and cold, especially if the life line cuts through the Venus mount. Very often a strong love affair can actually increase the size of this mount.

## The Mount of Luna

Located opposite the mount of Venus just above the wrist, the mount of Luna represents the receptive, passive, and emotional aspects of the personality. It is the home of our subconscious impressions and unconscious drives, instincts, and imagination.

Ideally, this mount should be broad and lightly rounded in shape. It points to an interest in religion and mysticism and a desire to perceive more than meets the eye. People with medium-size lunar mounts have an imagination that's good but balanced by reality.

The stronger and more prominent the mount, the greater the imagination and subconscious drives, especially if the head line slopes downward toward its center. Intuition is enhanced, along with the potential for creativity.

A large mount of Luna can also reveal a strong desire to protect and nurture others, especially if accompanied by a series of short vertical lines (known as Samaritan lines) on the Mercury mount. Many of the most interesting people in literature, the arts, and science have well-developed mounts of Luna.

The presence of small diagonal lines tends to reveal a heightened degree of intuition, as found on the hand of the respected Colombian psychic (and the author's first palmistry teacher) Teresa Gómez de Barberi.

When this mount is deficient or lacking, the individual tends to be too realistic, unimaginative, and dull. Fantasy is of no interest, and imagination is seen as the indulgence of fools.

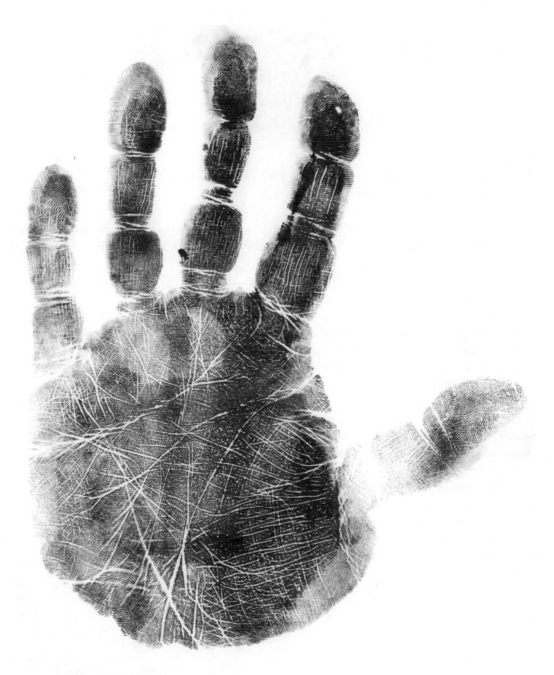

Figure 5.5. A handprint showing a large mount of Venus.

# chapter 6

# THE FINGERS

WHILE THE MOUNTS AND THE BASIC FORM OF the hand provide the fundamental information needed to analyze a person's character, it's the shape, size, and relative position of the fingers that offer a wealth of more specific information concerning both personality and major avenues of self-expression. In some cases, the fingers can tell us more about a person than any other single aspect of the hand.

When studying the fingers, it is important to consider each finger as an individual unit and also as an integral part of the hand. In addition, we must understand the relationship of each finger to the others.

We can determine a finger's relative importance in the hand by opening the palm completely, with the fingers held together. If the fingers tend to lean toward one in particular, that finger is the dominant finger of the hand and provides us with the keynote of an individual's character. Figure 6.1 shows a hand with a dominant Saturn influence, because all the other fingers (including a strong Jupiter finger) bend toward Saturn.

## FLEXIBILITY

The degree of flexibility of the fingers provides an important clue to a person's character. Ideally, the fingers should arch gently backward, revealing a capacity to adapt easily to new ideas and situations. When the top phalange of a finger bends back as well, strong creative talent is present. For example, when the tip of the Mercury, or little, finger bends back, it is a sign of writing or public speaking ability.

## LENGTH AND WIDTH

The length of the fingers must be judged in relation to the length of the palm. A balance exists when the middle, or Saturn, finger is the same length as the

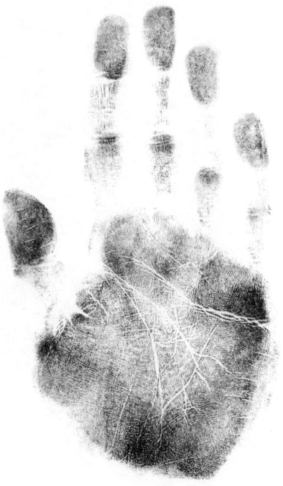

FIGURE 6.1. A hand showing a dominant Saturn influence.

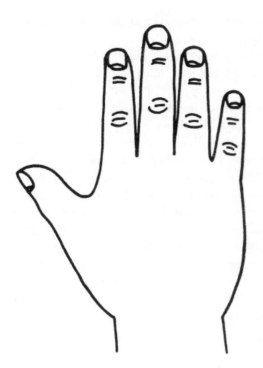

Figure 6.2. Short fingers.

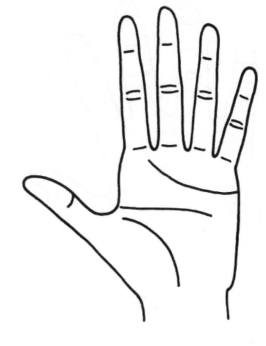

Figure 6.3. Long fingers.

palm itself. The "ideal" length of the neighboring fingers (those of Jupiter and Apollo) reaches halfway up the top phalange of the Saturn finger.

Generally speaking, short fingers (Figure 6.2) are found on people who are intuitive, impatient, and impulsive; these individuals are quickly able to grasp the essential points of an issue or situation. They tend to see things on a large scale, be they philosophical concepts, projects to be undertaken, or panoramic views of the countryside. Unless their fingers are knotted, they also tend to overlook details.

Long fingers (Figure 6.3) indicate the opposite qualities. Patience, love of detail, and a penchant for analysis are common traits of long-fingered people. They like to focus on the minutiae of daily life, and tend to relate to the world in an intellectual (as opposed to an intuitive) context. Long fingers often reveal an introspective nature, with the tendency to hold grudges and harbor resentment.

People with thick, fleshy fingers are basically sensate. They enjoy luxury, comfort, sex, good food, and other pleasures. Thin fingers tend to reveal an intellectual person who is often removed from the material, three-dimensional world.

## KNUCKLES

Smooth fingers (Figure 6.4) have an absence of developed joints, and people with smooth fingers tend to be intuitive and impulsive. They often are impatient with details and have difficulty breaking down a problem into its component parts. Their decisions are based primarily on hunches rather than careful analysis of the facts. Psychologically, they are often in touch with their feelings and find it relatively easy to express anger, love, and joy. If the fingers are short and smooth, impulsiveness, impatience, and aversion to detail are accentuated. Long, smooth fingers tend to strengthen the intellectual and analytical aspects of the personality.

Knotty fingers that are not due to arthritis (Figure 6.5) reveal a strong analytical mind. Their owners are rarely seduced by appearances and tend to penetrate deeply into an issue using logic, detail, and analysis. Psychologically, people with knotty fingers tend to lack spontaneity and find it difficult to express their feelings directly to others.

The handprint shown in Figure 6.6 features knotty fingers. It is the hand of a university professor and researcher considered by his peers to be one of the most original, influential, and controversial scholars in the fields of anthropology and contemporary culture. He is the author of six scholarly books and nearly one hundred articles, and his research currently focuses on the impact of globalization on indigenous communities.

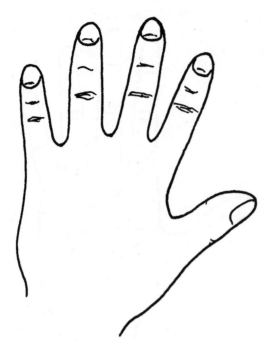

FIGURE 6.4. Smooth fingers.

## THE PHALANGES

The index, middle, ring, and little fingers are divided into three parts, or phalanges (Figure 6.7). The top phalange is that of mental order, the middle phalange is that of practical order, and the bottom phalange is called the phalange of material order.

When the top phalange is the longest of the three, it indicates that thinking absorbs most of its owner's attention. A long middle phalange shows that the primary keynote of the personality is action, a trait that becomes more specific depending on a particular finger's significance. A long and thick phalange of material order reflects a person who is grounded in the material aspects of life—money, products, property. For example, a long and thick phalange at the base of the Jupiter finger is a sign of a materialist who is very much interested in accumulating money, property, and possessions. This individual may also be a good businessperson. Remember that the comparative length of the phalanges may vary from finger to finger.

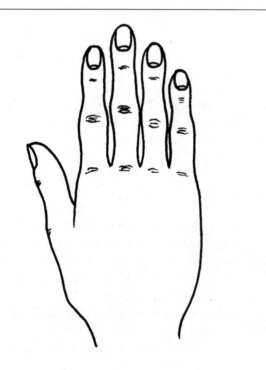

FIGURE 6.5. Knotty fingers.

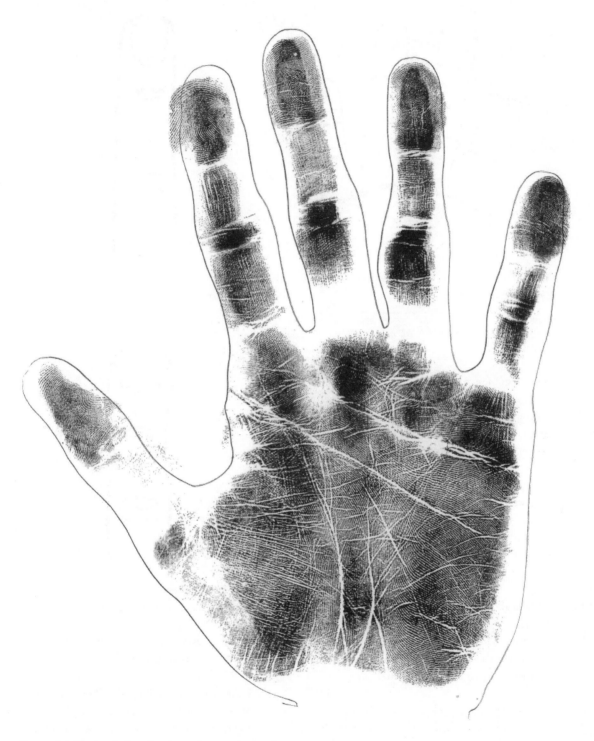

FIGURE 6.6. The hand of a university professor and researcher.

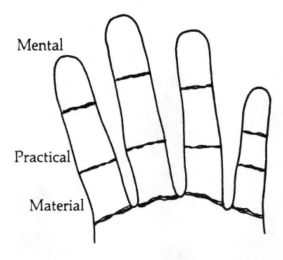

Mental

Practical

Material

FIGURE 6.7. The three phalanges of the fingers: mental, practical, and material.

FIGURE 6.8. Squarish fingertips.

## FINGERTIPS

Fingertips come in five basic shapes. Each shape reveals a specific core quality of the personality. Since most hands have a number of these types, look at the qualities governing each individual finger as well as the fingertips' basic form.

- Squarish fingertips (Figure 6.8) reveal order and regularity. The qualities of perseverance, foresight, structure, and organization are strong in individuals with this type of fingertip. People with squarish fingertips have the capacity for rational, decisive action.

- Spatulate fingertips (Figure 6.9) reveal an energetic, active, and impulsive person. Owners of spatulate fingers tend to be adventurous, self-confident, and down-to-earth in their approach to life.

- Conic fingertips (Figure 6.10) show a receptive and sensitive nature. People with conic fingertips tend to respond strongly to stimuli and are governed by impulse and

FIGURE 6.9. Spatulate fingertips.

first impressions. Conic fingertips are often found on artistic people.

- Pointed, or psychic, fingertips (Figure 6.11) are somewhat rare. They reveal a tendency to be strongly affected by events, conditions, and surroundings, and indicate a dreamy and intuitive mind that is easily inspired.

FIGURE 6.10. Conic fingertips.

FIGURE 6.11. Psychic fingertips.

FIGURE 6.12. Round fingertips.

Many hands contain a combination of these types. We need to take into account the qualities governing each individual finger as well as a finger's basic form as we make our analysis.

## THE THUMB

In Hindu palmistry, the thumb is considered so important that many hand readers restrict themselves to studying the thumb alone when they analyze an individual's character.

The thumb relates to our ego strength and our level of energy or life force. Because it permits us to accomplish a wide variety of tasks in daily life, the thumb also symbolizes our ability to express this energy and power in the world.

The size of the thumb is a guide to the basic energy level of the individual. Normally, the tip of the thumb reaches the lower phalange of the index (or Jupiter) finger. A long thumb (Figure 6.13), often known as a capable thumb, indicates an abundance of energy in addition to a forceful personality.

Individuals with short thumbs (Figure 6.14) tend to be weak willed and are not known for a strong

• Round fingertips (Figure 6.12) are the type most commonly found. They reveal an adaptable, well-rounded, and balanced personality. People with rounded fingertips are often active yet receptive, mental yet emotional.

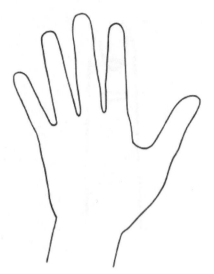

FIGURE 6.13. A long thumb.

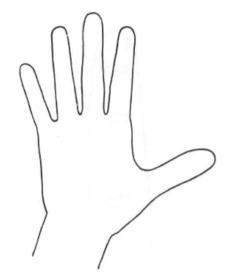

FIGURE 6.15. A low-set thumb.

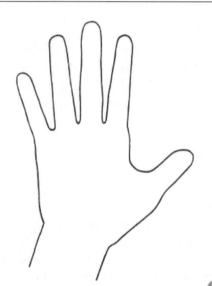

FIGURE 6.14. A short thumb.

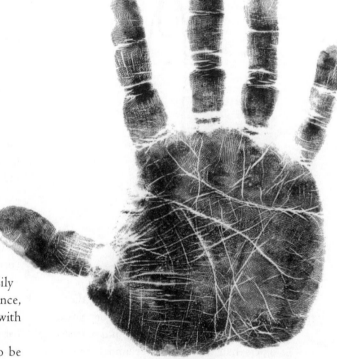

FIGURE 6.16. A long head line with a slight upward curving at the end.

character, especially if the thumb bends back easily under pressure. They often lack self-confidence, forcefulness, and the ability to follow through with a project or other endeavor.

However, before we proclaim a thumb to be long or short, we need to take into account how the thumb is set on the hand. A low-set thumb can easily be positioned at a ninety-degree angle to the index

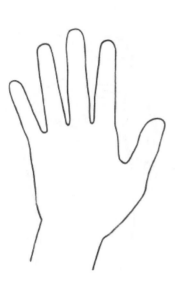

FIGURE 6.17. A high-set thumb.

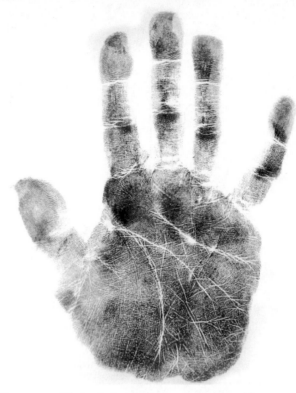

FIGURE 6.19. The handprint of a computer technician with a high-set thumb

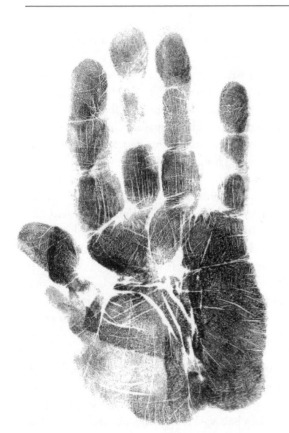

FIGURE 6.18. The handprint of a woman with a high-set thumb.

finger, as shown in Figure 6.15. It reveals an adaptable and independent person who takes risks.

The low-set thumb of a twenty-two-year-old Uruguayan exile (Figure 6.16) who was active with the Tupamaro revolutionary forces in the 1970s while a university student reveals his commitment to political action, love of adventure, and desire for independence. When I met him in Sweden, where he had sought political amnesty, I was impressed by his outgoing nature and supreme self-confidence.

To the degree that the thumb is set high on the hand (Figure 6.17), a person tends to withhold energy. There is a fear of letting go and going with the flow. In popular jargon, this individual would be described as uptight unless modifying aspects in the hand are present, such as overall flexibility and a separation between the life and head lines at their commencement. Generally speaking, people with high-set thumbs, like the woman whose hand is shown in Figure 6.18 and the highly competent—and somewhat shy—computer technician whose hand is shown in Figure 6.19, tend to be conservative and socially traditional.

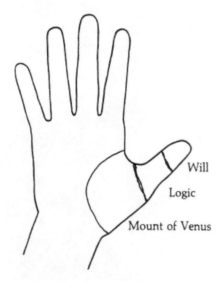

FIGURE 6.20. The three phalanges of the thumb.

FIGURE 6.22. A "murderer's" thumb.

FIGURE 6.21. A flat thumb tip.

Like the index, middle, ring, and little fingers, the thumb is divided into three parts, or phalanges (Figure 6.20). The nail phalange is called the phalange of will, and the second phalange is called the phalange of logic. The third phalange is the mount of Venus.

A strong phalange of will—one that is well rounded, long, and wide—indicates decisiveness, staying power, and the ability to transform thoughts into deeds. When this phalange is conic in shape, it indicates a person whose energy tends to scatter when he or she is confronted with a major project or serious problem. If this phalange is thin or flat (when viewed from the side), its owner tends to be high-strung and nervous (Figure 6.21). When the thumb tip is squarish, there is an ability to organize and execute projects. A spatulate tip is the sign of a dynamic individual with a zest for living. Things *happen* around him.

Some people have a thumb with a phalange of will that has a bulbous or clubbed appearance. Palmists have called it a murderer's thumb (Figure 6.22). Although it does not necessarily indicate homicidal tendencies (I have known several delightful people with murderer's thumbs), it is often a sign of a person who tends to withhold energy to such an extent that strong, sudden bursts of temper can result. This holding of energy may also result in physical problems, such as high blood pressure and other stress-related diseases.

The phalange of logic reveals our degree of reasoning power. Ideally, it should be the same length and strength as the will phalange, which would indicate a balance between thought and action. The longer and thicker the phalange, the more the ego will exert strong control over action. In extreme cases, people with long logic phalanges will think

FIGURE 6.23. A waisted thumb.

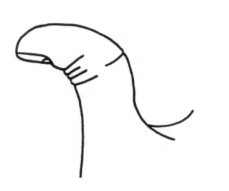

FIGURE 6.24. A supple thumb.

FIGURE 6.25. A stiff thumb.

something through so persistently that they are no longer capable of action. This is especially true if the thumb joint is knotted. A thick phalange of logic has been interpreted by palmists to mean that the owner tends to be frank and blunt with others. A "waisted" phalange (Figure 6.23) is an indicator of tact and diplomacy. Others believe it means that logic is not a major component of the personality.

Determining the flexibility of the thumb is important in understanding personality. A supple thumb (Figure 6.24) bends back at the joint and indicates emotional versatility and a willingness to adapt. Its owner is generous, although such generosity is rarely indiscriminate. When the thumb is extremely flexible (bending back ninety degrees or more), it indicates a person who can be generous to a fault. He or she is likely to be extravagant with money, especially if the rest of the hand is flexible as well. Willpower in this individual tends to be poor.

A moderately flexible thumb bends back only slightly under pressure. It reveals a practical individual who relies on common sense. Although it indicates a strong and determined will, this individual nevertheless retains a degree of open-mindedness and the ability to adapt.

A stiff thumb (Figure 6.25) will not bend back under pressure. Owners of stiff thumbs tend to be stubborn and prudent and have tremendous difficulty adapting to new ideas and situations. On the positive side, they are generally very stable and highly responsible. They can be relied on for almost anything. The qualities of a stiff thumb can be offset by a flexible hand.

## JUPITER

Like its corresponding mount, the index, or Jupiter, finger represents leadership, ambition, and the drive to succeed in life. Ideally, it should be the same length as the ring, or Apollo, finger, and slightly shorter than the middle, or Saturn, finger.

If the Jupiter finger is longer than the Apollo finger, the ego is strong, with a healthy amount of self-esteem. People with long Jupiter fingers like to be in charge and like to be the boss: they are natural leaders and are often involved in running a business, a school, or another institution in which they can use their executive or administrative ability. However, a long Jupiter finger (especially if it curves inward) can reveal a tendency to be vain, domineering, and controlling.

To the degree that Jupiter is shorter than Apollo, there is a corresponding lack of self-esteem and self-confidence. A person with a short Jupiter finger tends to underestimate his or her talents and accomplishments, especially if the head and life lines join each other.

If the Jupiter finger bends toward Saturn, its owner tends to be insecure, a trait that often shows up as jealousy, possessiveness, and acquisitiveness. People with bent Jupiter fingers can often be found browsing in antiques shops or flea markets or surfing Internet sites like eBay for something to add to their collection.

When the Jupiter fingertip is conic or pointed, religious feelings are strong. Such fingers are often found on people who have the ability to inspire and motivate others, especially if the finger is long. A spatulate index fingertip adds a streak of dynamism to the personality. A squarish tip reveals executive or administrative ability.

## SATURN

The middle finger is named for Saturn. It is the finger of propriety, responsibility, and introspection. It serves as a "balance finger" between the subconscious aspects of the personality represented by Apollo and Mercury and the more active, conscious qualities of the thumb and Jupiter finger.

A long Saturn finger reaches high above the other fingers. It reveals a person who treats life with the utmost seriousness. People involved with scientific research and businesspeople who deal with large amounts of money tend to have long Saturn fingers.

When the finger is unusually short (the same length or shorter than the Jupiter or Apollo finger) the owner tends to be careless and does not like to take on responsibility. Most of us have a Saturn finger that is neither abnormally long nor abnormally short.

When the Saturn finger is straight, there is a harmonious relationship between will and emotion, as well as a balance between liking to be with people and wanting to be alone. When it curves slightly toward Jupiter, its owner tends to be spontaneous and outgoing and enjoys being in the company of others as much as possible. A slight curve toward Apollo indicates a need to be alone. A prominent curve or bend toward Apollo (that is not the result of arthritis or accident) can indicate chronic melancholy or depression. When you observe such a formation, take special care to look for confirming or modifying aspects in the rest of the hand, particularly on the head line.

## APOLLO

Like its corresponding mount, the ring, or Apollo, finger rules creativity, the love of art and music, and the capacity for self-expression, especially in the public arena.

A long, straight Apollo finger is found on many artists, actors, dancers, and others who show their work to the public. When the finger features a spatulate tip, the individual's desire to display his or her work is enhanced; this feature is often found on public speakers, teachers, actors, and singers. A conic tip reveals a strong artistic sensibility as well as a good sense of style. Straight Apollo fingers indicate an ability to judge others quickly and accurately. A ring finger that bends slightly toward Saturn betrays a tendency to overestimate others. This often results in disillusion when others don't live up to our high standards. According to some hand readers, an Apollo finger that bends sharply toward Saturn is a sure indication of a gambler and libertine.

## MERCURY

The little, or Mercury, finger rules communication. The longer the Mercury finger, the greater the ability to communicate with others, both one-to-one and in larger groups.

Ideally, this finger should reach the top phalange of Apollo. In some cases, it is set low on the palm, which makes it appear shorter than it really is. If this is the case, place the Mercury finger over the Apollo finger of the other hand to determine its length.

A high percentage of successful public speakers, evangelists, actors, writers, dancers, politicians, lawyers, and businesspeople have long, well-developed Mercury fingers. Some palmists believe that a long Mercury finger is also the sign of a good lover, because such an individual can communicate on an intimate level as well in the public arena.

A short little finger can indicate difficulty in relating to other people, both publicly and privately. When this finger is short, it is not easy to make oneself understood, and close relationships are often difficult to establish and maintain.

A straight Mercury finger indicates honesty, frankness, and trustworthiness. A slight curving toward Apollo reveals astuteness and diplomacy. A sharp bending toward Apollo (not the result of arthritis or accident) indicates a tendency to be manipulative and even dishonest. When the hand features a sharply bending Jupiter finger as well, its owner will stop at nothing to obtain what he or she wants.

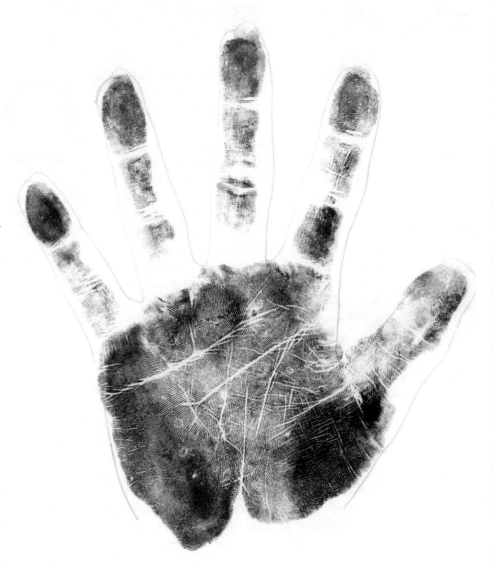

FIGURE 6.26. A hand with the fingers spread widely apart.

## FINGER SPACING

Like the fingers themselves, the spatial relationships between the fingers have specific meanings. When the fingers on an open hand are held closely together (as they are in Figures 6.1 and 6.18), it indicates an individual who tends to be contracted and fearful, lacking in self-confidence and independence. The wider the spacing between the fingers, the greater the openness, daring, and independence (Figure 6.26).

When the Jupiter finger breaks away from the rest of the hand, leadership and self-reliance are increased.

Very often, a shy, insecure person with a short index finger attempts to overcome his shyness by becoming overly aggressive, and this overcompensation will manifest itself as a separated Jupiter finger.

The separated Jupiter finger shouldn't be confused with one that juts out like a flag. A distinct gap between Jupiter and Saturn (as seen in Figure 6.26) is often called the Manager's Sign among palmists and is primarily an indication of initiative, the talent to see what needs to be done, and the ability to do it. It is also a sure sign of liking to be self-employed, or at least to have a good degree of independence at work.

If the Jupiter finger noticeably juts out from the rest of the hand, it is a sign of wanting to be the center of attention. Many actors, models, and other public figures have this trait, as do many people who yearn to have their proverbial fifteen minutes of fame.

If the space between the Apollo and Mercury fingers is wide (again, as seen in Figure 6.26), it reveals an independent, unconventional thinker. Such a person sometimes feels out of the mainstream. Viewing oneself as an outsider is often a stepping-stone to creativity, and many writers, artists, people in show business, and entrepreneurs have this feature on their hands. However, because these individuals do not conform to the expectations of society, this pattern is also found on people with emotional problems.

## NAILS AND PERSONALITY

Although the fingernails are most useful in medical diagnosis, they can also help us evaluate character. Ideally, the nails should be slightly longer than wide and should be slightly curved as opposed to flat, as shown in Figure 6.27.

People with long nails are often drawn to artistic pursuits and like to think and analyze.

Narrow nails reveal an individual with a narrow, dogmatic outlook on life who is generally not open

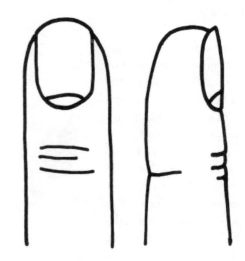

FIGURE 6.27. A normal nail.

to new ideas. Broad nails reveal a broad-minded personality. Short nails (that are not the result of nail biting) indicate an impatient and often critical personality.

Nail color is primarily an indicator of physical vitality, although it can reveal personality traits as well. People with reddish nails tend to have an abundance of energy and passion. They are also prone to flashes of anger and need to find creative outlets for their excess energy. Bright pink nails tend to reveal strong vitality, yet their owners tend to enjoy a balance between the physical and emotional expressions of love. Pink nails reveal good circulation, body warmth, and an outgoing, affectionate character.

People with bluish nails (especially if there are no complaints of poor blood circulation) are somewhat cool and reserved and may have difficulty expressing affection in a physical way. Although they don't lack passion, they often need some time to warm up to someone in a relationship.

Pale nails, like pale skin, indicate low physical vitality and low sex drive. However, this interpretation can be modified by other hand characteristics, such as a large Venus mount.

# THE LINES

THE LINES OF THE HAND, KNOWN SCIENTIFICALLY as flexion creases (Figure 7.1), can be compared to the expressways, city streets, and country lanes of a road map. They indicate the major talents and energies we have at our disposal, our capacity to manifest these talents, and the probable directions in which these talents and energies will take us. In essence, the lines of the hand form a "holographic" map of our life's journey, offering insights into our past, present, and future potential. At the same time, the network of lines allows for occasional detours and changes in direction dictated by our free will.

Even though palmistry dates back some five thousand years, hand analysts are not exactly certain why the lines appear on the hands. However, over the centuries a reliable system has evolved that helps us understand our physical constitution, mental and emotional characteristics, sexuality, and creative ability, the major influences that affect our lives, as well as probable travel, potential relationships, innate healing ability and psychic power, and the degree to which we are fulfilling our major goals in life.

Nor do we fully understand how the lines are formed. Some feel that they represent "rivers of energy" that come through the fingers and into the palm. Physicians have found that the lines are affected by messages from the brain to the nerves in the skin of the hand; this is especially noticeable in the case of an accident to the

shoulder or arm affecting nerve transmission to the hands. We also know that along with skin ridge patterns (such as fingerprints), the three major lines of the hand (life, head, and heart) first appear within several months after conception and are subject to

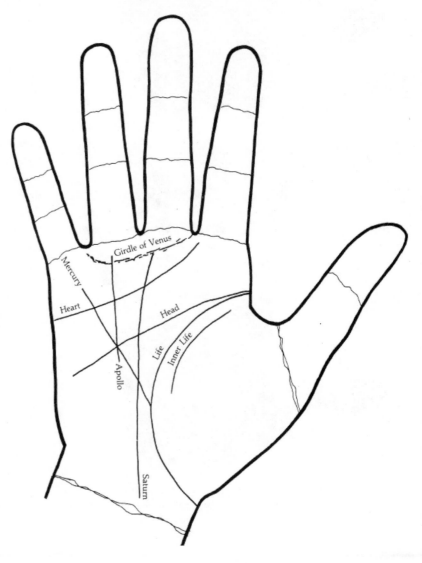

FIGURE 7.1. The major lines of the hand.

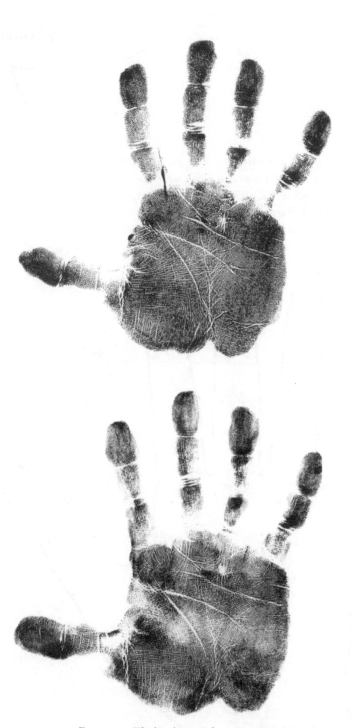

genetic influences and factors relating to a child's environment in the womb during pregnancy.

Yet, unlike skin ridge patterns, which always retain their original form and contours, the lines in the hand change gradually throughout the lifetime. We know that the form and number of lines are not dependent on hand movements, nor are they especially related to what we do for a living. However, sedentary individuals often have more lines in their hands than those who perform heavy manual labor, and many people who practice the same profession often share a number of distinct line and skin ridge characteristics. Digging ditches or playing a sport like handball without a glove will likely create calluses on the hand, making it more difficult for fine lines to appear.

In some cases, the lines of the hand can change in a matter of weeks, although most changes happen over the course of a few years. They are affected by the introduction of life stressors (such as exposure to a dangerous virus or drug abuse), as well as by attitude modification and changes in behavior. Learning how to meditate, cutting down on cigarettes, and devoting more time and energy to making a relationship work can alter the lines of the hand dramatically.

A case in point involves the handprints of a twenty-year-old university student taken six weeks apart (Figure 7.2). During this time, the young man changed his major from business administration to inhalation therapy, became a vegetarian, began to study theosophy and related metaphysical subjects, and told his father (a retired colonel) that he was not going to join the army reserve as planned.

Of particular interest are the longer heart line, the stronger career line, and the longer union line. As he began his studies in healing, the young man met his future wife, who was one of his classmates. Chances are that they would never have met if he had remained in business school. Although the man's life continued to evolve over the next thirty-five years (he is now a successful chiropractor, and he and his wife are the proud parents of four sons), his hand never again went through the kinds of dramatic changes it went through in those six weeks of drastic transformation.

FIGURE 7.2. The handprints of a university student, taken six weeks apart. Note the increase in the number of lines and the lengthening of the heart, fate, and union lines.

## LINE QUALITY AND QUANTITY

The ancient Chinese believed that the lines in the hand are similar to the distinctive grain found on a fine piece of wood. They thought that, as channels of life energy, or *chi*, hand lines that are clearly and beautifully formed reveal an intelligent, sensitive, and kind person who enjoys a happy and prosperous life.

Western palmists also believe that the lines of the hand should be clear and well defined and should have a color complementing that of the skin, whatever our racial heritage may be. Line depth and width should be even. A particularly deep line reveals abundant energy, while a broad, shallow line indicates a lack of strength and focus. Generally speaking, the stronger the line, the stronger its influence.

The number of lines on the hand is also important. An abundance of lines, as shown in Figure 7.3, indicates hypersensitivity and nervousness. It can also show that an individual has many paths in life through which to express his or her talents.

Few lines on the hand, as seen in Figure 7.4, generally indicate a thick skin and limited channels for life expression; the early Chinese believed that a person whose hands contained only three or four basic lines would have a circumscribed number of opportunities in life.

Splintering, or splitting, of a line (Figure 7.5) dissipates the line's strength and focus. In some cases, a split indicates a change or a new phase in a person's life, so its existence is not necessarily a negative sign, especially if the line remains strong. A split on the fate line, for example, could indicate a new career.

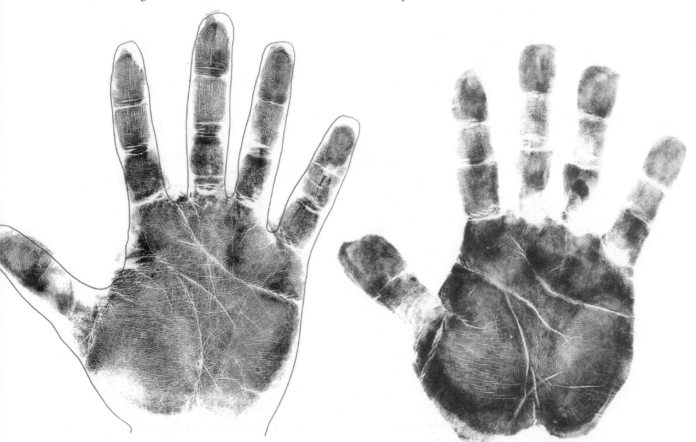

FIGURE 7.3. A handprint showing an abundance of lines.

FIGURE 7.4. A handprint showing few lines.

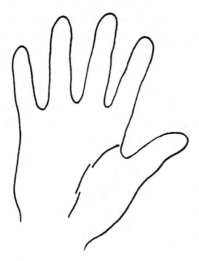

Figure 7.5. Splintering, or splitting, of a line.

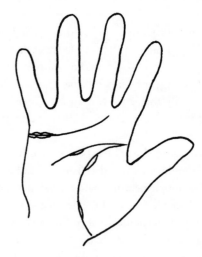

Figure 7.7. Islands on a line.

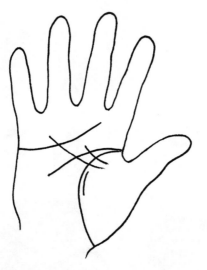

Figure 7.6. Lines of influence.

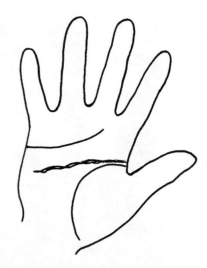

Figure 7.8. A chained line.

Lines of influence (Figure 7.6) are small lines that cross or run parallel to the major lines. Islands (Figure 7.7) form where a line splits from another line and reunites with it later on. Rarely a positive sign, islands impair a line's strength and indicate a lack of focus and a dissipation of energy. However, such formations also offer the opportunity to relinquish old patterns and adopt new insights into

one's physical or psychological well-being. A chain (Figure 7.8) is composed of many islands together and indicates a prolonged period of vacillation, a lack of focus, and a tendency to scatter energy. The line as a whole is weakened as a result.

A fork (Figure 7.9) appears as a split at the end of a line. Depending on its location, it can either indicate a dissipation of the basic energies represented

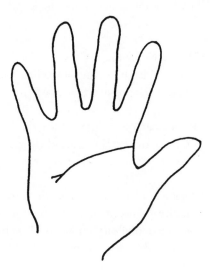

FIGURE 7.9. A forked line.

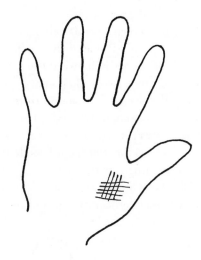

FIGURE 7.11. Lines forming a grille.

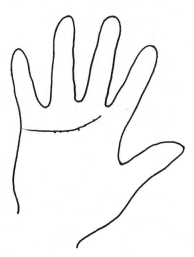

FIGURE 7.10. A dotted line.

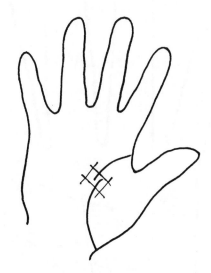

FIGURE 7.12. Lines forming a square.

in the line or reveal balance, adaptability, or even a special ability or talent.

A dot (Figure 7.10) appears as a slight colored indentation on a line. Depending on its color and location, the existence of a dot could indicate a physical or emotional setback of some kind.

Numerous fine lines that crisscross each other form what palmists call a grille (Figure 7.11). It generally indicates a period of diffused and scattered energy, although its meaning will depend on its location.

A square (Figure 7.12) is formed by four independent lines that create a rectangle. It is a sign of protection and preservation and often repairs a broken line. A square can reveal a special talent or ability, the nature of which depends on its location on the palm.

## THE LIFE LINE

The life line (known scientifically as the thenar crease) is the principal line of the hand. It begins at the edge of the palm between the thumb and forefinger and arcs downward around the mount of Venus. It is the primary indicator of the strength of our physical constitution and our level of vital force. This line records periods of disease, accidents, and other major events that touch our lives. It also indicates the *possible* length of time we can expect to live. Figure 7.13 shows how to gauge time in terms of age on the life line and other major lines of the hand.

When we want to determine the length of life, remember the following:

• When the life line is the same length on both hands, the ending of the line could indicate the possible time of death.

• If the lines are of different length, the line on the active hand is more likely to be correct.

• A long head, heart, or career line can modify a short life line, just as an abrupt termination of one or more of these lines can modify a long life line.

• *Never* predict a time of death. In the first place, there is a good chance you may be wrong. Many people with short life lines have been known to live to become great-grandparents, while others with long life lines have been known to die at a relatively young age. Also, by predicting the time of death, you may be planting a destructive thought in a person's mind, which can have unfortunate, self-fulfilling results.

Whenever you see a short or broken life line, be sure to mention that the lines of the hands are not set in concrete and that they can change according to our attitudes and habits. The life line is one of the most responsive to changes in attitude and lifestyle. I once read the hand of a pack-a-day smoker who quit immediately after the reading. Within three months, her life line had grown half an inch!

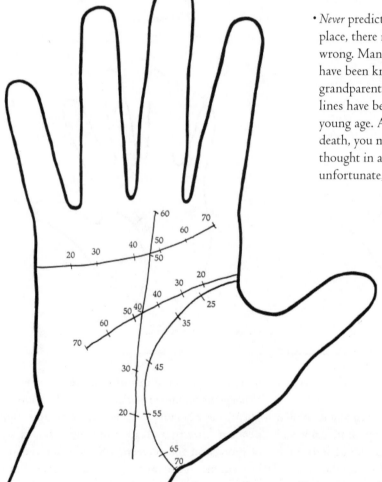

FIGURE 7.13. Gauging time on the hand.

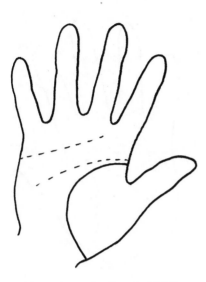

FIGURE 7.14. A long, clear, and well-marked life line.

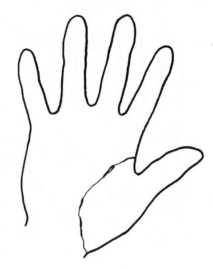

FIGURE 7.16. A long, weak life line.

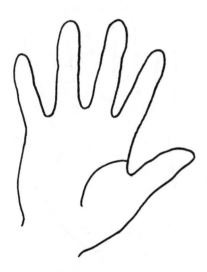

FIGURE 7.15. A short, clear, and well-marked life line.

No two life lines are the same, although most conform to the following brief descriptions:

- Long, clear, and well marked (Figure 7.14): This indicates a strong physical constitution, good health, vitality, and resistance to disease; the ability to meet life's challenges; and a probable long life.

- Short, clear, and well marked (Figure 7.15): This indicates intensity, good health, and possibly a short life. Check the length of the other major lines for confirming or modifying factors.

- Red and deep: This means powerful energy, intensity, and an aggressive or even violent disposition. Observe other hand characteristics for possible modifying factors.

- Wide and not well marked: This shows a personality that is easily influenced by outside stimuli; this person's life may tend to drift and lack clear direction.

- Long and weak (Figure 7.16): This indicates a weak constitution, vulnerability to disease, and a tendency toward nervousness and indecision.

- Accompanied by islands (Figure 7.17): This can mean periods of illness, general physical weakness, or periods of vulnerability to disease; it can also mean periods of confusion, indecision, or lack of focus in life.

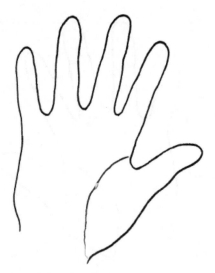

FIGURE 7.17. Islands on the life line.

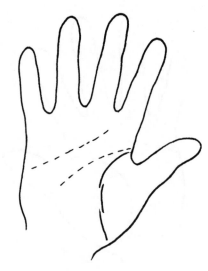

FIGURE 7.19. An overlapping break on the life line.

FIGURE 7.18. Breaks on the life line.

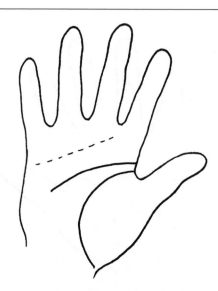

FIGURE 7.20. The life line separated from the head line.

• Broken in places (Figure 7.18): This indicates interruptions in the tenor of life, which can be physical, psychological, or both. A broken life line can also be a sign of accident or death, especially if "sister" lines—nearby parallel lines that can add strength to a weak or broken line—are lacking.

• Accompanied by an overlapping break (Figure 7.19): This might indicate a close call with death due to illness or accident, or a major shift in life direction on either a physical or psychological level.

• Separated from the head line (Figure 7.20): This indicates impulsiveness, impatience,

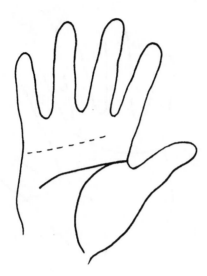

FIGURE 7.21. The life line connected to the head line.

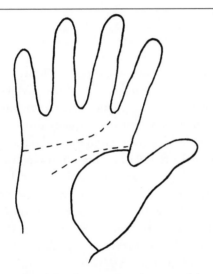

FIGURE 7.22. The life line forming a broad arc around the Venus mount.

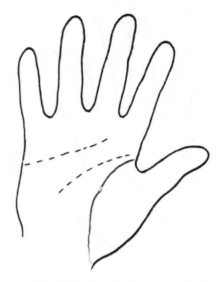

FIGURE 7.23. The life line hugging close to the thumb, cutting into the Venus mount.

self-reliance, and extroversion; depending on other features of the hand, it can also be a sign of recklessness.

- Connected to the head line (Figure 7.21): The owner of this hand is careful and cautious and takes a long time to make decisions. The point where the lines separate indicates the

age of independence from the family, either physically or psychologically. In general, the greater the distance over which the lines are connected, the longer it takes a person to make decisions and act independently.

- Forming a broad arc around the Venus mount (Figure 7.22): This is an indicator of a warm, affectionate, and emotionally responsive nature.

- Hugging close to the thumb, cutting into the Venus mount (Figure 7.23): This indicates an inhibited, cold, emotionally remote, and unresponsive character.

- Moving toward the mount of Luna (Figure 7.24): This reveals a naturally restless disposition; the owner of this hand loves to travel and enjoys frequent changes of scene.

- Branching from the life line and moving up toward the Jupiter finger (Figure 7.25): This is a sign of optimism, ambition, and a desire to overcome life's obstacles.

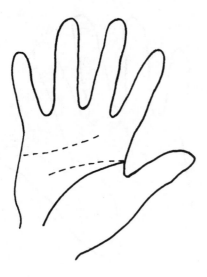

FIGURE 7.24. The life line moving toward the mount of Luna.

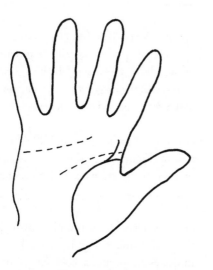

FIGURE 7.25. A branch from the life line moving upward toward the Jupiter mount.

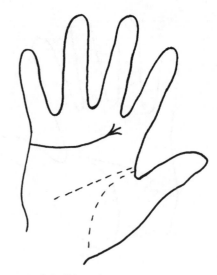

FIGURE 7.26. An "ideal" heart line.

The inner life line (also known as a "sister line") provides added strength and protection to the life line. It increases vitality and lends support (either physical or psychological) in the event of an accident, health problem, emotional trauma, or other difficulty.

## THE HEART LINE

The upper transverse crease, or heart line, is the emotional barometer of our lives. Moving from beneath the Mercury finger across the palm toward the Jupiter finger, it reveals the quality of our emotions, our degree of sensitivity, and our capacity for love and affection. This line can also provide important information regarding the physical condition of the heart as well as the strength and type of our sexual desire. In Chinese palmistry, the heart line is known as the Line of Heaven, since the ancient Chinese believed that the stars and all the heavens were a source of energy that gave life to both the human heart and spirit.

The ideal heart line (Figure 7.26) is smooth, of good color, and relatively free of islands and breaks. It curves upward slightly and ends between the Saturn and Jupiter fingers, indicating a balance between the mind and emotions. Two or three small branches sometimes appear at its end, revealing a balance among sentiment, common sense, and physical passion.

A straight heart line (Figure 7.27) reveals a mental type of lover. Fantasies, images, and romance are important aspects of this person's sexuality, which is primarily receptive in nature.

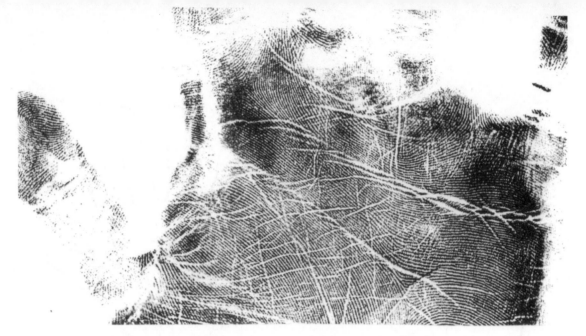

FIGURE 7.27. A straight, "mental" heart line.

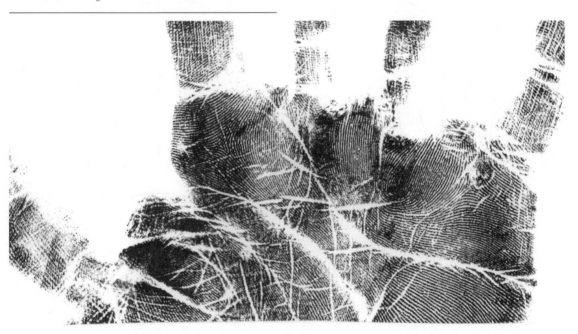

FIGURE 7.28. A heart line curving upward.

When the heart line curves upward (Figure 7.28) a physical or instinctual sexuality predominates. Sexual expression will likely be active and assertive.

Basic heart line descriptions include the following:

• Ending under Saturn (Figure 7.29): This reveals a predominantly physical type of sexuality; its owner is ruled more by the

head than the heart in love relationships. The individual with this type of heart line has a tendency to be emotionally cut off but also has strong sexual instincts.

• Ending between Saturn and Jupiter (Figure 7.30): This indicates a balance between reason and emotion in relationships; the

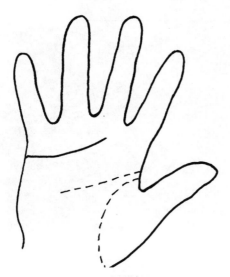

FIGURE 7.29. A heart line ending under Saturn.

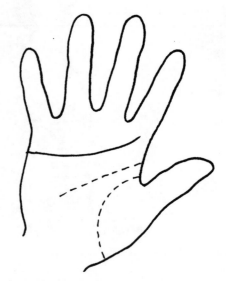

FIGURE 7.31. A heart line ending under Jupiter.

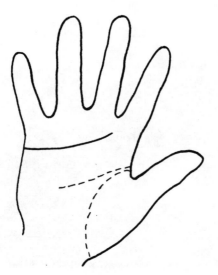

FIGURE 7.30. A heart line ending between Saturn and Jupiter.

FIGURE 7.32. A heart line dropping to the head and life lines.

person with this type of line is warmhearted, generous, and sympathetic by nature.

- Ending under Jupiter (Figure 7.31): This indicates idealism; the person with this type of line is ruled more by the heart than by the head in relationships and is a romantic, devoted, and poetic type of lover.

- Dropping to the life and head lines (Figure 7.32): This indicates strong conflicts between the heart and the head in relationships; a person with this type of line is prone to emotional extremes and finds it easier to love humanity than to love individuals.

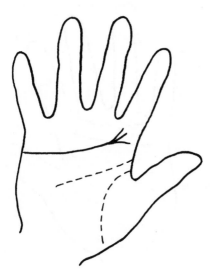

FIGURE 7.33. Branches at the end of the heart line.

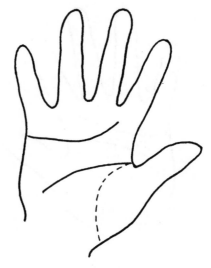

FIGURE 7.35. A wide space between the heart and head lines.

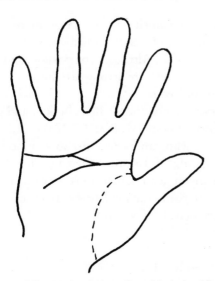

FIGURE 7.34. A line joining the heart line with the head line.

• Having chains: This reveals a high degree of sensitivity; a person with this type of line is easily hurt and emotionally affected by others. There is a desire for intimate contact with an accompanying fear of commitment, as well as a tendency to fall in and out of love frequently.

• Having branches at the end (Figure 7.33): This reveals a receptive nature.

• Having dots: This could possibly indicate heart disease.

• Connected to the head line (Figure 7.34): This reveals a balance between the emotions and the intellect in relationships.

• Widely separated from the head line (Figure 7.35): This shows a broad-minded, often unconventional outlook on life. A person with this type of line likes to share feelings with others but is impulsive and impatient, especially if the life and head lines are separate as well.

• Narrowly separated from the head line (Figure 7.36): This reveals a tendency to be narrow-minded and secretive. It might also indicate a repressed personality, especially if the head and life lines are joined.

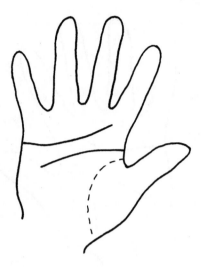

FIGURE 7.36. A narrow space between the heart and head lines.

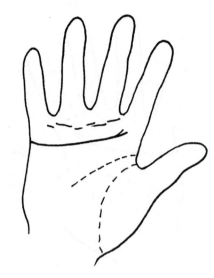

FIGURE 7.38. A broken and poorly formed girdle of Venus.

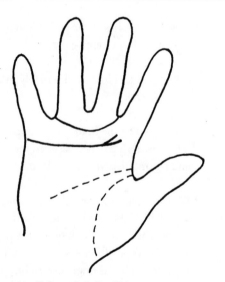

FIGURE 7.37. A well-formed girdle of Venus.

## THE GIRDLE OF VENUS

The girdle of Venus is like a second heart line and is located between the heart line and the top of the palm. Found on perhaps 10 percent of the population, its presence indicates sensitivity and emotional responsiveness. The clearer and more well defined this line is, the more balanced and

properly channeled a person's emotions will be. An example of a well-formed girdle can be seen in Figure 7.37. Altruism, compassion, and sexual responsiveness are strong attributes of such a girdle of Venus.

However, if the girdle is broken and poorly defined (Figures 7.38 and 7.27), it indicates a person who can be promiscuous, moody, and self-indulgent. Examine the entire hand before arriving at such conclusions, since other hand characteristics can modify the effects of a poorly formed girdle of Venus.

## THE HEAD LINE

The lower transverse crease, or head line, begins at the beginning of the life line and moves horizontally across the hand. It reveals our intelligence, our way of thinking, and our psychological disposition. The head line also records periods of emotional difficulty, mental illness, and any accidents or illnesses that affect the head.

A good head line is long, clear, and free of islands, dots, and breaks. It should slope gently downward and end with a small fork, denoting a balance

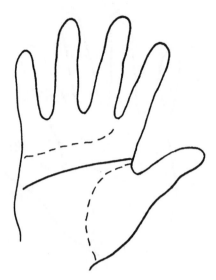

FIGURE 7.39. A long head line.

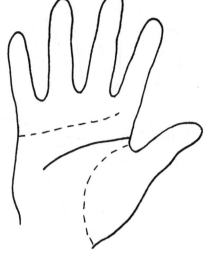

FIGURE 7.41. A strong head line.

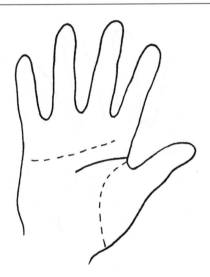

FIGURE 7.40. A short head line.

between realism and imagination. This feature is often found on the hands of writers and is known in palmistry as the writer's fork. Basic descriptions of the head line include the following:

- Long, ending beyond the Apollo finger (Figure 7.39): This indicates intelligence, mental and emotional flexibility, and a

wide range of intellectual interests.

- Short, just reaching the Saturn finger (Figure 7.40): This reveals a limited range of intellectual interests and a mind devoted primarily to mundane concerns.

- Strong (Figure 7.41): This indicates good mental capacity and an ability to concentrate on difficult problems.

- Weak (Figure 7.42): This indicates difficulty concentrating and may also indicate emotional difficulties.

- Accompanied by islands (Figure 7.43): This also indicates difficulty concentrating as well as a tendency to worry and suffer psychological disturbances.

- Wavy (Figure 7.44): This reveals a tendency to vacillate; the person with this type of line often changes his or her mind.

- Moving straight across the hand (Figure 7.45): This indicates practicality, realism,

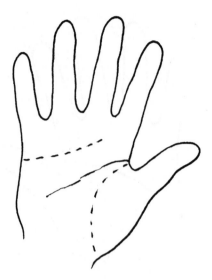

FIGURE 7.42. A weak head line.

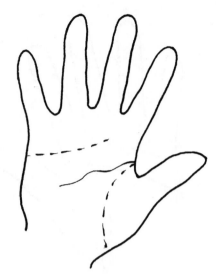

FIGURE 7.44. A wavy head line.

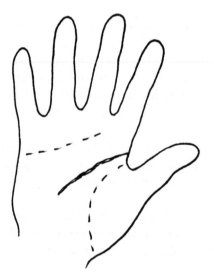

FIGURE 7.43. An islanded head line.

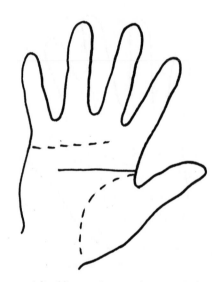

FIGURE 7.45. A head line moving straight across the hand.

and analytical tendencies; the person with this type of head line may lack imagination in dealing with problems.

- Sloping slightly downward toward Luna (Figure 7.46): This indicates a person with an imaginative approach to problems as well as a creative intellect.

- Sloping strongly toward Luna (Figure 7.47): This indicates a strong and fertile imagination. The person with this type of head line has a tendency to live in a dream world, where small problems can develop into major crises. If the line is broken, there may also be suicidal fantasies.

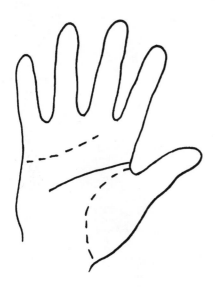

FIGURE 7.46. A head line sloping toward the mount of Luna.

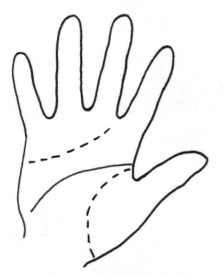

FIGURE 7.47. A head line dropping strongly toward the mount of Luna.

## THE SIMIAN LINE

The single transverse palmar crease, or simian line, exists when the heart and head lines appear to join together as one. It appears as a straight line across the palm, as shown in Figure 7.48.

At times, the simian line forms a clear channel across the hand. Yet is it also possible for a fragmentary heart or head line to be attached to a simian line in one way or another. These fragments look like broken pieces associated with the main line, the most common appearing as a fragment of a heart line floating above a loose simian bar. Amateur palmists often consider this line a girdle of Venus, but it is simply a piece of line left over when the simian pattern was formed.

The simian line is often misunderstood. Many palmists feel that it represents brutality and other animalistic tendencies, but this is not true. In general, this line tends to intensify both the mind and the personality. People with simian lines are often of strong character and tend to alternate between one emotional extreme and another, a situation in which feelings often conflict with the intellect. People with simian lines also have great tenacity of purpose, enjoy challenges and hard work, and have a strong potential for accomplishment.

Owners of simian lines often have difficulty relaxing and may have problems relating to others. You can find a good many simian lines among people who stand apart from the mainstream of society, including members of fringe religions and peripheral political or social groups. People with simian lines have a great deal of restless energy. When simian lines are found in hands with coarse skin, bent fingers, or poor line patterns, destructive or antisocial activity can result. However, for the majority of people with simian lines, this restless energy can be better released through hard work or dynamic exercise such as handball, squash, or martial arts.

The owner of the hand shown in Figure 7.48 is an eighty-two-year old Taiwanese grandmother who overcame tremendous hardship during much of her life. Born into poverty, Kim Mei was sold to a middle-class family as a little girl and served the family as a housekeeper. She was later forced to marry one of the sons, an alcoholic. She eventually had to support her sick husband and five young children. Kim Mei managed to study nursing part-time while taking care of her family and became a registered nurse. She eventually became one of the

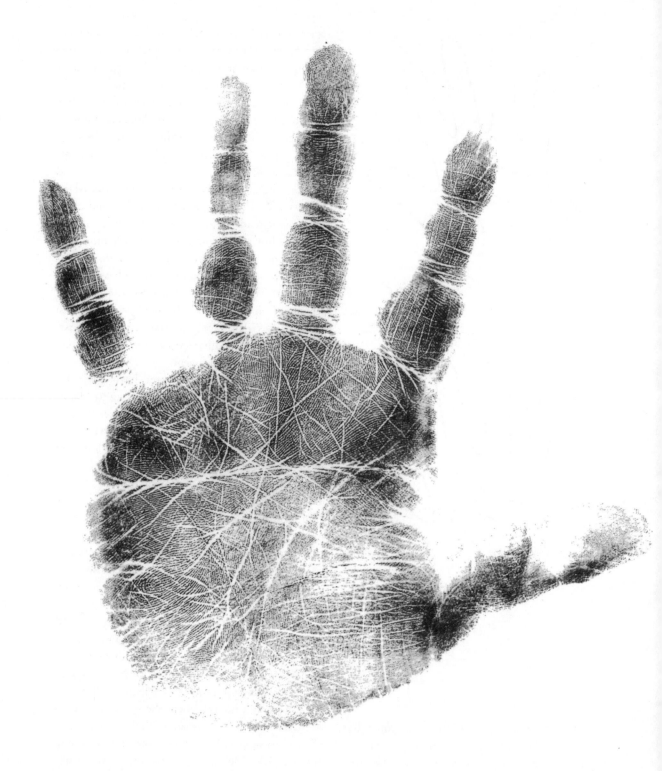

FIGURE 7.48. A hand with a clearly formed simian line.

most respected health-care providers in her community and is still consulted by neighbors who seek her advice. Now retired, Kim Mei has seen all her children go on to college and professional careers. She also enjoys an active life that includes mountain climbing, dance, and travel.

Like Kim Mei, many people with simian lines are tough but emotionally sensitive. However, if the skin texture, mounts, and fingers indicate a coarse personality, the owner of the simian line can be violent and unpredictable. Be sure to examine the entire hand carefully before making your evaluation.

## THE LINE OF SATURN

The vertical distal crease, or line of Saturn (Figure 7.1), is also known as the fate line, destiny line, career line, or line of life task. This line normally moves upward from just above the wrist toward the mount of Saturn. It should really be called the line of achievement, because it shows the degree to which we have fulfilled our most important goals in life. It indicates our level of personal success and self-fulfillment as well as recording the obstacles, changes, and restrictions that challenge us during our lifetime. In Indian palmistry, this line is known as *Indira rehka*, after the Hindu goddess of wealth.

The implications of this line are highly subjective. A bank president who is frustrated with his career direction can have a weak or broken Saturn line, while the man who cleans the executive's office and is satisfied with his work can have a line that is strong, long, and free of breaks.

Like the other major lines, the Saturn line should be deep, clear, and free of islands, downward branches, or dots. The further up on the hand it begins, the later in life a person will likely find happiness in his or her life's work.

## THE LINE OF APOLLO

This vertical line is found on the mount of Apollo, as seen in Figure 7.1. Long Apollo lines are rare, and

most consist of a small dash (or a series of overlapping dashes) beginning at the top of the heart line and extending to slightly below the ring finger.

The presence of this line, which was called the line of capability by the famous American palmist William G. Benham, indicates the potential for achievement in life. It points to honors, success, money, and creative ability, especially in areas involving art and music. It can also be a sign of deep personal fulfillment. Many well-known artists, musicians, actors, and writers have a strong line of Apollo, although this line is also found on the hands of people who simply love music, art, and other things of beauty.

## THE MERCURY LINE

Known also as the health, or stomach, line, the line of Mercury (Figure 7.1) indicates the degree of balance in a person's body and his or her basic nervous state. Ideally, this line should not appear at all, but when it does, it moves from the base of the life line toward the Mercury, or little, finger.

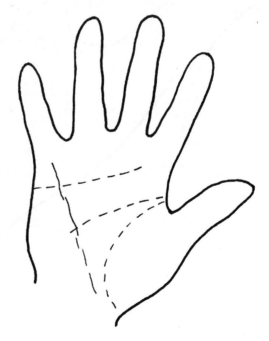

FIGURE 7.49. Breaks in the line of Mercury.

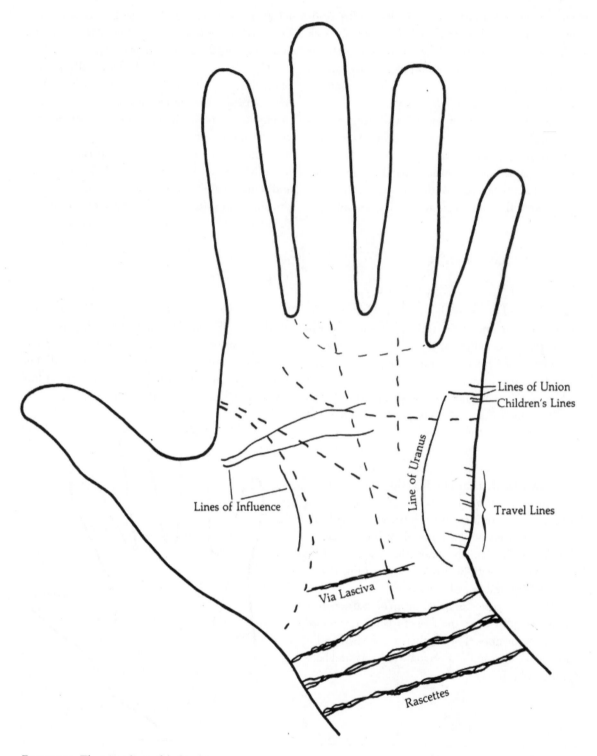

Lines of Union

Children's Lines

Line of Uranus

Travel Lines

Lines of Influence

Via Lasciva

Rascettes

FIGURE 7.50. The minor lines of the hand.

When the Mercury line is deep and free from breaks, it indicates a strong physical constitution and good digestion. Breaks in the line (Figure 7.49) reveal stomach and intestinal problems due to nervousness, repressed emotions, or physical factors such as poor diet or intestinal parasites. It may also indicate gynecological problems in women.

## THE LINE OF NEPTUNE

The line of Neptune, or via lascivia, is considered one of the minor lines of the hand. However, its appearance has become increasingly common in recent years, and recognizing its presence can be of vital importance for those who have it on their hands. This line (which is often a series of small overlapping lines) normally branches off the base of the life line and moves toward the lower mount of Mars or the mount of Luna, as seen in Figure 7.50.

The existence of this line reveals a strong sensitivity to drugs, tobacco, alcohol, and other toxic substances. It is also found on people who are prone to become dependent on one or more of these substances, which can also include much-loved foods containing caffeine and sugar, such as coffee, soft drinks, chocolate, and pastry. People who are prone to food allergies often have this line on their hands as well.

Those who have this line on their hands must be careful when taking prescribed or over-the-counter medications. In addition to having a higher-than-average sensitivity to each individual drug, they are also more likely to experience adverse side effects when drugs are combined.

Ironically, people whose hands feature the via lascivia often have a strong interest in natural therapies such as herbal medicine and homeopathy. The line is also found on the hands of doctors of naturopathy and other types of natural healing; many of them likely reacted strongly to food allergies or drugs as children and eventually developed an interest in helping others attain good health through natural means.

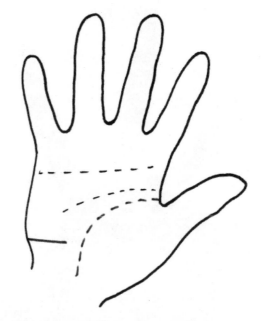

FIGURE 7.51. A long travel line on the mount of Luna.

## TRAVEL LINES

Travel lines are tiny horizontal lines located on the outer edge of the palm. Each line stands for an important journey, and the position of each line is determined by a person's age at the time of the journey. Trips represented may be important in terms of distance, duration, or their overall impact on the life of the traveler. For a businessperson who is constantly traveling all over the world, a month-long visit to the Far East would probably be of minor importance, whereas a two-hundred-mile journey to Milwaukee would appear as a major travel experience on the hand of a farmer who rarely ventures out of northern Wisconsin. The more important the journey to the individual, the longer and deeper the travel line.

Some people have a line that at first closely resembles a travel line, but is deeper, longer, and located only on the mount of Luna (Figure 7.51). Although hand readers do not generally agree on its significance, this line appears to be found on people who are extremely fond of adventure and risk, whether physical, psychological, or both.

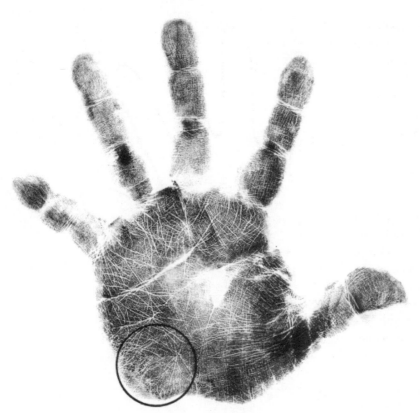

FIGURE 7.52. The handprint of a young Uruguayan revolutionary with a low-set thumb.

## THE LINE OF URANUS

The line of Uranus, or the intuitive crescent, begins on the mount of Luna and moves in a gentle arc toward the mount of Mercury, sometimes moving parallel to the Mercury, or stomach, line (refer to Figure 7.49).

While this line rarely exists in its perfect form, it indicates a powerful intuition with strong psychic abilities. It is often found on clairvoyants, mediums, and healers.

This line is more common in its incomplete state and appears as a short line (or several short parallel lines) moving diagonally across Luna toward the center of the palm, as seen in Figure 7.52. It indicates intuitive perception.

## LINES OF UNION

These short horizontal lines are found on the mount of Mercury and run from the edge of the hand toward the center of the palm. Formerly called marriage lines, the lines of union indicate important relationships that impress the person deeply. These relationships do not necessarily involve marriage. They can be with either a man or a woman and may or may not include sex. The stronger the line, the deeper the potential union.

To determine the age at which these potential unions might occur, measure upward from the heart line. Midway between the heart line and the base of the Mercury finger should be the point that indicates approximately thirty-five years of age. However, rely on your intuition to determine the exact age.

## CHILDREN LINES

The existence and location of so-called children lines are subject to controversy among hand readers. From my experience, they appear as tiny horizontal lines located beneath the lines of union. Like other aspects of the hand, they reveal potential only.

In places like Latin America, where contraception and abortion are less common than in other regions of the world, the correlation between the number of children a person has and the number of children lines on his or her hand is fairly accurate. There, six tiny lines under the line of union would almost always indicate six children.

However, in countries where birth control is routinely practiced, predicting the number of children a person might have is more difficult. Miscarriages and abortions are recorded on the hand as potential children, as are children conceived by artificial means. In general, children lines can be read with greater accuracy on the hands of women (after all, it is they who give birth), although these lines can occasionally be found on the hands of men. On rare occasions, adopted daughters and sons can appear as children lines, although these lines indicate biological children as a rule. As I have told many palmistry clients, beloved companion animals like cats and dogs are *not* represented as children lines on the hand!

## RASCETTES OF VENUS

The rascettes are lines that appear on the underside of the wrist (Figure 7.50). Each strong, unbroken line is said to represent thirty years of good health. Weak, broken, or chained rascettes reveal a weak physical condition and have been linked to gynecological problems in women. Be sure to examine other aspects of the hand for confirmation.

## LINES OF INFLUENCE

Influence lines are small lines that can modify the meanings of the major lines of the hand. There are two basic types:

1. Lines that run parallel to the vertical and diagonal lines of the hand (such as those of life, Saturn, and Apollo) strengthen these lines. In many cases, they repair a split or strengthen a section of a line that is islanded or chained.

2. Lines of influence can also emanate from the mount of Venus and move horizontally across the hand, as shown in Figure 7.6. Generally speaking, these horizontal lines indicate obstacles, traumas, and times of testing.

This second type of influence line is not necessarily negative in meaning; it often records an event that provides wisdom and valuable life experience. A loss of a job, for example, can open the door to new and better career opportunities. In contrast, winning the lottery is often seen as a wonderful event, but difficulty in adapting to sudden wealth has destroyed many marriages, ruined long-time friendships, and even led some jackpot winners to consider suicide.

If, at the point of crossing a line (usually the life or head line), a red dot is formed, a major illness or accident is possible. This would also hold true if an island or break follows the point of crossing. Examine other lines for confirming or modifying indicators.

# SKIN RIDGE PATTERNS

As PART OF OUR GENETIC HERITAGE, EVERY human being possesses a unique pattern of dermatoglyphics, the skin ridges of the hands and feet. Taken from the Greek words *derma*, meaning skin, and *glyphe*, meaning carve, the skin ridge patterns of the fingers and palms have fascinated humans since primitive times. According to Julian Verbov, MD, of the University of Liverpool, skin ridges help us retain a better grip on the objects we hold and may also improve our sense of touch.[1]

Archaeologists have found that fingerprints were used for identification as early as the time of Christ. As we saw in Figure I.I, Chinese contracts written during the Qing dynasty (1644-1912) bore the palm prints (and often the fingerprints) of the parties concerned. In addition to being a unique and reliable form of identification, skin ridge patterns can provide important physical and psychological information that can be useful for the palmistry student or professional hand consultant.

Because skin ridge patterns are genetically unique, they show basic inherited characteristics, attitudes, and tendencies. Deciphering these patterns can be an important part of an overall hand analysis because it can aid in evaluating health, career, relationships, and an individual's self-awareness. If the fingerprints are strong and clear, they intensify the meaning of each type of pattern and bring out its positive qualities.

## FINGERPRINTS

Although scientific interest in dermatoglyphics goes back to seventeenth-century Europe, it wasn't until 1823 that the great Czech physiologist and anatomist Jan Evangelista Purkinje (1787–1869)

FIGURE 8.I. The title page of Sir Francis Galton's book *Finger Prints* (1892).

became the first to attempt a systematic analysis of fingertip patterns. Sixty-five years later, the English polymath Sir Francis Galton (1822–1911) was the first to describe a practical classification of fingerprints, a method that is still in use today. The title page of his book *Finger Prints*, published in 1892, is reproduced in Figure 8.I. However, it wasn't until the twentieth century that the police finally accepted fingerprints as definitive proof of identity.

Today, fingerprint analysis is part of the field of biometrics, or the science of determining a person's identity through his or her unique physical features. Other modern branches of biometrics include face recognition technology, hand geometry, and iris recognition. While fingerprints remain important for identification, they are not as accurate as DNA. As a result, law enforcement agencies have focused more on DNA analysis and other means of identification when determining guilt or innocence.

Even if you are not wanted by the FBI or Scotland Yard, many palmists believe that your fingerprints are important because they represent the most basic and unchangeable elements of your personality. Although you can learn to modify the traits they represent, you can never completely be rid of them. Several medical texts discuss the genetic and physiological significance of fingerprint patterns, and dozens of scientific and medical journals have featured articles about them.

There are three basic types of fingerprint patterns: the whorl, the arch, and the loop. They account for most fingerprint patterns.

FIGURE 8.2. Fingerprint in the whorl pattern.

### Whorls

Making its appearance on an estimated 25 percent of hands, the whorl (Figure 8.2) is the sign of the individualist and the specialist. A person whose fingerprints are mainly of the whorl type tends to be an original thinker and has clearly formed opinions. People with whorls often seek to carve out their own niches in life and become experts in some specialized area.

When whorls predominate on the fingers, a person can become a law unto himself and will disregard convention if it gets in the way of his personal desires. People with whorls also tend to dislike others interfering in their personal affairs. Whorls are often found on the hands of social reformers and career criminals because they both defy social convention and are unhappy with the status quo.

Positive qualities of the whorl include:

• Independence

• Love of freedom

• Capability in many fields of endeavor

Negative traits include:

• Tendency toward isolation

• Secretiveness

• Self-obsession

### Arches

The arch (Figure 8.3) is a sign of capability and trustworthiness and is found on an estimated 5 percent of hands. People whose fingerprints are primarily of the arch pattern tend to be practical, hardworking, efficient, and good with their hands. They often work as craftspeople, farmers, mechanics, and surgeons. They are often better able to express themselves through actions than through words.

Positive aspects of the arch include:

• Steadiness

• Realism

• Practicality

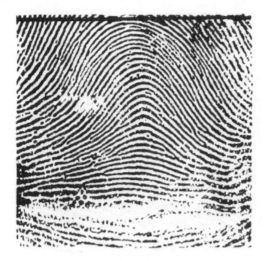

Figure 8.3. Fingerprint in the arch pattern.

Figure 8.4. Fingerprint in the loop pattern.

Negative traits include:

• Emotional repression

• A suspicious nature

• Reluctance to accept change

Generally speaking, the higher the arch, the more skillful and idealistic the individual.

### Loops

The loop (Figure 8.4) is by far the most common fingerprint pattern and is found on approximately 60 to 70 percent of all hands. It represents an easy-going, adaptable, middle-of-the-road personality.

Owners of hands where loops predominate are generally easy to get along with and are able to adapt easily to new and varied social situations. They are also able to grasp most intellectual concepts with little difficulty, and react quickly to changing social situations, especially if their hand is flexible as well.

Positive qualities of the loop include a flexible personality and an ability to sustain a well-rounded view of the world.

The primary negative aspect of this pattern is the tendency to lack individuality. Wherever a loop is found, it reflects the basic middle-ground tendencies of that particular finger.

### Other Fingertip Patterns

• The tented arch (Figure 8.5) earns its name from the vertical line—resembling a tent pole—that appears in the middle of the arch. Although it still reflects the qualities of the ordinary arch, it a sign of a heightened degree of emotional sensitivity, idealism, and enthusiasm.

• The high loop (Figure 8.6) looks like a normal loop pattern, except that it reaches higher up on the fingertip than a regular loop. It reveals high intelligence and an optimistic personality.

• The composite pattern is also known as the double loop, or twinned loop. It is composed of two loops curling around each other, as seen in Figure 8.7. This pattern is a sign

FIGURE 8.5. A tented arch fingerprint.

FIGURE 8.7. A composite fingerprint.

FIGURE 8.6. A high loop fingerprint.

of duality—a natural ability to see both sides of any issue. It is often found on the fingertips of mediators, analysts, therapists, lawyers, and counselors, for whom an objective, well-balanced outlook is useful. However, people with twinned loops often have difficulty making decisions because they need to research a situation thoroughly before feeling competent to choose. They may take forever to make a

purchase in a store or to make a change in a job or relationship, especially if the lines of life and head are connected at their commencement.

## SKIN PATTERNS ON THE PALM

Palmar ridge patterns serve as an additional guidepost as we endeavor to achieve a clear, specialized understanding of human personality traits. Everyone's fingers show distinct patterns like the whorl, loop or arch. Yet while every person's palm contains skin ridges, not everyone possesses clearly defined and distinguishable loops, whorls, and other skin ridge patterns on their palms.

As a general rule, black people tend to have thicker skin ridges than whites or Asians do, and men tend to have thicker ridges than women do. At any point on the palm, the skin ridges can run close together or far apart and can be thick, thin, composed of numerous broken points, or formed in clear, unbroken lines. A loop can be so vague that you may have trouble seeing it without a strong magnifying glass or so bold that it seems to jump out at you. This is something that can be learned only after examining and comparing the skin texture of a good many hands.

## The Raja Loop

The Raja loop (also known as the loop of charisma) is found between the Jupiter and Saturn fingers, as seen in Figure 8.8. Although extremely rare, it is always a good pattern to have, since it reveals a strong ability to lead and inspire others. People with Raja loops often gather a following of devoted admirers. The Raja loop can be found on successful politicians, entertainers, and religious leaders, as well as on people who are considered an authority in their chosen field of work or study.

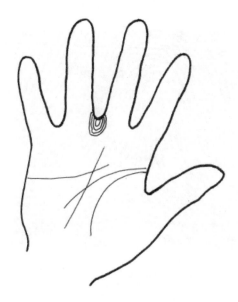

FIGURE 8.9. The loop of seriousness.

mission in life. They don't like to waste time and are driven toward achieving their career goals. As a result, they often make money and can be found in the upper echelons of their chosen profession.

Some loops of seriousness can easily be seen with the naked eye, while others require the use of a magnifying glass. Like other skin ridge patterns, the loop of seriousness should be large and well defined in order to reveal its full meaning.

## The Loop of Humor

The loop of humor (Figure 8.10) is located between the Apollo and Mercury fingers. In contrast to individuals with the loop of seriousness, people who have this loop tend to value comfort and pleasure over status and financial rewards. They tend to take life easy, laugh things off, and have a sense of the ridiculous.

They tend to choose a profession that provides them with interest and enjoyment over one that pays well. Some of the funniest people I have ever met have loops of humor on their palms, including an editor for *Mad* magazine.

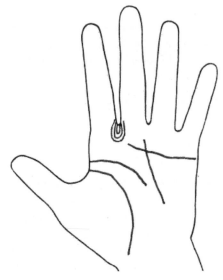

FIGURE 8.8. The Raja loop.

## The Loop of Seriousness

The loop of seriousness (Figure 8.9) is located between the fingers of Saturn and Apollo. It is far more common than the Raja loop and can be found on approximately 20 percent of all hands.

The presence of this loop reveals a serious, responsible, and often ambitious individual. People with this loop tend to have a definite purpose or

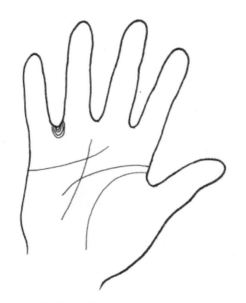

FIGURE 8.10. The loop of humor.

FIGURE 8.11. The vanity loop.

The presence of both a loop of seriousness and a loop of humor on the same hand indicates that the individual can have both a serious approach to life and the ability to enjoy it at the same time.

### The Vanity Loop

The vanity loop is somewhat rare. It consists of a large loop that entirely encompasses the Apollo mount, as seen in Figure 8.11. In general, the presence of this loop has two meanings that can be considered either together or separately: (1) it reveals a person who is excessively preoccupied with his or her appearance, and (2) it betrays a tendency to be overly sensitive to criticism.

### The Memory Loop

The so-called memory loop is found on perhaps 10 percent of all hands and is usually located in or just above the mount of Luna. In addition to revealing a good memory (whether for facts or for emotional impressions and experiences), the presence of this loop is said to provide insight into the minds and motives of others.

When located near the mount of Mars, this loop reveals a practical type of memory, while a loop located deep in the Luna mount can indicate psychic ability. It is often found among clairvoyants, astrologers, palmists, and card readers.

The handprint reproduced in Figure 8.12 is unusual for the number of interesting dermatoglyphics it contains. In addition to a whorl on each fingertip, it features a larger than average memory loop, a Raja loop, a loop of seriousness, and a music loop set high on the Venus mount at the thumb joint. The hand belongs to a multitalented man who works as an information technologist in Latin America.

### The Nature Loop

The nature loop (Figure 8.13) is normally located on the mount of Luna, well below where the head line ends. It is often found on people who have a strong affinity with nature and who are able to receive inspiration from being in a natural environment. This loop can also indicate psychic ability,

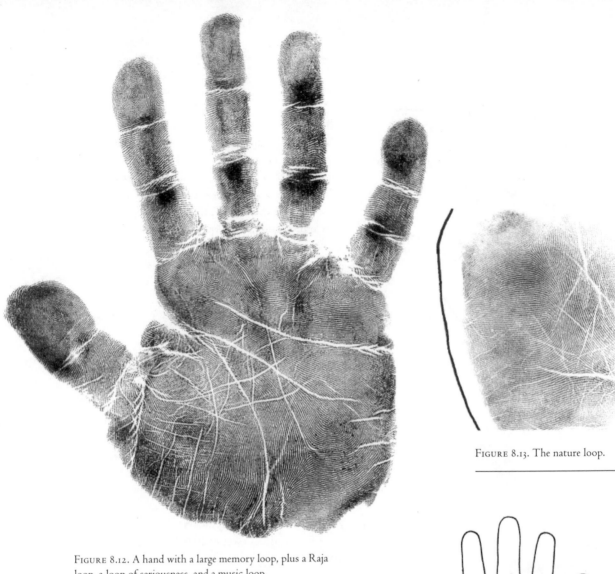

FIGURE 8.12. A hand with a large memory loop, plus a Raja loop, a loop of seriousness, and a music loop.

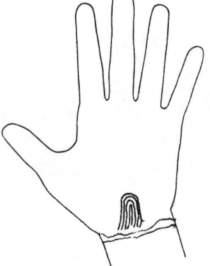

FIGURE 8.13. The nature loop.

especially where it concerns nature. Owners of this loop often have a special ability to communicate with animals and plants, as well as with the subtle forces in nature known as *devas*, or nature spirits.

### The Empathy Loop

Somewhat uncommon, the empathy loop rises from the wrist area just where skin ridge patterns begin on the hand, as seen in Figure 8.14. People with this loop tend to take a special interest in others and are able to feel compassion for them.

FIGURE 8.14. The empathy loop.

FIGURE 8.17. The loop of courage.

FIGURE 8.15. The music loop.

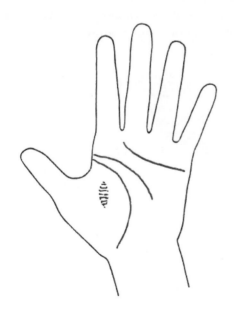

FIGURE 8.16. The bee.

### The Loop of Music

The music loop can be found toward the bottom of the mount of Venus, as shown in Figure 8.15. Although rare, this loop is occasionally found on people who are deeply moved by music. If the loop is clearly marked on both hands, the individual may choose to make music a career, whether as a composer, a performer, or teacher.

### The Bee

The bee (Figure 8.16) is found on people who have a strong love for music made by stringed instruments such as the guitar, cello, or violin. Located near the center of the Venus mount, it is sometimes found on professional musicians.

### The Loop of Courage

Although rare, the so-called loop of courage (Figure 8.17) is located on the lower mount of Mars. When it exists, it is a sign of courage and fearlessness.

FIGURE 8.18. A whorl on the mount of Luna.

## Whorl on Luna

A whorl pattern on the mount of Luna (Figure 8.18) is also rare. When it exists, it is a sign of a powerful imagination and a strong ability to visualize. Some palmists feel that it is a sign of clairvoyance and psychic ability.

## Composite Pattern on Luna

A small number of individuals, like the psychotherapist whose hand is shown in Figure 8.19, possess a twinned-loop pattern on the mount of Luna. Sometimes called the S-bend pattern, it is a sure sign of strong creative and instinctual abilities. When confronted with a problem or other issue they need to deal with, people with such a pattern may find that the solution will appear in their dreams or during meditation.

Some palmists feel that this pattern is found on people who strongly feature psychological traits popularly identified with the opposite sex. For example, men with this pattern would tend to be very gentle and sensitive, while women with this pattern would be tough, competitive, and assertive.

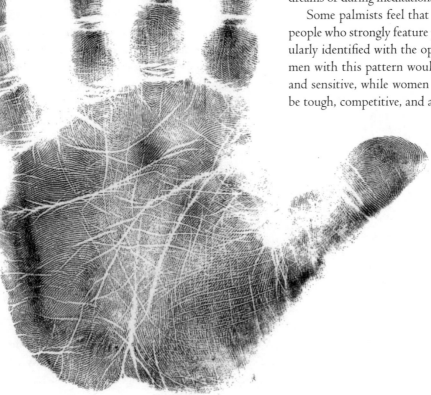

FIGURE 8.19. A composite S-bend pattern on the mount of Luna.

# Part II

# THE HAND AND YOUR INNER WORLD

# INTELLECT, IMAGINATION, IDEATION

Perhaps the most outstanding feature of hand analysis is its ability to offer an objective and deep understanding of our intellectual potential: our level of intelligence, our memory, our ability to concentrate, and the extent of our creative imagination. Since the vast majority of us use only a small amount of our brain power, palmistry can offer clues that can help us expand our interests and train our minds to become more flexible, more broad, and more powerful.

Emotion is one of the primary characteristics of our human makeup. It serves as both a motivator and a bridge that propels us and transports us toward new spheres of understanding, new levels of consciousness, and new levels of existence. Like the intellect, palmistry can help us better understand our emotional nature. Our capacity for sensitivity, emotionality, and joy can easily be seen in the hand, as can our tendencies for melancholy, depression, and anger.

The hands also reveal our capacity for inner strength. In a world that is often insecure and chaotic, an understanding of the human hand can help us better assess our ability to resist outside pressures and adapt to change.

Moreover, by learning how to read hand gestures, we can perceive the subtle messages we and others are communicating. Unlike the voice and even the muscles of the face, hand movements offer a more spontaneous and truthful message because they are largely subconscious.

## YOUR HAND-READING IQ

Intelligence works on both concrete and abstract levels and involves a variety of factors, including understanding what others are saying, being able to express ideas to others, the ability to see similarities and differences between objects and issues, the ability to work with numbers and compute data, and the capacity to find an underlying rule or structure in a series of events, objects, or numbers.

Memory is another big part of intelligence. It not only involves our ability to recall smells, visual impressions, and sensations related to touch, hearing, and taste, but also includes an ability to recall people, places, events, and other concrete phenomena dating back to earliest childhood.

The head line is the hand's primary indicator of intelligence. Other factors, including the shape of the hand, the presence of a memory loop on the palm, hand consistency, and hand flexibility, can reveal the intensity of our intelligence and the direction in which it can be expressed.

## THE INTELLIGENT HEAD LINE

The head line shows the range of our intellectual interests. The longer the line, the more numerous the interests. Some feel that the head line reveals the level of our intelligence and how we use it in daily life as well. A long head line also indicates that one's thinking is careful, detailed, and comprehensive.

Perhaps one of the most brilliant people of the twentieth century, Albert Einstein (1879–1955) was a German-born theoretical physicist and Nobel Prize winner who is best known for the theory of relativity, specifically his theory of mass-energy equivalence: $E = mc^2$. His head line ran almost to the end of his palm, as seen in Figure 9.1.

Einstein's palm was long and broad, and his fingers were short and smooth. His life line was separated from his head line, revealing an impatient

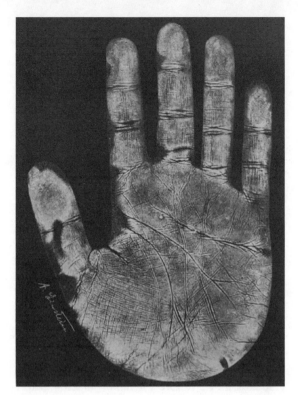

FIGURE 9.1. The hand of Albert Einstein. From *Hand und Personichkeit* by Marianne Raschig (Hamburg: Gebruder Enoch Verlag, 1931)

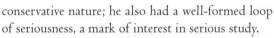

and impulsive nature. Yet Einstein's closely held fingers and high-set thumb indicate a conservative nature; he also had a well-formed loop of seriousness, a mark of interest in serious study.

Einstein's head line was long, deep, clearly formed, and completely free of islands and frets. It not only drooped down toward the mount of Luna, revealing a powerful imagination, but had a branch moving toward the mount of Mars about three-quarters of the way down the line, betraying a practical view of life. I've often seen such long and deep head lines on people with genius-level IQ.

The small diagonal lines moving up from the mount of Luna indicate strong intuition, which likely contributed to Einstein's scientific discoveries. He also had a well-formed charisma loop (located between the Jupiter and Saturn fingers) and a long, straight Mercury finger, an indicator of honesty and excellent communication skills. In addition to lecturing and teaching, Einstein wrote several books,

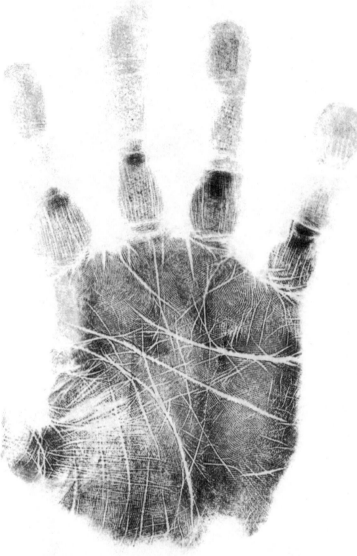

FIGURE 9.2. The handprint of an individual with a genius-level IQ, showing a long, clear head line.

and his private correspondence between 1912 and 1955 totaled more than thirty-five hundred pages.

Whorls can be seen on his thumb, index, and ring fingertips, attesting to his original intellect, independent nature, and powerful creativity. In addition to being a scientist, Einstein was a noted humanitarian, as confirmed by his long and sensitive heart line. In addition to physics, he lectured and wrote extensively on religion, racial equality,

FIGURE 9.3. A long head line with a slight upward curving at the end.

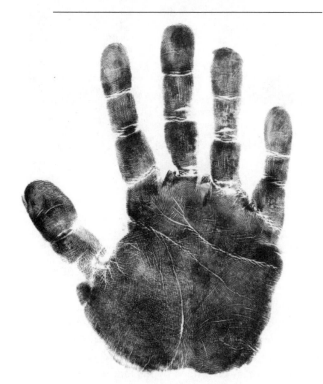

FIGURE 9.4. A handprint showing a weak, fretted head line.

philosophy, world peace, and psychology. One of his early books was coauthored with psychiatrist Sigmund Freud. In 1999, Einstein was named "Person of the Century" by *Time* magazine. Even more than fifty years after his death, his name is equated with the term *genius*.

Another long head line, seen in Figure 9.2, belongs to a woman who scored second in a series of intelligence tests given to twenty-eight hundred pre-university students by the New York City Department of Education, placing her in the 99.9th percentile. Her hand features a very clear memory loop, located just under the final quarter of her head line. Another sign that reveals above-average intelligence is a predominance of high loops on the fingertips.

Another type of head line indicting superior intelligence I've occasionally come across is long and gradually moves toward the mount of Luna before changing direction and moving slightly upward, as seen in Figure 9.3. The head line reproduced here is of a Taiwanese electronic technician who is one of the brightest people I've ever met. He presently oversees maintenance at a nuclear power plant and has taken graduate-level courses in his line of work. This type of head line reveals a mind that is highly adaptable and seeks a balance between imagination and realism.

Before we gloat (or despair, as the case may be) over the length and shape of our head line, remember that a short head line does not necessarily mean that one is short on intelligence. Rather, it reveals a person whose thinking is simple, practical, and to the point. Thought processes are limited to mundane affairs.

None of us uses our mental power to the fullest anyway. On the average, we utilize only 5 to 7 percent of our intelligence during our lifetime. So an individual whose head line barely clears the space under her Saturn mount may be using quantitatively more intelligence than her neighbor, whose head line crosses her entire palm. Remember as well that the head line can grow longer or shorter over time.

A lot depends on how we exercise the brain. Do we spend our leisure time passively, or do we devote our free time to expanding our range of knowledge? The extent to which we use our inherent mental talents and abilities depends on us!

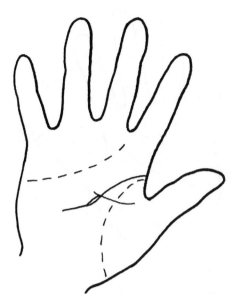

FIGURE 9.5. An island, formed by an influence line, on the head line.

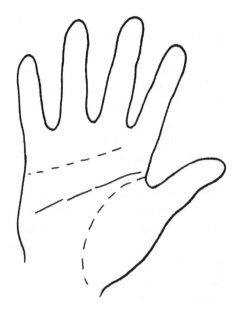

FIGURE 9.7. Breaks on the head line.

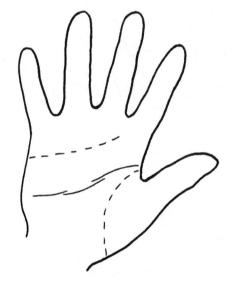

FIGURE 9.6. Overlaps on the head line.

The clarity and strength of the head line are also reliable indicators of present capability. A clear, well-defined head line reveals a good ability to evaluate concepts and situations, a strong memory, and a clarity of purpose that can lead to concrete action. Head lines that are weak, chained, islanded, or fretted, as seen in Figure 9.4, reveal a less grounded type of mental energy, which undermines clear thinking and diminishes our capacity to focus and act.

Islands have several meanings on the head line. They indicate difficulty in concentration, confusion, and the tendency to be scatterbrained. Neurotic behavior, such as anxiety, phobias, or depression, may also be indicated, although these signs can be found in people with every type of head line. The existence of islands on the head line may also be related to the abuse of drugs or alcohol—as a cause, a result, or both. As a rule, the larger the island, the more serious the mental or emotional difficulty.

When an island begins where an influence line from the Mars or Venus mount cuts the head line (Figure 9.5), chances are that a powerful trauma or other event set off a period of psychological difficulty.

By the same token, an influence line may appear at the end of an island, indicating that the event or influence brought the period of difficulty to an end. When the influence line leaves a dot on the head line, the cause of mental or psychological weakness is primarily physical in origin, such as an accident or illness.

Breaks on the head line indicate periods of transition. When lines overlap for a time (Figure 9.6), the changes are probably gradual, while an abrupt break (Figure 9.7) indicates something immediate, possibly an accident or some other trauma.

The quality of the head line at the point of breakage provides a good indication of how a person reacts to transition. Often when we experience a period of difficulty, we view it only in a negative way, when in reality it may open the door to important insights and new opportunities. When people go through difficult emotional transitions, we need to recognize the positive aspects of the dilemma and encourage them to overcome obstacles and move forward. Since the lines in the hand change (and breaks in the head line are especially prone to mending), such encouragement can be a real service to the person seeking our help.

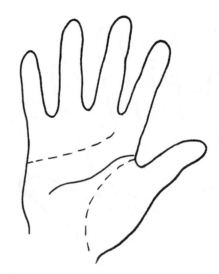

FIGURE 9.8. A wavy head line.

## THE CREATIVE HEAD LINE

Creativity is closely related to intelligence. However, unlike intelligence, it is primarily a measure of divergent thinking ("How many uses can you find for a kitchen knife?") rather than convergent thinking ("What is the capital of Costa Rica?").

According to psychologists, good indicators of creativity include unconventional thought processes, nonconformity, fluctuating moods, a strong intellect, and an interesting, arresting personality. Through the careful study of the shape, texture, and flexibility of the hand, along with an examination of the mounts, finger formation, tips, and spacing, we can have a good idea of the direction of a person's creativity and how it will be expressed.

Certain skin ridge patterns also have been linked to creativity. A predominance of whorls on the fingertips is a sign of an original, independent, and unconventional thinker. A whorl on the Apollo finger alone is a sign of artistic ability and is found on many graphic artists, architects, designers, and painters. Any unusual skin ridge pattern on the mount of Luna (the seat of the imagination) reveals a strong instinctual nature and a fertile, imaginative mind.

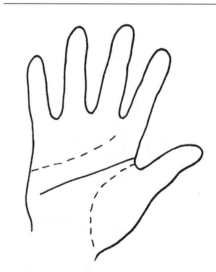

FIGURE 9.9. A straight head line.

As is the case with intelligence, the primary measure of creativity is the head line. However, it is the form of the line, rather than its length, that determines how creative ability is applied and whether a person's creativity is grounded or scattered.

- A wavy head line (Figure 9.8) reveals an original (and often unusual) mind that can conceive new ideas and understand unconventional points of view.

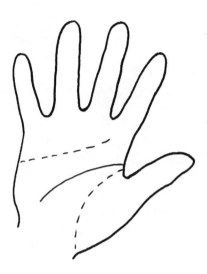

FIGURE 9.10. A curved head line.

• A straight head line (Figure 9.9) may run across the hand or can slope downward. It indicates clear and concentrated thinking regardless of the direction in which it moves.

• A curved head line (Figure 9.10) reveals a mind that likes to experiment and play with new ideas.

Generally speaking, a head line that moves straight across the palm indicates an individual with a strong convergent mind, as seen in Figure 9.2. While he or she may possess an abundance of information, this individual has a tendency to view the world primarily in practical terms. Imagination and creativity play a relatively minor role in life. People with this type of line like to follow rules and tend to dislike innovation. Their realistic, practical traits are often strengthened if their hands are rigid and their fingers are squarish in form.

A creative head line should slope gently downward toward the mount of Luna, which indicates a balance between the realistic and the imaginative. When the line ends in a small fork (which is either a part of the head line or extremely close to it), this sense of balance is strengthened, and there is a union of practical and imaginative ideas

that creates an ability to see both sides of an issue. This fork is often found on the hands of professional writers and hence is called the writer's fork. When this branch is extremely long and wide, it indicates more of a split between the imaginative and the practical than a balance.

Figure 9.11 shows the handprint of the celebrated American humorist, lecturer, satirist, and writer Mark Twain and features a clear writer's fork. Of special interest is the strong, clear, and realistic head line, which is slightly separated from the life line at its commencement. The mount of Luna is very well developed and is filled with strong lines of intuition. As can be expected, the Mercury finger is very long, revealing excellent communication skills, while the Jupiter finger is separated widely from Saturn, showing that Mark Twain enjoyed being in the public eye.

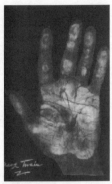

FIGURE 9.11. The hand of Mark Twain.

The more a head line slopes toward the mount of Luna (Figure 9.12), the greater the divergent or imaginative thought processes. Like other aspects of the hand, this sign has both positive and negative connotations. People with strongly drooping head lines are able to come up with creative ideas and solutions to problems that others cannot. Yet if they have a problem, their fertile imagination can blow it way out of proportion.

To learn whether or not a person's imagination is well grounded, we must ask ourselves the following questions.

• Is the head line strong, or is it broken or chained?

• Does the flexibility of the hand show emotional stability?

• Does the space between the life and head lines show a capacity to think before acting?

• Are the fingers conic, square, or spatulate?

• Is the Saturn line strong or weak?

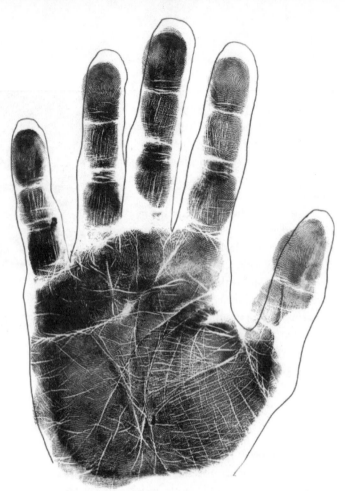

FIGURE 9.12. A head line plunging toward the mount of Luna.

Islands or breaks in a strongly sloping head line indicate that a person might go off the deep end into a world of fantasy. If the space between the head and heart lines is narrow, the fantasy world is even more secret and internalized. When these characteristics are coupled with a bent Saturn finger (indicating depressive tendencies), strong feelings of depression and fantasy can lead to suicidal thoughts. If a drooping head line contains islands or breaks toward the end, psychotic behavior can become evident later in life.

If a drooping head line is also broken or fragmented (Figure 9.13), a person can even be suicidal, especially if the Saturn finger bends strongly toward the Apollo finger. If you are reading the hand of someone with this type of head line, tactfully verify your suspicion by asking questions. Refer the individual to a competent professional if necessary.

## SIGNS OF MENTAL ILLNESS

It is difficult to make a specific psychological diagnosis from the hand. In the first place, it is well documented that normally rational and well-balanced people are capable of irrational, bizarre, and even violent behavior when placed in the appropriate conditions, especially during periods of extreme stress.

In addition, medical professionals sometimes place a label of *crazy* or *deviant* on individuals who do not conform to certain standards of behavior. Some of the most creative individuals in history— including numerous composers, inventors, writers, and artists—were condemned as "mad" by their contemporaries, only to have later been recognized as creative geniuses.

Some people commit suicide through neglect (such as the man who continues to smoke even though his doctor has said that smoking will kill him), while another may decide to kill herself by jumping off a bridge. Their hands may reveal different tendencies (the latter may include a classic suicide head line, while the former may appear completely normal), but the outcome (death by suicide) is the same.

We also have to consider the motivations of a person who commits suicide. For example, I knew an elderly woman with heart disease and severe diabetes. She walked with a prosthesis because one of her legs had been amputated due to her illness. Several years later, she decided to commit suicide soon after learning that her second leg was to be amputated. Rather than be dependent on others for her welfare, she chose suicide as a practical solution to her problem. Her hand would probably have been very different from that of a manic depressive who committed suicide after his wife left him.

For these reasons, we need to consider the hand as a *total unit* rather than make judgments based on one or two features alone. And if we choose to read hands either as a hobby or professionally, we also must strive to be as respectful, open-minded, and nonjudgmental as possible when we study a hand from a psychological point of view.

However, there are several major indicators on the hand that can show potential for mental illness. They reveal strong distortions of the basic core qualities that the lines, fingers, and other hand characteristics represent. They include the following:

- Hands and fingers that are abnormally small or large when compared to an individual's body size

- Jupiter and Saturn fingers of equal length, or Saturn and Apollo fingers of equal length

- A finger that is abnormally short in comparison to the others (such as a Jupiter finger that does not reach the top phalange of Saturn)

- Fingers that are severely twisted or deformed (especially the Mercury finger), when not the result of arthritis or accident

- Severely chained, broken, or islanded head lines

- Head lines that are missing (especially in both hands), or head lines that are extremely weak

- Hands, fingers, or fingertips that are extremely rigid or hyperflexible

- A thumb that is abnormally short, deformed, or placed extremely high on the hand, resembling the thumb of an infant

- A simian line on a poorly shaped hand or on a hand featuring one or more of the characteristics listed above

Remember that the existence of one or two of these traits does not mean that an individual is mentally ill. As mentioned before, the features of the hand reveal *potential*, which is always subject to change. Also, remember that apparent difficulties often open the door to opportunities that can lead to experience,

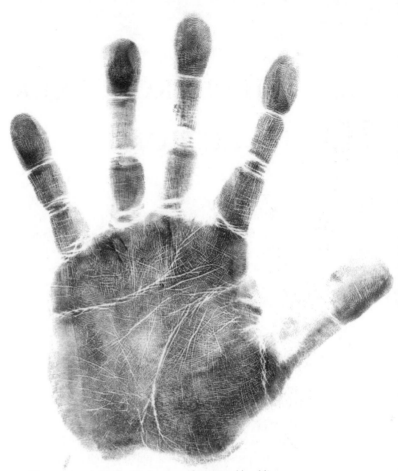

FIGURE 9.13. A handprint showing a fragmented head line.

transformation, and self-realization. A woman with a very long Jupiter finger, for example, can be dictatorial and overbearing. Another woman with a similar characteristic can develop the positive aspects of Jupiter and become a revered spiritual leader known for her ability to inspire, motivate, and teach. Indeed, in his autobiography *The Story of my Experiments with Truth*, Mohandas K. Gandhi acknowledged his tendencies towards fear, anger and jealousy as a teenager. By learning how to transform these negative traits into a positive force, Gandhi was able to transform his life and change the destiny of his country.

Hands reveal the essential specialness of every individual. They reflect a unique combination of character traits, life history, talents, and goals. As hand readers, we need to program our intuition to receive any subtle energetic messages the hand may offer us, since the study of the human hand is based on more than what we can see with our eyes.

# chapter 10
# WILL: FROM INERTIA TO ACTION

WILL HAS BEEN CALLED A DIVINE ASPECT OF the universe and is a potent source of strength and power. It enables a plant to break through concrete as it grows and gives many animal species their tenacious and often uncanny ability to adapt and flourish in a hostile environment.

In humans, will is connected with the soul, or what we can call the "essence, substance, animating principle, or actuating cause of life."

The will stands behind our ability to survive, to grow, and to manifest our talents and abilities. Without will, humanity would not have been able to evolve. It is the power that helps us explore new horizons and create cities, nations, and civilizations.

On a psychological level, will is closely connected to the ego, or our "I-am"-ship. It is concerned with one's awareness of oneself as a distinct human being capable of love, creativity, and self-realization. In esoteric philosophy, such as that taught by theosophists such as H. P. Blavatsky, we possess two egos: the mortal, or personal, which governs basic needs and desires, and the divine ego, which represents the spirit, the "Christ within," or the higher self.[1]

As expressed through the mortal ego, will represents our basic instinct to survive as well as the desire to achieve and maintain the family structure. Will is also involved in more complex psychological issues, including our need for pleasure, power, status, and security. Will is often connected with issues of control, possessiveness, and domination, especially with one's spouse and children. When expressed in the context of the workplace, will can manifest itself as greed, competition, or—in a positive form—leadership. In a social environment, will can involve the struggle to obtain benefits such as popularity and respect.

As we become more mature, and when our souls transmute from lower levels to higher levels of consciousness, the energy of will is changed to reflect the divine ego. This level is connected with feelings of inclusiveness, the application of inner wisdom, and the ability to be open to God's will. The more the personal ego can work harmoniously with the higher self, the greater the degree of personal integration, inner peace, and self-fulfillment.

In the hand, will is primarily reflected by the strength, form, and position of the thumb, the power of the mounts, and the clarity and scope of the major lines. By understanding our strengths and weaknesses, and by transforming negative energies into positive energies, we can harness the power of will and make it work as a force for good.

## THE THUMB: EGO INCARNATE

The thumb represents our individuality and the ability to assert ourselves in the world. Its association with the ego is so strong that infants tend to hide their thumbs from the world until they reach a point in their development when they feel more comfortable in their environment. Adults going through periods of fear or extreme stress often cover their thumbs with the other fingers in a regression to their protected lives as infants.

The more prominent the thumb, the greater the ego strength. A long, firm, and "expressive" thumb (see page 36) reveals courage, stability, and will-power. The type of tip adds character and direction. A spatulate tip, for example, reveals an individual of action who likes to throw himself into business deals, creative projects, and all kinds of adventures. A squarish tip shows that the ego will probably express itself in organizational and administrative affairs, while a conic tip favors artistic ability and

FIGURE 10.1. Aaron Copland in concert.

the desire to create, whether it be a sculpture, computer program, or musical composition.

Figure 10.1 shows the strong thumb of the American composer and conductor Aaron Copland (1900–1990), whom I was privileged to meet several years before his death. His thumb is a good example of how will plays an important role in creativity. In addition to the strength that the thumb imparted to his hands in general, the expressiveness of the thumb was especially present when the maestro conducted.

Skin ridge patterns on the thumb can also reveal aspects of will. An arch pattern on the thumb reveals a practical, commonsense approach. People with arches on their thumbprints are doers. A whorl print on the thumb tends to strengthen willpower. It is often found on people who tend to be abrupt and independent in their way of doing things. A loop fingerprint on the thumb has no special significance in regard to will. It represents adaptability, emotional responsiveness, and mental elasticity. On the surface, a composite loop would be seen to decrease willpower because it reveals a person who may have trouble making decisions. However, it can also be a sign of strength because such individuals can be extremely stubborn and tenacious in the process of reaching their goal.

A short, thin, flat, and waisted thumb generally reveals a lack of self-confidence and self-assertion. The individual tends to underestimate his or her talents and abilities and has difficulty overcoming adverse situations.

While a flexible thumb reveals adaptability, generosity, and spontaneity, it can also be a sign of poor willpower. People with flexible thumbs often have a difficult time arriving at appointments on time, sticking to a diet, or adhering to a budget. However, a hand of firm consistency, limited motility, strong mounts of Mars and Venus, and a long, prominent Jupiter finger can strengthen a weak thumb.

In general, the longer the phalange of will, the greater the willpower and the ability to put thoughts into practice. The phalanges of the thumb are discussed in greater detail in Chapter 6.

The position of the thumb is also important. The further the thumb is held from the other four fingers, the greater the degree of courage, self-confidence, and independence. Strong thumbs that separate from the hand (at an angle of sixty degrees or more) are found on many executives, military leaders, and others who need to make decisions and stand behind them. The low-set thumb of a twenty-two-year-old

Uruguayan exile (see Figure 6.16), who was active with the Tupamaro revolutionary forces in the 1970s while a university student, reveals his commitment to political action, love of adventure, and desire for independence. When I met him in Sweden, where he had sought political amnesty, I was impressed by his outgoing nature and supreme (and almost annoying) self-confidence.

Conversely, a high-set thumb located close to the rest of the hand reveals a more careful and contracted personality who may have difficulty asserting him- or herself, especially if the thumb is also short, thin, or flat. The print reproduced in Figure 6.19 belongs to a highly competent—and somewhat shy—computer technician.

Although the thumb is the principal indicator of ego strength and willpower, other aspects of the hand can reveal important information that can modify the essential qualities that the thumb reveals. For example, a Jupiter finger that is longer than the Apollo finger can strengthen the thumb. Egotism, optimism, and the ability to lead and inspire are several of the qualities indicated by a strong Jupiter finger. The desire to stand apart from others and prove oneself can often be revealed by a wider space between Jupiter and Saturn than is found between the other fingers of the hand.

Also, when the head and life lines are separate at their commencement, the power of Jupiter is increased. The individual with this type of configuration has a great ability to inspire, execute, and act in a natural leadership role. He or she also has a great degree of self-confidence and self-reliance.

When the head and life lines are connected, a long Jupiter finger indicates a need for domination and control. The strong ego is eroded by lack of confidence, which is an expression of weak will. The message is "I have to be the boss, or someone else will dominate me." The person with this configuration needs to be on top of a situation and generally is not open to the natural flow and movement of life.

The mounts and related skin ridge patterns can also strengthen and detract from the qualities of a strong thumb. A strong Jupiter mount (one that is more elevated than the other upper mounts of the hand) increases self-confidence and leadership ability.

A Raja loop, also known as the loop of charisma, enhances these personal qualities. A strong Saturn mount indicates a tendency toward emotional stability and thoroughness. Ambition, seriousness, and the will to succeed in life can also be revealed by a clearly marked loop of seriousness located between the Saturn and Apollo fingers.

A prominent upper mount of Mars increases courage and resistance, especially when the individual is confronted by outside pressures. When this mount is weak or soft, the person has difficulty standing up for him- or herself and can be controlled easily by others.

A strong lower mount of Mars (it often appears as a raised pad or "tumor" on the palm—see page 27) is a sign of assertiveness. If it appears in the form of a callus (especially if it is reddish), it reveals aggression and a strong temper.

A prominent mount of Venus imparts energy and power to the thumb, strengthening the individual's ability to move forward and create.

When evaluating a hand, it is important to offer an integrated view. We need to focus on the truth of what we see and, when appropriate, offer guidance to help the person whose hand we are reading resolve areas of weakness or difficulty. In addition, we should bear in mind that negative traits as revealed in the hand are often distortions of positive core qualities.

For example, a long Jupiter finger can reveal a dominating and controlling personality. However, with awareness and resolve, these traits can be transformed into an ability to inspire and lead others to discover their own inner strengths and abilities. A stiff thumb may indicate stubbornness and inflexibility but also can reflect a person who is inwardly stable, yet open to change. A high-set thumb may indicate fear and a reluctance to experience life, yet it can also reflect a healthy caution and a quiet sense of self-worth.

By dealing with issues of self-esteem and will with sensitivity and respect, we open ourselves to intuitive perceptions. As a result, we can truly help those we counsel to see themselves as they are. We can also inspire them to work with areas in their lives that require attention and transformation according to their circumstances and abilities.

# HAND GESTURES, POSTURES, AND MOVEMENTS

As newborns, our first acts in life involve using our hands to express ourselves. Babies use their hands to communicate all kinds of images, thoughts, and desires. The hands enable an infant, as Dr. Sandor Ferenczi, Freud's close collaborator, put it, "not only to signalize such wishes as immediately concern his body but also to express wishes that relate to the changing of the outer world."[1]

The grasping reflex is very strong in an infant. For example, if you put the hands of a newborn girl on a small rod, she will hold herself there until released, even if you do not hold her yourself. In that way, the newborn baby is like a tiny, defenseless animal to whom a tree offers safety and security, a means of escape from the dangers on the ground. The girl who clings to the rod is like the animal who grasps a tree branch firmly or clings to her mother's fur. Her grasping reflex demands the return of the state of security once enjoyed inside the mother's womb.

When infants become acquainted with their new world and become more sure of their environment, they gradually give up the grasping reflex. Dr. H. M. Halverson observed that a newborn who is comfortable quite often fails to exhibit any indications of grasping under repeated stimulation of the palm. The infant clutches firmly at the beginning of feeding and grasps weakly or not at all at the end of feeding.[2] This shows that there is a very definite relationship between satiation and grasping. Although the child loses the grasping reflex after four or five months, he or she maintains a grasping-like posture by holding the thumb firmly in a clenched hand, especially if disturbed or hungry.

Every hand analyst has recognized the significance of hand gestures and posture. Dr. Charlotte Wolff, the noted medical palmist and author of *The Hand in Psychological Diagnosis*, stated that subconsciously executed gestures of the hand are a more valuable mirror of personality than gestures of the face because, unlike facial expressions, gestures of the hand are beyond our control and therefore are impartial.[3]

This is especially true among gamblers. For example, men with "poker faces" may deceive some of their partners, but they can't deceive those who study their hands. The significance of hand gestures in relation to the so-called poker face was portrayed revealingly by Stefan Zweig in his 1927 novella *Twenty-four Hours in the Life of a Woman*:

> *Man betrays himself in gambling. I know it's a truism . . . but I maintain that it is the hand that is the traitor. Just because the gambler concentrates his attention on controlling his face, he forgets his hands and he who watches them . . . reads everything from them . . . the hands disclose the innermost personality.*[4]

## GESTURES OF THE THUMB

One of the most revealing manifestations of our inner world is the thumb, which represents the ego. For the first two years of an individual's life, he or she has a completely inactive thumb because the ego has not yet begun to develop. Occasionally, some children make gestures that indicate an active thumb before two years of age. They hold the thumbs far out from the palm and separated from the other fingers. This shows the beginning of independent mental attitudes. Eugene Scheimann, MD, the author of *A Doctor's Guide to Better Health Through Palmistry* and *Medical Palmistry*, wrote:

*I remember well an instance of this precocious thumb development. I visited a colleague of mine and marveled that his month-old daughter held her thumb outside her clenched hand while she slept. Her father replied that she almost never hid her thumb. I prophesied that this little girl would grow up to have a strong ego and would be very independent and secure of her own judgment. On her first birthday, I noticed that she now held her thumb far away from her index finger in an unclenched position and I added to my original prophecy that she would eventually dominate her household. Now every time I see my colleague he reminds me of that prophecy and comments that it was all too true. His little girl had indeed grown up to be a very strong young woman who takes life into her own hands!*[5]

Just as a grasping reflex in a child over six months old represents emotional insecurity, adults who hold their thumb in a clenched fist are manifesting a retrogression to childhood or a state of anxiety. Two other indicators of anxiety or emotional stress are the posture of hiding the thumb with the other hand and bending the thumb and holding it close to the outstretched palm.

Conversely, the thumb that stretches far out from the hand, forming a complete right angle with the index finger (as seen in Figure 6.16), demonstrates that a person is conscious of his or her ego. The opposite of anxiety is self-assuredness, and the more the thumb is held away from the index finger, the more that individual shows strength and self-confidence. This trait is commonly observed in very shy children, who generally keep their thumbs close to their index fingers. Their thumbs may also be positioned close to and bent slightly toward the outstretched palm (as seen in Figure 6.18). This reveals that that their lives are dominated more by insecurity and doubt than by confidence. Adults whose hands show these traits tend to be introverted, cautious, self-conscious, and secretive. As a consequence, they are often "bottled up" emotionally.

The person whose thumb is held far from the other fingers is liberal and generous by nature. This individual usually is friendly and likes to help others but does not like to be closely attached to someone, to be obligated, or to be dominated, because he or she likes freedom and independence.

## OTHER REVEALING GESTURES

Like the thumb, the index finger also shows the degree of a person's independence. It, too, carries a demonstrative, persuasive power. It is the most helpful assistant to the thumb. The beckoning index finger expresses an attempt to make the ego attractive to someone, while the pointing index finger emphasizes what it is pointing to. Depending on the intent behind the action, the pointing index finger may be dismissive or accusatory, or it may highlight a person or thing in a positive way. The index finger is also used to accentuate statements (president John F. Kennedy used this gesture frequently) or to make authoritative, menacing gestures.

People who hold all their fingers separately (Figure 11.1) tend to be nonconformists and are often extremely unconventional; they enjoy alternative lifestyles or involve themselves in unusual careers or hobbies. In contrast, if an individual holds all the fingers closely together, it is a sign of formality and conventionality. Such a person may tend to be stingy and self-centered.

If a person hides his hand from sight as he enters and crosses a room, it indicates that he has ideas or thoughts he does not wish to have exposed. He is likely to be deceitful or hypocritical. This gesture is also typical of schizophrenics.

## HAND MOVEMENTS ANALYSIS

Walter Sorell, in his book *The Story of the Human Hand*, states that movements of the hand are instinctive and we become aware of them only if they are used excessively or if our attention is called to them.[6] The position of the hands, the movements of the hands, and the gestures made with the hands reveal much about a person.

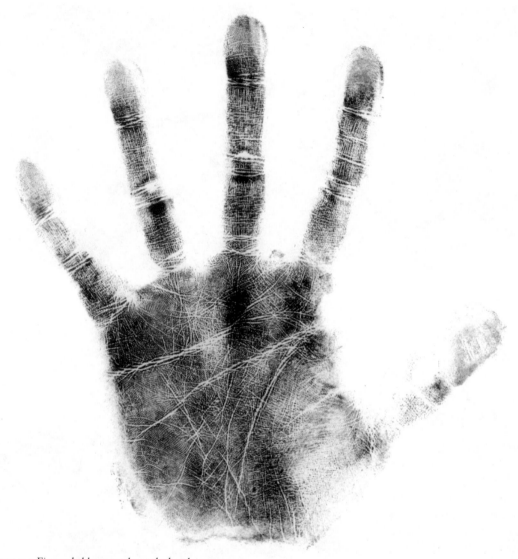

FIGURE 11.1. Fingers held separately on the hand.

Individuals whose hands are separated from each other in repose are self-assured, calm, and spontaneous. Persons who keep their hands together are never as free or able to follow impulses as those whose hands are separated.

Hands usually move in either a vertical or horizontal direction. The so-called offering gesture—which involves a horizontal movement with the palm open and turned upward—shows a hand that conceals nothing and a willingness to cooperate (Figure 11.2).

However, people who use this gesture often make poor diplomats because they are too outspoken.

Hands that move forward in a partly horizontal direction are seen in realistic people, especially if the fingers are short and fat. However, this movement is seldom seen in even-tempered, balanced people. When the hands move in a vertical direction with the palms outward and the hands close to the body at chest level, an individual is retreating behind a wall; in other words, the person is prepared for

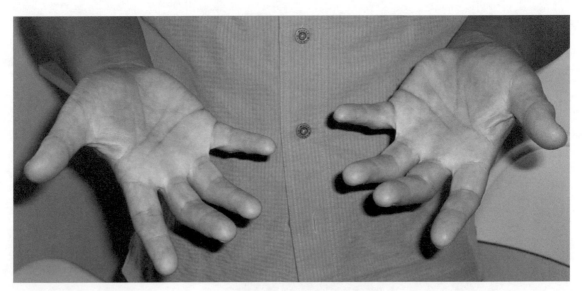

FIGURE 11.2. The "offering" gesture.

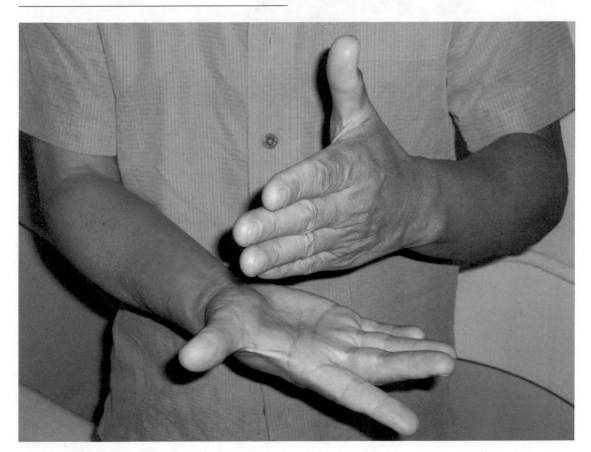

FIGURE 11.3. The "chopping" gesture.

attack and is getting ready to resist. When the arms are outstretched with this gesture, a person not only is prepared for an attack but also is ready to carry on the fight.

The chopping gesture (Figure 11.3) is seen in highly emotional and resolute people with a tendency toward extroversion. President Lyndon Johnson used the chopping movement frequently whenever he made an important point. Today, many politicians and other public figures are carefully coached in the hidden meanings of hand gestures, and they consciously use them to better express themselves in public.

Crossed arms held to the chest, which may appear to be a gesture of relaxation, indicate defense and defiance. This movement is seen, for example, in a child who does not dare to verbally contradict an adult. The desire to hide one's hands in a pocket, behind the back, behind a table, or otherwise out of view indicates anxiety, which forces a person to protect his ego. This gesture may have its roots in a trauma that happened to a person long ago.

Not only are hand gestures personally idiosyncratic, but they also reflect the society or culture in which we live. Italians, for example, are renowned for their hand gestures, which form an essential part of their verbal communication. More than thirty different Italian hand gestures have been identified to express specific meanings.[7] As can be expected, the significance of specific hand gestures tends to differ by country. On my first visit to Colombia, a friend waved her hand downward, meaning "come over here." As a North American, I interpreted her gesture as "have a seat." The signal that means "okay" in New York means "f*** you" in Brazil. Making the "peace" sign with the index and middle fingers raised and the palm facing toward you is a friendly gesture in America but is considered an insult in England with the back of the hand toward you.

Although I've given only a few examples of involuntary, instinctive gestures in this chapter, this fascinating subject is worthy of further study. There is no doubt that hand gestures and movements are as varied and unlimited as humanity itself.

# LOVE, RELATIONSHIPS, AND SEXUALITY | Part III

# THE SEVEN TYPES OF LOVER

Perhaps the most pronounced discontent in our society is frustration in our sexual lives—the difficulty of establishing and maintaining deep and satisfying romantic relationships with others. While we have more material knowledge about the philosophy of sex and the finer points of sexual technique than ever before in human history, many of us are ignorant about the true nature of our sexual selves and are not in touch with our own affectional and sexual needs.

When we come into the world, we arrive with character traits that eventually create the basis for our sexual personalities, and from the time we are born, we are given a sexual education. We first learn about trust, caring, and unconditional love from our parents, although we often learn about cruelty, withholding, and betrayal as well. In addition, those of us who have received a traditional religious education may have early memories about sexual teachings that have produced confusion, guilt, and self-loathing in our adult lives. For many of us, coming to terms with early childhood images about sex has been a major struggle, often requiring the help of psychologists and other health professionals.

For most of us, experiencing a close relationship with someone we love is both our fondest wish and most cherished life goal. Although much of our time and energy are devoted to achieving good health, having a fulfilling career, creating a happy, stable family life, maintaining a comfortable home, and enjoying good friends, the one single thing most of us want more than anything else in the world is simply to love someone and be loved in return.

Coming to terms with love, sexuality, and relationships isn't easy. It's also one of the most important personal tasks we face. While the sexual revolution of the 1960s and the rise of feminism during the following decade brought a new sense of individual awareness, freedom, and equality, and the breaking down of sexual stereotypes, we are now living in an age when total sexual freedom is being seriously questioned. Promiscuity, sexually transmitted diseases, the rising divorce rate, and a growing sense of alienation between women and men are all signs that we need to play by a new set of rules.

On one side, we struggle to claim our personal independence and integrity and enjoy both satisfaction and responsibility in our relationships. At the same time, we are challenged to relate to others more deeply, honestly, and faithfully, balancing strength and vulnerability. These challenges call for a new and healthy interpretation of love and sexuality that can give birth to a personal belief system and code of behavior that support us in our quest for health, happiness, and personal growth.

Relationships are essential for both our spiritual progress and our psychological well-being. The quality of our relationships with others can be a reliable guide to our own degree of personal integration and self-fulfillment. Like astrology, numerology, and handwriting analysis, the field of palmistry helps us know others and ourselves better. Through a careful, systematic study of the human hand, we can learn about our basic instincts and personality traits and how they are expressed in daily life, especially in our relationships with others.

## METHODS OF CLASSIFICATION

Over the years, many hand readers have sought to classify the hands into distinct categories. Some are based on the four elements, such as earth, fire, water, and air, and some are based on the different shapes

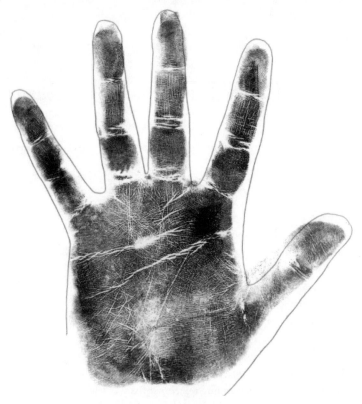

FIGURE 12.1. A receptive hand.

FIGURE 12.2. A realistic hand.

of the hand, such as square, spatulate, or conic. My own classification is a combination of these two systems. It recognizes the basic distinction, common to all classifications, between a receptive hand and a realistic hand.

A receptive hand is often fragile in appearance and is usually long and conic in shape, as seen in the woman's hand shown in Figure 12.1. Its owners tend to be highly sensitive, emotional, and romantic. Generally speaking, their emotions are strongly evident in their relationships and can manifest themselves as powerful mood swings, dramatic outbursts, and emotional instability. A rich line pattern, signifying a highly complex personality and a tendency for nervousness, is common.

The realistic hand, by contrast, appears more outgoing and assertive. The hand shown in Figure 12.2, also belonging to a woman, is strong and broad, giving an impression of substance and determination. Depending on the hand's skin texture and consistency, its owner is likely to be strongly grounded in three-dimensional reality and to have a strong interest in the physical aspects of sex.

Keep in mind that all the categories below fall into one or the other of these two basic types. The characteristics of receptivity or realism amplify the traits of the following seven classifications.

## ROMANCE AND THE ELEMENTARY HAND

People with elementary hands (refer to Figure 3.6), who are almost always men, have a tough physical constitution and are often very strong. They can also be conservative and set in their ways. People with these hands, which have only a few basic lines, are steady and reliable. They like to be independent and their values are often material ones. When threatened, they can be violent. People with elementary hands are often slow to react and are not likely to easily reveal their feelings, especially those of vulnerability and affection.

### The Lower Elementary Hand

The pure, or lower, elementary hand belongs to a person who is primitive, basic, crude, and unrefined. Intelligent reasoning and in-depth understanding are often lacking. The owner of this type of hand has a robust constitution, along with great strength and endurance. He has strong sexual drives and needs a partner who will satisfy those desires. When basic needs are met—food, sex, and shelter—he is happy. Yet if these needs are threatened, he can be abusive, especially when under the influence of alcohol. Jealousy is a common trait.

The pure elementary type can be difficult to get along with. Yet with a strict, controlled influence from a strong partner, he can be "domesticated" and reveal himself to be a hard worker and good provider. Good partners for this type include others with elementary hands, as well as those with strong hands that are somewhat squarish in form.

### The Higher Elementary Hand

A higher elementary type may still have the characteristic shape of the elementary hand, but the consistency of the hand is more elastic and the skin may have a finer texture. This reveals a more sensitive and flexible person who is receptive to new ideas and feelings and has a relaxed, responsive personality. This person is also likely to have a longer heart line (indicating a greater capacity for affection) and a longer head line (revealing more reasoning capacity).

Usually, owners of higher elementary hands can be described as follows:

- Physically earthy but gentle behind the tough exterior

- Unlikely to be demonstrative

- Likely to repress feelings

- In need of confidence boosting in a relationship

- Creative, especially with carpentry, repairing things, cooking, and working with animals or plants

- Dependable and reliable in providing and protecting

## ROMANCE AND THE SQUARE HAND: PRACTICAL AND REALISTIC

Owners of square hands (refer to Figure 3.8) love order, method, and stability. Common sense rules their emotions. They don't like confusion and often have difficulty adapting to new circumstances and situations, especially when the hand or thumb is rigid.

Although they are often thorough, competent, and careful with money, they tend to lack spontaneity. People with squarish hands prefer rules and structures. They like the tried and true and like to follow a fixed routine. People with squarish hands tend to be formal in their approach and are usually polite and reserved when dealing with others. Square hands also give their owners an inordinate ability to persevere and to cope with difficult situations.

Square-handed people tend to be conventional and are strict observers of social customs. Life is a matter of routine, order, and system. The same is often true of their sex life. It tends to be the same day after day, for this is the way they prefer it—the same time, the same place, the same person, and the same way, unless other hand patterns (such as an imaginative head line and separated head and life lines) are evident.

The square person is loyal and seldom commits adultery. If your partner has such a hand, start your relationship with a routine and either arrive (or be ready) for meals and appointments on time. Whether you are a woman or a man, try to be as neat and orderly as you can in your domestic life.

Usually, owners of squarish hands can be described as follows:

- Controlled and restrained at the beginning of relationships

- Sincere, honest, and direct when expressing affection

- Sometimes moralistic in their attitude

- Inflexible and resistant to change

- Punctual and reliable

- Sometimes dull and unadventurous

- Good workers and providers

- Careful with money

## ROMANCE AND THE SPATULATE HAND: ACTIVE AND REALISTIC

Owners of spatulate hands (refer to Figure 3.9) are often original and inventive and are known for their restless and exploring personalities. People with spatulate hands are energetic, tenacious, innovative, and self-confident. They are also independent, self-reliant, and curious about new ideas and unusual experiences. People with spatulate hands tend to be creative and impulsive. They are generally extroverted, dynamic, and exciting to be with.

Like the elementary hand, the spatulate hand is primarily sensate. When flexible and pliable, a spatulate hand indicates an interest in sensual pleasure at the expense of work and other responsibilities.

Owners of this type of hand are energetic and restless. They love action, excitement, and adventure and cannot tolerate monotony and restrictions. This characteristic also applies to their sexuality. If, for example, you are dating a person with a spatulate hand but you are sexually inhibited or prefer predictable romantic encounters, then you could be in trouble. Your partner is likely to become bored with you and may even seek out other partners.

However, if you choose to remain with a person with spatulate hands, keep yourself physically fit and attractive and learn new tricks as the years go by. Your partner is likely to keep coming back to you no matter how far he or she strays.

Usually, owners of spatulate hands can be described as follows:

- Interested in variety and adventure in romance

- Sometimes irritable and critical

- Lacking in tidiness, especially when it comes to personal appearance

- Very involved in career and sports

- Possessed of a healthy sexual appetite

## ROMANCE AND THE CONIC HAND: ARTISTIC AND RECEPTIVE

Conic hands (refer to Figure 3.10) belong to people who are often emotional, intuitive, and changeable. This type of hand is especially common among women.

People with conic hands are governed by impulse and first impressions. Unlike those with squarish hands, who are ruled by reason, conic-handed people are sentimental, intuitive, impulsive, capricious, and romantic.

Inconsistency can be a major problem with those who possess conic hands. They often begin a project with great enthusiasm, and then leave it for someone else to complete, especially if the hands are flexible. Although they tend to support the efforts of others, they shift loyalties often and have difficulty with commitment.

Creativity is high in the individual with conic hands. If the hand is firm and the lines well formed, creative energies are channeled toward mostly intellectual pursuits. When the hand is bland and fat, there is a strong sensuous nature. Rich foods, money, abundant sex, and comfortable surroundings are counted among the primary needs of a person with this type of hand.

People with conic hands enjoy sex to the fullest only if they are surrounded with mood-producing stimuli such as music and perfume and visual excitement such as erotic clothing. If your partner has this type of hand, you must make it your business to create the mood that inspires love and excitement. Try not to become caught up in routine. Be spontaneous. Make everything you do seem romantic and appetizing.

Usually, people with conic hands can be described as follows:

- Emotional, intuitive, and changeable

- Idealistic, with high aspirations in relationships

- Materialistic and opportunistic

- In need of constant stimulation; easily bored

- Averse to routine and predictability

- Emotionally available

- Appreciative of an unexpected compliment or gift

- Sensuous, especially if the hand consistency is thick

## ROMANCE AND THE PSYCHIC HAND: INTUITIVE AND RECEPTIVE

The psychic hand (refer to Figure 3.11) is relatively rare but also quite distinctive. It is essentially an extreme version of the conic hand.

Like people with conic hands, owners of psychic hands are very sensitive and have a strong interest in beauty. They also have a tendency to be high-strung and impressionable, and many people with this type of hand have strong psychic ability.

People with psychic hands are motivated by their deepest feelings. They are highly creative and possess a strong imagination. Common sense is not one of their primary attributes. They often need a partner of the realistic type who can help them deal with practical matters.

Owners of the psychic hand (usually women) are highly sensitive, idealistic in love, and appreciative of all that is beautiful and refined. Their aspirations are more spiritual and romantic than practical and down-to-earth.

A person with psychic hands needs to commit. She is often an inspiration to others and wants to help them improve themselves. However, she often places her partner on a pedestal, with frequent disillusionment. If your partner has this type of hand, be sensitive to her needs and offer protection and support. Allow her to rely on you; don't let her down.

Usually, people with psychic hands can be described as follows:

- Giving to friends and lovers

- In need of constant love and reassurance

- Averse to arguments and confrontation

- In search of security in a relationship

- Compatible with sensitive yet practical and realistic partners

## ROMANCE AND THE PHILOSOPHICAL HAND: THOUGHTFUL AND IDIOSYNCRATIC

Though not a pure hand type—that is, neither realistic nor receptive—the philosophical hand is easily recognized because of its long palm and long, bony fingers, which have large joints and long nails (Figure 12.3).

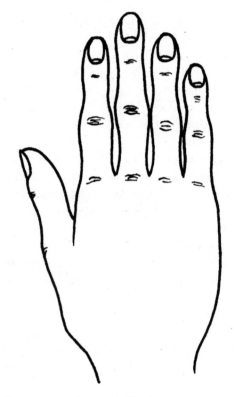

FIGURE 12.3. A philosophical hand.

Owners of this hand have analytical and inquiring minds. They examine everything, try everything, and then form their own opinions. Such people are independent and do not depend on hearsay. Whenever possible, they get their information firsthand.

Communication is the key to happiness with a partner who possesses this type of hand. Learn to talk about your problems and your feelings, and be open to hearing from your partner as well. People with philosophical hands love to analyze, and it often takes them a long time to make decisions.

For this reason, they are rarely spontaneous, especially when it comes to sex and romance. While this can be frustrating (especially if you possess smooth,

short fingers), becoming aware of this psychological trait can foster understanding and compassion.

Usually, owners of philosophical hands can be described as follows:

- Complex and contradictory

- Curious and interested in others

- Not easily deceived; naturally skeptical

- Individualistic—interested in maintaining a sense of self in their relationships

- Very sensitive to criticism

- Patient and considerate of others

- Protective of their solitude

## ROMANCE AND THE MIXED HAND

Very few hands actually conform to any of the previous hand types in their pure form, although one type may predominate over the others. By definition, the mixed hand (see Figure 3.13) contains characteristics of one or more of the previous hand types. The hand may be primarily squarish, yet one or two fingers may be spatulate in shape. Alternatively, the hand may be primarily conic, yet it also may contain elements of the more practical square hand.

The basic shape of the hand should serve as the foundation of a careful hand analysis. The fingers, mounts, and lines, as well as modifiers such as hand consistency and size, skin texture, flexibility, and skin ridge patterns, can often provide highly specific information regarding character analysis and individual life expression.

# PERSONALITY AND SEXUAL EXPRESSION

Our sexual personality is influenced by many factors. Aside from the obvious physical characteristics we inherit from our parents, we also receive subtle psychological and hormonal influences from our ancestral gene pool. These don't just govern body metabolism, but influence our psychological reactions to the world around us, such as how we deal with rejection or handle a stressful day at work. When someone tells us, "You think exactly like your mother," this observation (whether we agree or disagree) is based not only on the notion of external conditioning (which affects us more than most people believe) but also on inherited genetic traits. This is why, in many cases, children's hands have a lot in common with those of their parents.

In addition to inherited traits received at conception, our environment also plays a role in psychosexual development. It has been well established that prenatal trauma can affect children's development just as much as it would affect them after they are born. Our primary relationships with our mother and father, as well as our relationships with siblings and others during the first months and years of life, influence how we relate to other people later on. An act of psychological betrayal by a parent at even two months of age can adversely affect us for decades, even if the traumatic event has long faded from conscious memory.

Other childhood traumas, such as the death of a close relative or friend, a chronically dysfunctional family situation, or the more serious (and often overlooked) problem of physical or sexual abuse, also contribute to psychological and sexual development. In addition, powerful cultural influences from family, friends, school, religion, and the media all condition us to adapt to "acceptable" standards of society. Teaching a boy that "real men don't cry"

or telling a girl that a "good girl" plays with dolls instead of toy trucks or guns are just two of the most obvious examples of the cultural influences that help mold our psychosexual characters.

All these elements of personality and emotional makeup—including inherited characteristics, environmental influences, and past events—can be seen in the hand and can be interpreted in light of our lives as romantic and sexual beings. Remember that the hand reveals primarily tendencies and predispositions, and that individual lines can change over time. In addition, one characteristic does not a personality make, so several features in the hand—for example, the presence of a long, humanitarian heart line along with a rigid murderer's thumb—should be considered together before arriving at any final evaluation.

## ROMANTIC OR REALISTIC?

Chances are that a person's general attitude toward relationships—like attitudes toward health, career, and other aspects of life—can be roughly categorized as either romantic or realistic, depending on a person's basic hand type.

You can spot romantic people by their intensity. When they fall in love, their hearts begin to pound, their stomachs grow weak, and their minds often go blank: for them, love is instinctual and often "at first sight." Their relationships are often deeply emotional and include a powerful sensual component. As a result, sex among romantics tends to be varied, stimulating, and frequent.

The major way palmists identify a romantic is by looking at his or her heart line, which is usually deep and long and extends well into the mount of Jupiter.

Chances are that a romantic's heart line is also of the "mental" variety, which indicates both heightened emotional sensitivity and impressionability. Conic or psychic fingertips (especially on the index finger) reveal a tendency to be easily inspired by others and tend to strengthen romantic devotion.

If a person's hand features a large, pink mount of Venus, deep passion will also play an important role in his or her romantic life. A girdle of Venus may also reveal a strong romantic nature, especially if accompanied by the mental heart line described earlier.

The head line of the pure romantic will probably droop down toward the mount of Luna. This betrays a strong imagination and the tendency to indulge in romantic imagery and sexual fantasies, for better or for worse.

By contrast, the hands of the realist tend to be squarish, featuring square or spatulate fingertips. The surface of the palm is likely to be broad as opposed to narrow, and the head line, which is probably clear and long, moves straight across the palm toward the upper mount of Mars.

Unlike the romantic, the realist's heart line is of the "physical" type and usually ends under the mount of Saturn or just beyond. Remember that many romantic individuals try to portray themselves (usually unconvincingly) as realists in matters of the heart, despite their conic fingertips and long, chained, and broken heart lines. However, this duality could be present if their hands are squarish and the head line practical.

Disillusionment is common among romantics. They often place the object of their desire on a pedestal and expect more than can realistically be given. At the same time, the romantic is likely to overlook important warning signs that lead to heartbreak. For example, a romantic woman's boyfriend may already be in a relationship he has no intention of leaving ("He kept promising me that he would leave his wife") or a romantic man's girlfriend may simply be taking

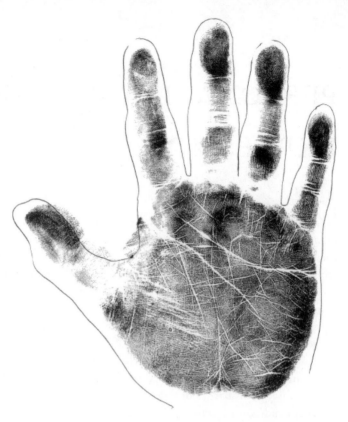

FIGURE 13.1. A Mercury finger curving toward the Apollo finger.

advantage of his innate generosity ("She told me that she loved me, but she only loved my money").

A tendency to overestimate others is found when the Apollo finger bends toward the Saturn finger. By contrast, if the Apollo finger is straight, our primary instinct about others is usually correct, especially if our hand features lines of intuition moving upward from the mount of Luna. However, whether or not we follow our instincts is another story!

A Mercury finger curving slightly toward the Apollo finger (Figure 13.1) reflects an astute, streetwise person who is not easily deceived by others. People who are especially charming or seductive (sexually or otherwise) often have this type of finger and often enjoy successful careers as salespeople, public relations agents, media personalities, and politicians. A straight Mercury finger (Figure 13.2) is a sign that its owner can be too trusting and naive. Though trusting others is an admirable quality, it can often lead to disappointment in a relationship, especially when we are not good at judging other people and their motives.

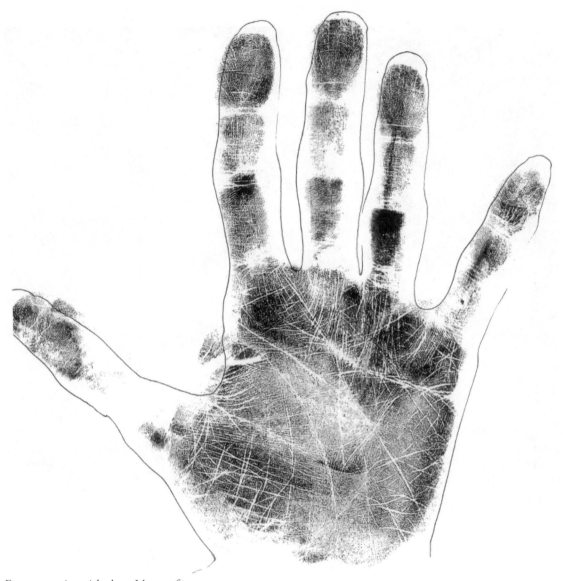

FIGURE 13.2. A straight, long, Mercury finger.

## COMMUNICATION: THE KEY TO RELATING

Our ability to communicate with another person is essential for a relationship, whether sexual or not. In palmistry, a long Mercury finger (i.e., one that reaches well into the top phalange of the Apollo finger) is the primary indicator of good communicating ability.

Remember that since many Mercury fingers are set low on the hand (as seen in Figure 13.1), the finger may appear to be shorter than it really is. Aside from using a ruler, the easiest way to measure the length of this finger is to lay it directly atop the Apollo finger of the other hand with the bases of the fingers aligned, as seen in Figure 13.3. Using this measurement, the little finger shown in Figure 13.1. can be classified as long.

Often found on the hands of accomplished

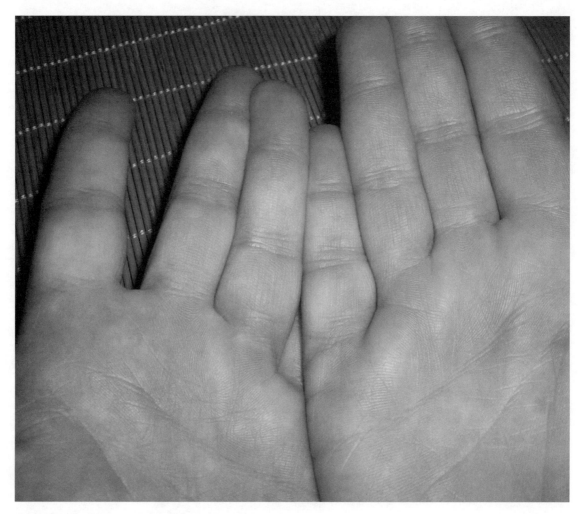

FIGURE 13.3. Comparing the length of the Apollo and Mercury fingers.

actors, writers, teachers, and public speakers, a long Mercury finger reflects a person who is comfortable with others in social situations and reveals an innate ability to easily share thoughts and feelings. Many believe that having a large mount of Venus (a sign of a strong sex drive) makes a person a good lover, but this is not necessarily the case. Because communication is an essential part of lovemaking, some palmists believe that the longer your Mercury finger, the better you are in bed.

In contrast, a short Mercury finger (as seen in Figure 13.4) reveals difficulties with communication. Its owner feels ill at ease in social situations,

may express him- or herself awkwardly, and is easily misunderstood by others. If the Mercury finger is set low on the hand as well, communication problems may originate in difficult early relationships with parents. Because these issues often have a profound impact on a person's ability to establish—not to mention maintain—a fulfilling relationship, I often suggest counseling to increase self-understanding, or group therapy to gain experience relating to others in a safe and supportive environment.

A wide separation between the heart and head lines (Figure 13.5) reveals an individual who likes to share personal thoughts and feelings with others.

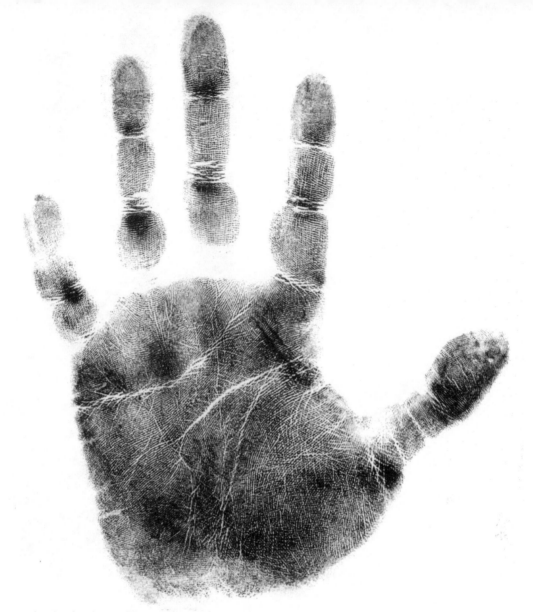

FIGURE 13.4. A hand with a short and low-set Mercury finger.

This openness is enhanced by fingers that are widely spaced (especially when the hand is held open), a low-set thumb, and head and life lines that are separated at their commencement.

By contrast, a narrow space (Figure 13.6) is a good indication of a secretive person who prefers to keep feelings and opinions to himself. This can be very frustrating in a relationship because it is often difficult to know what is going on with that person emotionally; he or she tend to keep feelings well hidden. Of course, if you want to share a secret of your own, a person with this type of line

configuration would be an ideal confidant, especially if the hands are firm or rigid.

Open-mindedness is another important part of communication. Generally speaking, people with broad hands, a low-set thumb, and large, broad nails are open-minded and emotionally accessible, making them easy to talk to. They are often interested in other points of view and are able to deal with the feelings of others. A chained or fretted heart line (especially if it is long) reveals a person who is sensitive to other people and cares about their problems.

However, a person with a narrow or elongated

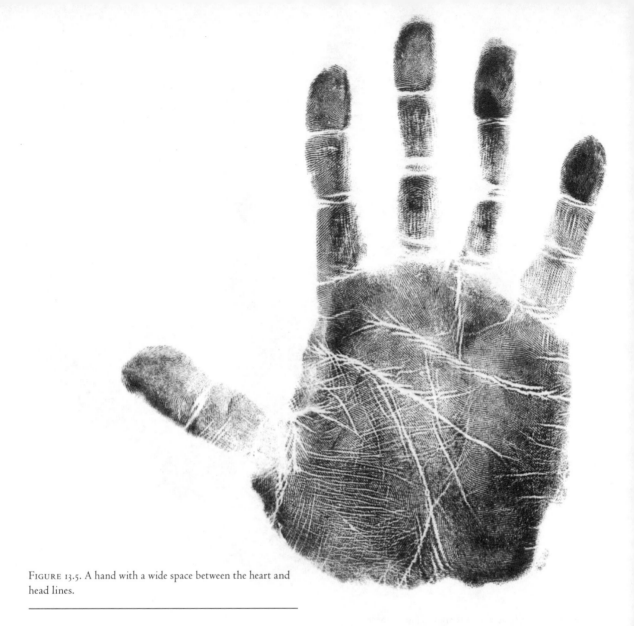

FIGURE 13.5. A hand with a wide space between the heart and head lines.

palm tends to be conservative and close-minded, especially if the hand is firm or rigid and the fingernails are narrow. Short nails (that have not been bitten) reveal a critical person who will likely be negative and bigoted toward other points of view. A person with short fingernails probably coined the classic phrase "Everyone has a right to my opinion."

## EXTROVERSION, INTROVERSION, AND SEXUAL INHIBITION

It will probably come as no surprise that the sex lives of extroverts and introverts differ substantially.

Studies have shown that extroverts generally have their first sexual experience at an earlier age than introverts and enjoy a more active, varied sex life throughout adulthood. They are also likely to experiment with a larger number of sexual partners, explore a greater variety of sexual techniques, and—among females, at least—experience orgasm more frequently than their more introverted sisters.

When you analyze a person's hand, ask her to open both hands as far as is comfortably possible. Pay special attention to the thumb. The greater the angle formed between the index finger and the open thumb, the greater the person's degree of extroversion and openness toward sexuality.

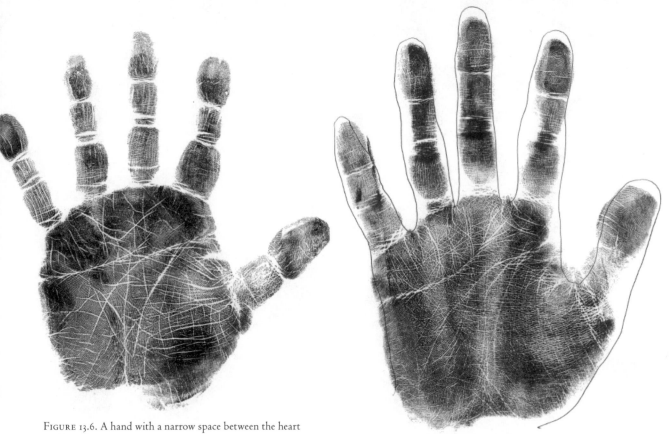

FIGURE 13.6. A hand with a narrow space between the heart and head lines.

FIGURE 13.7. A hand with a high-set thumb.

A high-set thumb, opening at a forty-five-degree angle to the index finger or less (Figure 13.7), is a sure sign that the owner is a Victorian in sexual attitudes. He or she is likely to be overly cautious, straitlaced, and sexually withdrawn and is often embarrassed about sexual matters, even to the point of avoiding them completely. This individual would likely be cautious in a relationship and have difficulty letting go sexually. In popular jargon, he or she would be described as uptight unless modifying aspects in the hand are present.

A thumb that is set at a sixty-degree angle indicates a greater degree of psychological openness. While more liberated than the Victorian, this person still has a fear of letting go emotionally or sexually.

A low-set thumb (Figure 13.8) can easily be positioned at a ninety-degree angle to the Jupiter finger. People with low-set thumbs tend to be self-accepting and are not overly concerned about what others think of them. They are generally more adaptable and more versatile and have a greater ability to "hang loose"

in a relationship than most other people. Because people with low-set thumbs are often independent, they are sometimes likely to pursue sexual adventure and experimentation.

Over the years, I've found it important to consider certain key modifiers when examining the angle of the thumb relative to the index finger. Spatulate or conic fingers, "generous" thumbs (i.e., those that easily bend backward), and flexible hands tend to increase extroversion, while stiff hands, squarish fingertips, and "stubborn" thumbs reveal greater self-control. A separation of the life and head lines at their commencement is a sign of impulsiveness, impatience, and self-reliance, which decrease sexual inhibition and self-restraint, especially when found in a flexible hand.

Knotted fingers can reveal increased sexual inhibition. Found mostly on people who love to analyze and focus on minutiae (especially if their fingers are long), knotted fingers indicate that their owners may well have a deep intellectual understanding about

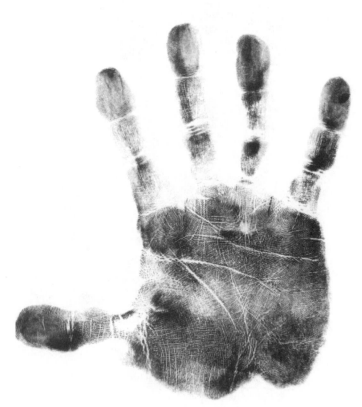

Figure 13.8. A hand with a low-set thumb.

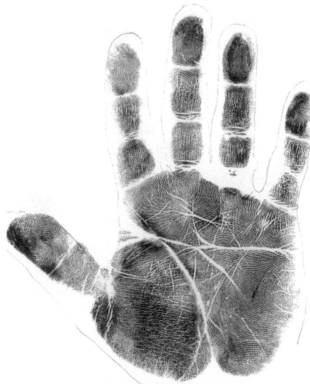

Figure 13.9. A Jupiter finger shorter than the Apollo finger.

sexuality and sexual technique but can experience difficulty putting their knowledge into practice. In fairness, such individuals are also likely to be patient and focused on details during lovemaking, which can make for a very exciting experience for their partners.

## FINDING SELF-ESTEEM IN THE HAND

Self-esteem plays an important role in our sexual lives. Because people with a high degree of self-esteem like themselves better, they tend to attract people and situations that favor them, too. As a result, they are more likely than others to make their fondest dreams come true, whether in business, sports, or relationships.

Like all other aspects of character, self-esteem is determined partly by our family gene pool and partly by childhood influences from parents, siblings, teachers, and friends. This is why it is important

to consider both hands when doing an analysis in order to learn whether self-esteem has increased or decreased over the years or has remained the same since childhood.

I've found that the two major indicators of self-esteem in the hand are (1) the relative lengths of the Jupiter and Apollo fingers and (2) the relationship of the life line to the head line at their commencement. Ideally, the Jupiter and Apollo fingers should be of equal length, indicating a good amount of self-esteem and a realistic view of inner strengths and weaknesses. The shorter the Jupiter finger in relation to the Apollo finger (Figure 13.9), the lower our basic level of self-esteem. People with this configuration tend to not give themselves credit where credit is due and to underestimate the many good qualities that they may, in fact, possess. In the hope of improving their self-image, they can sometimes become involved in romantic or sexual situations that are likely to end in disappointment.

Early childhood trauma can seriously erode our

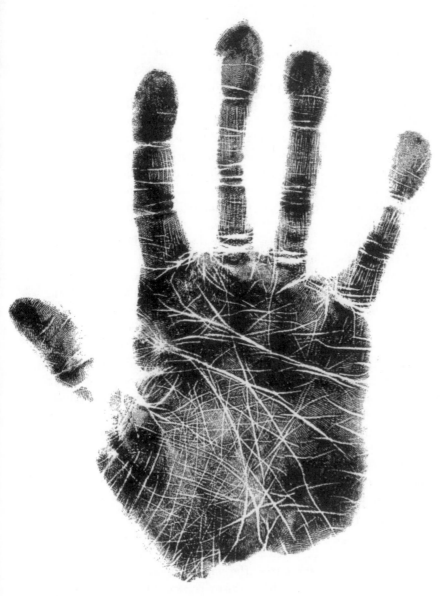

the impact or duration of the trauma, or both, is that much greater. Remember that not all traumas erode self-esteem. In some cases, a major trauma can have a powerful healing effect on the personality and lead us to feel better about ourselves than ever before.

Jealousy is one of the most common symptoms of low self-esteem in a relationship and needs to be recognized and dealt with right away. One strong indicator of jealousy is a Jupiter finger that curves inward toward Saturn, as seen in Figure 13.10. The greater the curve (as long as it is not due to arthritis or injury), the more innately jealous and possessive the person. By contrast, a relatively straight Jupiter finger reveals a more secure person who doesn't treat his partner like private property. A woman with such a hand would probably not be suspicious if her husband came home late from work, and a man might encourage his mate to take a coed dance class.

FIGURE 13.10. A Jupiter finger curving toward the Saturn finger.

inherited level of self-esteem. A hand reader can often identify the existence of a past trauma (whether it be physical, psychological, or both) by observing any influence lines that cross the life, head, and heart lines. A physical trauma, such as an accident or serious illness, often leaves a reddish or bluish dot on the line, while a psychological trauma would probably be free of such dots. If an influence line breaks or causes an island to form on a major line,

## SIGNS OF THE FAITHFUL PARTNER

Unfortunately, there is no foolproof indication of faithfulness in the hand. However, a strong thumb and firm-to-rigid hand, squarish fingers, and a relatively clear heart line ending under the mount of Jupiter serve as a strong sign of a person's feelings of responsibility, reliability, and loyalty toward a partner. In many cases, this sense of loyalty is not wholly dependent on sexual satisfaction, as sex for this person is usually neither more nor less important than other aspects of the relationship.

Very flexible hands, a generous thumb, and separate life and head lines tend to reveal a more spontaneous (and often less reliable) individual, especially if the head line is islanded and the upper mount of Mars is soft, indicating a lack of persistence and possibly of commitment. If the heart line is very long and chained, the person will likely be interested in a wide variety of partners and find it difficult to be completely devoted to only one.

By the same token, a person with a heart line ending under the Saturn mount tends to be more interested in sexual pleasure than loyalty to a mate. The tendency to seek multiple partners is enhanced by the presence of a broken girdle of Venus and an abnormally large Venus mount, indicating that sex (and sexual satisfaction) is a primary goal in life.

Another sign of seeking out multiple partners is a low-set Mercury finger (Figures 13.2 and 13.4). According to Andrew Fitzherbert, the author of *Hand Psychology*, a person with this trait has difficulty finding satisfaction in his or her relationship and will tend to shop around for the "ideal" partner.

## THE GENEROUS HAND IN LOVE AND MONEY

Most would agree that generosity is among the finest of human virtues and is an essential part of any happy long-term relationship. These days, generosity without conditions is rare, and the person who gives freely of money or time while expecting nothing in return is often considered unusual or eccentric.

The hand's primary indicator of generosity is a flexible thumb. The more the thumb bends back, the more inherently generous the individual, whether with money, possessions, time, or affection. Owners of flexible thumbs often make good romantic partners because they find it easy to give of themselves freely to others and place their lover's satisfaction above their own.

A flexible hand that is fairly soft in its consistency enhances generosity. A flabby upper mount of Mars can indicate difficulty resisting outside pressures, so a person with a generous thumb and a soft upper mount of Mars often has difficulty saying no to others. A stronger overall hand and a firm mount can temper this submissive tendency and lead to greater self-assertion.

The less flexible the thumb, the more circumspect and willful the individual. A man with a firm thumb may be generous to certain people but not to everyone. In general, the more inflexible the hand and thumb, the more inherently thrifty the owner will be on both the material and emotional levels. This doesn't mean that a person with a rigid hand and stiff thumb would not be a good partner in love or marriage. But such a person would need to be aware of his or her tendency to withhold feelings and would need to learn how to enjoy the pleasures of letting go in the context of a stable and trusting relationship.

## SENSITIVE HAND, SENSITIVE HEART

A person's degree of emotional sensitivity can often be detected in the texture of the skin. The basic rule is: the finer the skin, the more emotionally (and physically) sensitive a person will be. A profusion of tiny lines, in addition to fine skin, enhances sensitivity, especially if the heart line is long and chained and accompanied by a girdle of Venus.

Generally speaking, women tend to have finer skin texture than men do, but this is not always the case. While skin texture is basically an inherited trait, our daily activities also play a role. Hands that never wash dishes are smoother than those that do, while a person who digs ditches for a living has coarser palms than a person who trades stocks.

Another sure sign of a sensitive nature is the presence of soft tiny pads, which often resemble small tumors, on the fingertips. These pads reveal not only a refined sense of touch (which is especially useful for healers, artists, and craftspeople) but emotional sensitivity as well.

## DOMINANT/SUBMISSIVE

Unless your palmistry client is decked out in full leather, issues of sexual dominance and submission are difficult to read in the hand. In classical palmistry, we are taught that the hands of assertive and dominant people tend to have long, strong, and low-set thumbs, a long and thick Jupiter finger, life and head lines separated at their commencement, a clear head line (revealing mental focus and clarity), a firm and somewhat inflexible hand (betraying stubbornness), and strong mounts of Jupiter (revealing leadership) and Mars (indicating assertiveness).

A stereotypical passive individual possesses the opposite hand characteristics: a short, weak, and high-set thumb, a weak or short Jupiter finger, a soft mount of Mars, and so on. Yet most palmists overlook the fact that strong currents of domination and submission (or assertiveness and passivity) are normally found in the same individual and can change according to the particular relationship the person is involved in at the time.

We often find that supposedly passive individuals release their aggression when the right opportunity presents itself. This is why hand readers should be sensitive to all aspects of a person's hand and take contradictory features into account. Is a person naturally dominant, or does he or she take charge to compensate for a fear of being dominated by others? Is a person submissive by nature, or is he or she holding in assertive qualities because of fear of losing control or fear of being disliked by others if he or she acts them out?

## DESIRE DISORDERS

Although there are no clear-cut indications in the hand of so-called desire disorders—which include blocked sexual desire, inhibited sexual excitement, the inability to achieve orgasm, premature ejaculation, or outright aversion to sex—we may be able to spot certain markings on the palm that can offer insights into the problem. They include the following:

- A small, weak, or very soft mount of Venus and a thin, flabby hand, which indicate a low level of sexual vitality

- A life line cutting through a normal-size mount of Venus, which cancels out much of the warmth and passion this mount normally reveals

- A weak heart line, which indicates that sexual expression is not a priority

- An influence line joining or breaking the heart line, which may reveal a major emotional trauma

- Signs of physical illness on the life, heart, head, and stomach, or Mercury, lines, which may indicate impaired sexual interest and sexual function

Sometimes people withdraw sexually as a defense against their feelings. People with long, chained, and deep heart lines—especially those that droop down to join the head and life lines—can be afraid of their feelings to such an extent that they simply split off on both the emotional and sexual levels. Although these people may appear to be cold and aloof, the truth is that they are afraid of their feelings, whether they involve dependency, yearning, or anger. In addition, a lack of emotional expression is often connected with energetic blocks in the body, which inhibit the free flow of energy during sex.

# chapter 14
# SEXUAL VARIETIES, SEXUAL CHOICES

How do we become the sexual beings we are? We mentioned earlier that sexual expression is determined by several factors—genetics, early childhood experiences (especially with Mom and Dad), and education. If you believe in reincarnation, you may believe that experiences and lifestyles from previous lives may well have an impact on our sexuality in this life. According to some, an effeminate gay man may well have been a woman in several previous lives. Whether we believe in reincarnation or not, each relationship mobilizes different aspects of our sexual heritage in us. This is why we need to consider sexual expression as part of our overall being rather than as a separate compartment in life.

When it comes to dealing with unconventional styles of sexual behavior, most books on palmistry tend to ignore the larger issues involved or discuss unorthodox sexual expression with strong moralistic overtones. This is clearly not helpful to the person who comes to the palmist for assistance. As hand readers, we need to be as objective as possible when evaluating another person's sexual history, and we must be aware of our own fears, prejudices, and conditioning during the reading. We also must be wary about making broad statements about another person's sexual style, especially if it involves behavior we don't understand or never have experienced.

This doesn't mean that we should avoid being honest or direct when we share information with the person whose hands we are reading. Yet, given the seriousness of the subject—as well as the needs of those who seek our help—we should approach issues of unconventional sexual expression with sensitivity and respect.

## THE THREE TYPES OF SEXUAL FANTASY

Whether we dream of being kidnapped by a handsome stranger or wonder what it would be like to be alone on a tropical island with a famous movie star or model, fantasy plays an important role in our psychosexual makeup. Mental stimulation as well as physical stimulation is essential for sexual arousal and function. The tremendous popularity of Internet chat rooms (where people often assume fictitious identities and indulge in online conversations that can be incredibly rich in romantic and sexual imagery) show that fantasy is a major part of our emotional lives. Critics maintain that visiting online chat rooms is a waste of time and can involve users in dangerous situations; in some cases, they are right. Yet depending on how we understand (and learn from) our fantasies, we can not only enhance the quality of our relationships but also increase our level of self-understanding.

In my practice as a palmistry consultant, I've found that there are three basic types of fantasy:

- Escaping from boredom

- Realizing unfulfilled desire

- Going over the edge

The first type of fantasy takes the form of an escape from a boring, humdrum existence. An overworked housewife who dreams about being taken away by a handsome prince on a white horse entertains this kind of fantasy. Based on the sale of gothic romances (among women) and the popularity of magazines like *Playboy* and *Penthouse* (among men), this escape type of fantasy is perhaps the most common of all.

The second category of fantasy is deeply personal in nature and involves an unfulfilled desire or longing toward a specific person. A man who has sexual fantasies about his wife's sister and a woman who fantasizes about having an affair with her gardener are two such examples. In many cases, such fantasies can help us understand and come to terms with a problem in life that can be resolved within the context of an existing relationship, sometimes with the help of marriage counseling or short-term therapy. Whether this type of fantasy is shared with a partner, left alone, or acted on depends on the situation.

The third fantasy category is what psychologists call "deviant." It goes over the edge and may involve violence, humiliation, exhibitionism, or suffering. Far more serious than mere escapism, these fantasies are often related to deep psychological traumas from childhood. Because of strong feelings of guilt or shame, they are often kept secret, a repression that may lead the fantasizer to eventually act them out in real life, at tremendous harm to himself and to others.

## HOW TO RECOGNIZE A FANTASY-PRONE HAND

Since everyone experiences fantasies of various kinds and intensities at one time or another (psychologists claim that the average adult has a sexual fantasy every three minutes), a palmist should be careful making generalizations regarding a "fantasy-prone" hand. Nevertheless, we can find several features on the hand that reveal the extent that imagination and fantasy can play in a person's life. Whether this potential is channeled into writing a steamy romance novel or creating a bizarre sexual scenario can be seen by examining the hands carefully and noting the wide variety of messages they and their markings can offer.

Generally speaking, a head line that moves toward the mount of Luna (Figure 14.1) indicates that its owner has a richer fantasy life than a person who has a "realistic" head line, which moves straight across

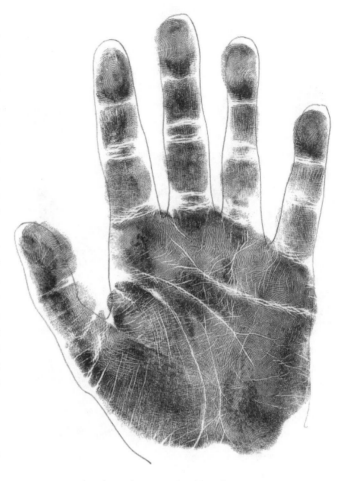

FIGURE 14.1. A handprint featuring a head line drooping toward the mount of Luna.

the palm (Figure 14.2). If the head line is clear and long, a person's sexual fantasies are likely to be both interesting and varied, although the fantasizer is still grounded in the reality of the here and now.

By contrast, if the head line is broken, weak, or islanded, neurotic tendencies may be present and the person can have difficulty distinguishing between fantasy and reality.

Other features in the hand that point toward unreality can include a weak thumb, a very flexible hand, and fingers that are conic, psychic, or strongly bent (especially the Saturn and Apollo fingers). If these features are accompanied by a long, chained, and deep heart line and a large mount of Venus, a

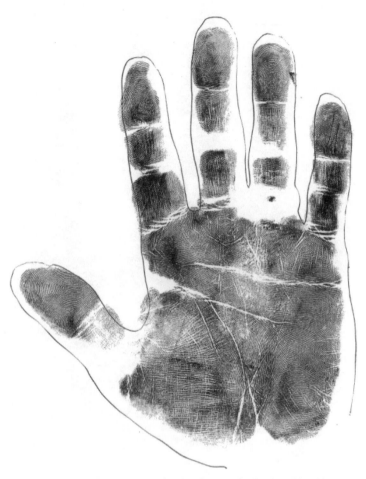

FIGURE 14.2. A hand with a straight, "realistic" head line.

person's fantasy life can hurt his or her chances for good relationships. In rare cases, they reveal a person whose fantasies are so strong that he or she is out of touch with reality.

When you evaluate the potential for fantasy, be sure to examine *both* hands in order to obtain a balanced and integrated view of the person. What is the degree of sexual inhibition? Is the individual basically sensitive or insensitive toward others? What impact might an unhappy career or relationship have on this person's fantasy life? For the most part, sharing sexual fantasies with others in an appropriate setting and trying to understand their message can be very useful. Yet we need to remember that the vast majority of palmists are not sex therapists and

shouldn't attempt to do sexual counseling unless trained (and certified) to do so. Clients should be referred to a qualified professional.

## GIVING YOURSELF A HAND

Closely related to sexual fantasy is autoeroticism. Although masturbation is almost universally practiced among human beings throughout the world, it's also one of humanity's most persistent sexual taboos. For those interested in word origins, *masturbation* appears to be a corruption of the Latin *manu stuprare*, or "to defile with the hand."

In years past, "touching yourself" was viewed with horror and was considered an act so vile that in the sixteenth and seventeenth centuries only veiled references to it were accepted in polite company. Even in the early 1900s, "scientific" books claimed that masturbation would lead to blindness and insanity. *Dr. Foote's New Book on Health and Disease*, published in 1903, claimed that masturbation was responsible for "tapping the very fountains of neuro-vitality, and drain from the blood all its purest and most strengthening qualities." The book also claimed that masturbation could lead to a variety of diseases, including "neurasthenia, mental depression, and insanity."[1]

Most palmistry books steered clear of the subject, and those who discussed it taught that masturbation was perverted and sinful. People who practiced "self-abuse" could be identified easily by features such as sweaty palms, blotches on the backs of the hands, or a large red grille on the mount of Venus.

Although sexual self-stimulation is discussed today in a more enlightened manner, it still produces a good deal of misunderstanding—not only among teenage boys who are worried about losing their eyesight or developing hairy palms. Masturbation should be of concern to the palmist only if sexual guilt, stemming from moralistic views, and sexual repression seem to be major problems for the person whose hands we are reading.

Today, psychologists and sex therapists consider masturbation a positive, even therapeutic, outlet. In addition to discharging sexual energy and relieving tension, masturbation releases endorphins, which have been found to enhance the immune system, relieve pain, produce relaxation, and even help postpone the aging process. Autoerotic activity can bring us into deeper emotional contact with our body and its sensations. Many women, and also men, practice masturbation in order to achieve more fulfilling sexual relations with their partner. In addition to claiming that masturbation fights yeast infections by increasing blood flow into the pelvis, Cathy Winks and Anne Semans, the authors of *The New Good Vibrations Guide to Sex*, report that masturbation can also provide a good cardiovascular workout and burn calories.[2]

A more controversial view of the therapeutic aspects of masturbation was put forth by the Sufi scholar J. G. Bennett, who believed that talkativeness, greed, hyperactivity, inquisitiveness, and even drug addiction are routinely used by the subconscious mind as ways to discharge excess sexual energy. He wrote, "For all those who are not committed to working on themselves for their transformation, masturbation acts like a safety valve for the sexual energy and allows it to be wasted without destructive consequences."[3]

Other than dangers encountered when a person doesn't use common sense—such as using an electric vibrator while sitting in a bathtub filled with water or becoming distracted while driving down the freeway at seventy miles an hour—the only real negative aspect of masturbation is when it becomes a compulsive act or a way to avoid entering into a sexual relationship with another person. In cases like this, a palmist can learn a lot about the situation by examining the lines of heart, head, and union, in addition to the mount of Venus and the Mercury finger.

For example, a person with a low level of self-esteem (as revealed by a short Jupiter finger and life and head lines that are joined), a sensitive, inward nature (as seen by a broken girdle of Venus and a long, chained, "mental" heart line that shares a narrow space with the head line), and problems with interpersonal communication (as shown by a short,

low-set Mercury finger) may likely use masturbation as a form of escape from relationships. This would be especially true if the mount of Venus is large, reddish, and grilled, indicating a strong sex drive and possible sexual excess. Through the insights gained by examining the entire hand, we can carefully point out some of the issues involved or recommend an appropriate counselor who can offer practical advice.

## GAY, BI, OR STRAIGHT?

Many people ask whether you can tell a person's sexual orientation by looking at his or her hand. Many early books on palmistry answered in the affirmative and in the process reinforced societal stereotypes about same-sex orientation. Some of the early classics portray the hand of a homosexual—invariably a male—as weak, with a supple thumb (revealing an unstable personality and a lack of willpower), a broken or islanded head line (indicating serious emotional problems), a long and broken girdle of Venus (betraying a sensitive nature and an obsession with sex), a long and chained heart line (showing that emotions rule over reason), and pointy fingers (revealing artistic tendencies, capriciousness, and lack of emotional balance).

However, some recent research also seems to suggest that hands might reveal a person's sexual orientation. A study of 720 men and women on the streets of San Francisco, conducted by researchers from the University of California at Berkeley, found that the index fingers of straight men are normally shorter than their ring fingers, while straight women tend to have index and ring fingers of equal length. But they also found that gay women tend to have index fingers substantially shorter than their ring fingers, as do gay men who have several older brothers. Believing that genetic influences can have an impact on the length of the fingers, Dr. Marc Breedlove, one of the researchers, opined that younger brothers are being exposed to larger levels of the hormone androgen in the womb and thus have shorter index fingers than their brothers.[4]

In other research, J.A.Y. Hall and Doreen Kimura at the University of Western Ontario in Canada found a relationship between the number of fingertip ridges on men and their sexual orientation. They compared the number of ridges on the index finger and thumb of the left hand with the number on the corresponding fingers of the right hand. They found that 30 percent of the homosexuals tested had a surplus of ridges on their left hands, while just 14 percent of the heterosexuals did.

This is an interesting discovery because fingerprints are fully determined in a fetus before the seventeenth week of pregnancy; they never change after that time. This would seem to indicate that, for at least some gay men, sexual orientation is determined before birth, either at conception or by the end of the fourth month of pregnancy.[5]

Over the past thirty years, I've probably read the hands of more than twenty thousand people, including many who are gay. Though the findings mentioned above are interesting and worthy of further study, I do not believe that finger length—or any other factor in the hand—can reveal a person's sexual orientation. Why? Because people who prefer members of their own sex are found in every culture and profession and represent a wide spectrum of personality traits and human emotions. According to D. J. West, author of the classic book *Homosexuality,*

> *Some homosexuals suffer from neurotic fears and anxieties, and some are self-assured and hard as nails; some are vain and ostentatious and some are shy and quiet; some are cowardly and some are heroes; some are effeminate and some are brutes. Since all these types are represented, psychologists can too easily pick out examples to suit their pet theories.*[6]

Figure 14.3 shows the handprint of a forty-three-year-old gay man. A former banker, lumberjack, and gardener, he now looks after his Wall Street investments and those of his private clients.

His broad hands feature strong fingers with spatulate fingertips and a large mount of Venus, revealing a strong sensate nature, an open mind, a love of physical activity, and an ability to work well with three-dimensional reality. He also enjoys

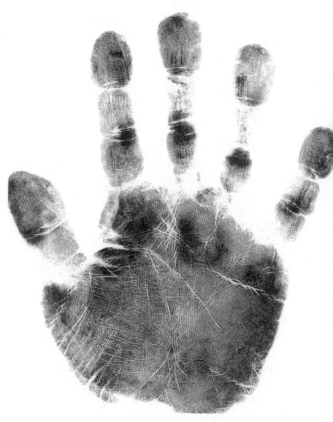

FIGURE 14.3. The hand of a gay man.

a reputation as an excellent masseur among both men and women. His abundant energy tends to be held in check, however, by the joining of the life and head lines, which indicate caution. The long, clear head line (especially as he enters middle age) indicates a focused mind and strong intelligence. While the heart line is somewhat chained at its commencement, it does not indicate an inordinate amount of emotionality or sensitivity. His ability to communicate (and business acumen) is found in his long Mercury finger. His "line of adventure," which moves horizontally across the mount of Luna, is primarily reflected in his love for travel.

Figure 14.4 shows the hand of a forty-year-old man—a hand that clearly resembles that of the stereotyped gay male described in early palmistry books. This man has a long, broken heart line, a

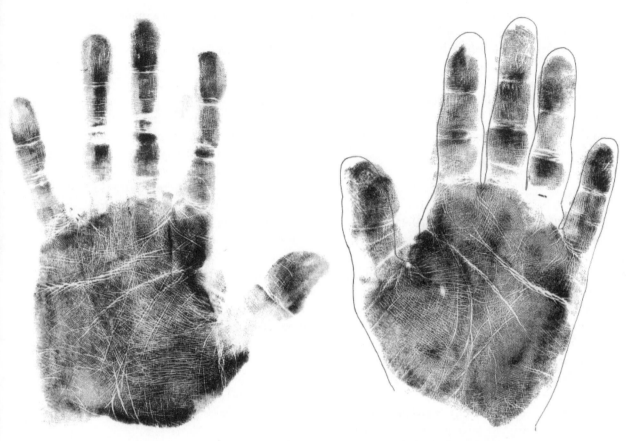

FIGURE 14.4. The sensitive hand of a male heterosexual.

FIGURE 14.5. The hand of a gay female nurse.

broken girdle of Venus, a flexible hand with a weak thumb, a weak, islanded, and imaginative head line, and numerous lines in general, which would indicate a tendency to be very emotional and high-strung. In life, he indeed exhibits all these psychological characteristics—and he is heterosexual.

Figure 14.5 shows the handprint of a fifty-five-year-old lesbian who works as a nurse and counselor. Featuring prominent Samaritan lines on the Mercury mount, her squarish hand reveals solid organizational skills, and her knotted fingers show a love of detail and analysis. She has a long, sensitive heart line, a girdle of Venus, and an "independent" Mercury finger. She has a prominent, firm thumb, which reveals strong willpower: a high school dropout, she decided to earn her nursing degree while in her forties and graduated at the top of her class. Her

Jupiter finger is slightly shorter than her Apollo finger, which supports the idea that lesbians have short Jupiter fingers. Yet since many straight women have a similar finger-length pattern, I feel that her hand is no different from those of other women (straight, bisexual, or gay) who are as dynamic and independent as she is.

I've never been fond of labeling people, and even psychologists would tell us that the boundaries between gay and straight are often quite vague. The hand can, of course, provide valuable insights into a person's sensitivity, impressionability, emotional responsiveness, and degree of sexual repression; it can also reveal issues with passivity and aggression, level of self- esteem and self-acceptance, and the capacity to love and enjoy fulfilling relationships. Whether such feelings are directed primarily toward men or women (or both) is sometimes difficult to figure out.

Of course, if you believe intuitively (or otherwise know in advance) that the person whose hands you are reading is gay or bisexual, your consultation can be guided accordingly. For example, instead of speaking of a husband or wife that person may have in the future, you can speak of a primary relationship, without referring to sex.

## POWER PLAY: THE DYNAMICS OF BONDAGE, DOMINATION, SADISM, AND MASOCHISM

During the mid-1980s, I began a correspondence with the late Gregory Leo, an English palmist who was deeply involved in the practice of bondage, domination, sadism, and masochism, collectively known as BDSM. He provided some of the background information I presented in the first edition of *Sexual Palmistry*, published in 1986.

Like the stereotyped homosexual, people who are involved in BDSM are largely misunderstood. In the past, palmists have often portrayed the "sadist's hand" as masculine, coarse, and deep reddish in color. The mounts of Venus and Mars are supposed to be large and hard and the fingers twisted, revealing severe mental disturbances. A murderer's thumb often completes the picture, revealing violence and a temper that is out of control.

The problem is that there are people with such hands who are not at all sadistic, while some individuals with long, slender fingers, elegant hands, and fine skin texture can be very delicate about their cruelty and act out their sadistic feelings every day of the week.

Those who enjoy sexual scenes such as bondage, domination, sadism, and masochism find that their erotic activities produce high amounts of endorphins in response to pain caused by spanking, whipping, biting, pinching, the use of hot wax or clamps, and other forms of consensual controlled physical and psychological assault. These intense feelings have been compared to nonsexual activities that produce endorphins, like long-distance running and eating chocolate or hot chili peppers.

People get involved with BDSM for a variety of reasons. Enthusiasts report that it gives them an emotional catharsis they would not normally experience during conventional sexual activity. Like my palmist friend, some are attracted to the dramatic and often theatrical aspects of role-playing, while others are drawn to the strong level of trust between partners during BDSM activity.

Others use it to attempt to expiate old guilt, to safely express feelings of cruelty or violence, or to fully experience an intensely dominant or submissive role that they cannot experience in daily life. In *A Sexual Profile of Men in Power*, the authors report a high frequency of sexual masochism (including being subjected to verbal abuse and being tied up, beaten, and humiliated) among the political leaders and power brokers they studied. They concluded that the conflict between the two impulses of aggression and submission among these political and business leaders could lead to behavior that swung widely between the opposite poles of ruthlessness (in the boardroom) and dependency (in the bedroom).[7]

Some psychologists believe that many who are involved with BDSM have difficulty getting in touch with their feelings. According to Dr. Jack Lee Rosenberg, author of *Body, Self, and Soul: Sustaining Integration*, "Whether they are thickly armored or split off, inability to feel the subtle pleasures of sensuality leads them to seek greater stimulation by inflicting and receiving pain."[8]

As hand readers, we need to understand the complexities of these issues and try to be aware of the underlying reasons behind these types of sexual expression. For the most part, people involved with BDSM are not "sick," and their hands may be similar to those who indulge in conventional sex. However, I've found that there are several features in the hand that can indicate a desire for intense forms of sexual experience:

- A strong, deep life line with a large mount of Venus, revealing an abundance of energy and stamina, especially if the thumb is strong and the hand has a firm consistency

- A strong and drooping head line, a deep and possibly chained heart line, or a simian line, all indicative of an intense personality and strong character

- Separated head and life lines, indicating sexual independence

- A Mercury finger standing far apart from the Apollo finger, revealing a feeling of being out of the mainstream of respectable society

- A Jupiter finger that stands out from the rest, revealing a desire to be the center of attention

- In cases where a person is fond of drama and role-playing, an Apollo finger that is long and well formed, and a long Mercury finger, betraying good communicating ability

- In the case of a person who likes being the "top" in BDSM scenes, a Jupiter finger that is longer than the Apollo finger, a strong thumb, and a large mount of Mars, especially if this role involves an active physical dynamic like whipping

While many of these traits are found in the hand of Gregory Leo (Figure 14.6), it would be wrong to conclude that most devotees of BDSM share similar hand characteristics. As with gay people, vegetarians,

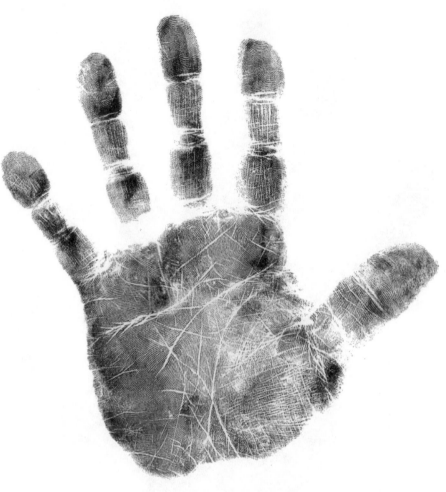

FIGURE 14.6. The hand of the late palmist Gregory Leo, a practitioner of sadomasochism.

and born-again Christians, people involved in bondage, domination, sadism, and masochism belong to all kinds of professions and political persuasions and represent nearly every personality type known to modern psychology.

Like the boundaries between gay and straight, the boundaries between having sadomasochistic or other BDSM inclinations and acting them out are often very fine. Psychologists tell us that nearly everyone has entertained thoughts of sexual sadism or masochism at one time or another, even though such feelings are seldom, if ever, expressed.

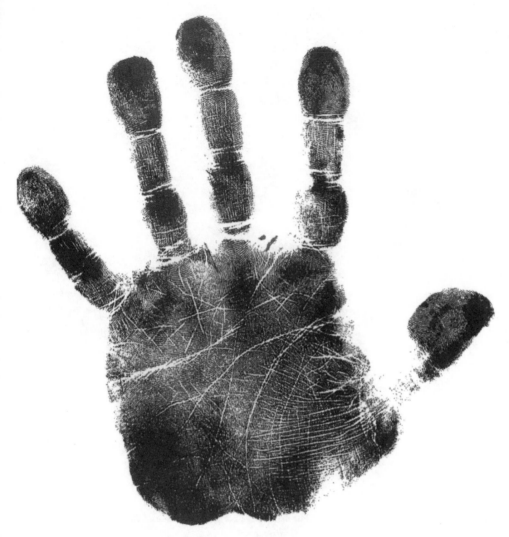

FIGURE 14.7. The hand of a male cross-dresser.

Some therapists feel that fantasizing about these practices (and acting them out) is a gesture of self-love and a way to assert sexual confidence and independence. Others feel that voyeurism, fetishism, exhibitionism, and cross-dressing are expressions of physical and psychological energy blocks that can have their roots in loneliness, sexual repression, fear, or lack of self-esteem. Like other sexual practices, they should be of concern if they interfere with a person's ability to work, study, or otherwise participate in daily life, or if they cause him or her to avoid deep relationships with others or bring about depression as the result of guilt or fear.

Figure 14.7 shows the handprint of a thirty-year-old male accountant who frequently dresses in women's clothing. The fact that he works for an elegant Fifth Avenue department store allows him to buy many of his expensive dresses, shoes, cosmetics, and hairpieces at a special employee discount. The palm itself doesn't offer any specific clues that would reveal his interest in cross-dressing. However, the strong Apollo finger and accompanying line of Apollo would indicate a love of beauty and a flair for style, and the whorl fingerprint on the Apollo finger shows strong artistic and creative ability. The man's long (and independent) Mercury finger reveals a nonconformist's way of viewing the world as well as an ability to communicate well with others; the Jupiter finger

## OTHER VARIATIONS

While phone sex, cybersex, talking dirty, using sex toys, and enjoying pornography are considered fairly normal among most adults today, other kinds of sexual expression—such as voyeurism, fetishism, exhibitionism, and cross-dressing—remain at least somewhat unconventional. Viewed as serious acts of perversion by "respectable" society in the past, such activities are seen today as relatively harmless, provided that they do not impose on children or unwilling adults.

separated from the Saturn finger reveals an interest in being the center of attention, which he often is. The sloping head line reveals a strong imagination, although it is held in check by an upwardly moving branch, adding an accountant's practicality. In general, this man is cautious, careful, and somewhat secretive, as seen by the joined head and life lines and the narrow space between the head and heart lines. I read his hands during a flight to Rio de Janeiro, where he was planning to make a pilgrimage to the Carmen Miranda Museum.

## SEXUAL ABUSE

Sexual abuse, especially of minors, is an extremely serious matter and has been a major issue in recent history, confronted by parents, educators, religious leaders, and law enforcement. As is the case with rape, a stigma is frequently placed on the young victim rather than on the perpetrator, who is often a relative or other trusted adult.

Most sex abusers were themselves sexually abused as children. In the hand, this past history can be seen as a major influence line crossing both the life and head lines, often causing breaks or islands in the head line. Sometimes, the influence line may even cross the heart line as well.

Sex abusers are emotionally disturbed. In many instances, this can be seen by an islanded head line as well as a string-of-pearls skin ridge pattern, an indicator of severe neurosis. Where sex drive is strong, a large, reddish mount of Venus is present. A tendency toward violence is indicated by large, coarse upper and lower mounts of Mars, reddish nails, and coarse skin texture.

We'd normally assume that people who impose themselves sexually on others would have no control over their actions (hence, a supple thumb or very flexible hand), but studies reveal that child abusers (and sex abusers in general) can be willful and stubborn. Many are often unable or unwilling to respond to psychological treatment.

I've found that it's difficult to look at a person's hand and say, "This person is a child molester," or "This guy is a rapist." This is why we need to carefully examine the entire hand and be open to what our intuition tells us about the person whose hands we are reading.

We mentioned earlier that there are a number of key indicators in the hand that can reveal serious sexual and psychological problems. They indicate not only abnormal behavior but the potential for violence. These behaviors go beyond the normal boundaries of adventurous sex into realms of conduct that can pose a danger to others. Indications in the hand of these types of behavior are worth repeating here:

- Hands and fingers that are abnormally short or long when compared to the person's body size

- Jupiter and Saturn fingers of equal length, or Saturn and Apollo fingers of equal length; Dr. Charlotte Wolfe, author of *The Hand in Psychological Diagnosis*, found that such configurations appear primarily in schizophrenics

- Fingers—especially those of Jupiter and Mercury—that are severely twisted or deformed when not the result of arthritis or injury

- Severely chained, broken, and islanded head lines

- Head lines that are missing (especially in both hands)

- Extremely weak or short head lines, particularly when accompanied by a strong, deep heart line and a large, reddish and coarsely textured mount of Venus

- Thumbs that are abnormally short, deformed, or placed extremely high on the hand to the extent that they appear similar to those of an infant

- An abnormally large, hard, and red mount of Venus, especially if the skin is coarse and grilled

- Abnormally large, hard, and reddish upper and lower mounts of Mars, especially when found with the type of Venus mount described above

- A simian line found on a rough and poorly shaped hand, especially when the hand features two or more of the characteristics listed above

Remember that the existence of one or two of these traits does not mean that the person is a sexual psychopath or a rapist. Features of the hand reveal potential. In addition, modifying factors in the hand have been known to counteract negative qualities found in hand shape, fingers, mounts, and lines. By the same token, it is entirely possible that a person with a "normal" hand can be a sexual predator.

When we counsel others through hand analysis, we have an opportunity to help them get in touch with their reality. At the same time, we want to strengthen this self-awareness with inspiration and constructive advice to help them take the next step.

By understanding our own hands, we can learn to appreciate and accept our own sexual nature, which can help other people on their own journey of discovery and self-acceptance. Whenever we encounter situations that go beyond our own knowledge or experience, we have a responsibility to refer the person to a professional who may be better able to help. By dealing with others with respect and compassion, we can serve as an effective catalyst for helping them realize their true potential for personal growth and happiness.

# COMPATIBILITY IN RELATIONSHIPS

I HAVE OFTEN BEEN ASKED TO READ THE HANDS of couples. On one level, it's interesting to analyze the hands of two people as a unit because I'm always curious about the dynamics of different relationships. On the other hand, doing a compatibility study of the hands of both partners to determine areas of harmony and potential conflict (as well as areas of jealousy, greed, and domination) can be compared to walking through a minefield and requires utmost sensitivity and tact.

While I've found that a sense of humor is essential when reading someone's hand, it's important not to embarrass the person whose hand is being read or intrude on a relationship with ridicule or judgment. I always try to follow what I like to call the Golden Rule of Speaking: make sure that everything I say is true, kind, *and* helpful. If it doesn't satisfy all three requirements, I hold my tongue and move on to something else.

There are many ways in which two people form a romantic relationship. Usually, they share common interests and enjoy each other's company. Alternatively, they may have a good sexual rapport but like to pursue their own personal goals in life. Some thrive on being with someone radically different from themselves, and many couples remain close through constant friction and conflict. Some are together because they like their partner's wit, good looks, or bank account. Others may be spiritually compatible or move in the same social or political circles. Believers in reincarnation feel that karmic ties from past lives may determine some relationships—in other words, the partners are together because they need to reestablish ancient ties or resolve old issues between them from a past life.

For many, a relationship can be a primary avenue for personal growth, especially if the relationship is shared on physical, emotional, mental, and spiritual levels. According to Julia A. Bondi, author of *Love-light: Unveiling the Mysteries of Sex and Romance*:

> When we begin to connect to our partners on all four levels of relating, we also begin to approach the true meaning of love. Love begins when sexual energy touches not only our genitals but also our mind, heart, and spirit as well. Love is sexuality enlarged, enlightened, and transformed. When we love, we see our purpose in life. We are motivated to move ahead toward union and completion not only with our partners but also in all areas of our lives.[1]

Whether we want to study our own hands or have the privilege of reading the hands of others, it's important to have a basic understanding of the dynamics of human relationships and how they can affect our lives. Being deeply involved with another person (whether this develops into marriage or not) brings up important emotional issues that we often avoid by being alone. Our ability to trust, make compromises, be vulnerable, and share feelings is constantly challenged in a close relationship.

When we are romantically involved, we are called on to accept a partner totally, despite his or her eccentricities or imperfections. As we learn to accept a partner, we come closer to accepting other people as well: a romantic relationship helps us to become at one with the world. In his essay "Practical Friendship," John L. Hoff wrote:

> We need to know how to build a relationship and how to use that field of force as energy to nurture and guide us: it is our primary resource for human evolution and spiritual development. It is in relationships that we collaborate with each other to create a better world.[2]

Many people are confused about marriage and committed relationships today. On the one hand, marriage has become an institutionalized ideal for every person, complete with tax benefits and other advantages for those whose unions are sanctioned by the government or church. According to popular belief, a marriage should be exclusive and last forever. On the other hand, the reality of a 30 to 50 percent divorce rate among couples living in industrialized Western countries such as the United States—with divorce's concomitant emotional, financial, and social trauma—points out the difficulties of this marriage ideal.

Though a romantic at heart, I've come to the conclusion that each person has unique relationship needs. For some, marriage is a perfect choice and can open the door to lasting happiness. For others, marriage (or even a committed relationship) may not be a good idea at all. Many people are not ready for marriage and shouldn't be coerced into it. For some, the freedom of being single, with its inherent versatility, independence, and freedom from compromise, may be more important than settling down with another person, not to mention raising a family.

Yet those contemplating an important relationship need to consider their true motivations. They also need to be aware of any fears or psychological blocks that can prevent them from achieving a pleasurable relationship that provides an opportunity for meaningful, intimate contact and personal growth. Those who are already in a relationship need to be reminded of the potential strengths and weaknesses in their unions so that they can reach greater levels of intimacy with their partners.

Aside from emotional compatibility, a couple should be physically compatible as well, because if a relationship has a good sexual foundation, its potential for long-term success is greater. For example, a woman with a low sex drive is not likely leave a husband who is not sexually demanding, nor will a highly sexed woman leave a man who is ready for lovemaking at any time. However, the key to a successful relationship involves more than good sex alone. According to Omraam Mikhael Aivanhov, author of *Love and Sexuality*, "The ideal is to agree on all three planes—to have a mutual physical attraction, a similarity of tastes and feelings . . . and most important of all, there must be a tremendous agreement in the world of ideas, a common goal, an ideal."[3]

The hand reader's basic task is to help others achieve greater self-awareness and self-knowledge so that their present or future relationships can be guided by their own genuine needs and aspirations. Therefore, the hand analyst must be extremely careful when making pronouncements on the advisability of establishing or continuing a relationship. While we can provide a valuable service by making people aware of the inherent strengths and weaknesses of their relationships, we need to leave any decisions about the future of the relationship to the parties involved.

## COMPATIBILITY AND THE HAND

If scientists realized the value of hand analysis in the study of compatibility between two persons, they would learn that the most reliable computer is the human hand. While a computerized dating service can match couples based on their known rational likes and dislikes, it cannot make a computation based on irrational or subconscious factors. These factors include personality, temperament, ability to communicate, and primal needs like sexual satisfaction or the urge for empowerment—all of which are of vital importance in relations between a couple.

Perhaps the most important computation a palmist can make has to do with a couple's similarities and differences. In *The Psychology of Sex*, authors H. J. Eysenck and Glenn Wilson point out that "partnerships are more successful if based on similarities rather than supposed complementation" and that similar personality traits and interests are crucial to successful long-term relationships.[4]

Some point out, however, that there is often more opportunity for growth in a relationship of opposites because each person can learn more about him- or herself and his or her partner through the friction generated by being with someone different.

Perhaps the ideal relationship would be with someone who is similar in areas of importance but different enough to help make the relationship more interesting. Ideally, each partner should share (or at least respect) the other's views on major issues such as religion, politics, and the desire to have children. The couple should also share basic views on matters such as diet, smoking, and sex. If they don't, each partner can at least respect the other person's point of view and strive to cherish the differences that come up over time, as they will in any relationship between two people.

## MARKS OF COMPATIBILITY

Because the shape of the hand reveals basic temperament, it should lay the foundation for a compatibility analysis. If one partner has squarish hands while the other partner's hands are conic, each probably has a very different way of seeing the world. While the owner of the squarish hands tends to be highly organized and practical and enjoys rules and structure, the other partner might tend toward the instinctual, spontaneous, and romantic.

Similarities in hand and thumb flexibility should also be noted because they indicate how harmoniously the couple is able to face challenges and adapt to change. However, don't write the couple off if their hands reveal major differences: if one partner has a stiff hand and the other has a flexible hand, for example, the two should be encouraged to acknowledge their differences and balance their divergent approaches.

From the mount of Venus and the shape of the little finger, we can determine an individual's sensuality. If the mount of Venus is well developed and the little finger is long, we probably are looking at the hand of a sensual person who loves physical contact, affection, and sex. Ideally, the partners should have mounts of Venus of comparable proportions.

If the mount of Venus is flat, the little finger short, and the consistency of the hand weak, chances are that sex will not play an important role in that person's life. If both partners have this type of hand, they will likely be compatible with each other. The

most important features of their relationship are probably mutual respect, intellectual compatibility, and shared interests, such as books, art, or the theater. If one partner is very sensual and the other is not, however, conflicts are likely to plague the relationship. One partner will feel sexually frustrated, while the other will feel that he or she is being imposed upon.

Another reliable mark of compatibility is the heart line. If both people share a deep, "physical" heart line, they will both gravitate toward the purely sexual aspects of love. They'd be right at home having sex in a car, in the bushes, or on the kitchen table. By contrast, people with "mental" heart lines place more importance on soft music, candles, cuddling, and emotional support. While personality variations between a couple are inevitable, a person with a short physical heart line ending under the Saturn finger and another with a long, chained mental heart line ending under Jupiter would probably not be compatible sexually.

Whether having different types and lengths of heart lines will be a problem can be determined by studying other aspects of the hand, such as the mount of Venus (the key indicator of sex drive), the Mercury finger (an indicator of the ability to communicate), the thumb (revealing the existence of sexual repression or lack thereof), and hand flexibility, which could reveal a person's ability to adapt to another person's sexual style.

Fingerprints also have a bearing on compatibility issues. Generally speaking, people whose fingerprints are primarily of the loop variety are the easiest to deal with in a relationship. They are by nature flexible and adaptable and have a well-rounded view of the world around them.

By contrast, owners of hands where whorls predominate tend to be the most difficult to get along with. They are independent and like to do things their way. In addition to being secretive, they are not likely to adapt to their partner's needs. However, other hand characteristics, such as a flexible hand and a supple thumb, can modify this trait.

I've found that people with arch fingertip patterns like to build or fix things: they enjoy working

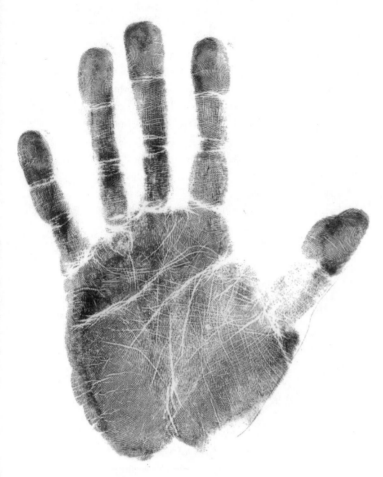

FIGURE 15.1. A sensitive male hand.

Double loops reveal a person who is extremely thorough and who likes to consider all sides of an issue. Although this is a perfect trait for a counselor or judge, it contributes to difficulty in making domestic decisions. If your partner has this pattern and needs to go shopping, avoid frustration by letting him go by himself. He is likely to insist on visiting every clothing store in the mall before buying that pair of pants, especially if his fingers are long and knotted.

A fine skin texture with lots of lines is a clear indicator of a sensitive nature. If both partners tend to be very sensitive (see the sensitive handprint shown in Figure 15.1), their relationship could be somewhat difficult, since each partner could easily overreact to almost any conflict or problem. If one or both partners has a vanity loop as well, sensitivity is an even bigger issue. Generally speaking, if one person is slightly less sensitive than the other is, there is a greater chance for emotional balance in the relationship.

Stiff thumbs and rigid hands are sure signs of a strong will and stubborn personality. When both partners share this trait, neither would want to compromise over an issue or problem. If the couple is generally compatible in most areas of their life, this should not be a problem, but if there are many divergent issues between them, it almost definitely will be. In such cases, a good hand analyst should point out the need for both people to become more aware of their willfulness, develop the ability to compromise, and strive to understand the other person's point of view.

A well-developed, long index finger with an enlarged muscular pattern at the base signifies a dominating nature (Figure 15.2). Such people like to be in charge and enjoy being in control. They like to be on top in their relationships.

This isn't likely to be a problem if the dominant person's partner is submissive or dependent by nature. Couples seldom engage in adultery or get divorced when one who has to dominate to be happy chooses a partner who likes to be dominated. The best results are obtained when one partner is as dominant as the other is submissive.

on their cars or computers, like to spend time in the garden, or like to experiment with new recipes in the kitchen. If their nonarch partner understands that these activities are normal for people with arch fingerprints, domestic tranquillity can be guaranteed.

If one partner has a hand with mostly loop fingerprints while his partner has mostly whorls, he will likely adapt to her needs. If both partners have loops predominating, they can be so adaptable that it may be difficult making decisions together. Yet when both partners have whorl fingertip patterns, harmony in the relationship will likely be a challenge, especially if their hands and thumbs are firm or rigid.

FIGURE 15.2. The hand of a strong woman who likes to be in charge.

You don't need to be a professional marriage counselor to understand what happens when both partners are dominant types: their domestic life can resemble a battleground. Because the dominating partner is usually quite vain, he or she succumbs to a partner who is generous with praise and affection. When dominating people receive enough attention, they often sublimate their dominating natures.

By contrast, dominating partners who feel neglected are another story. They tend to have frequent explosions of temper. Because domineering people need to assure themselves of their attractiveness, they are likely to flirt and may even have sexual relations outside their primary relationship.

## ANALYSIS: A LONG-MARRIED COUPLE

The handprints reproduced in Figures 15.3 and 15.4 show a couple who recently celebrated their sixty-fifth wedding anniversary. While each person is different in character and professional interests (the wife, whom we'll call Mildred, is a former artist, while her husband, whom we'll call Michael, recently retired from teaching college-level math), they find that their long life together features both strong similarities and strong contrasts.

Their joined head and life lines indicate a shared caution toward life and a tendency to depend on each other. Both have a loop of seriousness in their hands. Both are intelligent and have a broad range of intellectual interests, as seen by their long, strong head lines; they also have comparable mounts of Venus and similar heart lines (which show that they understand each other emotionally). They share an ability to communicate well with each other. They both love music, reading, and travel.

Although they are in basic agreement on most important issues, they have different ways of seeing the world. Michael tends to be conservative and rational (he's a mathematician, after all) while Mildred is rebellious and eager to explore new ideas and trends. In addition, she tends to be more restless, as seen by the tiny lines moving from her life line toward the Luna mount. Although they enjoy each other's company, each partner has always given the other lots of physical and psychological space to follow personal interests. Both Michael and Mildred have more than one union line, a fact that reveals other deep friendships in addition to their marriage.

When problems arise in the relationship, they make an effort to seek compromise, since their stiff thumbs and relatively rigid hands betray a shared stubbornness. As is typical of people whose hands are squarish, they are both fairly rational and practical in the way they deal with new situations.

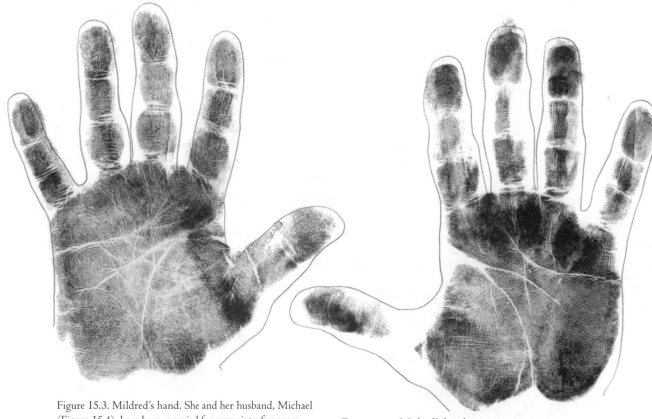

Figure 15.3. Mildred's hand. She and her husband, Michael (Figure 15.4), have been married for over sixty-five years.

FIGURE 15.4. Michael's hand.

The essence of their long and happy relationship involves a balance between interdependence and dependence, with a strong sense of shared affection, loyalty, and respect for each other's needs.

## A FINAL NOTE

Because the lines on the hand can change (and the union line is among the most changeable of all), hand readers should be careful about making predictions like "You will divorce by the time you are forty" or "You'll never get married." In addition to the probability of being wrong, you may also be creating self-fulfilling prophecies in a person's life. In fact, if you see a problem that warrants professional intervention, it's best to refer your clients to a qualified marriage counselor or psychotherapist.

The primary value of psychologically oriented palmistry is to help the person whose hands we are reading achieve greater self-understanding. A clear, accurate, and objective reading will remind him of aspects of his personality he may already be aware of and can offer new insights into areas of his character he may have ignored. This is doubly true when you are reading for a couple. After you have shared the information you see in the hands, it is up to the person (or couple) to take the next step.

This does not mean that you cannot comment on trends that you see in the hand, such as conflicts in the relationship or even separation. Almost every intimate relationship between two people requires work, and you do your client no favor by ignoring potential problems. Yet the way you present the information is crucial: If you see a possible separation, for example, it's most helpful to say something like, "I see a possible breakup unless you and your husband work on this relationship." You not only point out a potential problem but also help the person take control of the situation rather then leave it to fate.

# PART IV

YOUR
HAND AND
HEALTH

# chapter 16
# ELEMENTS OF MEDICAL PALMISTRY

Although the ancient science of hand analysis is thousands of years old, doctors are reevaluating its use as a guide toward understanding the dynamics of health and disease. While orthodox physicians have studied the color of the nails and the temperature and texture of the skin for decades, an increasing number of physicians feel that the flexibility, ridges, and lines of the human hand also provide important guidance for the prevention and diagnosis of disease and the alleviation of symptoms.

## WHAT IS HEALTH?

According to *Stedman's Medical Dictionary*, health is not only freedom from disease or abnormality but also "a state of dynamic balance in which an individual's or a group's capacity to cope with all the circumstances of living is at an optimum level."[1]

Health is determined partly by heredity but is mostly dependent on how we are able to adapt to our environment: fighting germs, dealing with stress, avoiding accidents, and resisting the threat of environmental pollution. Healthy diets, stress management, a positive mental attitude, adequate rest, and regular exercise are all major factors in achieving and maintaining good health. Since only unhealthy bodies provide fertile ground for disease, maintaining a strong, healthy body should be one of our primary goals in life.

Since the time of Hippocrates, health practitioners have considered the hand a reliable indicator of hereditary conditions, emotional makeup, and physical constitution. In addition, modern medical researchers have found that our thoughts, emotions, and attitudes can have a profound impact on our physical health. Because the hands reflect the *whole person*, medical palmistry can serve as a tool to help us understand our total health picture and work toward achieving the level of well-being we deserve.

Any competent palmist will report that hands show tendencies and not always definite facts, and the lines of the hand can change dramatically, sometimes in a matter of just weeks. Therefore, the fact that you have a long life line is no guarantee that you won't die of a heart attack at a young age or be run over by a taxi on your way to work. Having a sign indicating a tendency for cancer does not mean that you won't live a long, cancer-free life.

However, because a hand consultant can recognize a predisposition to certain health problems, palmistry can be a valuable tool in both the prevention and cure of disease. In addition to providing indicators to possible ill health, the structure, texture, and lines of the hand offer hope to those of us who want to achieve our maximum health potential.

For example, many people are unaware that each of the five fingers is associated with a different organic system of the body. Dr. Charlotte Wolff associated the thumb with vitality and the general state of health, the index finger with the respiratory system and the stomach, the middle finger with the liver and intestines, the ring finger with the kidneys and blood circulation, and the little finger with the feet and the sexual glands.[2]

The human hand is like a complex ecosystem that changes constantly. By understanding individual characteristics—like temperature, consistency, and lines—and by making logical and intuitive connections regarding their relationships, you can use the hand as an ongoing guide to ensure your own good health and the well-being of those who seek your counsel. In addition, by periodically taking handprints of your clients, you can keep detailed records of their hands over a period of years, enabling you to observe any changes that could affect their health.

## THE HAND AS COMPUTER

Modern scientific medicine is advancing rapidly. New diagnostic tests and new drugs are being developed so quickly that physicians simply cannot keep up with them. As soon as a doctor learns how to interpret one diagnostic test, for example, others come along. The physician cannot afford to ignore the new tests and must incorporate them into the diagnostic procedure. If something goes wrong with a patient or if the doctor fails to make a correct diagnosis, he might be sued for malpractice, especially in a country like the United States, where malpractice suits are common.

In an effort to improve this situation, the modern physician, like everyone else today, has been introduced to the computer. Nearly all modern medical centers from Cleveland to Chengdu have been at least partially computerized. Increased reliance on computer technology is projected for all medical facilities in the future.

While computers may well help diagnose disease more quickly and more accurately than traditional diagnostic methods, some doctors believe that computers may help the doctors but not the patients. It will never be possible to program a computer for empathy, individual experience, and human wisdom, which are all required to understand the patient as a whole. Nor will a computer be able to detect the etiological factors in disease (i.e., those relating to cause or origin) that have to do with temperament, constitution, the unconscious, and the nonquantifiable aspects of a patient's lifestyle, such as love, libido, and loneliness.

Many medical doctors, like the late Eugene Scheimann, have found that there is one "computer" that has always been with us, though. It is always available, it is always accessible, and it does not involve complicated technical equipment. It can enable doctors to gain a better insight into a patient's disease, as well as help them develop a better understanding of the patient as a whole. This computer is the human hand.

Has mainstream medicine recognized the hand as a diagnostic tool? An editorial published in the *Journal of the American Medical Association* more than fifty years ago, recognizing the importance of the study of the hand in the diagnosis of subacute bacterial endocarditis, had the following to say:

> *Despite widespread and sometimes unnecessary use of numerous laboratory tests in the day-by-day clinical practice, diagnostic methods that require no special apparatus and that depend only on simple observation can play an effective role in obtaining clinical information about patients. In this connection, the human hand is a unique organ from which an extraordinary amount of clinical information may be derived.*[3]

Keep in mind that this editorial does not come from a pulp magazine catering to sensation-seeking mystics. It is from a professional journal whose reputation in the medical world is beyond question. It continues, "Diagnosis of the disease is sometimes established initially by *information supplied solely by the hand*" (italics added). It concludes with a comment on the hand's role in diagnosing shock: "The color and temperature of the skin of the hands sometimes yields more information of *impending* shock than either the pulse or the blood pressure" (italics added). Surely these observations should increase our respect for palmistry as a diagnostic aid.

To illustrate the diagnostic significance of the hand, let's consider a common disease such as arthritis. We all know that a cure is not yet available for this disease. However, according to the consensus of all arthritis specialists, symptoms could be more effectively relieved *if treatment is started within six months after the first sign of the disease*. One of the reasons for the frequent failure of treatment is that the crippling or dangerous symptoms of arthritis are not recognized early enough. In the case of rheumatoid arthritis, which involves swelling of the knuckles or joints at the base of the fingers, and osteoarthritis, which involves swelling of the joints nearest the tops of the fingers, physicians could begin more effective treatment if they were able to diagnose the condition earlier.

In his book *The Hand as a Mirror of Systemic Disease*,[4] Dr. Theodore J. Berry associates certain configurations of the hand with no fewer than fifty diseases, including those that are congenital and those that are acquired after birth. In addition, a review of current medical literature throughout the world reveals that physicians and other medical researchers are performing ongoing research linking abnormal handprint patterns with dozens of major physical and mental health problems. These include childhood leukemia, schizophrenia, diabetes, congenital heart defects, epilepsy, chromosomal aberrations, thyroid cancer, and Alzheimer's disease. Surely, with this weight of testimony in favor of the hand as a diagnostic aid, one would expect medical palmistry to be more widely employed than it is.[5]

## PERSONALITY AND DISEASE

The primary message of this book is that palmistry is a valuable way to study and analyze personality. Many people might not realize that personality has an important impact on health and disease, as well. For one thing, the hands are open for inspection and do not require a person's cooperation to reveal information. This eliminates the probability of coming to a wrong conclusion because an individual may be deceptive or may otherwise withhold important information from a health practitioner.

This is why hand analysis can be especially valuable for the psychotherapist. In many cases, the client can withhold important information that he or she has repressed or does not want to share, such as a serious trauma or behavior considered too shameful to reveal. Withholding such information can lead the therapist—and the course of therapy—in the wrong direction.

Through hand analysis, the therapist is able to immediately discover the psychological essence of the client in an objective, holistic, and nonjudgmental way. He or she can point out, for example, a personality characteristic or traumatic event in the hand that can encourage the client to open up and discuss it in more detail. This not only can reduce the time necessary to arrive at a clear diagnosis but can shorten the overall course of therapy as well.

In addition, the characteristic features of the hand are often evidenced in early childhood, well before the time when handwriting, the Rorschach ink test, and other psychometric or technical tests can be applied.

Dr. C. W. Cutler, a well-known hand surgeon, said that if one examines it closely, the hand reveals much concerning its owner.[6] In it is written a record of age and sex, health or disease, occupation and habit, skill or ineptitude, accident and misuse, work or indolence. One does not need to know palmistry to know that there is something of the past, a good deal of the present, and even a little of the future in the hand.

But how can medical palmistry benefit a person—especially those of us who don't practice medicine? How can self-understanding gained through medical palmistry help prevent disease and improve overall health?

- Perhaps the most important benefit of medical palmistry is that it helps a person develop intuition.

- In addition, medical palmistry can help prevent diseases by making us more health conscious in daily life. For example, if, like most people, you have an interest or at least a dependency on cars, you become "car conscious." You may study the car manual or watch the mechanic as he treats your car's ills. You gradually become so familiar with your car that you recognize certain noises or irregularities indicating that something may be wrong. Similarly, your study of the human hand will help you recognize certain irregularities of your body's mechanics. By being alert to certain signs, you may consult a physician or urge a friend to seek professional help before a disorder progresses beyond the treatable stage.

- In certain cases, especially in psychosomatic ailments caused by mental difficulties, medical palmistry may be able to help someone when medicine fails to do so. Because a hand consultation can offer a deep level of psychological insight, it can inspire a person to have faith and hope in the healing process. This may sufficiently relieve anxiety enough to allow nature to effect a cure. Remember that hope is one of the best medicines for the sick.

- Medical palmistry can persuade patients to observe the warning signals they receive from physicians. The modern doctor knows a great deal about the causes of disease and can offer guidance about how to achieve a healthier way of life. Unfortunately, few patients listen to their physicians. The insights offered through medical palmistry can persuade many people to live a healthier life.

- Medical palmistry reveals a great deal about human nature. The hand gives information to the layperson as well as to doctors.

## ADVICE TO THOSE WHO ARE STARTING OUT

As the world's foremost expert in medical palmistry, Dr. Eugene Scheimann taught that, to become adept at the practice, one must have more than intuition and the ability to influence others. One also must have knowledge, reason, and wisdom. He believed that if we possess these qualities, we can help our fellow humans—as well as ourselves—maintain better health.

In order to achieve this beneficial aim, he taught that we must observe certain immutable guidelines, described below.

### Be Skeptical

Do not believe the information presented in this book (or in any other palmistry book) until you subject it to analysis, tests, and actual readings. Only through firsthand experience will you learn the most important aspects of palmistry. For example, let's say you've read that a long index finger (i.e., an index finger that is longer than the ring finger) is a sign of dominance, pride, or a strong ego.

Before you accept this statement, you should observe at least ten people with long index fingers. If the majority of them (at least 80 percent) admit to being proud or having a strong will to dominate, then you have a right to draw a general conclusion. However, in order to be sure, you should also examine the hands of ten people with short index fingers, which would supposedly signify dependency, lack of pride, and a weak ego. If you again observe eight out of ten subjects correctly, you can be positive.

Yet suppose you discover, as is often the case, that many people with short index fingers show dominance, pride, or a strong ego. You must then learn whether these traits constitute a person's overcompensation for feelings of inferiority and dependency by questioning that individual about his or her background. This example emphasizes the very important point that *the hand shows only tendencies that we can overcome.*

### Beware of Fortune-Telling

Telling fortunes can be dangerous to anyone who is searching for improvement in physical or emotional health for the simple reason that you can be utterly wrong. *It is not up to us to predict.* In ancient times, the Oracle at Delphi purposely kept her predictions ambiguous. Even today's physicians have a difficult time forming an accurate prognosis. A doctor may predict a patient's imminent death, only to have the patient ultimately outlive him. Similarly, a complete medical checkup may show that a patient is in excellent health, but the next day the patient may die. If you are interested in telling fortunes, do it for fun. Don't take yourself seriously.

## Be Humble

Even if you think you have mastered the art of palmistry, do not be too sure of yourself. I have been reading hands since 1969, and I still make mistakes and am still learning new things.

Don't try to impress others with your specialized hand knowledge, but always continue to learn. A thousand years ago, medicine was sure of everything. Now, with the benefit of millions of case histories, libraries, and clinics, the practice of medicine is more mature and practitioners are often more aware of what we do *not* know than they were in the past.

In spite of the astonishing number of medical advances over the past twenty or thirty years, there are still many diseases—including lupus, multiple sclerosis, Lyme disease, and chronic fatigue syndrome—that are often misdiagnosed by physicians. In addition, there are still many diseases for which medical science has not found a cure, including diabetes, cystic fibrosis, leukemia, psoriasis, and even the common cold. If the doctors themselves are not sure, then palmists have no right to give a diagnosis based on an analysis of the hands. We can only tell the person who comes to us for a consultation that the hand indicates certain factors that can indicate a predisposition for certain medical problems. To find out whether your impression is valid, try to obtain a case history, as a physician does, or let the subject do the talking. Evangeline Adams, the famous astrologer, stated that she learned much more from what people told her than from what she saw in their horoscopes![7]

## Be Confident

Although you should be humble and skeptical, you should also have confidence in your own intuition. If there is an idea of which you are convinced, don't be afraid to explore it. Medical palmistry is still comparatively young and can benefit from new discoveries.

## Do Not Attempt to Practice Medicine

Unless you are a licensed physician, it is illegal, as well as unwise, to practice medicine. However, if you are serious about exploring the field of medical palmistry, you should observe one of a physician's most important rules: *do not predict doom*. Few doctors tell their patients that their condition is hopeless.

Rather, if you are convinced that certain signs indicate illness or an accident, consider them warning signals on the highway: DANGER AHEAD; SLOW DOWN; DRIVE WITH CARE. You may tell your client to take it easy, or you may suggest general changes in diet or lifestyle.

In any case, you should not practice medicine. If you see a serious medical or psychological problem in the hand, suggest that the individual consult a qualified health practitioner for further examination and analysis.

## Do Not Depend on One Sign Alone

I cannot emphasize enough that palmists must study the hand as a whole. Some diseases or symptoms show up in different ways in individual hands. To learn the significance of the total hand in health and healing, you must evaluate the following characteristics:

- Texture, temperature, and color of the skin

- Consistency, flexibility, and moisture of the hand

- Nail color, shape, and condition

- Configuration of the fingers and the palm

- Dermatoglyphics (skin ridge patterns on the palms and fingers)

- Chiroglyphics (the lines and other markings of the palm)

# THE BASICS OF MEDICAL PALMISTRY

*chapter*

# 17

The famous smile of Leonardo da Vinci's *Mona Lisa* has captured the imagination and curiosity of many observers. Her smile may be mysterious or even deceitful, but her hands are not mysterious to the experienced observer. Their smooth texture indicates that she has noble characteristics!

The texture and the temperature of the skin have been important to doctors and palmists since ancient times. Doctors have always considered them to be a barometer of mood, disposition, age, and health. When people are healthy, happy, and young, the skin is smooth, elastic, and warm. When a person is sick, old, or tense, the skin is probably wrinkled, and coarse, or cold and clammy.

## SKIN TEXTURE

A fine, soft skin texture, only slightly coarser than a baby's hand, signifies a refined and emotionally impressionable person who doesn't like anything rough or coarse. This individual tends to avoid the company of vulgar people and only reluctantly performs manual tasks, such as washing dishes or changing a flat tire. On the contrary, skin that is coarse, hard, or wrinkled indicates a coarser individual who can be quarrelsome, critical, and rough. This type of person loves to perform manual labor and often chooses to work as a farmer, mechanic, or construction worker.

The texture of the skin is determined by our hormones, which are also influential in forming our personality. Therefore, we could consider skin texture an indicator of our inner nature. As William G. Benham put it in his classic book *The Laws of Scientific Hand Reading*: "Refined texture softens everything; coarse texture animalizes it."[1]

Because of the close relationship between the texture of the skin and the endocrine glands, skin texture and temperature are important in the diagnosis of thyroid disorders. In the case of overactive thyroid glands (a condition known as hyperthyroidism), the skin is smooth, satiny, and warm. However, in the hand of a person with hypothyroidism (an underactive thyroid gland), the skin is doughy, dry, cold, and coarse.

Dr. Scheimann once described the case of a woman who was tired and very nervous. She went to her physician for a physical examination. The doctor gave her a complete checkup and found nothing wrong with her. All the laboratory tests performed during the examination came back negative. She was not satisfied with this doctor's findings and went to see Dr. Scheimann.

The first thing Dr. Scheimann noticed was that her hands were doughy, dry, rough, and cold, and her nails were brittle. He immediately suspected that she might have an underactive thyroid gland. When taken previously, a basal metabolism test had been negative. He repeated the test, which was again negative. But because her hands indicated a thyroid deficiency and he could find no other evidence of disease, he prescribed thyroid medication. In three months she improved considerably. This improvement was also reflected by the condition of her hands; they were warmer and the nails were firmer.

## SKIN TEMPERATURE

The temperature of the skin can provide definite information concerning changes in blood circulation. In winter, if a person's hand remains cold despite the warm indoor temperature, or if the hand is persistently cold in any kind of weather, you must consider whether that person has a circulatory disorder called vasospasm, a constriction of the tiny blood vessels (known as capillaries) in the hand. Vasospasm is controlled by our nervous system. If the nerves are stimulated, changes will take place. The most common causes of constriction are drugs (such as adrenaline), certain illnesses, starvation, cold, and emotion, such as pain, fear, or anxiety. However, if a person undergoes, for example, a satisfying sexual experience, the blood vessels will dilate and the hands will be warm. Over the years, I have observed that people who suffer from insomnia and sexual frustration tend to have cold, clammy hands.

The best way to determine a person's skin temperature is to check both the back of the hand and the palmar surface of the fingers. It is important that you compare the temperature on both hands. A difference in skin temperature between the two hands is an indication that some local abnormal condition (such as blockage of circulation in the colder hand) exists. When this is the case, the person should be referred to a doctor.

## SKIN COLOR

Blood circulation determines not only the temperature but also the color of the hand. The normal color of the hand is rosy or pink, no matter what an individual's racial background. Any other color is an indication that there is something wrong either with a person's health or with his or her temperament. In fact, it is not an exaggeration to state that the color and temperature of the hand, when considered together, are two of the most important signs of life and death, because the hand is a highly reliable indicator of the overall condition of the cardiovascular system.

There are three main color changes in the skin that are of interest in medical palmistry: rubor, pallor, and cyanosis.

Rubor, or extreme redness, is generally associated with increased temperature of the hand. This occurs when the blood vessels are dilated as a result of changes in temperature, illness, or another dysfunction.

Rubor is a common symptom of a disease known as erythromelalgia. Other symptoms of this disease include increased skin temperature, a burning or tingling sensation, and profuse perspiration. The disease sometimes occurs suddenly in response to exercise or heat. At other times, it is associated with internal diseases such as high blood pressure, gout, rheumatoid arthritis, and diabetes.

In a condition known as palmar erythema (or "liver palms"), rubor is limited to only a part of the hand, usually the part of the hand that would come in contact with a surface. This condition is common in persons with liver disease as well as in pregnant women. It is also associated with vitamin deficiencies and chronic pulmonary tuberculosis.

Pallor, or paleness of the skin, is accompanied by decreased temperature. It is the most important sign of anemia or anxiety. You can perform a great service for a person with skin pallor by recognizing it as a possible early sign of anemia or internal bleeding. First, extend and bend back your client's palm. If you notice that the main crease lines are pale, the best thing that person can do is consult a physician, because chances are that he or she has anemia or possibly even an internal hemorrhage.

Occasionally, a pale or white hand is also a sign of certain character traits. Persons with pale hands are often unrealistic, selfish, and unemotional. In contrast, individuals whose hands are an intense red usually adopt an extremist attitude in their behavior and their thinking.

Cyanosis, or a bluish discoloration of the hand, occurs most frequently in cases of congestive heart failure, congenital heart disease, and local circulatory disturbances. Unlike other color changes, cyanosis can be accompanied by either an increase or a decrease in skin temperature. A warm bluish hand may tell us that there is something wrong with the general blood flow, while a cold bluish hand may indicate that there is a local circulatory disorder or some degree of persistent vasospasm. When a warm, pale hand suddenly becomes cold and bluish, it is a sign of impending shock.

In an interesting illness known as Raynaud's disease, all three colors—red, white, and blue—are present. This disease occurs most often in young women who have an underactive thyroid gland. Raynaud's disease is a vasospastic disorder that is precipitated either by cold or by emotional distress. During the onset of this disease, the tips of the fingers of both hands first become pale, then cyanotic, then an intense red, with throbbing and swelling. The attack usually ends spontaneously after the patient calms down or after the hands are placed in warm water.

## HAND CONSISTENCY

According to the Hindus, palmistry has three main functions: *darsana* (seeing), *sparsana* (touching), and *rekha vimarsana* (reading the lines). For the purposes of medical palmistry, *sparsana* includes touching not only to determine the skin's texture and temperature but also to determine the hand's muscle tone, vigor, and mobility.

The consistency of a hand, which is measured by its resistance to pressure, is a sure indication of the quantity of energy a person possesses. The hand's muscular development and fatty deposits also contribute to its consistency. Based on these factors, we can classify hands into three types: the flabby hand, the firm hand, and the hard hand.

A lack of muscle tone and lack of resistance to pressure or palpation characterize the flabby hand. This type of hand is usually small, broad, and fat. The fingers are very soft and "boneless," resembling small sausages.

This type of hand is often present in persons who have a sluggish or underdeveloped thyroid gland. Such people love worldly pleasures, comfort, and luxury. They like to eat, drink, and be merry. Those who possess such a hand tend to have poor willpower and little self-discipline in the face of their pleasure-seeking instincts. Although these people are friendly and very sociable, they are generally unreliable.

The firm hand is firm because it contains more muscle and less fat. Despite its firmness, there is some degree of elasticity. In comparison to the flabby hand, which indicates lack of energy or laziness, the firm hand is a sign of activity, vigor, and energy. People with firm hands are usually reliable and have positive personalities. They show their loyalty to their friends through deeds and action, not just words.

The hard hand is firm and has a strong resistance to pressure. It is an obstinate, unreceptive hand, indicative of a person filled with an immense store of energy that must be expended in physical labor. The hard hand is large and the skin has a coarse texture, signifying that its owner is unrefined and uncultured.

People with hard hands have a tendency to shut themselves off from others and harden themselves to the outside world. The hard hand, unlike the flabby hand, has an extreme form of rigidity.

## MOBILITY OF THE HAND AND ITS IMPORTANCE

The mobility of the hand reflects the mobility of the mind and emotions. Flexible hands show a flexible mind, and stiff hands a stiff mind. Some hands are so flexible that the fingers can be bent back almost to a forty-five-degree angle, while other hands are so rigid and cramped that the fingers cannot be straightened at all.

A rigid or stiff hand is indicative of a contracted or nonadaptable personality. Such an individual is reserved, egotistical, stubborn, and often stingy. A flexible hand denotes adaptability, versatility, and generosity. However, if flexibility is extreme, there is a danger that the individual may have a tendency to diversify his or her energy or talents, thus becoming a jack-of-all-trades. Another danger to persons with extremely flexible hands is that they are likely to be easily influenced by others and become slaves or easy victims of undesirable people.

Dr. Scheimann observed that there is a definite relation between the mobility of the hand and the space between the upper and lower transverse (or flexion) lines (the heart and head lines). The space is

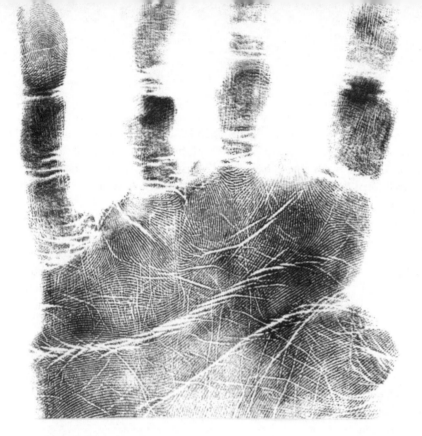

FIGURE 17.1. A hand with a girdle of Venus.

very narrow in the hand of a person with an extremely contracted personality, whereas in the hand of a person with a flexible personality, the space is wide.

In cases of extremely flexible personalities, we often find an additional flexion line (also known as the girdle of Venus) at the base of the fingers (Figure 17.1), which is a sign that its owner is very sensitive to nervous and emotional stimuli. Although this is certainly not the case with every person whose hands possess this marking, Dr. Scheimann believed that it often appears in the hands of psychiatric patients, notably in schizophrenics.

The skin ridge patterns of the palm rarely change, but there are times when mobility changes in the dominant hand. If, for example, the left hand of a right-handed person is flexible and the right hand is rigid, that individual's personality has become more rigid over time: he or she has become more cautious and stingy and less versatile or adaptable. However, if the left hand is stiff and the right is flexible, that individual's personality has become more released and flexible over the years. When both hands have equal mobility of the hand and equal spacing between the crease lines, we can assume that the personality has remained the same as well.

## HANDWRITING: CONTRACTION AND RELEASE CONNOTATIONS

Changes in mobility are more revealing if we study a person's handwriting as well, because it is a good indication of the flexibility of the fingers.

The keynote of modern handwriting analysis is the so-called contraction and release hypothesis. According to the experts, if a person's handwriting is considerably contracted, his or her personality also is contracted. In contrast, if a person's handwriting is very loose or released, his or her personality is open and flexible. When contraction is predominant, the handwriting tends to be cramped and restricted. When release is predominant, the writing is expanded and loosely executed.

Over many years of evaluating patients, Dr. Scheimann noticed a correlation between a contracted or released personality, the consistency and mobility of the hand, and handwriting. For example, a strong ego, vanity, and dominance are revealed by high and ornamental capitals or heavy writing. His findings are summarized in the following table.[2]

| Type | Handwriting | Structure Of Hand |
|---|---|---|
| *Contracted* | Slowness | Immobile joints |
| | Contraction of letters | Stiff fingers |
| | Narrow, cramped writing | Narrow space between flexion lines |
| | Excessive pressure | Well-developed muscular pattern |
| | Carefully drawn letters | Heavy, thick, short fingers |
| | Deliberate regularity | Uniformity of crease line |
| *Released* | Speed | Mobile joints |
| | Amplification of letter contours | Flexible fingers |
| | Wide, loose writing | Wide space between flexion lines |
| | Little pressure | Lack of muscular development |
| | Simplified letters | Long, thin fingers |
| | Irregularity | Irregular crease line patterns |

Dr. Scheimann believed that graphology can also prove valuable when there is a discrepancy between the mobility of the finger and thumb—in other words, in instances where the fingers are flexible and the thumb is rigid or the fingers are stiff and the thumb is flexible or double-jointed. He believed that such a contrast denotes a person's attitude toward his or her material possessions. For example, if a person has flexible fingers but a rigid thumb, he or she tends to freely give away money or possessions but may have difficulty becoming emotionally involved with others. If a person has a flexible thumb and stiff fingers, he or she may tend to be emotionally generous but will not be generous with material things. Such an individual will do everything for a friend as long as it does not involve financial or material sacrifice.

Many palmists believe that handwriting analysis can be a useful adjunct to palmistry in that it helps determine the true character of the individual. For this reason, many recommend the study of graphology for the serious palmist.

# THE NAILS IN MEDICAL DIAGNOSIS

PHYSICIANS HAVE BEEN USING THE HUMAN fingernail as a diagnostic tool for hundreds of years. Fingernails are easily damaged by a reduction in blood supply and can be discolored or deformed by poor circulation, disease, or trauma. A wide variety of systemic diseases, including congenital circulatory disorders, syphilis, endocrine disturbances, and anemia, leave imprints in the fingernails. That's why studying the nails should be an important part of any health-related hand analysis. A drawing of a "normal" nail appears in Figure 18.1.

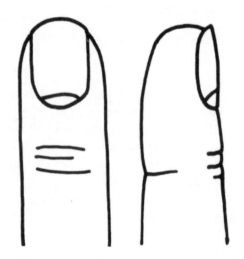

FIGURE 18.1. A normal nail.

The nail beds are located at the point where the nail begins to come out of the finger. They are usually the simplest and easiest place to evaluate blood circulation and overall physical health. A nail bed that is a healthy pink, for example, reveals good blood circulation, while a bluish nail bed could be a sign of cyanosis or poor circulation.

Liver trouble could be indicated by a yellowish tinge to the nail bed, while a nail bed that is pale pink in color is often a sign of anemia. In addition, the nail beds are usually the first places where one can observe an early sign of jaundice or gallbladder disease.

A doctor using a special type of microscope known as a capillaroscope can detect very early signs of diabetes, arteriosclerosis, and even mental illness by studying the nail beds. Emotional disorders may change the nails by creating pitting, thinning, and splitting.

In certain diseases that involve poor blood circulation, the cuticles widen and the nail bed becomes thin. In some cases of hardening of the arteries, the blood supply to the nails is diminished and the nails become twisted and distorted.

Dr. Alfred Hauptmann, a noted psychiatrist, found that 88 percent of 304 of what he diagnosed as "constitutionally neurotic" persons showed abnormal capillaries (tiny blood vessels) in the fingernail, whereas only 4 percent of the patients with acquired neurosis showed abnormal capillaries. He also observed that most of the schizophrenic patients he examined had immature capillary formations resembling the capillaries of children and infants. In addition, he found that most of the patients with manic-depressive psychosis had twisted capillaries.[1]

At least twenty-four nail configurations have been associated with more than fifty different diseases by medical science. Ongoing studies of the nail as a diagnostic tool are being undertaken in universities and medical centers in both Europe and America.[2]

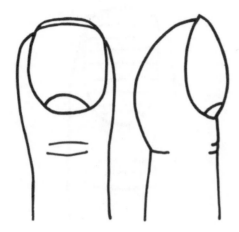

FIGURE 18.2. A Hippocratic nail.

FIGURE 18.3. A clubbed finger.

## HIPPOCRATIC NAILS

One of the classic symptoms of an abnormal health condition, known to every medical student, is the presence of Hippocratic nails, also known as watch-glass nails. In this condition, the nails, as the nickname indicates, are lustrous and curved outward in the shape of a watch crystal, as seen in Figure 18.2. Watch-glass nails are frequently found in patients suffering from tuberculosis, lung tumors, asthma, chronic heart disease, and cirrhosis of the liver. They are also found in people who are prone to heart and lung disease and are common in those whose hearts may overreact to certain stimuli, such as caffeine. I remember taking a Chinese guest who has watch-glass nails with me to a local café for her first cup of coffee. After a few sips, she began having heart palpitations. Apparently she didn't realize that, like green tea (which she never drinks because it causes heart palpitations), coffee contains caffeine!

I've also found that many heavy smokers possess Hippocratic nails. Sadly, I have also seen numerous second-hand smokers with these nails as well. Many of them are adults whose parents smoked in their presence when they were children.

Watch-glass nails sometimes accompany so-called clubbed fingers, as seen in Figure 18.3. Clubbed fingers have thickened tissue at the fingertip, causing them to appear rounded, like a club. When circulation in the heart or lining of the heart is poor, the ends of the fingers often become swollen and bluish. Clubbing of previously normal fingers is a clue to the presence of this disorder. However, some healthy teenagers may show this phenomenon as a normal, inherited family trait.

It is important to remember that the nail can also reflect positive changes in health. For example, bluish nails and clubbed fingers can become normal if a person gives up smoking or recovers either from a disease like tuberculosis or from surgery to correct a congenital heart disorder. However, the shape of a Hippocratic nail is not likely to change and should be considered a predisposition to heart or lung trouble.

## SPOON NAILS

Unlike watch-glass nails, spoon nails (as seen in Figure 18.4) are flat or concave on the outer surface. This disorder, also known as koilonychia, is the result of the thinning and softening of the nails due to illness or diet.

Spoon nails are found primarily among individuals with nutritional deficiencies (especially iron-deficiency anemia), syphilis, skin disorders, and

FIGURE 18.4. A spoon nail.

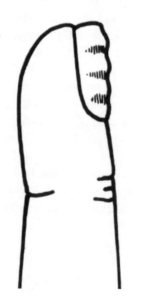

FIGURE 18.5. Beau's lines.

hypothyroidism, or an underactive thyroid gland. Koilonychia can occasionally be found in the fingernails of individuals suffering from mental illness or mental retardation.

FIGURE 18.6. Mees' lines.

## BEAU'S LINES AND MEES' LINES

This nail abnormality known as Beau's lines is named after the French physician Joseph Honoré Simon Beau, who discovered it in the middle of the nineteenth century. It consists of horizontal or transverse ridges (Figure 18.5) that start at the root of the nail and move toward the top as the nail grows.

Beau's lines are primarily associated with acute infection, systemic diseases, or other severe disabilities that can temporarily interfere with the normal growth of the nail. Diseases such as scarlet fever, influenza, measles, mumps, coronary thrombosis, pneumonia, and typhus have been linked to the appearance of Beau's lines. Physical traumas caused by accidents, as well as nutritional deficiencies and nervous shock, can also be recorded in the nails as Beau's lines. Since it takes about 160 days for a nail to grow, it is often possible to determine the date of the onset of the illness or accident that produced these lines.

Similar to Beau's lines are Mees' lines, named after the Dutch physician R. A. Mees (Figure 18.6). They are transverse white lines but do not cause any

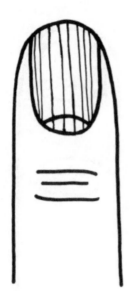

FIGURE 18.7. Longitudinal ridges.

ridge or dent in the nails. They occur in cases of high fever, arsenic or thallium poisoning, kidney failure, and coronary heart disease.

## LONGITUDINAL RIDGES

Unlike Beau's lines, longitudinal ridges (Figure 18.7) exist in the nail for a long time because they are associated with chronic diseases such as colitis, dermatitis, and hyperthyroidism (an overactive thyroid gland). They are also an important symptom of rheumatic disorders, especially if there is evidence of this condition in the family. Therefore, if you notice these ridges in a child, it would be well to advise the parents to be alert for signs of rheumatic fever or rheumatoid arthritis and to consult a physician for a detailed analysis.

## NAIL SYMPTOMS IN ENDOCRINE DISTURBANCES

The development of all the structures in the hand is determined by the endocrine glands. Therefore,

changes in the nail could very well indicate the onset of glandular disturbances. In her book *The Human Hand*, Dr. Charlotte Wolff stated that she had several times diagnosed pituitary and thyroid malfunctions from the nails when no clinical symptoms were present. She discovered that thin, brittle, ridged, short, and moonless nails are indicative of an underdeveloped thyroid gland, as well as a sign of underactive gonads (sex glands) and an underactive pituitary gland. If this type of nail is found in a broad, spongy hand with sausage-shaped fingers and a tapered little finger, it is an indication of hypothyroidism. If the hand is slim and flexible and the little fingers are deformed and shorter than normal, these nails signify underactive gonads. In a hand with broad, square, very flexible, and short fingers, this type of abnormal nail indicates hypopituitary function. A long, narrow, shiny nail with a large moon is a sign of hyperthyroidism.[3]

## NAIL COLOR AND DISEASE

Ideally, nails should be a healthy pink, with a smooth, lustrous surface. This indicates good blood circulation, adequate nutritional intake, and an overall level of good health. Red nails indicate strong blood circulation and a tendency for flashes of anger, overexcitement, and hypertension (high blood pressure). Blue or bluish nails indicate circulatory problems. If all the nails on the fingers are blue, poor circulation affects the entire body, while only a few blue or bluish nails indicate a localized problem in the hand or fingers.

Pale nails, like pale skin, reveal low vitality and poor nutrition. They may also indicate anemia. Although yellowish nails may reveal liver trouble, such as hepatitis or cirrhosis, a yellow tinge to the nails (especially the nail beds) may also be a sign of an excess of beta carotene in the diet. Health-minded individuals who consume large quantities of carrot juice often have yellowish nail beds. When you observe a person with yellowish nails, be sure to ask if he or she drinks lots of carrot juice before you diagnose liver disease. According to Robert Baran, MD, of the

FIGURE 18.8. A fan-shaped nail.

FIGURE 18.10. A short nail.

## NAIL SYMPTOMS IN NERVOUS AND MENTAL DISORDERS

The presence of nervous disorders and mental illness can also be detected by examining a person's nails. The most common indicators of these problems are the white spots that, according to many physicians and palmists, occur in tired, tense, nervous patients and disappear when anxiety and stress are eliminated. If you find these spots, you may assume that your client is suffering from anxiety or depression.

Another sign of neurosis is the softened, fan-shaped nail, shown in Figure 18.8. People with this type of nail are very sensitive and are seldom satisfied. They often complain, tend to nag, and delight in finding fault with others.

The nail that is long and narrow (Figure 18.9) occurs primarily in women and is an indication of nervousness. The possessors of such nails are usually frustrated artists, actors, and intellectuals who have trouble expressing themselves.

Very short, or "critical," nails (Figure 18.10) are a sign of a peculiar (and annoying) neurotic behavior characterized by an urge to contradict everyone and

FIGURE 18.9. A long, narrow nail.

Centre Hospitalier in Cannes, France, brown nails can be an indicator of nervous injury or malnutrition; nail beds that are slate gray can reveal the presence of malaria, and nail beds that are amber or brownish can indicate syphilis.[4]

to argue. They are a sure sign of someone who is self-critical and critical of others as well. People with critical nails often have a negative attitude about life in general. They often have some degree of repressed rage, especially when the hand reveals strong vitality and lack of flexibility and the head and life lines are joined at their commencement. This is why many palmists believe that people with critical nails are candidates for stress-related diseases such as heart attack and stroke.

## GUIDELINES FOR NAIL ANALYSIS

When we examine nails in the context of medical palmistry, we need to keep in mind that nail abnormalities not only are reflections of medical or psychological problems that affect the individual as a whole but also may reflect problems affecting the nail itself.

For example, an allergy to a certain detergent or constant wetting and drying of the nails may cause splitting or discoloration. Personal habits such as chronic nail biting and picking at the nail can produce ridging and other malformations. Certain fungal diseases can produce changes in the nail bed itself in the absence of systemic disease. With this in mind, be careful not to make any definitive statements in your examination without evaluating other signs in the hand. When in doubt, refer your client to a qualified health professional for further evaluation.

# DERMATOGLYPHICS: THEIR MEDICAL SIGNIFICANCE

$A$LTHOUGH THERE IS EVIDENCE THAT THE STUDY of dermatoglyphics began more than two thousand years ago, it was not until 1943 that skin ridge patterns were recognized as an indicator of medical and emotional disorders.[1] Over the past thirty years or so, dermatoglyphics has received a good deal of attention in the medical community, and dozens of ongoing investigations of the subject are being carried out by medical doctors and other scientists, primarily in the United States, Europe, India, and Japan. The International Dermatoglyphics Society published its first bulletin in 1972, and regular symposia dealing with the latest discoveries take place in different parts of the world.

These patterns, or skin carvings, as one researcher calls them, develop in the first four months of a child's life in the womb, when the fetus is most susceptible to viral infections and other harmful conditions. Unlike the lines in the hand, skin ridge patterns remain largely unchanged throughout a person's life. However, they increase in size and can be altered as a result of injury or disease. Students of dermatoglyphics believe that if negative or unhealthy environmental factors interfere with the growth of a fetus, they not only cause congenital diseases (such as heart defects, mental and neurological disorders, and schizophrenia) but also create abnormal palm print patterns.

In the last several decades, more than four hundred scientific papers have been published on this subject. Dr. James R. Miller of the Health Centre for Children at Vancouver General Hospital in Vancouver, British Columbia, who evaluated one thousand schoolchildren, urged that the study of dermatoglyphics be a part of a child's routine examination. He found that it provides information that might be critical in making or confirming a diagnosis of abnormal mental or physical development. Many other researchers agree with him.[2]

Remember that a study of skin ridge patterns shouldn't be a substitute for a thorough physical examination or chromosomal analysis. However, a study of the skin ridge patterns of the palm and fingers can enable a doctor to become more aware of potential health problems before they actually manifest themselves as a physical or mental disease, especially if these problems are genetic in origin. By the same token, even a careful dermatoglyphic analysis by a layperson can help make a physician aware of a possible problem.

In fact, one of the greatest advantages of palm print studies in evaluating genetic disorders is that they are easily available and cost almost nothing to obtain. Skin ridge patterns can be observed by a layperson with a simple magnifying glass in good, direct lighting. However, to obtain a permanent record, or for research purposes, I advise the taking of palm prints (see page 271). By contrast, the chromosomal test known as a karyotype, taken by swabbing a smear from the mouth, is expensive, and relatively few laboratories can administer it. According to Dr. James B. Thompson of the University of Toronto, dermatoglyphic studies may establish a diagnosis in doubtful cases without karyotyping.[3] In fact, an editorial in the *New England Journal of Medicine* called dermatoglyphics "the poor man's karyotype."[4]

## MEDICAL DERMATOGLYPHICS: THE BASICS

For the beginner, I suggest learning about three basic factors in the study of fingerprints and palm prints:

FIGURE 19.1. A loop fingerprint.

FIGURE 19.3. A whorl fingerprint.

FIGURE 19.2. An arch fingerprint.

(1) the formation, number, and location of ridge patterns, (2) the location of the axial triradius and the degree of its angle, and (3) the loop ridge count on the fingers.

Remember that there are five main skin ridge patterns: loops, arches, whorls, composites, and tented arches.

- The loop is the most common. It has a center or a core, and a triangle called a triradius, as seen in Figure 19.1.

- The arch is, as the name implies, a plain arch. Unlike the loop, it has no triradius (Figure 19.2).

- The whorl is a design in which the majority of ridges make a circle around a central core or hub. It has two triradii, as seen in Figure 19.3.

- Composites combine two or more patterns and usually look like twin loops. They form an S pattern (Figure 19.4).

- The tented arch is characterized by a vertical line running through the middle of the arch, resembling a tent pole. Unlike the simple arch, this pattern often features a triradius, as seen in Figure 19.5.

All five patterns can also occur in the palm on the base of the middle and ring fingers, and on the mounts of Luna and Venus, scientifically known

FIGURE 19.4. A composite fingerprint.

FIGURE 19.5. A tented arch fingerprint.

as the hypothenar eminence and thenar eminence, respectively.

In medical palmistry, the triradii in the palm are more significant than those in the fingers. There are two types: the digital triradii are known in medical circles as A, B, C, and D and are located on the bases of the second, third, fourth, and fifth fingers. The axial triradius, known as T, is located at the base of the palm, between the mounts of Luna and Venus, but can be displaced elsewhere, which indicates an abnormality. Lines drawn from the A and D triradii to the axial triradius form what is known as the ATD angle. Two variations of the ATD angle are shown in Figures 19.6 and 19.7. The normal ATD angle is around forty-five degrees.

The loop ridge count on the fingers is measured from the triradial point to the core (Figures 19.8 and 19.9), and the A-B ridge count on the palm, as shown in Figure 19.10, is measured from the triradius located under the index finger to the triradius found under the middle finger, as shown. To count accurately, you must have a magnifying glass and a long needle. Most important, though, you must count along a straight line. In a normal hand, the average loop ridge count on the fingers is between twelve and fourteen, and the A-B ridge count on the palm is thirty-four.

In order to avoid confusion when you study the skin ridge patterns in the hand, try to remember the following major points:

- In an average hand, there are usually no patterns on the palm itself, except on the base of the fingers and occasionally between them. If you find patterns on the mounts of Venus or Luna, for example, consider them an additional sign of genetic abnormality.

- Monkeys have patterns of the same type on all ten fingers. This is a simian or animalistic trait, and hands such as these are called monomorphic hands. From my own observations, I would estimate that fewer than 5 percent of human beings have monomorphic hands. In her book *The Human Hand*, Dr. Charlotte Wolff concluded that

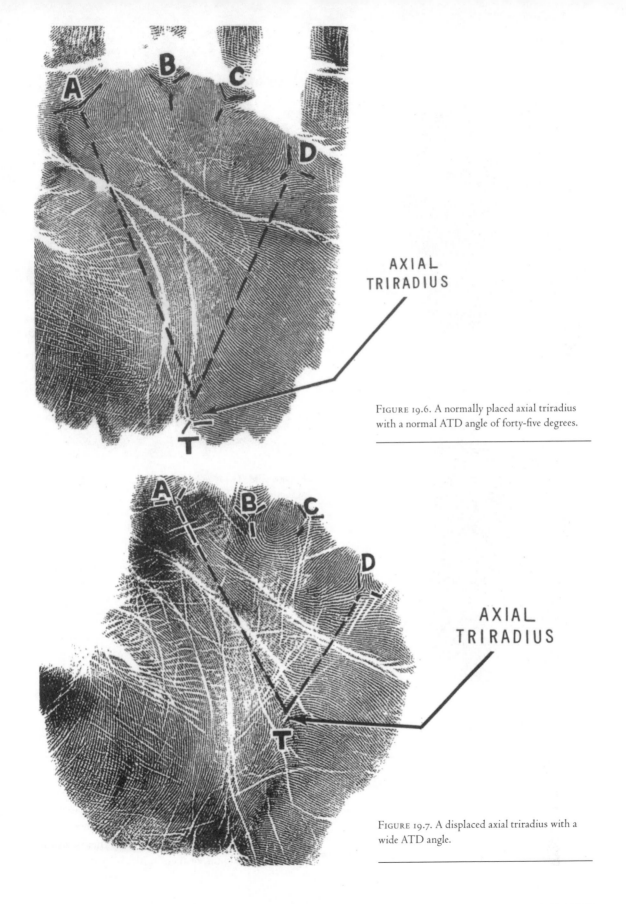

FIGURE 19.6. A normally placed axial triradius with a normal ATD angle of forty-five degrees.

FIGURE 19.7. A displaced axial triradius with a wide ATD angle.

FIGURE 19.8. A hand with a normal loop ridge count of twelve.

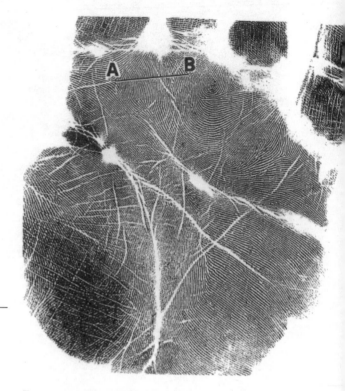

FIGURE 19.10. The A and B triradii. The normal ridge count, as shown, is thirty-four.

FIGURE 19.9. A hand with a low loop ridge count of eight.

people with monomorphic hands have an abnormality of some kind in their genetic makeup.[5]

• Abnormal ATD angle. A normal ATD angle is approximately 45 degrees, and an "abnormal" angle would be at least ten degrees more or less than 45.

• Abnormal loop-ridge count or abnormal A-B ridge count or both. According to Dr. Scheimann, in a normal hand, the average loop ridge count is 12 to 14, and the AB ridge count is 34.

If you find three of the four factors abnormal, you may conclude that your client may have certain congenital defects that can manifest themselves in physical, emotional, or mental illness.

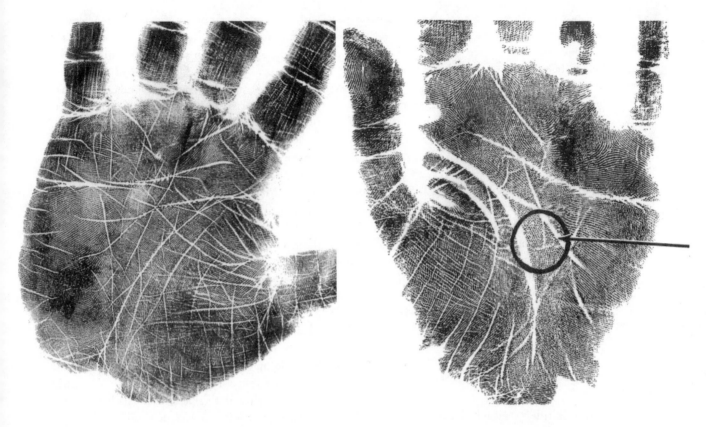

FIGURE 19.11. A hand with a normal skin ridge pattern.

FIGURE 19.12. A hand with a string-of-pearls skin ridge pattern.

## THE STRING OF PEARLS

According to the late British palmist David Brandon-Jones, conditions such as depression, cystitis, colitis, certain heart conditions, fibromyalgia, and many more common afflictions can produce alterations in the skin ridge patterns of the hand.[6] In addition, glandular imbalances can produce disintegration of the dermatoglyphics of the palm and fingers.

The most common disintegration of the ridge pattern is known in palmistry as the string of pearls. Figure 19.11 shows a hand with a normal skin ridge pattern, which can be compared with the hand in Figure 19.12, showing a string of pearls. For the medical palmist, a string of pearls is one of several signs of present or potential ill health. When health is restored, the ridge patterns (as well as some of the lines of the hand) can repair themselves.

## SPECIFIC DISEASES REVEALED

When you study a person's hand, keep in mind that while dermatoglyphics are inherited, the lines of the hand appear to be due to both genetic and environmental factors. Therefore, your study of an individual's hands should, ideally, also include a study of the handprints of his or her parents. If your client's hands resemble those of his or her parents, the patterns were inherited and therefore should be interpreted differently from the way you would interpret them if they were formed by environmental factors.

As a rule, doctors don't examine a patient's parents or the patient's hands. For this reason, the palmist has at least one advantage over the doctor: a palmist can examine the hands of both generations and possibly discover factors that the doctor has overlooked.

In recent years, dozens of medical studies have linked abnormal skin ridge patterns to a wide variety of physical and mental illnesses. These include cerebral palsy, diabetes mellitus, spontaneous abortion, leukemia, epilepsy, psoriasis, schizophrenia, celiac disease,[7] Down syndrome, and other chromosomal disorders like Patau syndrome (also known as trisomy 13), Edwards syndrome (also known as trisomy 18), and cri-du-chat syndrome (also known as 5p- syndrome). Although medical researchers have established many associations between certain skin ridge patterns and these diseases, more conclusive research is ongoing. According to a review of PubMed, an online database of the U.S. Library of Medicine and the National Institutes of Health, several dozen studies on medical dermatoglyphics were published in scientific journals between 2007 and 2009 alone.

### Congenital Heart Disease

Under the title "Congenital heart disease and sudden death in the young," an article appearing in the journal *Human Pathology* evaluated the possibility that unsuspected congenital abnormalities of the heart may occasionally be found in young people who die suddenly during physical exertion.

The goal of the investigation, undertaken by researchers from the Department of Pathology at the University of Padua Medical School in Italy, was to establish whether—and to what extent—sudden deaths among people 35 years of age and under may be ascribable to underlying congenital heart disease. The researchers conducted postmortem examinations of 182 young people who died of sudden cardiac death. They found that a total of 58 (32 percent) had congenital heart disease.[8]

A doctor in the department of pathology at the Sree Chitra Tirunal Institute in India later confirmed these findings in a study of 927 patients. In an article appearing in the *Indian Journal of Medical Research*, he reported that a distally displaced axial triradius occurred more frequently among males with congenital heart defects (it appeared in between 32 and 56 percent of those cases) than among the control population (in which its occurrence was 28 percent). In addition, the so-called Sydney line (see page TK) was observed in a significantly higher number of patients with congenital heart defects than among those without such defects.[9]

Researchers at the department of genetics at the University of Hawaii also carried out a study of dermatoglyphics and myocardial infarction (heart attack). Preliminary findings showed that Japanese males suffering heart attacks had a higher frequency of whorl patterns and a higher skin ridge count than the general population.[10]

### Rubella Syndrome

Much has been written about the fact that if a pregnant woman contracts German measles (rubella), her child may be affected with a congenital disease called rubella syndrome. After the birth, you might be able to help a mother determine whether this syndrome is present if you study her child's palm.

According to Dr. Milton Alter of the University of Minnesota, children who suffer from this syndrome differ from normal children in that they have a larger number of whorls on their fingers, a reduced A-B ridge count, a wider ATD angle, and more patterns on their palms.[11]

### Autism

To examine the role of the genetic component in the transmission of autism, a group of researchers at the Institute for Anthropological Research in Zagreb, Croatia, took finger and palm prints of 120 autistic patients (92 males and 28 females), their parents (92 mothers and 70 fathers), 32 healthy brothers and 28 healthy sisters, and 400 healthy controls (200 males and 200 females). An analysis of quantitative traits of skin ridge patterns on the fingers and palms (A-B, B-C, and C-D ridge count, as well as ATD angle) was performed.

The researchers found significant differences between the examined groups of autistic patients and their family members and the healthy volunteers. Autistic male patients differed significantly from the healthy controls in the ridge count on the fourth and fifth fingers and in the A-B ridge count and the ATD angle of both hands. Healthy fathers of autistic patients differed from the healthy control group in ATD angle. In addition, brothers of autistic patients differed in all palmar variables from the healthy control group. Mothers of autistic patients differed significantly from the healthy female controls in the ridge count of the first, fourth, and fifth fingers, in A-B and C-D ridge count on the palms, and in the ATD angle of both hands. The researchers concluded,

*We found significant differences in ridge counts on the fingers and palms between the affected patients and their healthy controls, but these differences also existed between family members of autistic patients and healthy controls. Particularly pronounced were the differences between healthy female controls and female family members, including not only autistic female patients, but also their healthy mothers and sisters. Since the mothers and their autistic sons showed higher statistically significant correlation in most of the examined variables, unlike the mothers and their autistic or healthy daughters, it is possible that there is a connection between a recessive X-chromosome linkage, as a genetic component in the etiology of autistic disorders, and the influence of the inactivation of the affected X-chromosome in the females.*[12]

Another study of autistic children was carried out by scientists at the Universidad del País Vasco in Bilbao, Spain, and reported in the *American Journal of Medical Genetics*. After comparing the fingerprints of autistic children with the fingerprints of members of the control group, the researchers concluded,

*We found significant differences between the digital dermatoglyphics of autistic boys and control boys. Autistic children have a higher frequency of transitional radial loops and a lower frequency of dicentric whorls; also the total finger ridge count (TFRC) and radial count are*

*lower in autistic individuals. There were no significant differences in the girls. In palmar dermatoglyphics, autistic girls have a lower frequency of radial loops in the hypothenar area, and the value of the "ATD" angle is higher than in control girls. These differences were significant. The a-b interdigital ridge count is significantly lower in autistic boys. Autistic children of both sexes have a higher frequency of aberrant palmar creases. The results obtained in the present study do not contradict the hypothesis that genetic factors may be important in autism of unknown cause.*[13]

## Irritable Bowel Syndrome and Constipation

Very often, physicians point to stress and anxiety as possible causes of chronic constipation and abdominal pain. However, the late Dr. Marvin Schuster of the Johns Hopkins University School of Medicine and Dr. Sheldon H. Gottlieb, then of the Francis Scott Key Medical Center in Baltimore, believed that these conditions may have a genetic cause.

They based their theory, which was published in an article in *Gastroenterology*, on the fact that the rare arch type of fingerprint pattern turns up with surprising frequency on patients suffering from abdominal pain and chronic constipation. The doctors found that 64 percent of patients who experienced constipation and abdominal pain before reaching ten years of age had one or more arch fingerprints, while only 10 percent of patients without constipation or abdominal pain featured digital arches. They also found that people with arches had a higher prevalence of chronic intestinal pseudo-obstruction, which is classified as an organic disorder, and a lower incidence of irritable bowel syndrome, considered to be a functional problem due to diet or stress. The authors concluded, "Identification of a congenital marker, digital arches, associated with early onset constipation and abdominal pain may help to differentiate a congenital organic syndrome from functional disorders such as the irritable bowel syndrome."[14]

## Breast Cancer

A recent study at Vardhman Mahavir Medical College in New Delhi was conducted on sixty confirmed breast cancer patients. Their fingerprint patterns were studied to assess whether an association could be established with certain features of the cancer. The researchers also studied a control group of sixty women in the same age-group who had no history of diagnosed breast cancer.

It was observed that the presence of six or more whorls in the fingerprint pattern occurred in a statistically significant number of cancer patients as compared to the controls. It was also observed that whorls in the right ring finger and right little finger were found more frequently among the cancer patients than among the controls. The researchers concluded, "The dermatoglyphic patterns may be utilized effectively to study the genetic basis of breast cancer and may also serve as a screening tool in the high-risk population. In a developing country like India it might prove to be an anatomical, non-invasive, inexpensive and effective tool for screening and studying the patterns in the high-risk population."[15]

Dr. Murray H. Seltzer and his colleagues at the New Jersey College of Medicine in Newark studied the fingerprints and palm prints of 78 breast cancer patients, 391 patients that were considered at risk for developing breast cancer, and 64 control patients for the purpose of finding a pattern that would identify those women with breast cancer or those who are predisposed to its development.

They found that a pattern of six or more digital whorls was identified more frequently in women with breast cancer than in those without the disease. This was a finding independent of known risk factors for breast cancer and was present in 28 percent of the cancer patients. They saw no correlation between palm prints and breast cancer. As a diagnostic tool, the researchers believe that the positive predictive value of six or more digital whorls was comparable to that of mammography and that of breast biopsy, and with increasing age, there was an increase in the positive predictive value associated with six or more digital

whorls. The researchers concluded, "Digital dermatoglyphics may have a future role in identifying women either with or at increased risk for breast cancer such that either risk reduction measures or earlier therapy may be instituted."[16]

## Thyroid Cancer

A major European study involving 293 persons made the connection between a predisposition to thyroid cancer and abnormal skin ridge patterns. In an article published in *Endocrinologie*, the authors revealed that thyroid cancer subjects had a lower total digital ridge count and a reduced number of papillar ridges between the A and -D triradii than the general population.[17]

## Alzheimer's Disease

Over the past few years, Alzheimer's disease has received much attention in medical circles and in the popular media. Known scientifically as senile dementia of the Alzheimer type (SDAT), this disease primarily affects elderly women. Although the origins of the disease are unknown, researchers believe that immunological factors may have a role in the development of SDAT.

An important study conducted by Herman J. Weinreb, MD, of the New York University Medical Center led him to postulate that, like patients with Down syndrome, sufferers of Alzheimer's disease showed "a marked increase of ulnar loops on the fingertips, with a concomitant decrease in whorls, radial loops and arches."

Among the general population, radial loops predominate and are found most often on the index finger and thumb. In radial loops, the "lariat" of the loop is thrown, as it were, from the side of the hand where the thumb is located. But in the ulnar loop, the "throw" is from the percussion side of the hand, nearest the little finger.

In Dr. Weinreb's study, 36 percent of the patients suffering from SDAT had eight or more ulnar loops on their hands, as opposed to 13 percent of the control group. Only 14 percent of Alzheimer's patients had fewer than seven ulnar loops, in contrast to 37 percent of the general population.[18]

In contrast, a study by Doctors Benjamin Seltzer and Ira Sherwin involving sixty-four men with early onset of primary degenerative dementia (occurring before they reached sixty-five years of age) and thirty-five men with a late onset of the disease (i.e., occurring at age sixty-five or older) found the opposite pattern than the one found in those afflicted with Alzheimer's, a group primarily composed of elderly women. In comparing these men with the general population (represented in this study by one hundred male control subjects), the researchers found that "patients with an early, but not those with a late, onset of dementia had significantly more ulnar loops than the control group."[19]

It has been suggested by some researchers that Down syndrome is related to deficiencies in immune response.[20] Because of the high presence of ulnar loops among SDAT patients and those suffering from Down syndrome, some researchers conclude that the presence of ulnar loops may signify an enhanced susceptibility to immune dysfunction, with consequent impairment of the nervous system.

### Deviations in Sex Chromosomes

The study of dermatoglyphics may also help us discover the existence of chromosomal abnormalities that delay or prevent the development of certain secondary sexual characteristics. The most important disorders of this nature are Turner syndrome and Klinefelter syndrome.

In Turner syndrome, a female person looks like a male, and in Klinefelter syndrome, a male person looks like a female. Usually, these conditions cannot be recognized until after puberty, when a person's secondary sexual characteristics fail to develop. Very often these patients seek professional advice only after it is too late for a doctor to help them.

Examination of the fingerprints and the palm prints of a child could give a palmist a clue to such a disorder before puberty, however. If you recognize the signs—such as a teenage girl whose breasts are not developed or who has not yet menstruated, or a boy whose sex organ is too small and whose breasts are too big—you could be extremely helpful by recommending that a sex-chromosome analysis be performed. If a diagnosis is made early enough, these individuals could be given satisfactory hormone therapy by a physician.

Many fingerprint patterns are typical of persons with Turner and Klinefelter syndromes. Dr. Anne Forbes, a professor at Harvard Medical School, observed that in persons with Turner and Klinefelter syndromes, loops constitute 81 and 54 percent of the patterns on the right thumb and middle fingers, respectively, as compared with 56 and 32 percent in the general population. These patterns are less frequent on fifth fingers, where whorls were observed on 25 and 33 percent of the right and left hands, respectively, as compared to 11.4 and 6.9 percent in the general population. She also found 15 percent of certain composites resembling the letter S on the mount of Luna, in comparison with 3 percent in normal subjects.[21]

In Klinefelter syndrome, there are two significant dermatoglyphic traits: an increase of arches in all fingers and a low ridge count. Dr. Forbes stated that the most striking difference between the hands of a patient with Klinefelter syndrome and a normal person is the ridge count on the right index finger. In her study, the average count on people with Klinefelter syndrome was 8.5, in contrast to the normal average of 14.5 for males.

In some sex-chromosome aberrations, especially in females, there are additional important features to look for, such as puffiness of the hand, underdeveloped nails, and a short, inward-curving little finger, which is usually widely separated from the ring finger.

# PALM LINES AND MARKINGS

Aʟᴛʜᴏᴜɢʜ ᴅᴇʀᴍᴀᴛᴏɢʟʏᴘʜɪᴄs ᴀʀᴇ certainly significant in the diagnosis of certain diseases and conditions, the most important part of medical palmistry involves the lines and other markings of the palm—also known as *chiroglyphics*.

Chiroglyphics can be classified into three groups:

1. Flexion creases (the major lines)

2. Accessory lines

3. Symbols (sometimes called accidental signs)

The flexion creases, which are located at the joints, are directly related to the movement of the hands. The accessory lines are only indirectly associated with flexion of the hands, and the symbols are like fingerprints—they are the identifying signs of an individual. In the words of Aristotle, "The lines are not written into the human hands without reason; they come from heavenly influences and man's own individuality."

Fɪɢᴜʀᴇ 20.1. A hand with a simian line.

## FLEXION CREASES

There are four major flexion creases that can provide information about a person's health:

1. The thenar crease (known in palmistry as the life line)

2. The lower, or proximal, transverse crease (known as the head line)

3. The upper, or distal, transverse crease (called the heart line)

4. A diagonal crease known in palmistry as the line of Mercury, line of health, or stomach line

These major lines are illustrated in Figure 7.1. A guide showing how to determine chronology on the lines of the hand can be found in Figure 7.13.

Flexion creases are formed at the same time as the skin ridge patterns—during the third and fourth months of a child's life as a fetus. As Dr. J. S. Thompson pointed out in his book *Genetics in Medicine*, chiroglyphics are formed in part by the same forces that determine ridge alignment. For this reason, it is logical to assume that the forces causing congenital aberration and abnormal ridge patterns could also produce abnormal crease lines—such as the simian line, which is formed when the heart and head lines appear to join together as one (Figure 20.1).[1]

The simian line is a very common feature in the hands of persons with congenital and chromosomal disorders, although it is found on the hands of many "normal" individuals as well. In their article "The Single Transverse Palmar Crease in Infants and Children," Doctors P. A. Davies and V. Smallpiece stated,

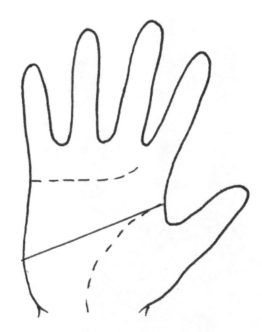

FIGURE 20.2. The Sydney line.

> *Few clinicians will have time to master the intricacies of dermal ridge patterns, but the presence of a single transverse crease . . . can be seen at a glance. The association of such a crease with mongolism has been known for some time, but it is not so widely appreciated that it may be found with other abnormalities, as well as in normal people.*[2]

The doctors also reported that abnormalities of the central nervous system are commonly associated with the simian line. They mentioned a wide range of other abnormalities, including thalidomide drug damage in infants as well as chromosomal disorders such as trisomy 13 and cri-du-chat syndrome.

Similarly, the Sydney line (which was, in fact, believed to have been discovered first in Sydney, Australia) at first glance resembles a normal head line. However, instead of stopping short of the percussion of the hand (also known as the ulnar border), it extends across the entire palm, as seen in Figure 20.2.

Researchers have found the Sydney line in surprising frequency among children with delayed emotional and mental development, learning difficulties, and minor behavioral problems. It has also been found with disproportionately high frequency among individuals suffering from Down syndrome, congenital rubella, childhood leukemia, and congenital heart defects. In one study, Sydney lines were observed in up to 24 percent of patients with congenital heart defects as opposed to 10 percent of the normal population.[3]

So chiroglyphics, as well as dermatoglyphics, can help a palmist diagnose genetic predispositions in the context of evaluating a person's overall health.

### The Life Line (Thenar Crease)

When it comes to health, the life line is by far the most important line to consider. It is associated with the movement of our most vital digit, the thumb. It begins between the thumb and the base of the index finger and encircles the mount of Venus, known in the medical community as the thenar eminence.

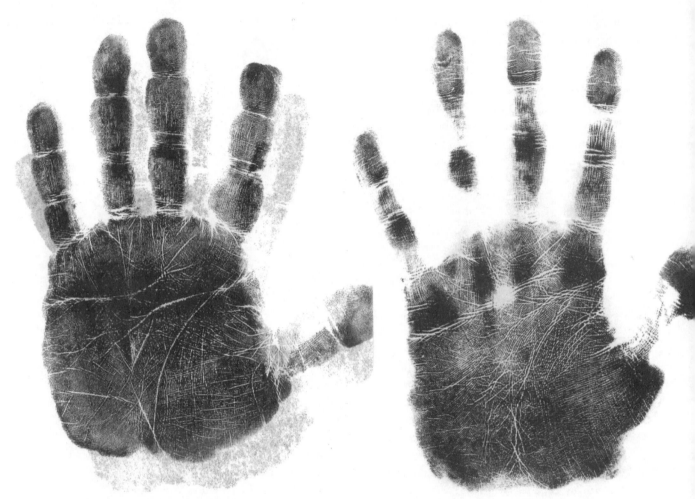

FIGURE 20.3. A hand with a strong life line.

FIGURE 20.4. A hand with a weak life line.

The life line is the mirror of our health, vitality, and constitution. That's why some palmists erroneously associate the strength and length of the life line with longevity. After reading the hands of thousands of people over the course of more than thirty years, I have met many who died young despite their long and well-developed life lines. I have also met many people who reached old age despite their short and weak life lines. Therefore, perhaps the most appropriate name for this crease should be the line of constitution.

A long, deep, well-marked line (Figure 20.3) is a sign of strong vitality and constitution, as well as the ability to bounce back from disease. A person

with this type of life line can spend the entire night eating and drinking to excess and still be able to make an appearance at work the following morning, looking and feeling good. The negative side is that many people with a strong life line tend to take their good health for granted and are thus more likely to not take good care of themselves.

By contrast, a short, thin, or faulty line (Figure 20.4) is an indication of a weak and delicate constitution with little or no vitality. Persons with the latter type of line often have less power to endure and resist diseases or injuries. A person with a weak life line must be especially careful with diet, exercise, and other personal habits. If such a person eats

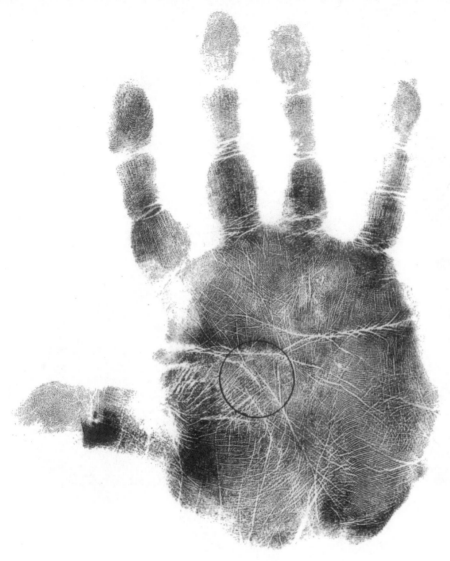

FIGURE 20.5. A hand with a broken life line.

individual's resistance and immunity to other ailments.

## The Significance of a Broken Life Line

The lines on the hands have both physical and symbolic meanings. On the physical level, a broken life line can mean a life-threatening illness or a close call with death. For example, if a broken life line is made up of two overlapping lines, its owner will likely survive. If the line is broken and does not overlap (or if a parallel accessory "sister" line is not present), he or she may not.

On the symbolic level, a broken, overlapping life line can signify a major shift in a person's life. Depending on the individual, this can include a marriage, a total change in life direction, a strong psychological change, or even a stint in prison. For example, over the years, I have read the hands of perhaps a dozen survivors of the terrorist attack on the World Trade Center on September 11, 2001. Several of them had broken life lines at the time of the attack. People who have the unusual ability to totally reinvent themselves during their lifetimes often have a broken, overlapping life line.

Figure 20.5 shows the hand of a woman who had her thyroid surgically removed in 1944, when she was in her mid-twenties. She was very ill before going to the hospital and had a fever of 108 degrees F for fourteen hours after the operation.

poorly, drinks too much, or does not get adequate sleep, the body's innate wisdom takes over and develops symptoms to show that something needs to be corrected. There is a greater chance of allergies to pollen, certain foods, and prescribed medications. In other words, such a person is more "healthy sick" than "sick sick" and develops symptoms in response the body's desire to achieve good health.

In many cases, you will observe that the beginning of the life line is chained or poorly marked. This indicates a history of childhood diseases, so it is a very common feature. If the rest of the line is deep, well formed, and unbroken, you could assume that the childhood diseases strengthened the

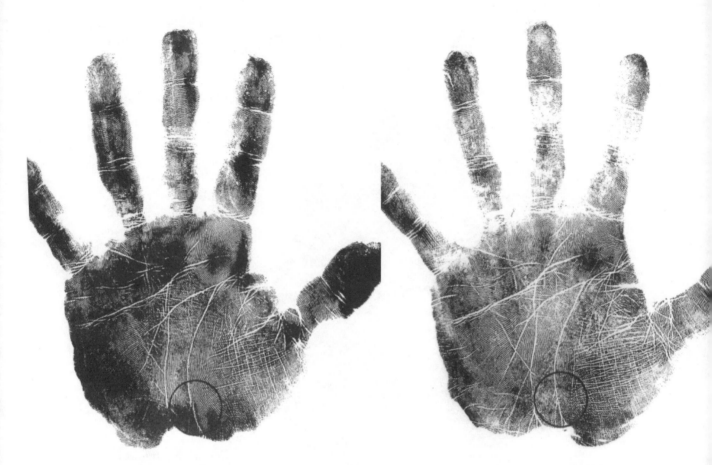

FIGURE 20.6. The hand of a thirty-four-year-old lawyer before lifestyle changes were made.

FIGURE 20.7. The lawyer's hand with a mended life line after lifestyle changes were made.

The young woman had to be placed in a bathtub filled with ice. No one expected her to survive the night (she told me that one of the nurses, coming to work to begin her day shift, exclaimed, "She's still here?"). The woman's close call with death is clearly seen by the break in her life line.

In most cases, palmists should consider a broken life line a warning signal meaning "danger ahead." People with broken life lines should be advised to be more health conscious and should try to avoid smoking, excessive stress, drug and alcohol abuse, and overeating. You might also suggest that when an individual with a broken life line develops a symptom such as pain or loss of appetite, he or she should consult a physician.

The prints reproduced in Figures 20.6 and 20.7 are those of a corporate lawyer from Colombia (note that he did not have a particularly stressful life). In Figure 20.6, the print—which was recorded when the man was thirty-four years old—shows a life line that is broken at the point where he would reach approximately fifty-six years of age, an indicator of a life-threatening disease. Concerned about this possibility, the lawyer decided to improve his diet and cut down on smoking. Within several years, the line mended completely (Figure 20.7).

In *Medical Palmistry*, Dr. Eugene Scheimann related the story of a woman who came to him after a hand reader told her that she would have an accident or a serious illness.

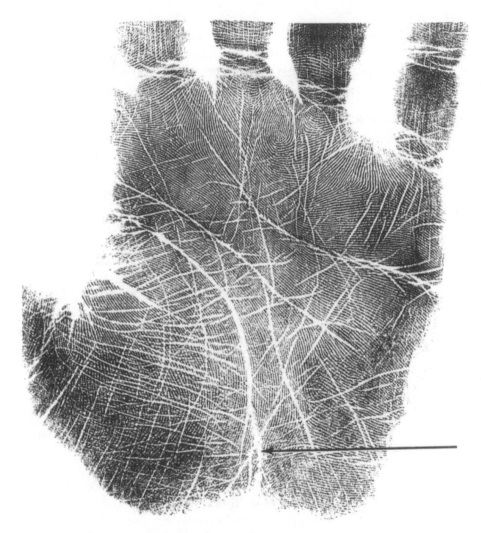

FIGURE 20.8. The palm print of a patient with terminal cancer. Note the large island at the end of the life line.

I reassured her that no one could predict the future or make any kind of prognosis by any one sign alone. I added that there was no other sign in her palm which signified an abnormal condition. Therefore, I suggested that she ignore that one particular sign. However, I advised her that during the next four years if anything unusual occurred, to consult her doctor promptly.

About eight months later the woman phoned me. She proceeded to tell me that a few weeks earlier she began to worry about her menstrual period because it had lasted longer than usual. At the time she made an appointment to see her gynecologist, and received an appointment three days hence. However, on the following day she developed sudden pain and insisted that the doctor see her at once. During the examination, he was able to diagnose an extra-uterine pregnancy and operated on her immediately. After the operation he remarked to her, "How very fortunate that you came to see me because your tubal pregnancy ruptured just one half hour before the operation."[4]

If you find a broken life line, don't come to any conclusion without considering other equally revealing signs of impending diseases. Remember that faulty crease lines—like abnormal ridge patterns—not only develop during fetal growth as a result of disease conditions but are also passed on genetically from the parents. If the latter is true, they will have no diagnostic significance.

For example, Dr. Scheimann reported that the parents of the woman in the story related above did not have a broken life line. If they had, the broken line in her hand would not have indicated impending danger in her life. But since her parents' palms differed from hers in this respect, he interpreted the broken line in her hand as a warning signal.

## Islands on the Life Line

In addition to a break on the life line, you should also look for one or more islands. In medical palmistry, an island is a sign of impending disease or a period of ill health.

In his classic book *The Story of the Human Hand*,[5] Walter Sorell concluded that an egg-shaped island on the end of the life line is a sign of oncoming cancer (Figure 20.8). I have seen the hands of dozens of people who were dealing with cancer since Sorell's book was published. Some did have an island, but many of them did not. Most probably, an island at or near the end of the life line may reveal a *predisposition* toward cancer rather than an absolute indication of the disease. Very often, a predisposition for cancer runs in the family. If you find an individual who has such an island (especially if it appears on both hands) try to find out more about his or her health situation before making any recommendations.

## Adjuncts to the Life Line

Some people have an "inner life line" that runs parallel to the line of life. This is a very good line to have, because it is believed to provide greater strength during times of illness or physical hardship. In the handprint shown in Figure 20.9, the inner life line provides added strength at the point where both lines (as well as the head line) are crossed by an influence line, which occurred when the owner of this hand was about twenty-eight years of age and experiencing a time of emotional trauma.

At times, the Saturn line, or fate line, takes over the task of a weak or disappearing life line, as shown in Figure 20.10. In this case, the Saturn line performs double duty and is both a supplementary life line and an indicator of career direction. At the time of this writing, the owner of this hand is nearing sixty years of age and enjoys excellent health.

### The Head Line (Proximal Transverse Crease)

Just as the life line reflects our general health and physical constitution, the head line denotes our mental health as well as the way we think. According to many observers, an ill-formed or broken head line is a signal of an impending nervous or mental breakdown. Although such predictions may be exaggerated, breaks on this line can reveal periods of severe mental stress and emotional difficulty. As with a break in the life line, a break in the head line can represent a powerful shift in the way we perceive ourselves and the world.

Dr. Charlotte Wolff studied the palms of 650 "mentally defective" patients and an equal number of normal subjects. She found that 70 percent of the mentally defective patients had faulty or broken head lines, compared to 30 percent of normal persons. She also observed that abnormally short head lines were a very common feature in persons with mild mental impairment.[6]

### The Heart Line (Distal Transverse Crease)

In our age of anxiety, perhaps one could state, as many palmists do, that the heart line is the most vital line of all. After all, many people become sick, commit suicide, and kill others because of disappointment in love. Millions die young because of heart failure. The heart line is the barometer of the emotions and

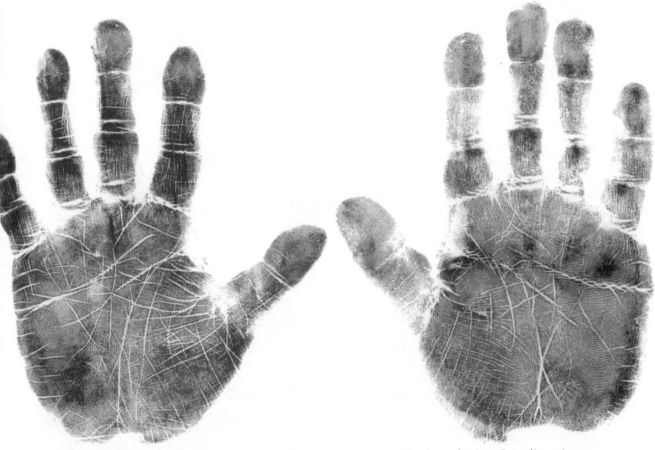

FIGURE 20.9. A hand showing an inner life line.

FIGURE 20.10. A handprint showing a Saturn line acting as a supplementary life line.

reveals how (and to what extent) we give and receive love and affection. As the name implies, the heart line is often indicative of our greatest emotional trauma—the "broken heart"—as well as one of our greatest physical traumas—heart disease.

Unlike the head and life lines, which begin near the thumb, the heart line begins at the percussion of the hand, under the Mercury, or little, finger. It can end under the middle finger or the index finger or between the two. In some individuals, this line moves completely across the palm.

Ideally, the heart line should be deep, clear, and well formed, with a minimum of islands, breaks, and chains. Very often the heart line tends to be somewhat chained near its beginning, which can indicate

emotional and possibly sexual turmoil, especially during a person's youth.

Whenever you examine a heart line and discover abnormalities, avoid diagnosing heart ailments. Only a physician with the aid of a stethoscope, X-ray, cardiogram, and physical examination can do that. Over the years, there have been a number of celebrated palmists who could recognize heart ailments from the hand, but even they experienced difficulties. In referring to these difficulties, William G. Benham wrote,

*You will constantly be called upon to judge whether some marking seen on a heart line is a health defect, an event in the life, or an indication of character, and this is a point*

*which has puzzled many
excellent practitioners.*[7]

In order to make an
accurate diagnosis, Benham
recommended that palmists
check to see whether the
nails are clubbed and the
bases of the nails are blue. If
either or both of these signs
are present, you can suspect
heart disease. He also suggested that the hand reader
check for any unevenness
in the life line—that is,
whether it splits or breaks
or is crossed by a line that
runs from the defect on the
heart line to the life line.
He concluded, "Not finding
any of these health defects,
it is evident the mark on the
heart line is one showing
some characteristic of the
affections and not disease."[8]

Similarly, Dr. Eugene
Scheimann wrote,

*In my own practice, I have observed
that the nodules on the heart line which
occur in coronary heart disease are often
associated with an island on the heart line.
Therefore, if you find any kind of defect (such
as a break, a chain, bluish dots or an island) on the
heart line below the little finger or ring finger, consider it
a possible sign of disease, especially if the individual also
exhibits certain contributory factors to coronary disease,
such as anxiety, overweight, high cholesterol, and high blood
pressure. You should also examine the dermatoglyphic patterns (especially the ATD angle and the axial triradius)
to determine if any genetic predisposition to heart disease is
present. If you find any abnormalities, remind the person of
the heart line defect and advise him or her to be conscious of
the need for a low-fat, high-fiber diet, proper exercise, and
stress management.*[9]

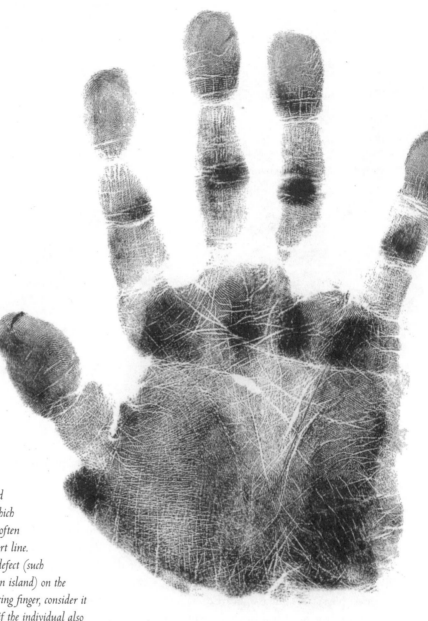

FIGURE 20.11. The palm print of a man with a long and
broken Mercury line.

## The Mercury Line

The diagonal flexion crease, or Mercury line, begins near the end of the life line and moves upward toward the little (or Mercury) finger. It has also been called the health line and the hepatic line. Ideally, it is better not to have this line in the hand at all, since its presence indicates a predisposition for problems of the stomach, intestines, liver, kidneys, and female reproductive organs.

While a strong, clear Mercury line indicates a degree of resistance to these problems, a weak, fragmented line reveals existing or potential stomach ulcers, intestinal problems (including colitis), chronic constipation, or other disorders. Very often, such maladies are due to stress or poor dietary habits.

The handprint shown in Figure 20.11 is that of a man who suffered from colitis for many years, which resulted in a colostomy. His Mercury line is long and clearly marked, with numerous breaks.

## ACCESSORY LINES: THE VIA LASCIVIA

Although not a major line on the hand, the via lascivia (or line of Neptune) is an important one. It normally branches off the life line and moves below and often parallel to the line of Mercury. The via lascivia is often weak and broken and is sometimes

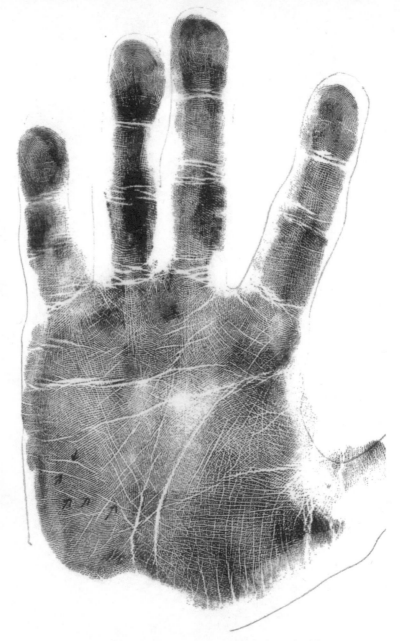

FIGURE 20.12. A palm print with the via lascivia.

formed by parallel lines, as seen in Figure 20.12 (and also in Figure 20.13). It has two meanings: sensitivity and addiction.

People with this "poison line," a sure sign of sensitivity to toxins, tend to react strongly to all kinds of chemical substances, including prescribed medications, chemical additives in food, alcohol, tobacco, and controlled substances such as marijuana and cocaine. They may also suffer from allergies to prescribed medications such as penicillin, as well as

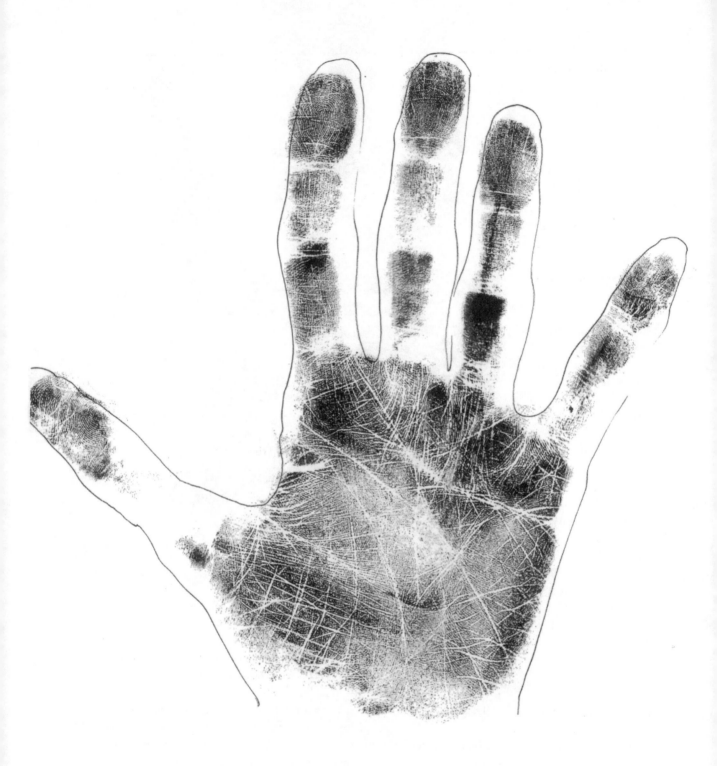

FIGURE 20.13. The handprint of a man in recovery from addictive behavior.

elements in certain foods such as lactose and gluten. They are often allergic to bee stings, cats and dogs, and pollen (hay fever) and can have adverse reactions to a wide variety of common industrial and household chemicals that make up so much of our modern environment.

The via lascivia can also be a mark of addiction. In addition to hard drugs, a person can also be addicted to elements found in common foods, such as salt, sugar, and caffeine. The person with a via lascivia would be very likely to consume endless cups of coffee or generous amounts of sugar on a daily basis. Compared with heroin or cocaine, these substances are relatively harmless, but they are not at all healthy, especially when consumed in excess. However, anyone with the via lascivia who takes hard drugs is almost certain to become addicted. That's why it is commonly found on the hands of drug addicts and alcoholics.

A person with the via lascivia could also be addicted to various forms of excitement, getting high from the adrenaline rush their body chemistry produces. Others can become food addicts, gambling addicts, or even sex addicts. I've seen this marking on the hands of many members of twelve-step groups such as Alcoholics Anonymous, Narcotics Anonymous, Sex and Love Addicts Anonymous, and Co-Dependents Anonymous.

Recent science has shown that addiction and addictive behavior—whether to heroin, alcohol, gambling, or sex—is not just due to social causes but has its roots in genetics, biological factors, and pharmacological factors as well. A study of the via lascivia can help a person understand the roots of his or her addiction and possibly prevent addictive behavior before it appears.

The hand reproduced in Figure 20.13 is that of a seventy-six-year-old man who has acknowledged addictions to prescribed medications, alcohol, and sex over the course of most of his adult life. In addition to several broken poison lines moving diagonally across the mount of Luna toward the mount of Mars, the hand shows a long and "romantic" heart line and a head line that droops strongly toward the mount of Luna, a sign of a rich fantasy life. The gentleman is now deeply involved in several different twelve-step programs and is considered a role model of sobriety to many of his peers.

Ironically, the via lascivia is also found on the hands of many natural healers, such as naturopaths, homeopaths, and chiropractors. It is probably because these people discovered early in life that their bodies react badly to medications and other chemicals. Childhood medications could have made them very ill, and they turned away from conventional medicine and sought help from herbal remedies, acupuncture, homeopathy, acupuncture, or other drug-free therapies. Inevitably, some of these people take up natural medicine as a career.

# chapter 21  ALTERATIONS IN THE HAND

A NUMBER OF YEARS AGO THERE WAS AN ARTICLE in a national news magazine about the medical research undertaken by Dr. Mark E. Silverman and Dr. J. Willis Hurst of Emory University School of Medicine in Atlanta regarding the hand in relation to disease. The physicians presented their findings to the American College of Cardiology, and the resulting excitement about their conclusions reached past the medical profession and into the national media.

The bulk of their research led them to state that a skilled physician's careful observation of the hands will yield valuable clues that a stethoscope and even an electrocardiograph may not disclose. In addition, they found that more than thirty different types of heart disease could leave distinguishable marks on the hands.

Most significantly, they confirmed that heart disease is often associated with changes in the fingers such as clubbing, which is a thickening of the tissue of the fingertip (Figure 21.1). When the circulation in the heart or lining of the heart is poor, the ends of the fingers often become swollen and bluish. Some healthy teenagers may show this phenomenon as a normal, inherited, family trait, but with heart disease, a clubbing of *previously normal fingers* is a clue to the disorder. In their article published in the *American Journal of Cardiology*, Doctors Silverman and Hurst point out,

> *Warm, moist hands with a fine tremor and occasionally clubbing of the fingers suggest hyperthyroidism [an overactive thyroid gland] with a possibility of high output cardiac failure [inefficiency of the heart], tachycardia, and atrial fibrillation [twitching of its upper chambers]. A cold hand with coarse, puffy skin may be due to hypothyroidism [an underactive thyroid], which may be associated with*

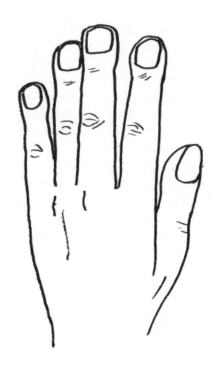

FIGURE 21.1. Clubbing of the fingertips, a common symptom of heart disease.

*pericardial effusion [fluid in the heart sac], hypercholesterolemia [a high level of cholesterol], or myocardial infarction [heart attack].*[1]

Since clubbing can be seen in childhood, before other symptoms appear, it is wise to examine the hand of any child who tires easily and does not keep up with other children. For instance, children who have heart disease should not run, jump, or exercise too vigorously. You may be responsible for saving the life of a child who has an undiscovered disease by examining his or her hand.

Dr. Eugene Scheimann and other physicians have observed that, in addition to clubbing, coronary heart disease causes palmar changes below the little finger and the ring finger, near where the distal transverse crease (heart line) is located. They believe that coronary diseases irritate a nerve center near the heart that is related to the ulnar nerve in the left hand. Irritation of this nerve causes a lump of scarlike tissue, or a nodule, in the palm of the hand.

Although nodules usually appear after a patient has had a heart attack, occasionally they appear without a patient having known that he or she suffered a heart attack. In this case, the individual has experienced what physicians call a silent heart attack. After the silent heart attack occurs, the hand may become swollen. The swelling eventually subsides but a lump of hardened tissue may be left in the palm of the hand. Naturally, this telltale evidence of a silent heart attack should warn of a larger, more damaging heart attack in the future, and measures should be taken to prevent a future occurrence.

Figure 21.2 reveals the changes made in the palm print by the presence of a nodule under the skin. The nodule causes a groove on the palm instead of the usual dermal ridge.

In his book *A Doctor's Guide to Better Health through Palmistry,* Dr. Eugene Scheimann wrote about several case histories of coronary patients and the changes he saw in their hands. The first was a fifty-nine-year-old woman whom he examined after she suffered a severe heart attack, and the second was a sixty-two-year-old man who had also suffered a heart attack.

**CHANGES IN THE PALMAR RIDGES**

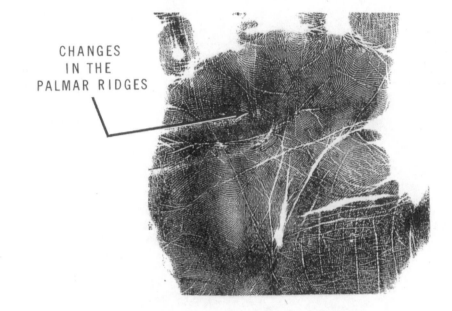

**CHANGES IN THE PALMAR RIDGES**

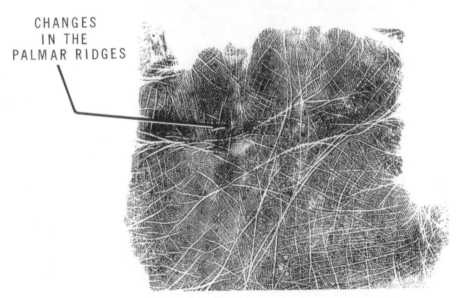

FIGURE 21.2. Changes in palmar ridges due to nodules that appear after a heart attack.

*I noticed that [the woman] had the indicated nodules present under the skin of her palm, and so I questioned her concerning her past history of heart attack. To her knowledge she had none, but several years earlier she experienced an abnormally severe attack of stomach pain. Later, of course,*

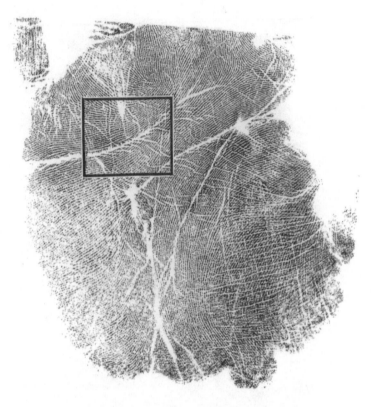

Figure 21.3. A normal palm print showing the "coronary area" under the ring finger, near the heart line.

*she had not noticed the appearance of nodules and the pain had eventually gone away without medication or a physician's attendance. I believe that the heart attack she suffered could have been prevented had the nodules been discovered earlier and her "silent heart attack" noted for what it was—a warning of the second heart attack.*

*Nodules have been observed as occurring simultaneously with genuine heart attacks in which the patient survives. I had an experience with this phenomenon when I attended a sixty-two-year-old man who suffered a classic coronary heart attack. He remained in the hospital for six weeks and was out of work for five months—a usual procedure in this type of heart attack. Two months after his heart attack I noticed nodules in his left palm for the first time. Since he had been a patient of mine for several years, I was aware that this was a new sign, which was*

*definitely associated with the cardiac infarction he had suffered.[2]*

In contrast to the last two individuals, whose palm prints show definite signs of heart trouble, Figure 21.3 shows the normal palm print of an elderly woman who consulted Dr. Scheimann with severe chest pains, resembling those of a heart condition. He did an electrocardiogram and discovered minor coronary insufficiency. He then advised her to go to the hospital for further tests and bed rest. Much to his surprise, she refused to go but wanted medicine to relieve the pain. He gave her medication and the pain subsided the same day and never reappeared, except mildly after she exerted herself too much.

Fourteen years after her visit to Dr. Scheimann, this woman was still working—long past the age of retirement—and appeared to be going strong. He found her to be as active and vigorous as a much younger woman in good health would be. Evidently, her anxiety at that particular period in her life brought on mild heart spasms, which subsided when she received the psychological assistance of medication.

As seen in her palm print, the coronary area, or the square that includes part of the heart line and the area under the ring finger, is absolutely perfect. That is not the situation with the previous two cases. Their palm prints show defects in this area, which are confirmed by their experiences.

## INDICATIONS OF DIABETES

Previously limited to a small number of seriously overweight adults, diabetes is reaching epidemic proportions in many industrialized nations, particularly among young people in the United States. Obesity and genetics play a role. While insulin—along with diet and exercise—is useful in controlling this disease, doctors agree that prevention is best.

The hand can show several warning signs that may reveal the presence of or potential for diabetes. One of them is muscle atrophy, or muscle shrinking. Atrophy

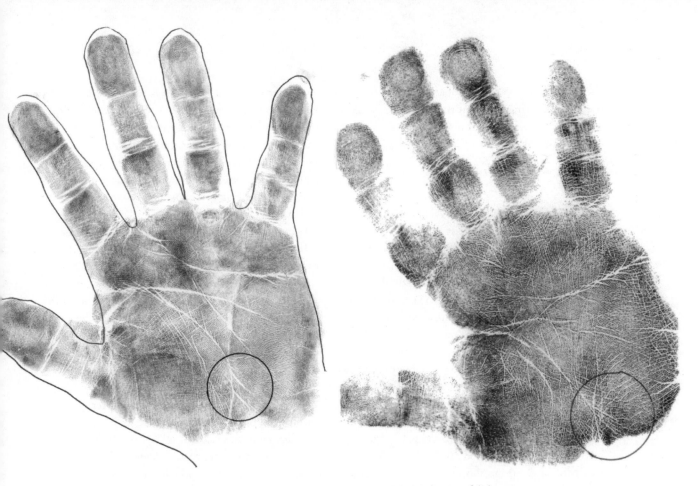

FIGURE 21.4. Lines of restlessness.　　　FIGURE 21.5. Lines indicative of diabetes.

may occur as a result of several diseases, sometimes before other symptoms appear. But if shrinking occurs and there is no neurological disorder, diabetes may be present. The late Dr. Max Ellenberg, then a professor at the Mount Sinai School of Medicine in New York City, stated that more than one out of every four diabetics shows signs of muscle shrinking, frequently long before the appearance of the usual symptoms of diabetes mellitus. He observed that this muscle shrinking takes place primarily in the space between the thumb and the index finger and on the bases of the thumb and little finger.[3]

Dr. Scheimann believed that if an individual has this type of muscle shrinking, or if a physician notices this condition in a patient, the presence of diabetes should immediately be suspected even if no other symptoms have appeared.

In addition, over the years I've noted that the palms of many diabetics (and prediabetics) have a grouping of small parallel diagonal lines moving away from the life line. Unlike the one or two small, fine lines breaking off the life line that are usually interpreted as a sign of restlessness and love of travel (Figure 21.4), these lines have a "feathery" appearance, as seen in Figure 21.5, which shows the hand of a woman with diabetes.

According to the National Center for Chronic Disease Prevention and Health Promotion, the incidence of diagnosed diabetes among adults between eighteen and seventy-nine years of age increased 43 percent between 1997 and 2004, from 4.9 per 1,000 people to 7.0 per 1,000 people in 2004. Similarly, age-adjusted incidence increased 41 percent, suggesting that the majority of the change was not due to the aging of the population.[4]

As can be expected from these statistics, "diabetes lines" are appearing on the hands of a growing number of people, especially those of high school and college age. When we observe these lines, it's important to remember that they are not necessarily a diagnosis of diabetes but reveal a predisposition to this disease. As the risk of diabetes is reduced, the lines tend to disappear.

## CANCER: SIGNS OF MALIGNANCY

Many years ago, an editorial in the *Journal of the American Medical Association* reported that palmar changes were observed in a large portion of patients with cancer.[5] These alterations are called palmar keratoses. They are usually few in number and located mainly on the mount of Venus and the mount of Luna. Palmar keratoses are pearly, yellow, or flesh colored and are translucent. Most patients are unaware of their presence, inasmuch as the lesions are asymptomatic.

In addition, Dr. R. L. Dobson and his associates studied 671 patients who had been diagnosed with various kinds of cancer. They found palmar keratosis in 46 percent of the men and 26 percent of the women. In a control group of 685 persons without cancer, palmar keratoses were seen in only 12 percent of the men and 5 percent of the women. These lesions were observed in all types of cancer, and the rate of occurrence varied only slightly among specific groups. For example, palmar lesions were found in 54 percent of the men with cancer of the skin, 45 percent with cancer of the lung, and 44 percent with cancer of the colon.[6]

In a controlled British study reported in the *Lancet*, British researchers looked at the prevalence of palmar keratoses in 69 bladder cancer patients, 66 lung cancer patients, and 218 hospital controls. They found that palmar keratoses were more common among the cancer patients, especially among those with cancer of the bladder. Above the age of fifty years, 87 percent of bladder cancer patients and 71 percent of lung cancer patients had one or more keratoses, as compared to only 36 percent of the controls. The researchers also found that prevalence of the lesions increased with age, and that keratoses were more common in males. However, no features could be found that distinguished the keratoses among cancer patients from those in the control group.[7]

Before writing *A Doctor's Guide to Better Health through Palmistry* in the early 1960s, Dr. Scheimann studied the palms of forty-two patients with all types of cancer and found that sixteen had palmar lesions. He concluded that the presence of palmar keratosis had the potential to be an important diagnostic tool.[8] Another possible sign of malignancy is an island at the end of the life line, as shown in Figure 20.8. Although it is no guarantee that whoever has one will indeed suffer from cancer, such an alteration in the hand can be viewed as at least a predisposition to the disease.

Patients who have been treated with chemotherapy can also experience a marked alteration in their hands. These alterations include a large increase in the number of lines, revealing a constitution that has become extremely sensitive, and the appearance of islands, breaks, and poor definition in the life line, which is a sign of a weakened immune system. These alterations can persist for many years after chemotherapy has been completed.

The handprints shown in Figures 21.6 and 21.7 are of a woman in her forties diagnosed with breast cancer. The print reproduced in Figure 21.6 was taken before the diagnosis, while the print in Figure 21.7 was taken two years after chemotherapy. The changes in her palm are typical of people who have been treated by chemotherapy.

Although she was declared cancer free after treatment, this patient reported that the chemotherapy "nearly killed" her, and she has subsequently undergone other health problems, including noncancerous tumors, irregularities of the parathyroid gland, and another possible cancer diagnosis involving the liver that doctors cannot confirm.

This woman's experience shows that we should never underestimate the ability of chemotherapy to weaken the body's immune system. The treatment may also make the body extremely sensitive to certain foods (especially those with chemical additives), cigarette smoke, and other environmental pollutants and stress. Natural healers often recommend that people who have received traditional cancer treatment undertake an aggressive program to help restore their immune system rather than continue to live as before their diagnosis.

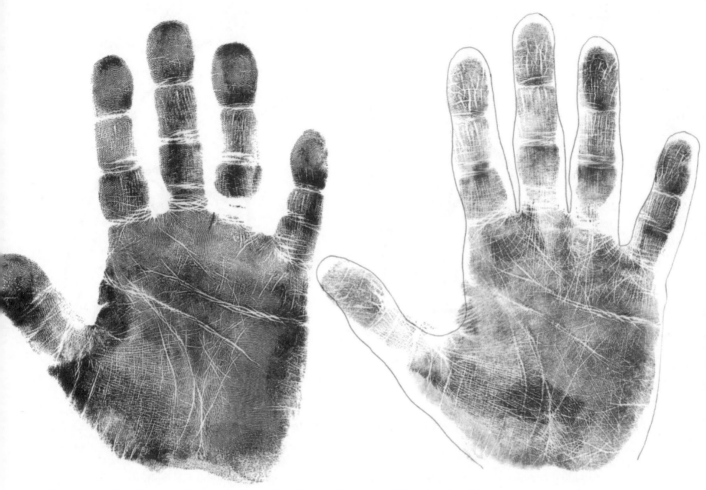

FIGURE 21.6. The palm print of a woman before undergoing chemotherapy.

FIGURE 21.7. The palm print of the same woman two years after chemotherapy.

## FINGER AND HAND MOVEMENTS AS DIAGNOSTIC AIDS

Dr. Eugene Scheimann taught that the posture of the fingers and movements of the hand are important diagnostic aids. If, for example, a person's thumb tends to remain bent, his palm is curled inward, and the rest of the fingers remain bent, you may suspect oncoming or existing spastic paralysis (Figure 21.8). When such paralysis occurs, a patient has difficulty straightening his fingers and thumb.

In contrast, a patient with flaccid paralysis not only can extend his thumb, but can also place it in back of his index finger, as seen in Figure 21.9.

In addition, involuntary movements of the hand, also known as tremors, are common symptoms of nervous disorders, certain toxic states, and internal disease. Dr. Scheimann identified the following varieties of tremor.

### Familiar Tremor

This type of tremor is often congenital and appears in the second and third decade of life; it usually affects men. A familiar tremor is not an indication of any specific disease. It is a fine, rhythmic trembling that tends to increase with emotion, especially if an

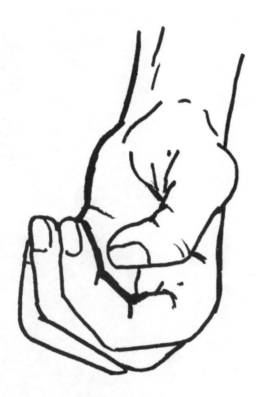

FIGURE 21.8. Flexed fingers, indicating spastic paralysis.

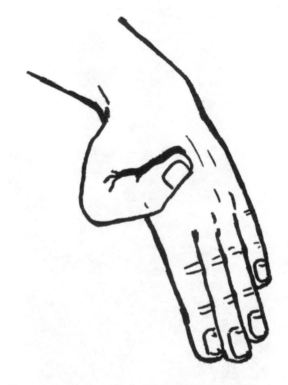

FIGURE 21.9. An extremely flexible thumb, indicating flaccid paralysis.

individual is aware of being watched. The subject is usually self-conscious and often gives the impression that he is nervous, alcoholic, or addicted to drugs. Sometimes a person with such a tremor is told to have a physical checkup, especially by an employer, because he may not be suitable for certain types of work.

We may include the senile tremor in this category. The senile tremor is very similar to the familiar tremor, except that emotion or tension does not increase it, and movement of the hand aggravates it. This tremor is often accompanied by shaking of the head and appears in the fifth or sixth decade of life.

### Parkinson Tremor

The Parkinson type of tremor is easily recognized by its characteristic "pill-rolling" movement of the index finger and thumb. Trembling associated with this tremor is coarse and of a large amplitude, and there usually are between four to eight movements per second.

The Parkinson tremor is present at rest and is increased by excitement; occasionally it stops when the patient uses his or her hand. It is the most characteristic symptom, as the name implies, of Parkinson's disease. However, it sometimes occurs if there has been a head injury or carbon monoxide poisoning or if there is arteriosclerosis of the brain.

### Cerebellar Tremor

In contrast to the Parkinson tremor, the cerebellar tremor is fine and rhythmic. It is absent at rest and becomes evident when a person approaches an object—for example, when he touches his nose or lifts a cup to his mouth. Therefore, it is called an intention tremor and is an important diagnostic sign of multiple sclerosis.

### Toxic Tremor

A toxic tremor occurs as a result of poisoning or intoxication from various substances, such as mercury, copper, alcohol, barbiturates, or narcotics. It disappears when the poison leaves the system.

If the tremor is caused by alcohol, it may mean that a person is an alcoholic. Dr. Scheimann wrote,

*A young man who came to me was worried about a woman he was in love with and wanted to marry because he had been told she was an alcoholic. He had been advised to observe her for a week and was told that if she drank liquor in the morning it would indicate she was an alcoholic. He did this and told me she never asked for a drink in the morning. I then asked him to watch her when she first got up in the morning to see if her hands shook. He said that both her hands and her lips shook. Evidently this young woman, who was an alcoholic, had controlled her desire for a drink but she could not control the tremor in her hands. Tremor in this case was an indication of alcohol addiction.*[9]

### Liver Tremor

A symptom of liver disturbance, the liver tremor resembles the Parkinson tremor except that it is not associated with rigidity, which is characteristic of Parkinson's disease. A liver tremor tends to become more severe when the patient holds his arms out at his sides because it resembles a wing-beating motion. Such a tremor is also an important indicator of early decompensation of liver function.

### Thyroid Tremor

One of the signs of an overactive thyroid gland is a fine trembling that is amplified when an individual stretches and spreads his or her fingers. The hand of a patient with a thyroid tremor is characteristically wet and warm, with smooth or satinlike skin.

### Nervous Tremor

The most common tremor, a nervous tremor, is associated with fear, anxiety, and hysteria. Unlike other tremors, this one has no pattern. It is not rhythmic but coarse and irregular. To diagnose a nervous tremor, a patient is usually given a tranquilizer and his or her reaction then carefully observed. In most instances, the trembling will stop.

However, if the trembling doesn't stop, the tremor may be associated with low blood sugar, which is sometimes brought on by dieting. In these instances, Dr. Scheimann recommended that instead of a tranquilizer, the person should be given a source of sugar or some orange juice.[10] If the trembling stops, its cause is likely to be dietary in nature.

# DISEASES OF ANXIETY TRACED THROUGH PALMISTRY

Before the discovery of vaccines, antibiotics, and vitamins, infectious diseases and nutritional deficiencies constituted humanity's greatest medical problems. Today, medicine faces an equally serious problem with the rise of psychosomatic—that is, mentally or emotionally based—disturbances. In fact, millions of patients who consult a physician suffer from ailments that often have an emotional component, including peptic ulcer, asthma, hypertension, colitis, cardiac arrhythmia, neurodermatitis, and hyperthyroidism.

It is generally understood within the medical community that each individual reacts differently to environmental stress. Some will suffer a nervous breakdown, some will be afflicted by physical diseases (such as high blood pressure, asthma, or skin disorders), and still others will develop tension headaches or chest pain or may be more prone to stomach and bowel disorders.[1] The hand can reveal much about the relationship linking anxiety, depression, and psychosomatic disease. In addition to providing insight into our level of emotional sensitivity, the shape, lines, skin texture, and flexibility of the hand can reveal how we adapt to everyday problems, the role of the imagination, and overall resiliency when faced with difficulty. At the same time, understanding the hand's message can offer practical strategies on how to achieve better emotional and physical health.

## ANXIETY AND BODY TYPE

A person's body type can influence how he or she deals with stress. Dr. William H. Sheldon (1898–1977), an American pioneer in constitutional psychology, believed that there are three basic body types, which are named after the three embryonic layers of cell development in the womb: an endomorph (named after the endoderm), a mesomorph (after the mesoderm), and an ectomorph (after the ectoderm).[2]

The endoderm, or inner layer of cells, develops into the digestive system and other inner organs of our abdomens. The mesoderm, or middle layer, gives rise to our body structure, including the bone, muscle, and connective tissue. The ectoderm is the outside layer and provides our skin, brain, and nervous system. Generally these layers grow in equal proportions, and an average person has equal amounts of these components. In some cases, however, one layer grows more than the other two and influences the appearance of the body and, to some extent, a person's behavior.

Endomorphs have an overdeveloped digestive system, so they have a large stomach, large abdomen, broad hips, and big buttocks. They also tend to be fat, with well-rounded faces. It is very easy for them to store fat, so obesity is often an issue for them.

Mesomorphs are characterized by a long torso, well-developed muscles, strong bones, and a well-developed heart.

Ectomorphs usually have thin, long, fragile bodies, often accompanied by flat chests and poor posture. Their upper bodies are short, and they have long arms and legs, long and narrow feet and hands, very little fat storage, narrowness in the chest and shoulders, and generally long and thin muscles.

No one can be classified as entirely one type; rather, everyone is a combination of all three types. These combinations are usually measured on a scale of 1 to 7 based on the level of dominance of the characteristics of each type. For example, someone who is mesomorphic (6), ectomorphic (1), and endomorphic (4)—that is, he or she has six out of seven mesomorphic characteristics, one out of seven ectomorphic characteristics, and four out of seven endomorphic characteristics—would be classified as an endomorphic mesomorph (well muscled but inclined to carry a lot of fat). Endomorphic mesomorphs make up the majority of individuals.

Although you can look at your body in a mirror or visit a body-oriented therapist who can determine your body type, a careful examination of your palm will tell you whether you are mesomorphic and need action when you are disturbed, whether you are endomorphic and need people when you are upset, or whether you are ectomorphic and need to be left alone when things are going badly. The science of body typing tells you how to best handle your emotional problems. If you have not recognized the need to handle these problems in the proper way for your body type, it is probable that you have added stress to your life instead of decreasing it.

A recent Bulgarian study published in *Reviews on Environmental Health* involved 524 men and 250 women. Of all participants in the study, 94.8 percent fell into five somatotype, or body type, categories; of these, 394 were endomorphic mesomorphs. The most common somatotype was endomorphic mesomorph for men and mesomorphic-endomorph for women.

The researchers found that in five disease groups, prevalence was significantly related to body type. Mesomorphic endomorphs most frequently suffered from digestive system diseases (40.6 percent), neuroses (30.1 percent), and radiculitis lumbosacralis (inflammation of one or more lumbar nerve roots) (15.4 percent). The prevalence of arterial hypertension in mesomorph-endomorphs (37.1 percent), endomorphic mesomorphs (35.5 percent), and mesomorphic endomorphs (34.3 percent) was about equal.

In both sexes, those with the highest endomorphy and mesomorphy and the lowest ectomorphy suffered most frequently from arterial hypertension and liver disease. The authors concluded, "Having a dominant mesomorphy and marked endomorphy constitutes a risk factor as a particular predisposition toward certain diseases and requires body weight control."[3]

## UNDERSTANDING ANXIETY THROUGH THE HAND

The human hand is an important guide to understanding anxiety and its consequences. It not only reflects our emotional state but also helps us recognize our particular body type and our possible reactions to extreme stress. Since recognizing our body types is an important factor in evaluating disorders due at least in part to emotional problems, we can use the infinite clues provided by the hand for both the treatment and prevention of anxiety and anxiety symptoms.

"The hand is one of the outstanding representatives of the emotions," stated Dr. Leland E. Hinsie, professor of psychiatry at Columbia University. "We speak of the heavy hand in states of oppression, of the slack hand denoting idleness, of the helping hand of cheerfulness and cooperation, of the light hand of gentleness, of the strict hand of severe discipline, of the strong hand of force, of the hand-in-glove of familiarity, of the hand-over-head of negligence, of the black hand of lurid crime, etc."[4]

By the same token, the first gesture of an infant—the grasping reflex or the grasping of the thumb—signifies anxiety about a new and unknown environment. When a child grows up, it will be the hand that expresses his or her anxiety when, as in infancy, insecure feelings come up.

### *Anxiety Neurosis*

An attack of acute anxiety (which often takes the form of feelings of impending doom) is manifested by physical symptoms such as sweating, choking, shortness of breath, heart palpitations, and extreme fatigue. These physical manifestations are often accompanied by oppressive feelings of sadness, hopelessness, and tension. Similarly, chronic anxiety is a steady, prolonged disturbance of mood with the same persistent physical manifestations as acute anxiety, except that it is less intense.

In the study of this common psychological ailment it is important to keep two factors in mind.

First, anxiety neurosis usually occurs in constitutionally predisposed individuals. Second, repeated anxiety attacks may cause some permanent personality disorders, such as obsessive-compulsive behavior, anticipating the worst of situations, and phobias like fear of certain animals, fear of flying, or fear of heights. It is essential that we learn to recognize early constitutional tendencies toward anxiety neurosis so that we may be able to prevent the development of a psychoneurotic personality and the physical ailments that often accompany it.

A comparison of your palm prints with those of your parents could help you discover whether you have a predisposition to anxiety. As Dr. David Henderson, professor emeritus of the University of Edinburgh, wrote, "How far is the habit of anxiety, which appears to favor the development of anxiety symptoms, based on inherited emotionality; how far a mere infection, as it were, from an anxious parent?"[5]

If your palm prints and those of your parents show similar dermatoglyphic patterns favoring the development of anxiety, Dr. Scheimann suggests that you may have inherited a predisposition toward the disorder, especially if your mother had repeated anxiety attacks during your early childhood.

The dermatoglyphic signs of inherited neurosis have diagnostic significance only if they are

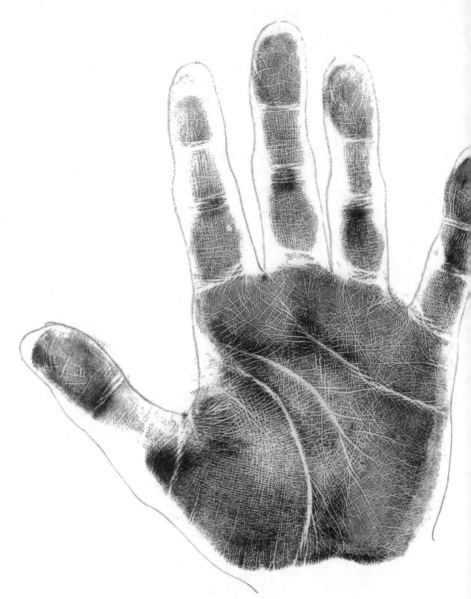

FIGURE 22.1. A hand with many lines, signifying a nervous temperament.

accompanied by other hand features that develop during early infancy or childhood. The most significant of such features include an abundance of accessory lines on the palm, a long and narrow palm, an elongated or excessively developed mount of Luna, and stress lines, all of which can signify acquired neurotic tendencies as well as inherited ones.

The palm print of most nervous and sensitive people is usually covered with many fine lines, resembling a spider web. Some observers believe that these lines are the direct result of the involuntary gestures and hand movements of a restless and nervous person during early childhood. According to Dr. Charlotte Wolff,

*The more frequent and complex are the person's nervous and emotional stimuli, the more will emotional tension and nervousness be produced in him, and this will affect the scale and variety of his involuntary movements and gestures and will be registered in the accessory crease lines of the palm.*[6]

We can safely assume that an abundance of crease lines (as seen in Figure 22.1) indicates a high-strung, receptive, and sensitive person. In contrast, the absence of accessory crease lines (Figure 22.2) signifies a calm individual who is relatively stable.

A hand with a long, narrow palm, especially if it is extremely flexible and graceful—with tapering fingers, long and narrow nails, and a skin texture that is fine and smooth—is a true mirror of a delicate and nervous constitution. This hand is known as the sensitive, or psychic, hand.

Those who possess such a hand are very sensitive to environmental stress and often get emotionally upset even in relatively normal circumstances. Like many children, these people frequently express their emotional instability or anxiety by complaining of symptoms of illness, such as pain, shortness of breath, rapid heartbeat, a lump in the throat, or what

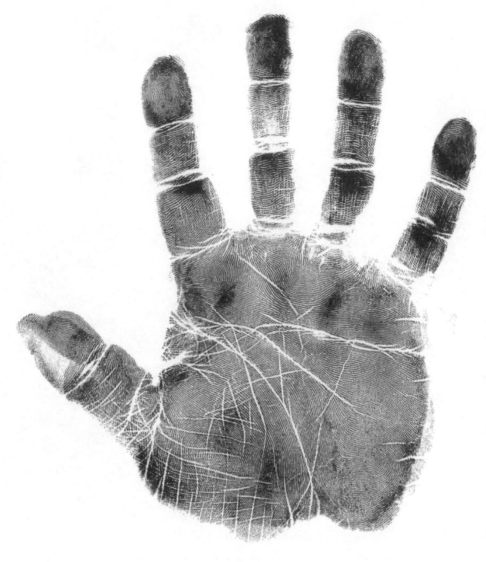

FIGURE 22.2. A hand with few lines, indicating a relaxed temperament.

I call the smelling salts syndrome: "I'm getting dizzy; I'm going to faint. Get me some smelling salts."

Many famous paintings of aristocratic women, such as Anguissola's Renaissance-era painting *The Chess Game* and Vigée-Lebrun's portrait of Marie Antoinette, show such hands, and one can assume that smelling salts or other stimulants were important items in their medicine chests.

The mount of Luna is an important part of the ulnar zone, the part of the hand located beneath the

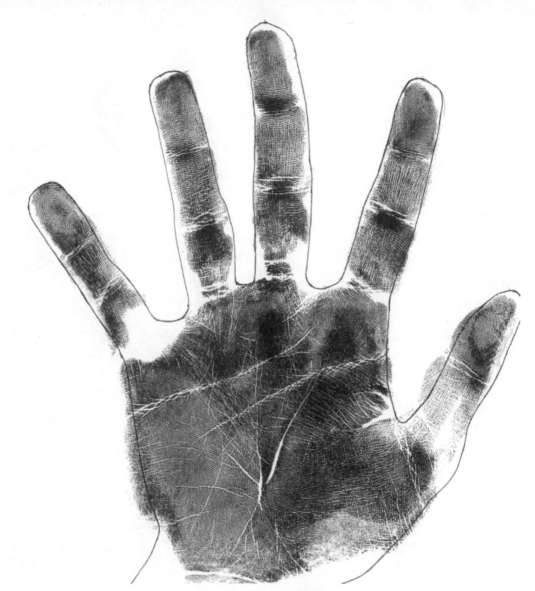

FIGURE 22.3. A hand with a line of intuition.

FIGURE 22.4. Stress lines on the fingertips.

little finger. It is the reflector of our unconscious impulses or energies, which are continuously seeking an escape. In other words, a large mount of Luna is a sign of accumulated unconscious tension. If the zone on a person's thumb side (which represents the conscience or the conscious mind) is relatively small when compared to the mount of Luna, he or she has trouble handling unconscious tension and will be a potential victim of anxiety neurosis or anxiety attacks. This tendency is increased by a head line drooping toward the mount of Luna, a sign of a strong imagination.

If the mount of Luna is encircled by a hypothenar line—the so-called line of intuition, as seen in the handprint in Figure 22.3—an individual's neurotic tendencies are even stronger. People with this line tend to have strong psychic ability and perceive subtle impressions from people and the environment that the vast majority of others do not. To quote Dr. Wolff: "The hypothenar line is the physiological consequence of an over-developed eminence and this stresses its psychological meaning: over-developed imagination, the factor which so often causes inadequate sense of reality and neurotic and hysterical disturbances."[7]

Another sign of possible anxiety is the presence of small horizontal lines located on the top phalanges of the fingers (Figure 22.4). These lines tend to appear during periods of stress and can disappear if a person learns how to manage tension. During an analysis of the hands of thirty young investment bankers at a major Wall Street financial institution shortly after the market crash following the attack on the World Trade Center in New York City, I found that the vast majority had these stress lines on their fingertips.

Similarly, long-term frustration manifests itself through a series of small horizontal lines on the lower phalanges of the fingers (Figure 22.5). These lines show that a person has experienced frustration in the area of life controlled by whichever finger or fingers the lines appear on. For example, frustration lines on the index finger are related to work and career, while lines on the

little finger can reveal frustration in a relationship or in the ability to communicate. These lines often appear in conjunction with the stress lines mentioned above.

## The Role of Anxiety in Physical Illness

The presence of a Mercury line on the palm is a sign of predisposition to problems of the stomach, intestines, liver, and kidneys. Whereas a strong, clear Mercury line indicates a degree of resistance to these problems, a weak, fragmented line reveals existing or potential stomach ulcers, intestinal problems (including colitis), chronic constipation, and other disorders.

These conditions may be due to genetic, emotional, or purely physical causes, but in my experience I have found them to be primarily of emotional origin. The abdomen and the solar plexus have been called the mirror of the emotions. When we repress feelings of anger, grief, and frustration, they can "implode" and cause abdominal pain and dysfunction.

It's the same way with heart disease. Numerous studies have been conducted on groups of coronary patients under the age of forty, and they all agree that prolonged emotional strain preceded a coronary occlusion in the vast majority of cases.[8] Although the vast majority of individuals who suffer heart attacks before forty years of age have been men, the growing number of female executives (especially in the industrialized nations of the world) has led to an increasing frequency of heart attacks among younger women. If extreme anxiety can so severely damage the health of young men and women, then we can assume that it is doubly damaging for older individuals.

You can force yourself to diet, to exercise, or to stop smoking, but many find that it is far more difficult to manage anxiety. Anxiety can be caused by conscious and unconscious tension. Those things that irritate and frustrate us consciously can be treated because they are obvious. However,

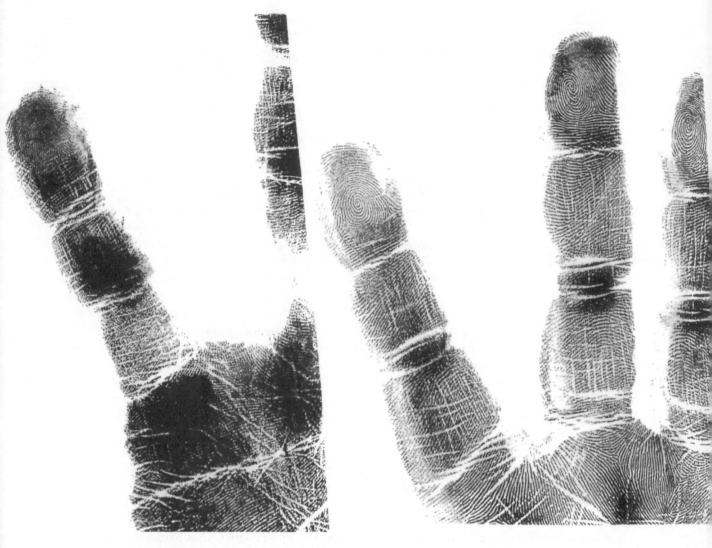

Figure 22.5. Frustration lines on the Mercury finger (left) and the Jupiter finger (right).

unconscious needs and frustrations, which may be even more damaging to our health, are hidden from our conscious minds and therefore often go untreated. Over the years, I have found that the key to finding the causes of conscious and unconscious tension is in the hand.

The handprint reproduced in Figure 22.6 belonged to my mother's first cousin. A typical endomorph, Frank was a fun-loving man with a good sense of humor. By the time he reached the age of

sixty-two, a large company bought his small video business, resulting in a financial windfall. Happy in his early retirement, Frank enjoyed short car trips with his wife and invited friends and family to enjoy his new hot tub and patio.

One day Frank received a call from the Internal Revenue Service accusing him of financial impropriety and threatening to put him on trial for income tax evasion. Even though Frank had done nothing serious (and the IRS later dropped most

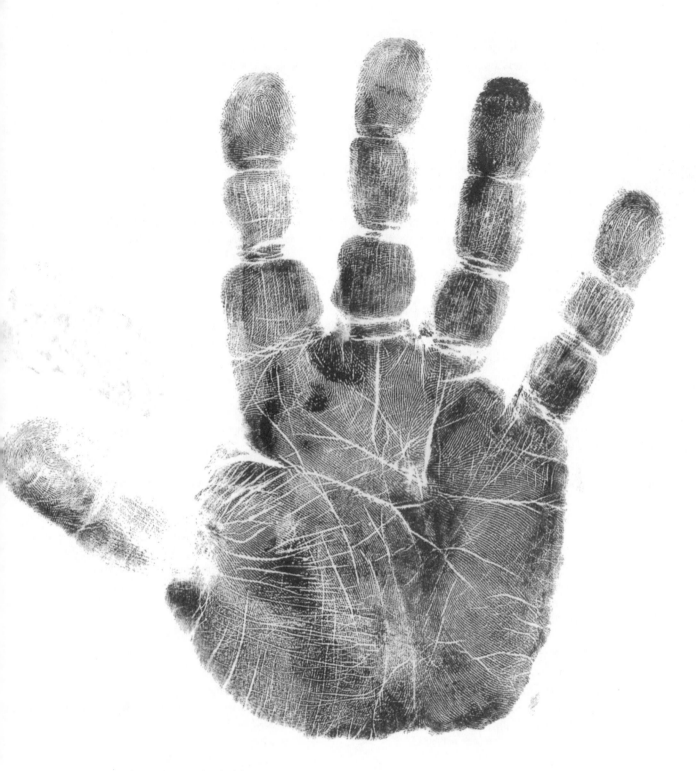

Figure 22.6. The hand of a man who died from a stress-related heart attack.

charges and settled for small fine), he was unable to handle the stress and died of a heart attack three days later.

As can be seen in the print, his hand contained many accessory lines, indicative of a sensitive individual. In addition to being tied to the life line, which indicates a tendency to hold in his feelings, his two-pronged head line droops toward a well-developed mount of Luna, showing a strong imagination. The fairly closed space between the heart and head lines indicates that Frank preferred not to tell others of his problems. Frank's age at the time of his death can be seen by the break in the life line, which occurred in a place corresponding to about sixty-three years of age.

During his many years of practice (he was seeing patients well into his nineties and was the oldest practicing physician in the state of Illinois), Dr. Scheimann collected many case histories. Through his wise counsel, many had the good fortune to gain a significant measure of self-knowledge, adjust to their environments, and achieve better health. Here is an example:

*Mr. M. was forty-two years old and a top executive in a large advertising agency. He consulted me because he had just recently lost his job through a company shakeup and had subsequently developed chest pains that he thought might be evidence of heart disease. His electrocardiogram revealed that he did have some circulatory disturbance in the arteries that resulted in coronary insufficiency. I also found that he had high blood pressure and a high serum cholesterol level. He was about ten kilograms overweight. He explained this by saying, "You know how it is, doctor, I work ten hours a day and at night I'm just too exhausted to do anything except eat and go to sleep." In addition, he was consuming large amounts of alcohol, and had not played golf or tennis—formerly his favorite sports—for more than five years. His palm revealed that he was a mesomorph with squarish fingers and nails.*

*From these facts, I advised him to find another job in a less anxiety-ridden field and to introduce a regimen or routine*

*into his life along with proper diet and exercise. Otherwise, he would have to face the possibility of a heart attack.*

*Mr. M. realized that he was the classic heart disease–prone patient and wished to save himself, although at first he could not accept the idea of changing his vocation. Instead, he decided to buy a motel in partnership with his father-in-law in Florida with the idea of using this investment as security to give him greater latitude when he chose another profession. He decided to give himself a six-month vacation from the "rat race" and moved to Florida to take over the management of this motel.*

*I did not see him again for two and a half years, but he told me then that he had never gone back to his former life because of the wonderful adjustment he had found in the new one. He had experienced no more chest pains, had lost weight, was tanned, and looked healthy. He had cut down considerably on his drinking and had greatly reduced his smoking. I was curious to find out what he had done to affect this marvelous "cure" and he told me the story.*

*He admitted, "I swim about five times a week in the motel pool. I go to the driving range for an hour on Mondays and Thursdays, and on Wednesdays I play golf with friends. On Fridays, my wife and I go out to see a movie or to visit friends. The motel keeps me busy most of the week, but I enjoy coping with the problems of running a first-rate motel and get considerable satisfaction out of the fact that we have a reputation for excellent accommodations and food. I have a few headaches now and then but nothing I can't handle. After all, I am the boss."*

*It is indeed unfortunate that all of us cannot be as perceptive and wise as this man was. After he came to understand his needs and realized the danger he was in, he very intelligently organized his new life so that he could enjoy the physical activity he needed. At the same time, he conditioned himself to enjoy this activity in a routine pattern, which he also needed. He followed my advice and now he enjoys not only good health but also peace of mind. The answer to his problems (and those of all of us) lies in the hand. However, one has to act on the knowledge found there.*[9]

Dr. Scheimann recounted another case history, this one of a man who owned a hotel that catered to long-distance truckers:

*He is a mesomorph with spatulate fingers and found his work extremely limiting and routine. On learning of his needs, he changed jobs and became—of all things—a truck driver. He found that driving satisfied him in two ways. The physical activity of driving and unloading a truck gave him the important opportunity to use his body. At the same time, the excitement of new places and people was satisfying to him emotionally. He is now a happy man because he heeded the message in his palm.*[10]

### Love Anxiety

No discussion of anxiety would be complete without mentioning "love anxiety." Love anxiety can happen at any time, but it usually starts in that period during the middle years, between forty-five and sixty-five, when men and women begin to have serious doubts about their sexual attractiveness or their ability to perform sexually. During menopause, women may become severely depressed and suffer physical trauma. And perhaps it's no coincidence that the "coronary attack" age for men—the time when men are, statistically, most likely to suffer a heart attack—coincides almost exactly with the age of their "masculinity crisis," or a perceived decline in sexual potency.

Some years ago Dr. Scheimann, who also wrote a book called *Sex Can Save Your Heart and Life*, told me about a study showing the importance of virility to good health.[11] Two Israeli physicians studied more than twelve hundred volunteers representing Jews from many different racial, cultural, and ethnic backgrounds. They found that the Yemeni, or Oriental, Jews enjoyed longevity, virility, and stamina that were the envy of European Jews. Two

important factors emerged—a better diet and a healthier mental attitude. In addition, before migrating to Israel, Yemenite men practiced polygamy—they married a new teenage girl every ten years, and thereby reinvigorated themselves sexually and emotionally.

I am not suggesting that people in their middle (or later) years seek out teenagers as sexual partners, or that they practice polygamy. Yet learning how to maintain good health and deeper intimacy in our relationships is key.

Figure 22.7 shows the handprint of a ninety-year-old man I'll call Bob. A former logger and construction worker, he married early in life and fathered nine children. Fifteen years after his wife died, Bob got remarried, at the age of seventy-seven, to an attractive widow a few years younger than he.

The outstanding feature of Bob's hand is the distinctively spatulate fingers, revealing a dynamic, adventurous individual with a strongly sensuous nature. The clear and well-defined lines (especially his life line and accessory "inner" life line) attest to both good health and physical energy, which also perhaps made him appear far younger than his years. His long Mercury finger and deep heart line also reveal a man who enjoyed sharing love, affection, and a sense of fun. Even though he lived before the age of Viagra, Bob's large mount of Venus reflects that he was sexually active until his late eighties at least (although at the time I visited with him, I was too shy to ask, and the narrow space between his head and heart lines reveal a man who treasures his privacy in any case). His wife once told me that she never experienced good sex until she met him and often commented that "Bob is the dessert of my life."

I once asked Bob the secret of his ability to stay so young. He replied, "I learn something new every day." A strict vegetarian, exercise devotee, and avid horticulturist, Bob took very good care of himself. He was physically active until just two months before his death at the age of ninety-one.

Like Bob, we have the choice of growing old in our fifties or deciding to remain young, romantic,

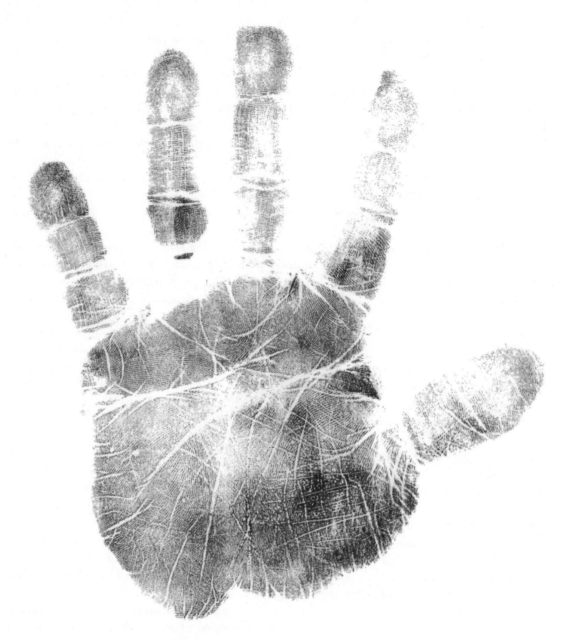

FIGURE 22.7. The hand of a sexy senior citizen.

and loving well into our eighties and nineties. Palmistry can serve as an important guidepost in this process. Like a sign on the highway, it can tell us that unless we seek to understand ourselves and prepare for a change in our personal and professional lives, we will have a difficult time of it. By becoming aware of our innermost needs, desires, and goals, we can take advantage of life changes and work with them. Then we can begin to achieve our highest potential as we enter this important phase of our lives.

PART V | LIFE TASK
AND
SPIRITUALITY

# YOUR CAREER AT YOUR FINGERTIPS

Next to health and relationships, our career, or life task, is our most important personal concern. For many, work is a source of tremendous frustration and dissatisfaction, which can continue until we reach retirement age. Gaining an understanding of our interests, aptitudes, and abilities can help us achieve fulfillment in our careers and make our working lives fun, challenging, and a continuation of the lifelong learning process.

Since the widespread introduction of computers, the job scene has changed dramatically. As we continue to move into the information age and away from the industrial age, our relationship to work and the kinds of tasks we perform will continue to change rapidly. The traditional pursuit of a secure job and fixed life goals has been challenged by the fast-moving and often revolutionary technological developments taking place throughout the world. Jobs that seemed absolutely secure have disappeared, while certain job descriptions—especially in the fields of computer technology, engineering, biological research, and telecommunications—would have been totally unrecognizable even ten years ago.

For those who desire to expand their career possibilities, these rapid changes have helped bring about creative new strategies. They call on us to mobilize our individual talents and challenge us to seek personal fulfillment in our careers. As an ever-changing blueprint of our lives, the hand can help us with these strategies. It can reveal many career-related personality traits, such as the tendency to overestimate or underestimate our abilities, and it can help us see the psychological forces that guide us to failure or success as well as help us analyze our ability to relate to others on the job.

It's also important to put work in proper perspective. Despite the advent of labor-saving devices to enhance productivity and facilitate communication, many people have become more addicted to work than ever before. For these people, their jobs compensate for a poor social life or serve as an escape from boredom, a difficult relationship, or another personal problem. When work is used to compensate for feelings of loneliness or despair, it will not create a feeling of personal well-being or satisfaction in the long run.

## THE CYCLES OF WORK

Age has much to do with professional well-being. Every seven to ten years, we move through important life cycles that emphasize different personal and professional needs. As I see it, our working lives can be roughly organized into the following chronological categories:

- The early years (age twenty to age thirty)—a time for opportunity and exploration

- The building years (age thirty to age forty)—a time to solidify career choices; this can also be a time of dynamic changes in the form of traumas, problems, and challenges

- The transitional years (age forty to age fifty)—a period of reduced economic pressure, with new opportunities for enjoyment and an increased desire for personal growth

- The mature years (age fifty to age sixty)
  —traditionally seen as years of lowered
  expectations and decline; this period
  can also be a time for new discoveries,
  enthusiasms, and professional
  redirection

- The golden years (age sixty and beyond)—
  usually considered a period of relaxation and
  retirement; these years can also be a period
  of loneliness and boredom; it's important
  to see these years for what they are—an
  opportunity for utilizing life experience
  and accumulated wisdom in new areas of
  creativity, leisure, and service

In past generations, the traditional notion of "career" involved adopting a single profession for one's entire working life. Many people would find a lifetime job at a specific company and work there until reaching retirement age; they often received an engraved gold watch from the company after thirty, forty, or fifty years of service.

By the dawning of the twenty-first century, this pattern had changed considerably. Many modern companies provide little long-term security for their employees, even in countries such as Japan, where workers traditionally remain with a single company throughout their working lives.

Many people begin in one career and after ten or twenty years decide to leave that career and move into another. For some, the new career may be related to the previous one. For example, a practicing psychologist may decide to teach psychology at a university or become a life coach to people enjoying good mental health. For others, a career change may be more dramatic, such as an English teacher opening a shop that sells surfboards.

In addition, there is a trend toward devoting oneself to two or even three part-time careers at the same time. In my own case, I balance my work as a writer with my work of practicing palmistry. For me, this offers interest and variety, along with a perfect balance between solitude and being with others. As people continue to expand their personal interests, the trend toward career diversification will become more accepted as the norm.

The midlife crisis is of special interest to the hand analyst. The vast majority, if not all, of the people whose hands I read experience this period during their lives, which often begins when a person has problems at work. A midlife crisis may bring about the need to make minor adjustments in career patterns and direction or may cause a traumatic break with the past and a profound reevaluation of one's life and its purpose.

Many people dread the midlife crisis, mainly because they don't like change. Yet if properly worked with, this period of transition can open the door to new and exciting career interests and a deep level of self-understanding. Rather than being a negative, a problem at work can signal the beginning of an exciting process of personal growth.

For some, the work cycle need not extend to the traditional retirement age of sixty-five or seventy. Our society glorifies people (especially men) who cling relentlessly to a career until they die or are otherwise forced to retire, especially if they accumulate vast amounts of money in the process. Very often, they don't live long enough to enjoy this money, which is usually shared by the the government and surviving relatives.

By the same token, many middle-aged men and women lose interest in their established career but continue working even though they don't need the income. They are using work to avoid being with their spouses or are afraid of the freedom that their new lives might bring. In some cases, they simply want to maintain the image of a responsible worker and provider.

For others, retirement at any age is out of the question. For many senior citizens, their work is their life, offering continuous enjoyment and challenge. One such case was my uncle Michael, who enjoyed a long career as a professor and chairman of the department of mathematics at a major East Coast university. After reaching the school's mandatory retirement age of seventy, he moved to California with my aunt and taught at several local colleges well into his eighties. He also served as a volunteer math tutor to local high school students.

One of the beauties of palmistry is that it objectively reflects the needs and abilities of each individual. Rather than encourage a person to conform to whatever patterns society deems acceptable, it offers a perspective through which we can evaluate our own needs without prejudice or coercion.

For many who approach retirement age, the best help a hand reader can provide is to encourage the exploration of new interests apart from work and facilitate the process of taking stock. Being free of traditional work patterns offers time for reading, travel, painting the house, working as a volunteer, planting a garden, serving as a mentor to a younger person, athletics, pursuing a hobby or craft, writing, fishing, dreaming, playing golf, socializing, or doing nothing at all. For those who are divorced or widowed, retirement can even provide the time and opportunity to begin a new romance.

The cycles of work show that life involves continuous change. We need to manage this change and adapt our activities to suit our needs. Ideally, a career should be more than just a job or an activity that contributes only to our basic survival. It should also be a vocation—an activity that produces a sense of self-fulfillment, a feeling of self-worth, or a contribution to the community. While it need not occupy all our talent, time, and energy, a career should be conducive to our personal, professional, and spiritual well-being. It should provide pleasure, challenge, and opportunities for personal growth.

## WHAT'S THE RIGHT AGE FOR CAREER COUNSELING?

Special consideration needs to be given to young people. Many parents today try to influence their children's career choice as early as the grade-school years and push them into activities that will get them into special career-track programs in middle school and high school. This may be because some parents feel that unless they guide their child into a

FIGURE 23.1. The hand of a future West Point cadet.

particular career, he or she will not be successful in life.

Other parents simply offer support and guidance and allow children to decide their own career paths. Such were the parents of the boy whose print is reproduced in Figure 23.1. Eight years after this print was taken, he became a cadet at the U.S. Military Academy. Similarly, the seven-year-old girl whose hand is shown in Figure 23.2 didn't decide to become a nurse until her senior year in high school.

Generally, I am opposed to advising preteens about specific career directions. In the first place, I feel that children have enough on their plate these days and should try to enjoy the pleasures of simply being children without having to focus on what they will do after they graduate from high school. In addition, the hands of children are especially prone to change, and any coercion—subtle or not—by adults can have a negative effect on both personality and career satisfaction in the long run.

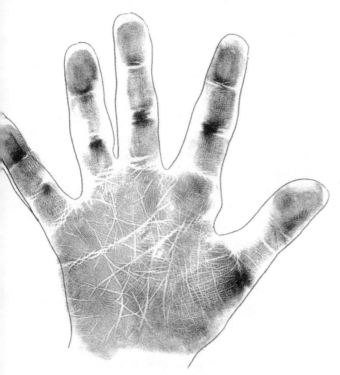

FIGURE 23.2. The hand of a future nurse.

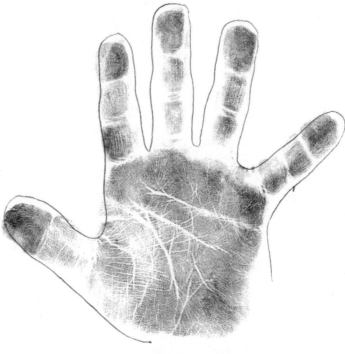

FIGURE 23.3. The hand of a future computer analyst.

Of course, if a young person shows a special aptitude or interest in a specific area, there should be no reason why he or she cannot receive encouragement and support from an adult. Like the parents of the future West Point cadet, the mother and father of the boy whose hand appears in Figure 23.3 allowed him to explore many areas of interest on his own, which included working with computers. He is now a well-paid computer analyst and Web designer.

For a palmist, reading the hands of young people is a special privilege. In a society where standardization and conformity are the rule, palmistry allows a child to see himself or herself as a unique individual with special gifts. A careful hand analysis can highlight at least several positive traits in the hands of any child or young teen that can confirm a talent or interest of which the child may already be aware. It can also draw attention to traits that may have been overlooked or taken for granted. Sometimes a hand contains a special marking that sets a child

apart from others. Acknowledging the presence of these tendencies can help build self-knowledge and self-esteem.

Perhaps the best time for a career-oriented hand analysis is during the high school years (between the ages of fifteen and eighteen), when young people are beginning to seriously consider future career plans. When we examine the hands of a teenager, we shouldn't immediately focus on specifics but should attempt to get a bearing on that person's general direction, taking personal interests and aptitudes into account:

- Is he or she extroverted or introverted?

- Is he or she "people oriented" or solitary?

- Is his or her hand the type that enjoys physical activity, or is it more suited to intellectual work?

By determining the type of hand a person has—along with its flexibility, thumb type, dominant fingerprint patterns, and finger formation and placement—we can gather an abundance of useful data. This in turn will give us a good overview of our client's personality and direction in life. From this general understanding, we can proceed toward a more specific and deep analysis of the hands.

## THE PALMIST AS CAREER COUNSELOR

For the serious hand analyst, proving career guidance through the careful examination and interpretation of the form and the markings of the hand is both a privilege and a responsibility. For this reason, we need to seek a balance between a caring and compassionate attitude and the desire to maintain high standards of accuracy and thoroughness when a person seeks our help.

Although our primary task is to provide general and specific information about an individual's character, career possibilities, and life path, we must at the same time avoid trying to control a person's life. We must recognize areas of talent and difficulty that we see in the hand, while offering clarity for and support of an individual's choice of career.

On occasion, for example, I have met people whose hands reveal no specific career direction at all, indicating that they aren't suited for any particular line of work. This often occurs with people who have never had any idea what they want to do in life. In such cases, it's useful to suggest one or two general career directions that are within the range of that individual's talent. If appropriate, encourage your client to stick to his or her chosen field rather than jump from one job to another.

The hand is a "living blueprint" of our professional life and career direction. Because the lines in the hand can always change, it can offer us continuing guidance. It is important to remember that luck does not create a vocation. By getting in touch with our deepest aspirations, talents, and skills, we can begin to attract people, circumstances, and opportunities that open the door to satisfying and purposeful careers.

## YOUR FINGERS AND YOUR CAREER

Many hand analysts believe that the fingers alone can tell us more about a person and his or her lifestyle than any other aspect of the hand. Remember that each finger has a specific meaning, or core quality, and reflects the type of energy that is channeled through it:

- The thumb relates to ego strength, willpower, and level of energy. Because it allows us to accomplish a wide variety of tasks in daily life, the thumb also symbolizes our ability to express this energy to the world.

- The Jupiter, or index, finger reveals our degree of self-confidence. By studying its size and shape, we can evaluate a person's leadership potential, ambition, and desire to succeed in life.

- The Saturn, or middle, finger reveals the serious side of our psychological nature. It is the finger of propriety, responsibility, and introspection. Depending on how it is developed, this finger will reveal business acumen, reliability, and steadiness. If undeveloped, it can betray a careless or frivolous personality.

- The Apollo, or ring, finger is the symbol of our creative and artistic qualities. The development of this finger is associated with a talent in the field of graphic arts (including drawing, design, and architecture), the fine arts, and acting. Some palmists believe that a well-developed Apollo finger is also related to successful careers in public speaking, teaching, advertising, and public relations.

- The Mercury, or little, finger reveals our ability to communicate. Our capacity to express ourselves through speaking, acting, and writing can be reflected through this finger. It also can reveal our talent for business, sales, languages, and broadcasting.

When studying the fingers, we need to consider each finger by itself and also as an integral part of the hand. In addition, we must understand the relationship of each finger to the others. We can determine a finger's relative strength by opening the palm completely with the fingers held together. If the fingers tend to lean toward one finger in particular, that finger is the dominant finger of the hand. It provides us with the keynote of an individual's character.

## FINGER CHARACTERISTICS

The degree of flexibility of the fingers provides an important clue to a person's character and his or her ability to adapt. Ideally, the fingers should arch gently backward under pressure, revealing a capacity to adapt to new ideas and unexpected situations.

The length of the fingers must be judged in relation to the length of the palm. A balance exists when the length of the fingers is proportionate to the length of the palm itself.

Generally speaking, people with short fingers, like the successful businesswoman whose print is reproduced in Figure 23.4, are quick thinkers. They tend to act on impulse and instinct and are able to grasp quickly the essential points of an issue. They also tend to view things on a large scale, be they philosophical concepts, business strategies, or specific tasks that need to be done. Unless their fingers are knotted, they tend to overlook details and can be less than thorough in completing assigned tasks.

By contrast, long fingers (Figure 23.5) indicate a person who tends to fuss over small details and likes to focus on the minutiae of daily life. Long fingers often reveal an introspective nature and suggest analysis, patience, and thoroughness. Knotted fingers

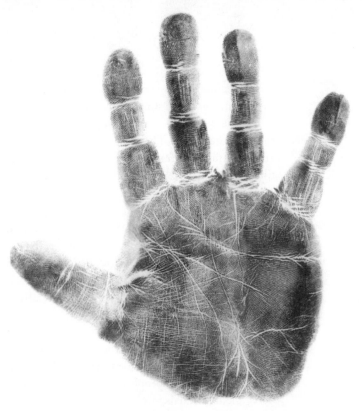

FIGURE 23.4. A hand with short fingers.

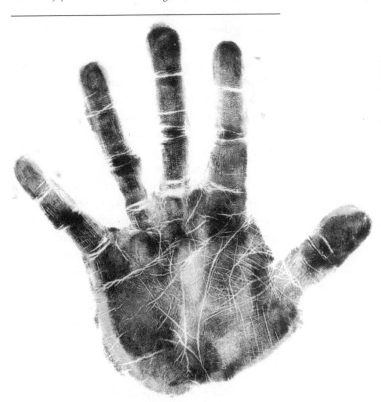

FIGURE 23.5. A hand with long fingers.

and a life line that is connected to the head line at their commencement strengthen this tendency.

People with thick, fleshy fingers possess a basically sensate nature. They enjoy luxury, good food, and sensate pleasures. As a result, they are sometimes drawn to careers such as cooking and catering and excel in careers grounded in three-dimensional reality, such as real estate and finance.

Thin fingers tend to reveal a more intellectual person who is often removed from the trials and tribulations of the everyday world. People with thin fingers tend to favor careers in research, library science, writing, and computer analysis, especially if their fingers are long as well.

Smooth fingers have an absence of developed joints and belong to people who rely on intuition rather than pure reason when making decisions. Artists, poets, actors, people involved in public relations, and individuals involved with sales and service normally have smooth fingers.

Owners of smooth fingers often have difficulty breaking down a problem into its component parts. Their decisions are based primarily on hunches rather than on a careful analysis of the issues. If the fingers are smooth and short, impulsiveness, impatience, and aversion to detail will be accentuated. Long fingers reveal intellectual and analytical tendencies.

By contrast, fingers with prominent joints, or "knotty fingers," that are not caused by arthritis (Figure 23.6) reveal a person with a strong analytical mind. Their owners often gravitate toward careers in scientific research, engineering, and systems analysis. However, this analytical component can often be applied to a wide variety of professions and usually means that a person loves details, minutiae, and analysis. Individuals with this characteristic are rarely seduced by appearances and tend to delve deeply into an issue using logic and careful attention to detail.

## THE PHALANGES

We mentioned earlier that all of the fingers of the hand are divided into three parts, or phalanges. The top phalange is that of mental order, the middle

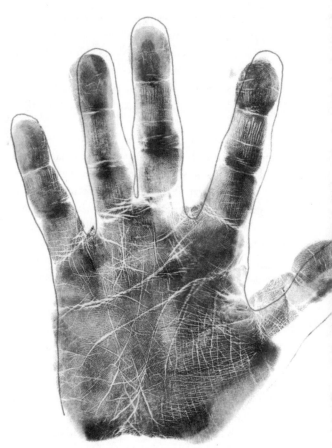

FIGURE 23.6. A hand with knotty fingers and a wide space between the Jupiter and Saturn fingers.

---

phalange is that of practical order, and the bottom phalange is called the phalange of material order.

When applied to an analysis of a person's career, long top joints on all fingers reveal a thoughtful person whose mental activities absorb most of his or her attention. Those involved in research, writing, and teaching are likely to have long phalanges of mental order.

A long middle phalange on all fingers shows skill in business and other practical types of work.

A long and thick phalange of material order reflects a person who is grounded in the material or instinctual side of life, such as those involved in real estate, construction, or the food industry. If other confirming signs are present on the hand, a thick phalange of material order can also indicate greed or self-indulgence. Pinched-in, thin bottom phalanges are an indication of fussiness.

Remember that the length of the phalanges may vary from finger to finger and that these variations influence the significance of each individual finger.

## FINGERTIPS

The tips of the fingers come in four basic shapes, and each shape denotes a special key quality of the personality. Since most hands have a combination of these types, we need to take into account the qualities governing each finger as well as each finger's basic form.

- Squarish fingertips show a lover of careful, neat, and thorough work. People with squarish fingertips respect order, rules, and regulations and like to follow an established method in the tasks they perform. They are practical, rational, and realistic in their approach to both work and life.

- Spatulate fingertips reveal a person who is energetic and down-to-earth and who loves physical activity and the outdoors. Spatulate fingers also reveal a strong intuition and an entrepreneurial nature. Unless modified by other aspects of the hand, they show a tendency to take risks.

- Conic fingertips are often found on artistic people who respond easily to outside stimuli. A person with conic fingertips is active yet receptive, mental yet emotional. Owners of these fingertips also have an easygoing way of doing things.

- Pointed, or "psychic," fingertips reveal a strong tendency to be affected by the outer environment and show a dreamy, intuitive, or inspirational type of personality. People with psychic fingertips tend not to be practical and often have difficulty surviving in the workaday world.

## FINGER SPACING

When the fingers are held closely together on an open hand, a person is likely to be introverted and fearful by nature, often lacking independence and self-confidence. He or she tends to conform to the rules and not rock the boat, whether on the job or in romance. By contrast, the wider the spacing between the fingers, the greater a person's openness, self-confidence, and daring. Very extroverted people, including small children, will lay their hands on the table with all their fingers splayed outward.

A gap between the Jupiter and Saturn fingers is an indicator of individuals who have the ability to make decisions for themselves and those around them. This feature can be seen in the hands of managers and other practical decision makers but not in the hands of those in executive positions who are not actually making the day-to-day decisions. When this gap is prominent, as it is on the hand of the nurse-practitioner and educator whose print appears in Figure 23.6, it indicates a person who enjoys being the center of attention. Many people who possess this trait enjoy being self-employed, working in the public eye, or having a job where they can be on their own or take the initiative.

A gap between the Saturn and the Apollo fingers usually occurs when the fingers of the hand are widely spaced in general. It shows independent thinking about the basic issues of life.

A wide space between the Apollo and Mercury fingers (Figure 23.7) indicates that its owner is likely to be an independent and often unconventional person who tends to think outside the box at work.

## FINGERPRINTS AND CAREER DIRECTION

The three basic types of fingerprints—the arch, the whorl, and the loop—account for approximately 95 percent of all fingerprint patterns and can offer valuable insights into work personality and career direction.

The whorl fingerprint is the sign of the individualist and the specialist. A person whose fingerprints

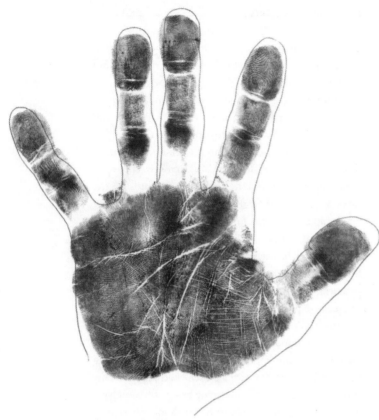

Figure 23.7. A hand showing a wide space between the Apollo and Mercury fingers.

are mainly of the whorl type tends to be his or her own person rather than a member of the group. He or she tends to have clearly formed opinions and do things the way he or she likes: people with whorl fingerprints rarely follow the rules. When all fingers have whorl fingerprints, the ability to keep secrets is strongly indicated. Very often a predominance of whorls can indicate a unique or unusual talent or ability or a special area of expertise that distinguishes an individual from others.

Positive qualities of the whorl fingerprint include originality and all-around ability; negative qualities include the tendency toward isolation and self-absorption.

The arch fingerprint pattern reveals a practical nature. A person whose fingerprints are primarily arches tends to be reliable, hardworking, and efficient. Such a person tends to be skilled with his or her hands and has the ability to make, mend, or repair things. Arch fingerprints are also found on people who are good organizers and who have the ability to fix problems and resolve difficult situations at work.

Positive aspects of the arch include consistency, realism, and usefulness. Negative aspects can include reluctance to accept change and difficulty responding to new ideas and unexpected situations on the job. A person with a tented arch fingerprint, which is distinguished by a little vertical line in the middle of the arch that looks like a tent pole, usually has a high degree of intelligence and enthusiasm.

The loop is the sign of a balanced, middle-of-the-road person who gets along well with others. Those with a predominance of loops on their fingertips tend to be easygoing, are good at dealing with a wide variety of people, and tend to make the most of their work situations. They are often team players who value consensus in the decision-making process.

Positive qualities of the loop pattern include flexibility, adaptability, and all-around capability. Negative aspects include a lack of individualism, a tendency to conform, and a tendency to capitulate when pushed around by others in the workplace.

People with composite-type fingerprints, which are made up of two loops curling around each other, have the ability to see two sides to every issue and can thoroughly evaluate a wide variety of diverse information. People with composite loops make excellent judges, counselors, and therapists, and other people often come to them for objective advice. However, when it comes to making personal decisions, owners of composite fingerprints can have great difficulty making up their minds unless other features of the hand modify the prints.

Remember that strong and clear fingerprint patterns intensify the meaning of each type and bring out its positive qualities.

## THE THUMB

The size of the thumb is an indicator of a person's basic energy level. It is considered long when it is higher than the lower phalange of the index finger.

A long thumb that's fairly thick and broad reveals abundant energy and a forceful, take-charge personality. Long, strong thumbs are found on people who usually have their way in any situation, whether at a staff meeting, closing a sale, or tackling a difficult project at work.

By contrast, people with short thumbs tend to be weak willed and can be dominated by others (i.e., those with normal-size or long thumbs). They may also lack self-confidence, forcefulness, and the ability to follow through on a project or other task.

Thumb length can be modified by how the digit is positioned on the hand. A low-set thumb reveals a person who is adaptable and independent and who is inclined to take risks both personally and professionally. A high-set thumb, which is held closely to the hand, is an indication of a careful and generally conservative person who is less likely to take risks.

A thumb that is both long and broad usually belongs to an individual who tries hard to achieve his or her professional goals (and who has the energy and force to do so). A long but fairly narrow thumb reveals the desire to achieve professional success but a lack of the energy and driving force needed to achieve it. This type of thumb is often found on intellectuals and others who tend to work quietly and persistently in their chosen profession.

A small, broad thumb reveals an abundance of energy and drive but a lack of staying power. A small, narrow thumb reveals an altogether weak personality who has difficulty achieving professional success. Yet a special talent or other ability can compensate for this problem.

Like the other fingers, the thumb is divided into three phalanges. The nail phalange is connected to willpower, the middle is the phalange of logic and reason, and the lower part—the mount of Venus—primarily reveals a person's baseline energy level.

A strong phalange of will—one that is well rounded, long, and wide—indicates decisiveness, staying power, and the ability to transform thoughts into deeds. Square-tipped thumbs reveal organizing ability and a sense of justice or fairness when it comes to making decisions concerning others. A spatulate phalange is a sign of a dynamic individual who is aggressive and has a fighting spirit. Yet if this phalange is narrow or pointed, willpower is often lacking, and the owner's energy may tend to scatter when confronted with a major project or a situation that requires long-term attention.

If the phalange of will is thin or flat (when viewed from the side), its owner is likely to be nervous and high-strung. Generally speaking, thick top joints show a person with a blunt, no-nonsense way of doing things, while a tapered tip reveals a more subtle personality. A thick-thumbed boss who wants to fire you will tell you immediately and in no uncertain terms (as in Donald Trump's famous line from *The Apprentice*, "You're fired!"). By contrast, a boss with a thin thumb would likely flatter you and invite you to lunch, yet would make sure that your termination notice is waiting on your desk when you return.

If the middle section of the thumb, above the mount of Venus, is broad (it sometimes can appear to be swollen), its owner will be blunt and straightforward when dealing with others. When the phalange is waisted, its owner tends to be diplomatic, tactful, and clever.

Ideally, both the top and middle phalanges of the thumb should be of equal length, which indicates a balance between will and reason. A long top joint and short middle joint reveal a tendency to act without thinking, while a long middle joint and a short top joint favor thinking and talking over action.

Determining the flexibility of the thumb is also important. A supple, or "generous," thumb reveals an individual who is changeable, adaptable, and generous. Yet people with supple thumbs can be unreliable and may tend to take on more responsibilities than they can realistically handle at work. If the thumb bends back to an angle of ninety degrees or more, the tendency to be unreliable is strengthened. Unless modified by other aspects of the hand, a person with such a thumb can be extravagant and generous to an extreme.

The less flexible the thumb, the greater the reliability and persistence. However, if the thumb is stiff and will not bend back under pressure, the person will be stubborn and have difficulty adapting to new ideas and unexpected situations. Flexibility in the other four fingers will modify these tendencies somewhat.

## JUPITER

As the symbol of self, the Jupiter finger represents leadership, ambition, and the drive to succeed. Ideally, this finger should be equal in length to the ring, or Apollo, finger and should reach slightly higher than halfway up the top phalange of the Saturn, or middle, finger.

A long Jupiter finger reaches more than two-thirds of the way up the top phalange of the Saturn finger and is often longer than the finger of Apollo. When this occurs, the owner has a strong ego with plenty of self-confidence. The person is sure of his or her abilities, likes to be in charge, and is very concerned with self-development and personal advancement. People with long Jupiter fingers are natural leaders and are often involved with running a business or a job that requires administrative or executive ability.

If the Jupiter finger is shorter than the Apollo finger, there is a corresponding lack of self-esteem and self-confidence. There may also be a tendency to doubt one's abilities.

While a short index finger may be ideal in a person who works for others, it may also indicate that a person is unable to handle stressful work or pressure from a boss or coworkers and may have a fear of failure. In that case, self-employment (or employment in a low-pressure environment) may be a wise career direction.

Very often, a shy, insecure person with a short index finger attempts to overcome his or her problems by becoming overly aggressive and independent. In these cases, the Jupiter finger tends to jut outward. People with this feature tend to break away from the influence of employers and coworkers. They either demand a high level of autonomy while working for others or simply choose to be self-employed. If a

hand with a short and "independent" index finger also reveals a degree of manual skill, a career as a carpenter, plumber, electrician, beautician, chef, or computer repairperson is favored. Salespeople often have this configuration as well. Although they may work for someone else, salespeople can often set their own hours and be their own bosses in other ways.

If the Jupiter finger bends toward Saturn, its owner will tend to be insecure. This is often manifested as jealousy, possessiveness, and acquisitiveness.

A squarish tip on the Jupiter finger betrays strong organizational and executive skills and is often found on the hands of administrators and planners. A spatulate tip, often found on the hands of innovative and brash entrepreneurs, reveals a streak of dynamism to the personality and increases the tendency to want to take risks. A conic or pointed Jupiter finger is a sign of inspiration. It is found on people who are attracted to mysticism, but it also gives an individual the ability to inspire others and help them overcome their problems. Religious leaders, teachers, mentors, life coaches, and inspirational speakers often have conic Jupiter fingers.

## SATURN

The Saturn, or middle, finger denotes seriousness and is the finger of propriety, responsibility, and introspection. It serves as a link, or "balance finger," between the subconscious aspects of the personality represented by the Apollo and Mercury fingers and the outgoing qualities represented by the thumb and the Jupiter finger.

A long Saturn finger reaches high above the fingers on either side. It reveals a person who treats life with the utmost seriousness and who is strongly interested in personal success. People who are deeply involved in scientific research, mathematics, philosophy, and engineering often have a long Saturn finger, as do businesspeople who deal extensively with money, stocks, and property.

If this finger is short, its owner tends to be careless and does not like to take on heavy responsibilities. For the vast majority of individuals, the Saturn finger is neither very short nor very long.

When this finger is straight, there is generally a

balance between liking to work with people and preferring to work alone. When the finger curves toward Jupiter, its owner enjoys being in the company of others most of the time. A slight curve toward Apollo indicates a need to work alone more often than not.

## Apollo

The Apollo, or ring, finger is the symbol of creativity on the hand. People with long and well-developed ring fingers are often attracted to careers involving art, music, and design. Over the years, I've read the hands of hundreds of students at the Fashion Institute of Technology in New York City, and many of them have long, well-developed Apollo fingers. Such fingers are also found on the hands of people in the entertainment industry. When the ring finger features a spatulate tip, the ability to work with the public is enhanced: it is often found on the hands of public speakers, teachers, actors, dancers, and singers. A pointed tip indicates artistic ability and a well-developed sense of style.

On some hands, the Saturn and Apollo fingers tend to bend toward each other. When this occurs, there is a tendency to sacrifice pleasure for duty. A person may stifle his or her innate creativity in order to achieve financial success or to otherwise fulfill certain responsibilities to others.

## Mercury

The Mercury, or little, finger rules communication. Ideally, this finger should reach the top phalange of Apollo. (Remember that in some cases, the little finger is set low on the palm, which may make it appear shorter than it really is.)

Generally speaking, the longer the Mercury finger, the greater the ability to communicate with others, both individually and in groups. A high proportion of successful entertainers, broadcasters, writers, lecturers, businesspeople, lawyers, and politicians possess long and well-developed Mercury fingers. This type of Mercury finger is also found on people with above-average intelligence.

A short little finger can indicate difficulty in relating to other people. Those who have one are often inclined toward emotional immaturity and have trouble acting as adults in office relationships. While in some cases this may have its advantages (people with childlike qualities are often very appealing to others), owners of short Mercury fingers are often misunderstood. Because such people often feel insecure and lack maturity in social situations, they may make comments that are inappropriate or do not express what they really want to say.

For the most part, a little finger that sticks outward from the hand indicates a person who feels out of the mainstream. Those with a wide gap between their Apollo and Mercury fingers are often fiercely independent and nonconformist. They do not feel part of the crowd and often suffer emotionally as a result.

The straighter the Mercury finger, the greater a person's innate level of honesty, frankness, and trustworthiness. A slight curving toward Apollo indicates a degree of shrewdness and is often found on successful businesspeople and political figures.

Many years ago I analyzed the hand of Mariano Ospina Pérez (1891–1976). President of Colombia from 1946 to 1950, he led his highly vulnerable government through one of the most turbulent and chaotic periods in the nation's history. The owner of a strong thumb and a long and slightly curved Mercury finger, Ospina had diplomacy and sagacity that earned him the nickname the Silver-Haired Fox. But when the Mercury finger bends strongly toward Apollo, there is a tendency to manipulate others and to be dishonest in order to achieve one's personal or professional goals.

Interestingly, the Mercury finger nearly always bears a loop fingerprint pattern, unless all the other fingerprints on the hand are of another type. In that case, the Mercury finger will bear the same pattern as the other fingers. However, when the Apollo and Mercury fingers are both marked with whorls—and if the prints on the other fingers are of another type—it indicates a subconscious mind that is especially active, revealing a high level of creativity. This can lead to precognitive dreaming as well as to hunches and mental impressions of all kinds.

# LINES, MOUNTS, AND CAREER CHOICE

*chapter*
## 24

Aₗₜₕₒᵤgₕ ₘₐₙy ₕₐₙd charac-teristics offer important guidelines regarding career direction, it is the lines on the hand that have the most direct bearing on career and self-fulfillment. A person with a weak life line, for example, would probably not be suited for work that is physically challenging. An individual with a straight head line that does not droop toward the Luna mount would likely excel in a job where a realistic, practical approach to problems is required.

## SATURN: THE LINE OF LIFE TASK

But it is the line of Saturn (also known as the fate line or the career line) that most clearly reveals how satisfied a person is with his or her career and the degree to which the individual is fulfilling his or her life task.

The stronger and clearer the line of Saturn, the more content we are with the direction of our life. If a prominent executive is unhappy with her vocation, for example, the line will probably be weak and fragmented, even if others regard her as a success. By the same token, the person who cleans her office every evening and is happy performing this work will probably have a Saturn line that is strong and clearly marked.

The line of Saturn normally begins at the base of the palm between the mounts of Venus and Luna

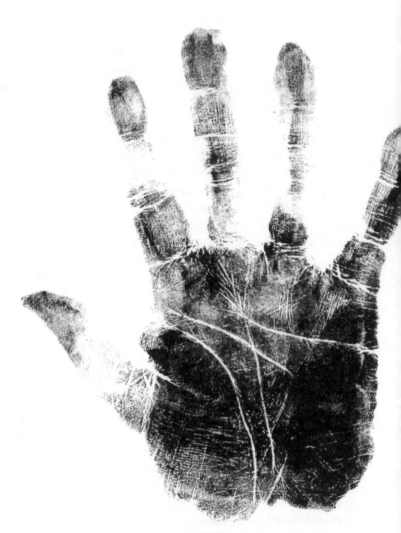

FIGURE 24.1. A strong and "independent" Saturn line.

and moves upward toward the Saturn finger, as seen in Figure 24.1. A line like this one indicates that the owner—in this instance an internationally acclaimed opera singer—has known her life path since she was a teenager. Her Saturn line continues

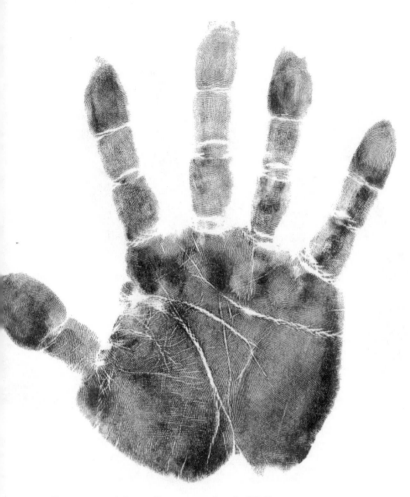

FIGURE 24.2. A Saturn line connected to the life line.

to be strong until it reaches the fifty-years-of-age mark, when it branches out, revealing a movement into several different areas of interest.

Generally speaking, the later the Saturn line begins on the hand, the later in life a person will find his or her true vocation.

When the Saturn line runs together with the life line at its commencement (as seen in Figure 24.2), it is often difficult to establish oneself in a career. This may be due to pressures or expectations from one's parents. When the fate line begins inside the life line, the influence from parents is especially strong.

When the line begins in the mount of Luna (Figure 24.3), a person's life path will be extremely varied, carrying the potential for several careers and frequent relocations. Some palmists believe that a

fate line beginning in the Luna mount reveals a profession in the public eye, which can include anything from movie star to teacher or beautician.

When the Saturn line continues deep into the mount of Saturn (also seen in Figure 24.3), its owner will probably remain happily active well beyond retirement age. Figure 24.3 shows the hand of an agronomist and teacher who served in the Peace Corps after his retirement. Before his death at the age of eighty-two, he continued to be actively involved in theosophy, his Masonic lodge, and his church, as seen by the three small branches at the end of the Saturn line, known in palmistry as the trident.

When the Saturn line ends deep in the mount of Jupiter, it reveals a career involving leadership. When it ends between the mounts of Saturn and Apollo, it indicates a career related to some aspect of the arts, or it can be an indication of money or fame. If the career line is strong and deep, its owner will realize the potential the line offers. A strong line also reveals self-confidence, determination, and satisfaction in work.

An additional vertical line running near the Saturn line may indicate an additional career or avocation. In the handprint of the agronomist, the short line that eventually crosses the Saturn line less than half an inch (one centimeter) above the heart line may represent his several years of university teaching. In many hands, a midlife crisis may be seen by the ending of the Saturn line and the appearance of another (often overlapping) line. This indicates a relatively easy shift into a new line of work at the age corresponding to the commencement of the new line.

In others, the Saturn line ends at a point roughly corresponding to the age of forty or forty-five years,

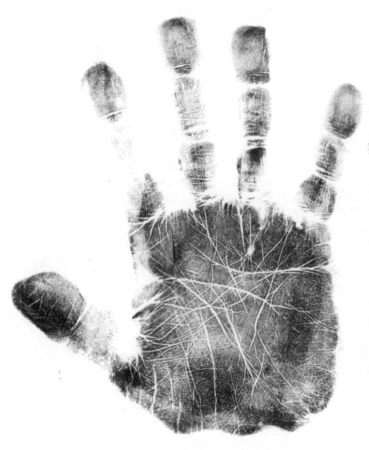

FIGURE 24.3. A Saturn line beginning in the mount of Luna and ending in a trident. Note also the loop of seriousness between the third and fourth fingers.

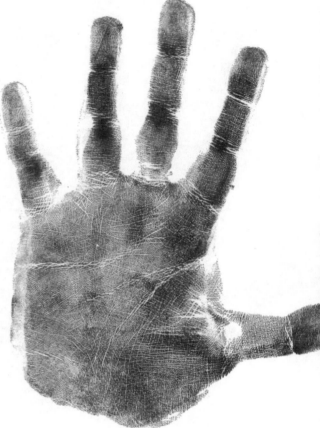

FIGURE 24.4. A hand with a thin, shallow Saturn line.

indicating a period of professional drift and unhappiness. This is often accompanied by a series of small horizontal lines on the lower phalange of the Jupiter finger, indicating frustration with work. However, a broken fate line may be followed by another fate line farther up the palm, revealing that after several years of uncertainty or dissatisfaction, a new career path begins.

If the fate line is thin, shallow, or absent (as in Figure 24.4, which shows the handprint of a young girl), there is often a struggle to fulfill one's career ambitions (if indeed these ambitions are defined at all). Frustration and lack of focus in life are common. Parents of a child with a weak or absent Saturn line can encourage him or her to expand into different areas of personal interest or can engage the help of a competent guidance counselor to help the child discover possible career directions.

Islands on the Saturn line reveal a need for greater focus of energy and ideas. Obstacles to a career are often indicated. Breaks on this line reveal periods of transition and possible lack of career direction.

A wavy Saturn line is a sign of irregular participation in a given career or direction. The person with a wavy Saturn line tends to be a jack-of-all-trades as opposed to a specialist in one or two fields.

Branches moving upward from this line add strength to the line at the age they appear, while downward branches indicate career disappointments.

## THE LINE OF APOLLO

The presence of a good line of Apollo, or sun line, tends to strengthen the Saturn line. It is found on the hands of many wealthy and successful people and is also associated with accomplishment in music, entertainment, and the arts. It also reveals a person's ability to land on his or her feet in the face of career challenges. People with a clear and long Apollo line are more prone to make an easy transition from a work routine to a life involving more personal choices. The presence of a good Apollo line is believed to be an advantage after retirement and reveals an ability to adapt to the new demands and opportunities of the situation. Seniors without strong Apollo lines often have difficulty getting along without the structure of regular employment.

Long Apollo lines are rare. They often consist of a small dash that runs from above the heart line to the base of the Apollo finger. The handprint in Figure 24.5 belongs to a psychologist, and it reveals one of the best Apollo lines I've ever seen. Although this individual became neither rich nor famous, he always enjoyed considerable career success and experienced what others have called amazing good luck in finding new opportunities and taking advantage of them. His hand also features several lines of Saturn (one beginning in the mount of Luna and one that is tied to the life line), a ring of Solomon, a near-perfect girdle of Venus, and a large memory loop just under the end of the head line.

## THE MOUNTS

The presence of many prominent mounts on a person's hand is a sure sign of enthusiasm, while a flat hand reveals a lack of vitality. A person with many mounts lives life to the fullest, but the individual with a flat hand rarely gets very excited or involved in anything. As a result, his or her life is generally boring and bland, with little passion or excitement of any kind. As you'll discover by observing many hands, most people have a mount pattern that lies somewhere between these extremes. Nevertheless,

FIGURE 24.5. A hand with an excellent line of Apollo.

if you find a person with prominent mounts—or someone with no strong mounts at all—the interpretation above is very reliable.

People with flat mounts are suited to quiet jobs that provide little or no adventure. Their favorite occupations include clerical work, office work, and any profession that provides a basic, reliable routine involving little emotional or physical exertion. Flat-mounted people seldom possess much physical stamina and have little or no desire for an exciting or stressful work environment.

By contrast, people with full mounts have difficulty adjusting to quiet work. They enjoy travel. People coming and going are a source of interest and pleasure for them. Constant, varied activity and a sense that "things need to be done" are also common among people with prominent mounts. These people work best when given plenty of work requiring a variety of skills.

The palmist Andrew Fitzherbert has suggested that the major pads near the Jupiter-Saturn, Saturn-Apollo, and Apollo-Mercury fingers develop equally, so if one is prominent, the others probably will be also.[1] For this reason, it's perhaps more useful to study the strength of each finger itself rather than the prominence of the mounts that lie between them.

### Markings on the Mount of Jupiter

The convergence of skin ridges under each finger creates what palmists call an apex. Its location provides important information about career and self-fulfillment. The most interesting of these apexes is found under the Jupiter finger. Ideally, the apex should be positioned directly under the middle of the finger, as seen in Figure 24.6. In some hands, it is slightly displaced toward the thumb, while in others it tends to veer closer to the middle, or Saturn, finger.

When the apex is displaced toward the thumb, it is said to be located on the radial side. Although rare, this placement reflects daring, independence, and a dislike for convention and authority. It is found on people whose actions tend to be unpredictable and unexpected. They need freedom, adventure, and constant challenge in their working lives.

A more common variation is for the apex of this mount to appear on the other, or ulnar, side, bringing it closer to the mount of Saturn. That placement is a sign of caution. The owner of this mark tends to be careful and restrained and likes to play it safe. While there are no specific jobs related to this pattern, people who have it tend to remain in the same line of work (or remain working for the same company) for their entire careers. This pattern often accompanies an index finger curving toward Saturn, tied head and life lines, and tied fate and life lines, all signs of a cautious and restrained personality.

If the apex is found directly under the Jupiter finger, a sense of balance exists between the extremes

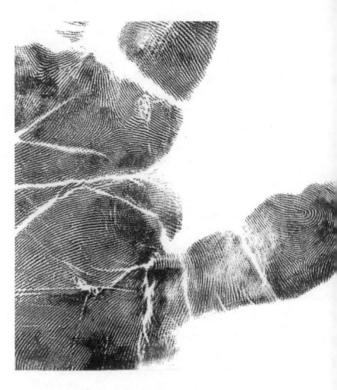

FIGURE 24.6. An apex on the Jupiter mount.

described above. A person with this type of placement is able to integrate a sense of adventure and unconventionality with the need for responsibility and stability in his or her working life.

Perhaps one hand in fifty shows a loop pattern between the Jupiter and Saturn fingers. This is known as the loop of charisma, or the Raja loop (Figure 8.8). A fine marking to have, it reveals an ability to take the lead, to rise to the top, and to earn respect and admiration from others. Leaders in many fields, including entertainers, radio and television personalities, and politicians, often have a loop of charisma on one or both hands. Loops of charisma are also found among gurus and other religious or spiritual leaders, but because the loop of charisma attests to their ability to gather disciples as opposed to their level of spiritual advancement, gurus and cult leaders of low morality or dubious spiritual achievement can also have such a loop on their hands.

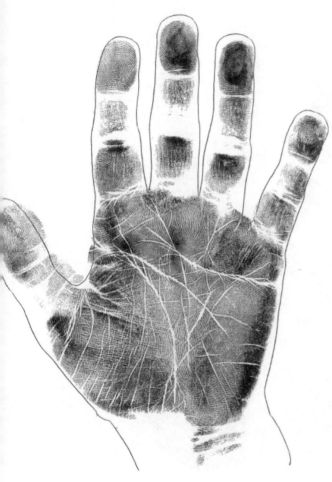

FIGURE 24.7. A hand with a teacher's square and a double ring of Solomon.

ring of Solomon. A clear and well-formed ring of Solomon (also seen in Figure 24.7) is considered to be a sign of mystical inclination, and it is often found on the hands of clairvoyants, seers, mystics, and spiritual counselors.

Because it is reveals an interest in what makes people tick, it can also be found on the hands of psychotherapists, social workers, career and marriage counselors, and many types of healers, especially those involved in alternative and unorthodox therapies.

### Markings on the Mounts of Saturn and Apollo

The mounts of Saturn and Apollo are of relatively little importance in regard to career. Nonetheless, there are traditions in palmistry that maintain that the Saturn mount is connected to occupations such as mining and farming as well as professions associated with death, such as cemetery worker or funeral director. Similarly, the mount of Apollo has traditionally been associated with the arts, including painting, acting, music, and poetry.

Early palmistry books placed much importance on the heights of these mounts and their "inclination" toward each other. However, because these muscular pads do not lie under the fingers but between them, traditional interpretations are often subject to debate.

On rare occasions, one might see a cross or star on one of these mounts. That can be a sign of a specialist, a person with unusual talent in the fields represented by a given mount. Many years ago, I noticed a small but distinct diamond pattern on the Apollo mount of a college art professor who was also a well-known songwriter, poet, and musician. Such markings are extremely rare and are also open to a wide variety of interpretations.

### The Loop of Seriousness

The skin ridge pattern found between the mounts of Saturn and Apollo is important indeed. Known as the loop of seriousness and seen in Figures 24.2

The teacher's square consists of a small but distinct square attached to a line that rises vertically from the life line, as seen in Figure 24.7, which shows the hand of palmist Andrew Fitzherbert. As the name indicates, this mark is related to a strong gift for teaching. Anyone who has this small marking can excel in giving lectures, running classes, and presenting workshops; in some cases, it reveals the ability to write textbooks, instructional software, and other training materials. The teacher's square often accompanies other marks on the hand related to healing and counseling.

Another interesting marking on the Jupiter mount is the seal of Solomon, also known as the and 24.3, it is found on people who have a responsible and serious attitude toward life and work. This loop is common among successful businesspeople as well as those involved in research, teaching, banking, and healing. Students with this loop study hard. Businesspeople with this loop are ambitious and make money. Writers with a loop of seriousness complete their manuscripts on time. The presence of a clear and well-defined loop of seriousness is a reliable indicator of material success.

## The Loop of Humor

The loop of humor has the opposite meaning. Located between the Apollo and Mercury mounts, it is often found on people who value comfort and enjoyment over proficiency and financial reward. In many cases, they will accept a low-paying job they enjoy rather than a high-paying job they don't like.

Owners of a loop of humor tend to be lighthearted, enjoy working at their own pace, and prefer to be in an environment that makes them happy. A high proportion of self-employed people and part-time workers have the loop of humor on their hands. There is nothing inherently lazy about them, although they generally do not have the "driven" quality associated with the loop of seriousness.

A classic case is that of the fifty-seven-year-old owner of the hand shown in Figure 24.8. Taiwanese by birth, Wei had a promising career in a large computer company before deciding to open a coffee shop with a friend. It was among the first coffee shops to open in Taipei, a city better known for its numerous tea shops.

After immigrating to the United States, Wei held a number of sales jobs and later became co-owner of

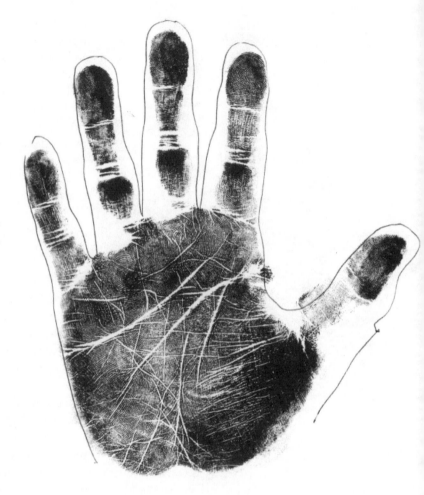

Figure 24.8. A hand with a loop of humor.

a Chinese restaurant. Although the venture was successful, he walked away from his investment after he discovered that his partner was stealing.

Although Chinese tradition calls for property to be passed to the eldest son, Wei, a second son, was bequeathed a valuable property in Taipei by his grandmother. After protest from his older brother's wife, he decided to transfer the property to his brother without compensation. Impressed by his generosity, Wei's parents-in-law bought him a three-family house in New York, which he rents out to tenants, providing an adequate income for himself and his wife. Aside from maintaining his property, Wei has not held a regular job for the past fifteen years. Even though he owns the property free and clear, he doesn't want to use his equity to purchase a larger, more profitable building. Wei spends his time working in his garden, going to the gym, playing the stock market, and visiting with friends.

The loops of seriousness and humor reveal our basic attitude toward life, and their influence affects everything we do. Employment is just one of these areas, so it shouldn't be considered something apart from the rest of our lives. There are times when we'll read the hands of a person with a loop of seriousness who is chronically unemployed or those of an individual with a loop of humor who has earned lots of money. However, for the most part, a well-defined loop of seriousness is a reliable indicator of a steady job with good prospects of material success.

Incidentally, contrary to popular belief, many top comedians have a strong loop of seriousness in their hands rather than a loop of humor. This may appear to be the opposite of what we might expect, but comedians such as Charlie Chaplin, Lenny Bruce, and W. C. Fields were all far from lighthearted people in real life.

When both loops are developed in the same hand, it reveals a person who has a serious approach to life and an ability to relax and enjoy life at the same time. Such people can take on almost any kind of job and make a success of it. The presence of both loops is a very favorable pattern!

### Markings on the Mount of Mercury

The mount of Mercury lies directly under the Mercury, or little, finger. The most interesting markings on this mount are known as the Samaritan lines, or medical stigmata. They are composed of a grouping of small vertical lines isolated from any other small lines that may be scattered about under the finger. A

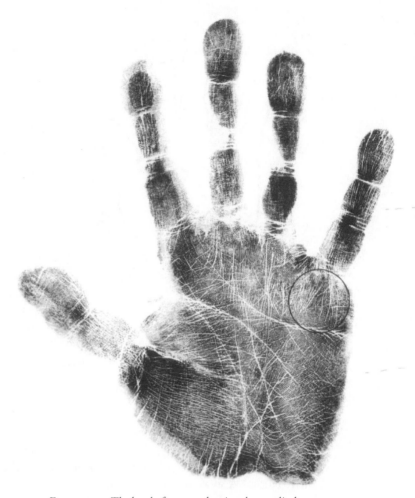

FIGURE 24.9. The hand of a nurse, showing clear medical stigmata.

good example of this pattern can be seen in Figure 24.9, which shows the hand of a nurse.

The medical stigmata are found on the hands of doctors, nurses, dentists, chiropractors, physical therapists, psychotherapists, social workers, Reiki and therapeutic touch practitioners, and others who are involved with health and counseling. They reveal an interest in helping and caring for others and, often, genuine healing ability.

Many people who are not health professionals have this mark. Yet these people often have an interest in healing or at least have the ability to give a good massage. While it is certainly possible to succeed in a healing profession without the medical

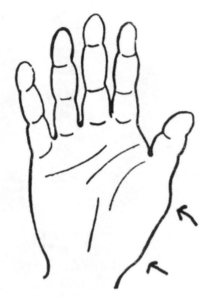

FIGURE 24.10. The angles.

stigmata, there is no doubt that those who have it can excel in any health-related field.

### The Mount of Venus

The mount of Venus is a prime indicator of our innate vitality. A weak and flabby mount reveals a low energy level, while a firm, high mount of Venus reflects plenty of energy and drive. A person with a weak mount of Venus is often unsuited for strenuous physical work, while those with strong mounts tend to be outgoing and exciting and enjoy physical and emotional challenges on the job.

Sometimes the Venus mount appears to be very large because the life line, which marks the boundary of the mount, swings out into the palm in a wide curve. This is a sign of an abundance of physical strength and is often found on the hands of professional wrestlers, weight lifters, dancers, and others with good physical skills.

Strictly speaking, the mount of Venus is actually the third joint of the thumb. People with strong musical talent invariably have strongly marked joints in the lower part of the palm. These joints are known as the angles (Figure 24.10) and are found on many

professional musicians, including instrumentalists, singers, and songwriters.

Skin ridge patterns on this mount can also reflect a musical person. In particular, a pattern known as the bee (see Figure 8.16) is sometimes found on people with a special ability to play stringed instruments. Professional guitarists and violinists have this sign, as do others who have never learned to play but nonetheless feel a special attraction to music played on stringed instruments.

### The Mounts of Mars

Just above the mount of Venus, where the web of the thumb appears, is the location of the lower mount of Mars, also known as Mars positive. In the average hand, it appears simply as part of the Venus mount, while on others, it appears as a separate and distinct pad of flesh that looks like a callus.

When present, this mount reveals a courageous and fighting spirit. Those who have it are willing to fight for what they believe in. People with this mount often gravitate toward careers in the military, although many police officers and firefighters have it, too. A well-developed Mars positive has also been found on a surprisingly large number of social workers and others who run homes and shelters for the sick and the homeless. Katherine St. Hill, who was president of the London Cheirological Society in the 1890s, noted that nuns who provided social services in the city's poorest and most dangerous neighborhoods often possessed a strong mount of Mars.[2]

Traditional maps of the hand show two mounts of Mars—Mars positive and Mars negative, or the upper mount of Mars, which lies directly opposite Mars positive on the outer edge of the hand. A developed Mars negative often appears puffy and is sometimes firm to the touch. The presence of this mount has often been linked to the ability to resist aggression and reveals courage and resistance. Because there's no distinct and separate pad of flesh to outline this particular mount, some palmists feel that there is little evidence to support its meaning. Yet I have often seen this mount on people who are brave and do not allow themselves to be pushed around by others. Like those with a well-developed Mars positive, people with a strong Mars negative can be found in the military, in police and fire departments, and in practitioners of martial arts.

Several years ago a very elegant woman whose hands had well-developed mounts of Mars came to me for a consultation. After I had expressed my surprise at seeing these mounts and explained their meaning, the woman told me that she was the founder and president of a company that provided security to businesses throughout the New York metropolitan area and that more than one hundred security guards worked for her. Many were former soldiers, bodyguards, and law enforcement officers.

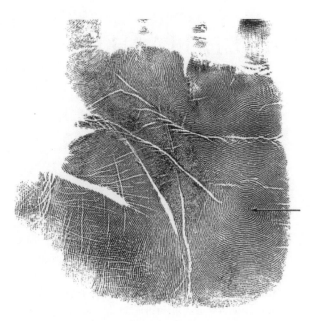

FIGURE 24.11. A whorl pattern on the mount of Luna.

## The Mount of Luna

The lower edge of the palm, lying opposite the mount of Venus, is known as the mount of Luna. As the seat of the subconscious mind, it is the realm of dreams, fantasy, and imagination. A well-padded mount of Luna reveals vigorous creativity as well as a strong desire to protect and take care of others. I've often found a prominent Luna mount on healers, counselors, teachers, and others in the so-called helping professions.

Markings on Luna are important. If the head line runs down onto this mount, its owner will have a strong creative imagination. Novelists, artists, designers, scriptwriters, songwriters, and others whose work involves invention tend to have this configuration.

A whorl pattern on the mount of Luna (Figure 24.11) reflects a strong ability to visualize. Although quite rare, it can be found on the hands of artists and writers. It would be a useful marking for an architect, playwright, or any person whose work demands the ability to communicate visions and impressions to others.

A nature loop (refer to Figure 8.13) indicates a strong affinity with nature. It is especially common among people involved in agriculture, including farmers, beekeepers, environmentalists, and dowsers. Although this loop is not strongly linked to any specific profession, those who have it always have a "feel" for the natural world and are often drawn to careers or hobbies related to nature.

A loop on Luna running the opposite way (i.e., from the center of the palm onto the mount) is known as the memory loop (refer to Figure 8.12). It is an indicator not only of an excellent memory (which can be applied to a wide variety of careers) but of psychic ability as well. It is common on clairvoyants and other psychic people of all types, including card readers, mediums, and psychometrists. Astrologers and palm readers often have this loop, including those who swear that their work is entirely scientific and has nothing to do with extrasensory perception.

The hands of some professional psychics feature a fine line that runs up the mount of Luna and then curves outward toward the lower mount of Mars. In palmistry, this is known as the line of intuition, or the line of Uranus (refer to Figure 22.3). Some individuals have one or more small lines that run diagonally up this mount from the wrist area but do not move in an arc. While not related to any particular line of work, these "intuition lines" reveal a person who has powerful intuition and strong psychic ability. This is a good mark to have if you are trading stocks or need to make a snap decision about a person or an idea.

# ABLE HANDS

IF YOUR PALM IS BROAD AND YOUR FINGERS ARE short, chances are that you're reading this book somewhere in the countryside. As far back as 1843, Captain Casimir Stanislas d'Arpentigny, considered the founder of modern palmistry in the West, noted that country people often have short, broad hands. His observations are still valid today. This type of "able hand" reflects a person with a strong affinity for nature, so it is not surprising that so many people who have it decide to make their home well outside the city limits.

The able, or elementary, hand usually features a squarish palm with short, stocky fingers. Fred Gettings (see page 10) named it the earth hand. You may expect that such a hand would be coarse and heavy, and indeed it sometimes is. However, there are plenty of earth hands that are supple and soft, in spite of their stubby appearance. Countrywomen often have soft, feminine hands that conform to the "square palm, short fingers" description formulated by Gettings.

Lines on the elementary hand tend to be deeper and broader than those found on other hand types. There are few subsidiary (or minor) lines to be seen. The ridges are often strong and clear and will stand out clearly on an inked print. Arches or low loop patterns are common on the fingertips, revealing a practical mind.

The life line on these hands may be either long or short, but it will almost certainly curve strongly out into the palm. This is a sign of strength and energy. Although all the major lines tend to be strongly marked, the life line is likely to be the strongest. The thumb is usually large and rigid, as is the hand as a whole.

Palmists have always associated the middle, or Saturn, finger with the earth, and this finger is usually thick and well formed on able hands. A strong Saturn finger appears to have an association with earth-related professions such as farming and mining.

On elementary hands, fate lines that come from the outer edge of the hand are rare. It is more probable that the destiny line will be tied to the life line at its commencement, which shows that a person is following a career that is predetermined by upbringing or parental influence. Since many farmers come from farming families, it is not surprising that they have fate lines of this type.

A farmer who runs his or her own farm will have signs of independence in the hand, while the farmhand who works for him probably will not. Independence is shown by a separation between the head and life lines at their commencement, as well as by an index finger that stands apart from the other fingers of the hand. Anyone who is self-employed is likely to have at least some space between these two fingers.

Farm work often thickens the skin and coarsens the fingers. This is not an inherent feature of the elementary hand and will begin to disappear if the farmer takes a long vacation. Don't assume that a hand has to be coarse in order to take up a profession like farming. However, most people with very fine skin will probably not take up farming in the first place because they would likely not enjoy strenuous physical work.

Among rural dwellers, farmers and farm laborers form the largest groups of elementary-handed people. There are no set rules on what a farmer's hand should look like other than that it features strong earthy tendencies. There is no reason why a farmer should not also be a musician, a poet, a philosopher, or a computer genius. In these cases, the hands will vary accordingly.

There are a host of rural jobs in addition to farming that may appeal to people with elementary hands. In those parts of the world where forestry is important, there is always work for skilled lumberjacks. Other possibilities include jobs in conservation, road building and maintenance, farm machinery maintenance and repair, landscaping, and mining. While there is no one particular feature of the hand that predestines people for these types of work, signs of strength in the fingers, the thumb, and the mount of Venus should be expected.

A good illustration of an able hand is shown in Figure 25.1. It belongs to a highly skilled automobile mechanic. Raised in the country, the man learned auto mechanics from his father, who was a lifelong tinkerer with cars and had more than a dozen cars on his property. His son was a good learner and eventually got a job as an apprentice mechanic. Within five years, he owned his own garage, specializing in foreign car repairs. He also became an expert in antique car restoration. Though his hand is "able" in appearance, the interesting fingerprints (especially on the Saturn and Apollo fingers) are a clear indication of a higher-elementary type of hand.

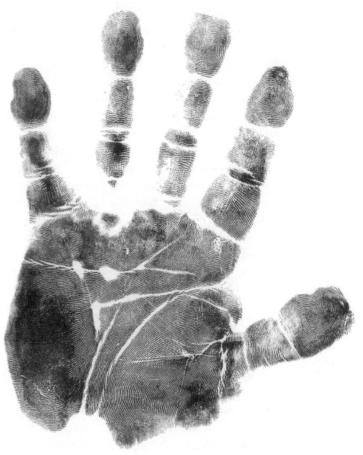

FIGURE 25.1. The hand of a highly skilled auto mechanic.

## FINGERPRINTS AND THE ABLE HAND

Arch fingerprints are found on skilled workers of all types. This doesn't mean that every manual worker will have a predominance of arch fingerprints—just one or two arches are enough to reveal that an individual is inclined toward manual work. While there are also excellent manual workers who don't have arches on their fingertips, nearly every person who has one is bound to take up some type of craft or handiwork as a profession or a hobby.

If you have arch fingerprints, you enjoy touching and handling things. You also probably have a practical mind. You like efficiency and insist that machines and other equipment work properly. You also tend to be impatient with anything vague, useless, or impractical.

If the owner of an able hand with arch fingerprints is highly intelligent, he or she will probably choose a profession that relies heavily on manual skills. Many intellectuals with arch fingerprints dabble in such fields as carpentry, leatherwork, or bookbinding as a hobby. If the IQ of a person with an elementary type of hand and arch fingerprints is average or below average, he or she will probably choose a profession that involves manual labor. Of course, there's nothing wrong with an intellectual choosing a profession involving manual skills: I once knew a housepainter who had doctoral degrees in mathematics and psychology.

Complete sets of arch fingerprints are rare and invariably occur on a person with an unusual and distinctive personality. You'll find them on those involved in professions such as stage design, jewelry repair, and watchmaking. A full set of arches reveals that an individual's career is specialized and highly demanding. It is far more common to find a manual worker with arch-dominant hands—those that contain only two or three arch fingerprints. They are most likely found on the thumb and the Jupiter and Saturn fingers, with loops or whorls on the rest.

If a hand has only a single arch print, it is usually found on the index finger. In such cases, the arch's qualities manifest themselves in personal areas of life and reflect the owner's hopes, goals, and ideals. A person who has a single arch print on Jupiter may well use his or her manual skills at home but will not make a career of them. Yet the psychological aspects of having an arch on Jupiter will come through in that person's efficient, sensible, and practical approach to his or her job.

A single arch on the Saturn finger is sometimes found on the hands of skilled manual workers, despite the presence of an intellect with which they could attain other career goals. An individual with an arch print on the Saturn finger is likely to perform some kind of manual work, even if it does not comprise his or her main career. If it is the only arch print on the hand, manual work at some point in that person's life is almost certain.

When an arch appears on the tip of the Apollo finger, it indicates that a person is likely to enjoy a craft-oriented hobby. It could be pottery, weaving, woodworking, quilt making, or another practical art form. Often this skill can earn a person money and may occasionally evolve into a part-time or full-time career.

Even after reading the hands of thousands of people, I've never seen a solitary arch on the Mercury finger and have seen only a few on the thumb. Arches are normally found on those fingers only when there are arches elsewhere.

Remember that manual workers need not have arch fingerprints. Although you will commonly find them among such workers, there are also many bricklayers, mechanics, and cabinetmakers without a single arch fingerprint. In these cases, other features are present in the hand that point to the type of work the owner is likely to select.

By contrast, loop fingerprints are more common and can turn up anywhere. What is uncommon among manual workers are "high loops" (see page 68), which indicate idealism and a tendency to aim for higher things. Ordinary loops should be regarded as neutral: a worker with loops could be good, bad, or indifferent on the job. Check other aspects of the hand for a more accurate analysis.

Whorl fingerprints indicate concentration, thoughtfulness, and a tendency to be self-contained. If whorl fingerprints are found on the hands of a manual worker, that individual will tend to be highly skilled at his or her work.

The print seen in Figure 25.2 belongs to a highly talented American artist and jeweler who designed accessories for the popular *Dynasty* television series. His work has been sold in major American

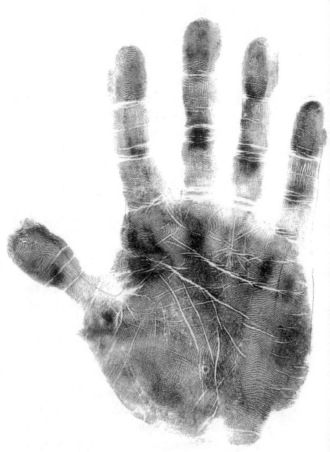

FIGURE 25.2. Arch fingerprints on the hand of a skilled designer and craftsman.

department stores such as Bonwit Teller, Saks Fifth Avenue, and Neiman Marcus, as well as the gift shops at the Dallas Museum of Art and the North Carolina Museum; it has also been featured in *Vogue*, *Harper's Bazaar*, *Savvy*, and other national magazines.

This is a large hand with the long fingers typical of a jeweler, who works on a very small and exacting scale. Arch fingerprints can be found on the Jupiter, Saturn, and Mercury fingers, while the loop on the Apollo finger looks almost like an arch. If you look carefully at the mount of Luna, the seat of the imagination and intuition, you will see that the entire area is covered with thick, swirling skin ridges. Although not a fully-fledged whorl pattern, it certainly lends great strength to the influence of the Luna mount. This jeweler reports that many of his designs come to him in his dreams.

## OTHER FEATURES OF THE ABLE HAND

Apart from the fingerprints, there are a number of structural features that can be found in most able hands. The skin texture tends to be firm, and the ridges of the skin tend to be coarser than you'll find in "mental" hands. The lines are never thin and spidery: they tend to be deep, clear, and well formed. For the most part, the palm is fairly broad and is square or rectangular in shape.

The fingers on the able hand are always strong and substantial. Their tips can be squarish, spatulate, or round, but they are never conic or pointed. Spatulate fingers are often found on outdoor workers or on those whose job involves a lot of physical activity and perhaps danger. Construction workers, bricklayers, and carpenters may have them. Manual workers with square-tipped fingers tend to be very organized and have a talent for working with calculations and measurements. Car mechanics are inclined to have squarish fingertips, as are many pipe fitters and turners. The occasional carpenter will have square-tipped fingers if he is methodical and accurate on the job. It is rare to find a lot of space between the fingers of people with able hands, as these people are rarely daring or adventurous.

Plumbers have no specific features in their hands, although their fingers tend to be short and roughly formed. The tasks of a typical plumber involve dealing with leaks and open sewers and working in tight, uncomfortable places: they put up with more problems than most other skilled tradespeople. A plumber is unlikely to be a precise, neat, or fussy individual, and his rough-and-ready hands often match a rough-and-ready personality.

By contrast, plasterers, locksmiths, and electricians tend to have long fingers, and their hands are usually more gracefully formed. Electricians in particular tend to be long fingered because their job entails concentrating on small details and making precise connections. Their hands and fingers can be any shape, but the length of their fingers usually shows attention to detail.

Some manual work requires even greater concentration than that of an electrician. Watchmakers and jewelers are obvious examples, and makers of optical equipment such as eyeglass lenses can join this group as well. These people invariably have large hands in proportion to body size. It is amazing to watch their large hands perform the most delicate of tasks. The jeweler's hand in Figure 25.2 is at least 20 percent larger than "normal."

## THE HAND OF A SUMO WRESTLER

Earth hands can often be found on athletes, particularly those involved in active, aggressive sports such as football, rugby, and hockey. One such hand belongs to Chiyotaikai Ryuji, one of the leading sumo wrestlers in Japan (Figure 25.3). Born Hiroshima Ryuji in 1976, he ran with local gangs and was involved in petty crime as a teen. Five and a half feet tall and weighing more than 176 pounds at the age of eleven, he was feared by many.

However, he showed considerable promise in judo, coming in third in the All-Japan Middle School Judo Championships. At his mother's urging, he decided to apply to a sumo club in Fukuoka at the age of sixteen and was accepted. So began one of the fastest ascents through the ranks in modern

FIGURE 25.3. The hand of the sumo wrestler Chiyotaikai Ryuji.

sumo history. Chiyotaikai has been an *ozeki*—a sumo of the second highest of nine ranks—since 1999 (at the time of this writing there are only four active *ozeki* in the world). When I first watched Chiyotaikai wrestle at a match near Tokyo in 2006, his agility and swiftness of attack impressed me.

Ozeki Chiyotaikai's large, strong, and fleshy hand is a superior example of a male elementary hand. He has a very large mount of Venus, revealing an abundance of physical energy, plus a long and deep life line. This is atypical of the life lines of many sumo wrestlers, which are often short and weak. Between the physical wear and tear on their bodies (it is not uncommon for two 350-pound wrestlers to tumble out of the ring and crash onto the floor during a match) and their formidable weight, many begin to experience poor health after they reach thirty-five or forty years of age.

The *ozeki* also has a well-developed mount of Luna, along with a very large and clear memory loop on Luna, revealing powerful instincts and an unusually active subconscious mind. His head line is long and clear, revealing a sharp mind and a wide range of intellectual interests. A second fate line appears to begin at approximately forty years of age and runs parallel to a strong and clear Apollo line. This would indicate a new career after Chiyotaikai retires as a sumo. The wide space between the Jupiter and Saturn fingers could indicate self-employment or perhaps a job in the public eye that will bring him stability, material success, and career satisfaction.

# CREATIVE HANDS

Creativity comes in many forms, and there is room to be creative in almost every job: over the years, I have seen creative cooks, creative electricians, creative teachers, and creative homemakers. As a profession, though, creative art—by which I mean the visual arts, such as painting, designing, and illustrating—is a difficult field. Although there are plenty of individuals who earn money by selling their artwork, few are able to support themselves and their families in this way. Even the most successful artists worked at other jobs for years before making a name for themselves and earning enough money to devote themselves full-time to their art.

Artistic ability is not particularly rare. In Victorian times, every young lady was taught to draw and paint. Most had the ability to do it successfully, whether through innate talent or through her own efforts. Today, many software programs offer the basic tools that allow people of even average artistic ability to create Web pages and other types of computer graphics without specialized training. My personal experience confirms that a great many people possess at least some artistic talent.

## FINGERPRINTS AND THE ARTISTIC HAND

Remember that the ring, or Apollo, finger—named for Apollo, the sun god and patron of the arts in Greek mythology—is strongly associated with artistic matters. Generally speaking, long Apollo fingers are common among artists. However, a whorl fingerprint on Apollo is a far more important indicator of artistic ability than length alone.

During the past several years, I have had the pleasure of reading the hands of many students at the Fashion Institute of Technology in New York City. Nearly all are learning to become fashion designers, and some have even created their own product lines. Of this group, most have whorls on their ring fingers. Although I've met many excellent artists and designers who do not have whorls on their ring fingers, you'll probably never meet anyone with a whorl on the Apollo finger who does not have some kind of artistic talent.

Artistic ability can manifest itself in many ways. Some nonprofessional people with whorls on their ring fingers may enjoy painting or sketching as a hobby or may have a talent for designing their own clothes. Nearly all those who have this sign possess a strong flair for color. They show a sense of style in the way they dress and in the way they decorate their homes.

The whorl on Apollo is almost always a sign of artistic ability, and among professional artists, I would estimate that nearly 80 percent have this mark. While it is possible to be talented artistically without having a whorl on the Apollo finger, having a whorl on your ring fingertip is a good mark to have if you enjoy art and want to work with it.

The whorl on Apollo is considered strong when no other finger bears the whorl print. When other fingers feature the whorl pattern, the owner may deny that he or she has a talent for drawing or painting. However, he or she would probably admit to at least some interest in design or decorating, or in building or making beautiful things. Andrew Fitzherbert, the noted palmist, told me that he once met a professional tree surgeon with several whorls on his hands. He was a simple man and claimed no artistic ability whatsoever. In addition to cutting and rehabilitating trees, he often trimmed trees in people's yards. When pressed, he admitted that he had won an award for the artistic way he could trim trees and hedges into any fantastic form the owner desired.

## APOLLO: LENGTH AND FORM

Long ring fingers reach more than two-thirds of the way up the top phalange of the middle, or Saturn, finger. Often this makes the ring finger appear longer than the index, or Jupiter, finger. However, don't use the Jupiter finger as a guide, because it, too, may be longer or shorter than average. Generally speaking, a long Apollo finger is associated with an interest in the arts, including music and theater as well as the visual arts. I've also found that some people who are interested in spiritual matters can have a long Apollo finger, as can compulsive gamblers, especially if the finger bends toward Saturn.

In ancient times, Apollo ruled over fame, wealth, the arts, and what we now call the humanities. For an astrologer, all these aspects are associated with the influence of the sun. Since long Apollo fingers can be linked to these fields of endeavor as well, the gambler, the artist, the actor, and the yogi may all possess them. Of course, if the finger features a whorl on the fingertip, its owner will likely be an artist of some kind. However, if there's no whorl present, examine other aspects of the hand in order to make an accurate analysis. For example, intellectuals and those dedicated to the service of humanity can have longer-than-average ring and little fingers.

## OTHER FEATURES OF THE ARTISTIC HAND

For the most part, you will find very few artists with knotty fingers, unless their work involves careful planning and tremendous attention to detail. The majority of artists have smooth fingers, revealing emotion and intuition. Knotty fingers tend to go with a logical mind that loves to reason, analyze, and investigate. Smooth-fingered individuals, however, work by intuition. The smoother the fingers, the more the person will depend on feelings, instinct, and hunches to move through life.

There is no reason why a logical thinker shouldn't be artistic, but in practice this seldom occurs. Hence, smooth fingers seem to predominate among serious artists. Perhaps the link that connects intuitive thinking, artistic ability, and smooth fingers indicates a dominance of the right hemisphere of the brain. It's also possible that other physiological influences are at work, since some children have knotty fingers while others never develop them, even into old age.

This smoothness can also apply to the texture of the skin. If the hand is smooth, soft, and tapering, it corresponds to Captain d'Arpentigny's vision of the artistic hand, as seen in Figure 26.1. He noted that many artists have particularly smooth hands, often with velvety skin. He found the palms of these hands to be fleshy, with long fingers tapering

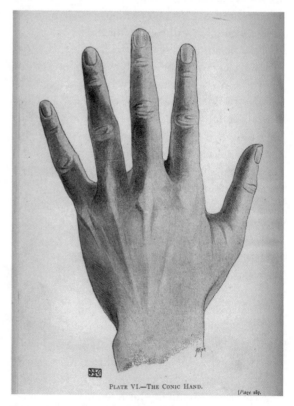

PLATE VI.—THE CONIC HAND.

[*Page 287.*]

FIGURE 26.1. A conic hand. From *The Science of the Hand* (Ed. Heron Allen; London: Ward, Lock and Co., 1886)

to conic tips. In the beginning of the twenty-first century, though, the "pure" conic, or artistic, hand is rarely seen. It may be due to natural selection but more likely is a result of the dramatic expansion and democratization of the art world and greater variety of artistic expression. This is one of the reasons why experienced palmists do not rely completely on d'Arpentigny's system of hand classification today. Yet it is possible to find an occasional example of a "perfect" artistic hand. Those who have this hand—usually women—are virtually certain to possess at least a moderate degree of artistic ability.

Another interesting feature of an artistic person's hand is the creative curve, which is formed when the ulnar edge of the palm arcs outward in a smooth curve. A true creative curve comprises the part of the hand you would thump against a table with your first clenched. A bulge at the top (the mount of Mercury) or at the bottom (the mount of Luna) should be considered an expanded mount rather than a genuine creative curve.

What does it signify? A painter without this formation may well produce competent works of art, but his or her work will probably not be groundbreaking. In contrast, a painter with a creative curve will be more likely to introduce new effects and fresh ideas and produce generally more interesting works of art. He or she will tend to experiment with new media and innovative techniques and will be more prone to establish a unique personal style.

The creative curve is found primarily in the hands of artists and writers and rarely appears in the hands of people who are not involved in those fields. The hand shown in Figure 26.2 belongs to a publisher who has designed three successful magazines known for their artistic layouts and graphics.

Artistic people often have droplets, or small protrusions of flesh, on the undersides of their fingers, as seen in Figure 26.3. A droplet is simply a high, soft padding and is unmistakable once you learn to recognize it. Strictly speaking, droplets are a sign of sensitivity in

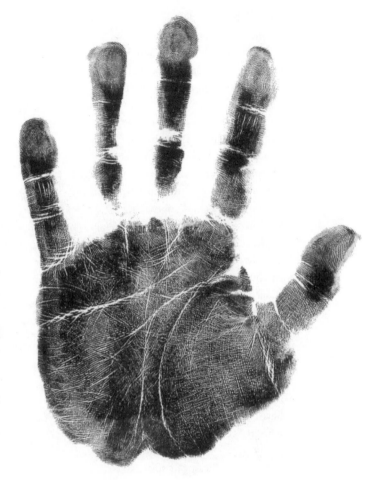

FIGURE 26.2. A hand featuring a creative curve.

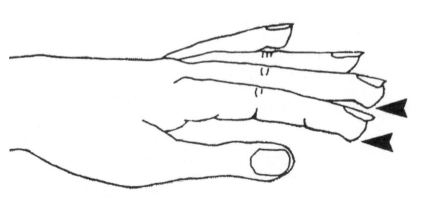

FIGURE 26.3. Sensitivity droplets, or pads.

general, but they denote artistic sensitivity in particular.

Of course, artistic sensitivity is not the same as artistic ability, although the two often go together. People with droplets on their fingertips love beautiful things: the ballet, fine antiques, and works of art. Droplets appear to be common among children but tend to disappear as a child approaches adulthood.

Many books on palmistry associate the line of Apollo, or sun line, with artistic endeavors. Indeed, many successful artists have well-defined Apollo lines on their hands. However, the sun line can have other meanings as well. Strong Apollo lines are often found on the hands of wealthy people and have also been found on people who are famous or live in the public eye. The Apollo line can also be an indicator of spiritual awareness or a deep sense of personal fulfillment.

Long Apollo lines are rare. In most cases, the line consists of a small dash that runs from just above the heart line to slightly below the Apollo, or ring, finger. Only a small percentage begin lower than the heart line and rise from the life line or from the mount of Luna. Although lines of this type may indeed suggest artistic propensities, they may just as easily reveal other meanings. In general, the longer and deeper the Apollo line, the stronger the meaning.

In a hand that reveals several artistic inclinations, a good Apollo line virtually guarantees success in an artistic field. But if supporting signs—such as droplets, a whorl on Apollo, or a pure conic hand—are absent, you'll need to make another interpretation. Like other lines in the hand, the sun line is capable

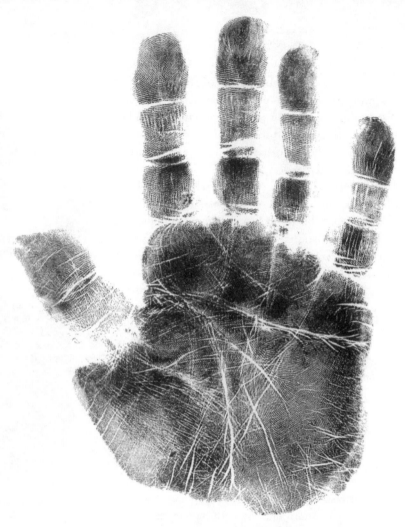

FIGURE 26.4. The hand of the Colombian painter David Manzur.

of growing longer, especially after the age of thirty. For this reason, don't lose heart if your Apollo line is weak or short!

Another place to look for artistic ability is on the mount of Luna. Any skin ridge located on this mount will provide information about the subconscious mind. Since most artists draw their inspiration from that area, it is not surprising that many of them have some kind of marking on the Luna mount.

While all skin ridge patterns on Luna have a particular meaning, none is specifically artistic. However, a whorl pattern will show that an individual has the ability to visualize things clearly, an important gift for all artists and designers. A whorl on Luna is relatively rare but is found more frequently on the hands of artists than in the general public.

There are no rules regarding artistic head lines, heart lines, or fate lines. Some hand analysts suggest that an artistic head line should curve down toward the mount of Luna (revealing a strong imagination), but experience has shown that this is not necessarily so.

However, a good example of an artist with a drooping head line is that of the celebrated Colombian artist David Manzur (Figure 26.4), whom I had the good fortune to meet when I was a university student in Bogotá. Manzur is a painter who works in the traditional techniques employed by classical artists, and his abstract paintings are known for interpreting dramatic events frozen in time. Manzur is a master of chiaroscuro, a technique described as "flashing beams of light with dramatic intensity across spaces murky with a velvety darkness."[1] He is still actively painting and teaching at the age of seventy-eight.

The simian line—a barlike crease across the palm, roughly where the head line would normally be—is another important indicator of artistic creativity. The line is formed before a child is born and is unlikely to change substantially during a person's life.

People with simian lines have a great deal of energy that can be released through creative channels. The owner of a simian line is always happiest when creating, and those who are physically oriented

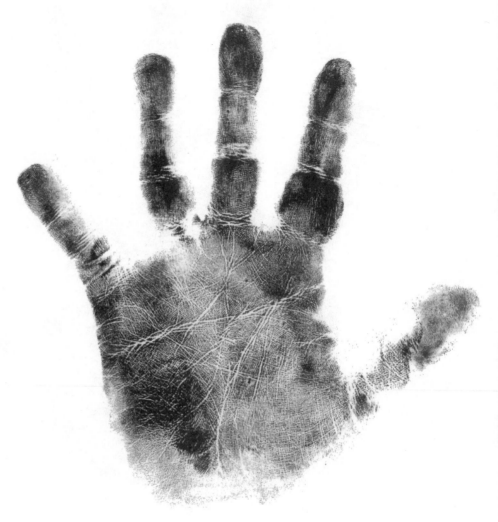

FIGURE 26.5. The hand of the Colombian painter and sculptor Enrique Grau.

love to build things such as furniture, machines, or houses. Mentally inclined people with this line create books, poems, or even entire philosophies. Any person with even a trace of artistic talent plus a simian line will derive great pleasure in painting, drawing, or designing.

The late Enrique Grau, whose hand is seen in Figure 26.5, was a member of the triumvirate of key Colombian artists of the twentieth century, which also included Fernando Botero and Alejandro Obregón. Grau not only had a simian line but also had a whorl on the Apollo finger.

FIGURE 26.6. The hand of an architect and builder.

Grau had a keen interest in palmistry and even created abstract drawings of hands with simian lines. He lived life with great intensity well into his eighties and was constantly working on new paintings, sculptures, or other projects. His dedication to his craft and amazing body of work are typical of an artist with a simian line.

## THE HANDS OF ARCHITECTS

Architecture is a specialized form of artistic work. It requires several years of university training and considerable mental ability in addition to artistic talent. Architecture seems to appeal to people of a quiet nature, and many of the architects I've met have a tendency toward introversion evident in their hands. Usually, their fingers, which tend to be long, are held closely together. However, the fingers can be of any shape, for this is the only artistic field where the usual rule about smooth fingers does not apply. Many architects do have smooth fingers, but sets of developed joints are not unknown among them.

You'll find a small number of architects with vigorous, muscular hands, like those of the architect whose handprint appears in Figure 26.6. Often, architects have worked in the construction industry in addition to having an architectural career, or they make their living as both an architect and a builder.

Spatulate fingers can be found occasionally, especially among architects who spend a good deal of time outdoors.

An architect's hands usually contain no more than one or two classic artistic signs. There may be a whorl on the Apollo finger, a simian line, a long ring finger, or a good Apollo line.

I have never seen d'Arpentigny's "artistic hand" on an architect. On the whole, the architect's hand appears as that of either an intelligent individualist with artistic ability or an energetic outdoor person with strong creative talent.

## THE HANDS OF DRAFTSPERSONS

Draftspersons sometimes don't have artistic signs in their hands, but this doesn't mean that they are devoid of creative talent. After all, it is possible to be a good artist without any signs in the hand at all.

Nearly all draftspersons have squarish fingertips. Indeed, this may be the only clue that a person follows this profession. Certainly, a set of squarish fingertips plus a whorl on the ring finger make drawing-board work a distinct career possibility. Because people with square fingertips love careful, methodical work, this feature, along with artistic ability, is a clear indicator of drafting skill.

Draftspersons tend to be inhibited folk, and it is common to see their head and life lines tied closely together. Their life lines and fate lines are often tied together as well. Generally speaking, there are no gaps between the fingers of draftspersons, with the possible exception of the chief draftsperson, who might have a small space between the Jupiter and Saturn fingers. Many members of this profession have one or more arch fingerprints, a reliable indicator of manual skill.

## THE HANDS OF LANDSCAPE ARCHITECTS

For the most part, the usual artistic features seem to be present on the hands of members of this profession. Those I have examined had certain "earthy" tendencies, or at least some indication that their owners like to spend time out of doors. All possessed spatulate or rounded fingertips, and most had practical head lines as well. None possessed a head line with much of a slope.

## THE HANDS OF INTERIOR DESIGNERS

An interior designer's hand usually has a less earthy appearance than an architect's hand. Smooth fingers are more common, and a whorl on Apollo is almost obligatory. Being primarily an indoor person, an interior designer will rarely have spatulate fingertips, and conic or rounded tips are more commonly found. Interior designers are also likely to have strong imaginative and creative signs on their hands, such as long, sloping head lines, skin ridges on Luna, and unusual fingerprints. You may also find a girdle of Venus, little fingers that separate from the rest of the hand, an abundance of lines, and other indications of a strongly emotional personality.

## THE HANDS OF COMMERCIAL ARTISTS AND WEB DESIGNERS

The hands of commercial artists and Web designers, of course, possess many of the same artistic features found in artists in general. A good example is the hand of Linda James, the commercial artist who created most of the original line drawings that appear in this book (Figure 26.7). Commercial and digital art and Web design often involve deadlines and require much personal and professional discipline. For this reason, features including squarish hands, strong thumbs, clear head lines, and firm hands are useful to have if one is to pursue a career in these fields.

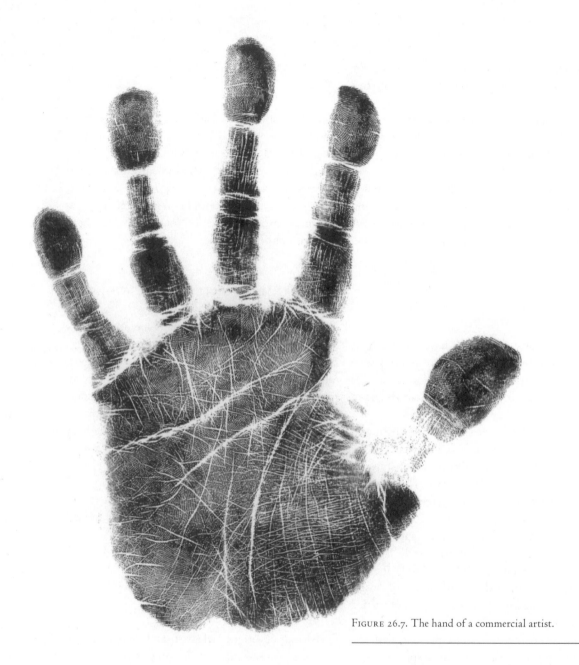

FIGURE 26.7. The hand of a commercial artist.

## THE HANDS OF COMPUTER GRAPHICS PROFESSIONALS

Although computer graphics is related to computer science, it is, by itself, an art form concerned with creating, digitally synthesizing, and manipulating visual content, such as animated movies and video games. While the hands of individuals involved in this exciting field are likely to possess the same creative signs found in those of commercial artists, you will also find indicators of practical ability, such as squarish fingers and arch fingerprints, especially on the Jupiter finger. You may also find an occasional whorl on the Saturn finger, indicating a unique talent or specialized area of study. Long, knotted fingers and joined head and life lines would likely be found on those who are involved with painstakingly detailed work in this fascinating field.

# COMMUNICATING HANDS

Tнe ability to effectively communicate knowledge, ideas, and feelings is a highly useful and important gift. In an information-hungry society in which new channels of communication—in print, audio, and video—are developing constantly, the demand for qualified writers, teachers, speakers, and other communicators is expected to remain high for many years to come.

Although many kinds of people are drawn to professions that involve writing, public speaking, and the media in general, I've found that quite a few of the professional communicators I've seen have hands that are squarish in the palm with longish fingers (also known as air hands), which are often found on people who love to communicate. If you are counseling someone about career direction, once you've determined that the hand you are reading is primarily of the air type, you can recommend a number of possible career choices for its owner.

## THE HANDS OF WRITERS

Let's begin our analysis of specific professions with people who choose writing as a career. Among writers, the largest group is composed of journalists who are employed by newspapers, magazines, and media companies that offer a wealth of information on the Internet. Others work as scriptwriters for the television and film industries. There are also many who earn a living writing books and articles on a freelance basis, as well as a select group of Internet bloggers who get paid for their opinions.

The print shown in Figure 27.1 belongs to the Australian writer Susan Drury, the author of more than thirty published books on a wide range of subjects. Her hand reveals many of the characteristics found in a professional writer, such as knotted fingers (revealing a love for analysis and detail) and a long and "independent" Mercury finger. She also has a clear "writer's fork" (see page 223).

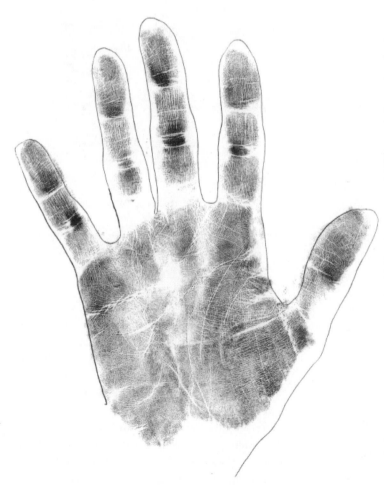

Figure 27.1. The hand of the Australian writer Susan Drury.

Pointed little fingers on a writer reveal someone who writes from inspiration. His or her writing tends to flow without effort, and ideas come into the mind seemingly out of thin air. By contrast, a squarish tip on this finger indicates a writer who is well organized and who works methodically. Sentences are hammered out with a good deal of effort, usually as a result of a number of revisions. This is more likely to happen if the fingers are knotted as well. Authors with square-tipped Mercury fingers are never vague or obscure in their writing. They make sure that every sentence is clear and conveys exactly the meaning the writer intended.

## The Head Line

The head line on a writer's hand is usually long and extends past the base of the Apollo finger. I've never found a short head line on a writer, and only rarely have I found one of average length on a writer's hand.

Straight head lines are found primarily on writers of nonfiction, especially those who focus on subjects of a practical nature, such instructional (how-to), historical, biographical, travel, and financial books. On poets and writers of fiction, the majority of head lines are somewhat curved and slope down toward the mount of Luna.

A head line that droops at the beginning and later moves upward slightly can be found on the hand of the American actor, playwright, novelist, screenwriter, director, and "drag legend" Charles Busch (Figure 27.2). He is the creator of many off-Broadway plays, the star of the films *Vampire Lesbians of Sodom* and *Die, Mommie, Die*, and author of *Tale of the Allergist's Wife*, which had a Broadway run of 777 performances.

His writing tends to be highly imaginative, with a heavy dose of humor. In addition to the slightly sloping head line, he has a composite fingerprint on the thumb, an unusual loop-type fingerprint on the index finger, and a long Mercury finger, a sign of good communication skills. There is also a whorl fingerprint on the Mercury

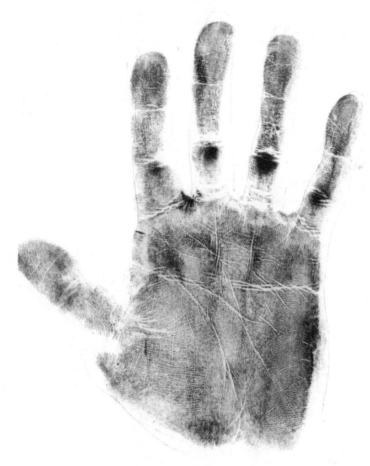

FIGURE 27.2. The hand of actor and playwright Charles Busch.

## The Mercury Finger

Every successful writer whose hand I've seen has an interesting Mercury finger, which is usually long and well formed. Because the Mercury finger normally reaches the joint line of the tip of Apollo, a Mercury finger that reaches higher than this can be classified as long. Nearly all good writers have a very long Mercury finger, sometimes reaching more than halfway up the tip of the ring finger. Although many little fingers are puny when compared to the other fingers of the hand, the writer's little finger has a healthy strength about it. Unlike a Mercury finger found on an earth hand, it is never clumsy looking.

finger and an interesting loop pattern near the top of the mount of Luna, both of which reveal a fertile and active subconscious mind. Although Busch is often flamboyant on stage, the connected head lines on both hands, the closely held fingers, the narrow space between the head and heart lines, the vanity loop, and the broken girdle of Venus reveal a shy and sensitive person. Busch's innate sensitivity is one of his finest assets as a writer and actor and has helped endear him to thousands of fans.

Instead of a regular head line, many writers' hands feature simian lines—Henry Miller reportedly had one—and I have met a number of playwrights who possess them as well.

### The Writer's Fork

Traditionally, a pattern known among palmists as a writer's fork is formed when the head line separates into two small branches at its end, as it does in the hand of the writer Susan Drury (Figure 27.1). This formation reveals a person's ability to draw equally from the imaginative and practical sides of his or her personality. A person with a writer's fork can easily see both sides of an issue and can approach a subject from more than one point of view.

This ability is virtually a requirement for a novelist, because without this multidimensional approach, a novel's characters will be flat and unconvincing. Nonfiction writers can also have this mark, because several perspectives are usually applicable to a discussion of any serious issue. The name *writer's fork* alone is an indication of how common it is to find this pattern on writers' hands.

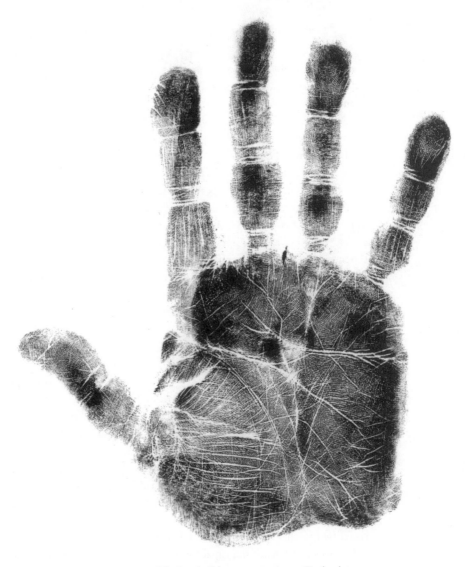

FIGURE 27.3. The hand of the composer Aaron Copland.

## THE HANDS OF COMPOSERS

Writing need not be limited to the written word. Composers of music are writers as well, though they have different abilities. Often the hands of someone who writes music and the hands of someone who writes books share some basic traits, such as an "airy" shape, a strong Mercury finger, a long head line sloping toward Luna, unusual fingerprint patterns, and perhaps a loop of seriousness, revealing a sober, disciplined approach to work.

However, the hand of a composer should also contain some of the traditional signs of musical ability, such as angles, strong lines, or unusual skin ridge patterns on the mount of Luna, revealing a strong intuition and a fertile imagination.

A good example of a composer's hand is that of the dean of American composers, Aaron Copland (1900–1990), shown in Figure 27.3. In addition to many of the features mentioned above, Copland's hand shows arch fingerprints on several fingers, perhaps attesting to a love of hard work and a practical, methodical approach to his craft. Note the clear and gently sloping head line and the lines of intuition moving up the mount of Luna. Of special interest are the unusually strong and clear line of Apollo (often related to creative brilliance, fortune, and fame) and the very long, straight, and prominent Mercury finger.

## THE HANDS OF JOURNALISTS

The hands of journalists do not usually reveal literary tendencies as strongly as the hands of other writers. Many newspaper people have considerable literary acumen, but they are often called upon to utilize skills far broader than writing alone, such as interviewing, reporting, research, and editing, often under the pressure of a deadline. For most journalists, writing is merely one aspect of a complex personality. For this reason, their hands often reveal a wide variety of talents and capabilities.

In addition, anyone who has ever visited a newspaper office knows what an extraordinarily busy place it can be. At first glance, it is a scene of confusion and chaos, with people rushing about, telephones ringing, and voices shouting across the room. A newsroom looks messy regardless of how often it is cleaned. Journalism is no place for someone with a placid disposition, who loves peace and quiet in the workplace.

Because the newspaper (or magazine) "game" requires speed and energy, many journalists tend to have "busy hands." For some, these features include:

- Many interesting-looking lines on the palm

- A large and well-formed mount of Venus

- A firm consistency

- A strong thumb

- A shape that corresponds with the spatulate, or fire, type, revealing energy and intensity

Newspaper editors tend to have short fingernails, as do many editors who work for magazine and book publishers. Short fingernails that are not the result of nail biting are an almost certain indicator of a tendency to find fault. People with short nails delight in pointing out one's mistakes. They notice anything that is wrong and immediately pounce on it.

People with short fingernails tend to be very skeptical and are always looking for a flaw in an argument or theory. An editor knows instinctively how to simplify a concept and reduce text to the bone. No wonder so many good editors have short fingernails and are often such difficult people to work for!

In journalists, arch fingerprints often accompany short nails, adding a practical component to the personality—another good quality for an editor to have. For the most part, experienced editors have risen through the ranks in a profession where a critical faculty and the need to be practical are absolute necessities.

## THE HANDS OF TEACHERS

Teachers make up another major group of communicators. Their profession is a complex and demanding one that utilizes communication as its backbone. It has been said that a good teacher must be a mixture of an actor, dictator, superhero, and sage. Indeed, many gifted teachers combine aspects of all four of these personalities. A good teacher takes delight in explaining things, has an ability to share inspiration, and a desire to teach others *how* to think instead of *what* to think.

The classic mark of a teacher is the so-called teacher's square. It is a small square on the mount of

Jupiter attached to a vertical line that rises from the top of the life line and could be likened to a flag. Indeed, the Indian school of palmistry calls it "the mark of the flag." This square is a sure indicator of teaching ability, and its owner will likely be drawn to a career involving teaching, tutoring, or lecturing.

Often, the teacher's square is formed around the ring of Solomon, a sign of psychological insight. The teacher's square is often found along with Samaritan lines, which reveal a desire to help others as well as an ability to heal them (potentially).

The teacher's square can also be found on the hands of teachers of yoga, cooking, or crafts. It reveals a person with a yearning and an ability to share information in an interesting and authoritative way. A young person with this square may pursue a degree in teaching at a university but will not seek out a teaching career unless other features that favor communication are present in the hand as well.

Julius Spier, the German palmist and author of *The Hands of Children*, observed that female schoolteachers tend to have long index fingers, while male teachers do not.[1] This tendency has probably changed as more traditionally male-oriented jobs have become open to women, especially in the more developed countries. From my own observations, mostly in the United States, I have found that the length of the Jupiter finger more reflects the individual teacher's personality rather than his or her gender.

A strong Jupiter finger is characteristic of people with a strong ego and the desire to take charge.

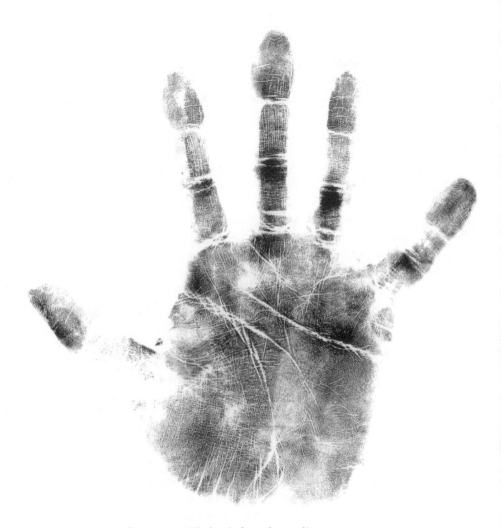

FIGURE 27.4. The hand of a professor of linguistics.

Many women who enter the teaching profession possess these qualities, and certainly those who make a career of teaching need them. Males with a long first finger tend to make strong teachers and good disciplinarians, but most men with long index fingers are more likely to take up other types of professions.

The handprint reproduced in Figure 27.4 belongs to a professor of linguistics at a major American university. In addition to a strong and independent Mercury finger, her hand features a teacher's square, a long and imaginative head line, a loop of seriousness, and a memory loop to the right of the end of the head line. All her fingerprints have high loops, revealing keen intelligence, optimism, and an ability to relate to many different kinds of people. Although this professor has a reputation as an excellent lecturer, she is best known for her pioneering research into the structure of Mayan languages.

The loop of seriousness is fairly common among teachers, as are strong Saturn, or fate, lines. Both these features are found on people who follow a stable and responsible career like teaching. In addition, teachers tend to talk a lot, and they often possess hand features associated with verbal fluency, such as long head lines and long, strong Mercury fingers. As can be expected, these characteristics are often found among members of other professions that involve talking, including announcers, politicians, salespeople, and auctioneers.

A long tip on the Mercury finger—as seen in Figure 27.4—indicates a skill with words. All sorts of wordsmiths, from poets to crossword puzzle enthusiasts, tend to have this long top joint.

## THE HANDS OF RADIO BROADCASTERS

Andrew Fitzherbert reported that radio and television broadcasters often have a special formation on their Mercury fingers.[2] He found that the top joint not only is longer than average but also is unusually wide. Unlike a spatulate fingertip, the entire joint is thicker than the two lower joints of the Mercury finger.

This natural thickening of the top joint is considered an infallible sign of talkativeness. While rare, it has been found on disc jockeys and talk radio hosts, who never seem to run out of things to say. Talkative people often have unusually long head lines as well.

For the most part, radio broadcasters tend to have strong, stable hands. In order to achieve success in such a highly competitive field, one must be both hardworking and patient: only a stable person can do this. The hands of these people are more down-to-earth than you might think from listening to them on the air.

The most provocative and interesting radio personalities often have broad, firm hands, with a strong thumb and the fingers held closely together—all features of a stable, conservative person. I have rarely come across a broadcaster who carried his or her fingers spread in an extroverted manner, unless he or she had hopes of switching careers from radio to television.

For all their talkativeness, many radio broadcasters are not true extroverts. Their work is done inside a tiny cubicle, either alone or with occasional guests. It is essentially solitary work, and few genuine extroverts would want to make a career of it. (Extroverts often go into television broadcasting instead.)

Two features in the hand that are useful for the radio personality to have are loop fingerprints and a wide space between the lines of the head and heart. Loops reflect an easygoing manner and the ability to get along with others. The radio broadcaster must appeal to a relatively wide audience and when interviewing guests must appear to be interested in what they have to say. These are skills that come easily for people with loop fingerprints. Individuals with other fingerprint patterns often lack this congenial nature and may need to make an effort to acquire it.

A wide space between the heart and head lines isn't essential for radio broadcasting, but it reveals a certain openness in viewing the world. People with this space tend to be tolerant toward different types of individuals and are more likely to listen to—and encourage—diverse points of view.

## THE HANDS OF TELEVISION BROADCASTERS

Like radio, television employs many people who are unseen by the general public, and most people involved in the television industry never appear on the screen. Although they may be offscreen, people with air hands love to work in the media, and they can often be found at radio and television stations working as secretaries, production assistants, researchers, and programming executives. They are curious and hungry for information, and they love working in the type of exciting and ever-changing environment that a television station provides. Some can even be found behind a camera and among the technical staff.

## THE HANDS OF ADVERTISING PROFESSIONALS

The final group of communicators comprises those who choose a career in advertising. Because advertising agencies provide jobs to a great many writers and artists, signs of these abilities are present in the hands of a number of people in this profession.

Advertising agencies offer people a wide range of jobs, but common to all of them is the need to be flexible yet accurate and punctual. As a result, many people who work in advertising agencies are bright and focused, as shown by a clear and well-developed head line. In advertising people, this line is usually long, with a strong bow-shaped curve, revealing a creative, imaginative way of thinking. Interesting skin ridge patterns on the mount of Luna are often found as well.

If the head line is straight, it is usually long and features a writer's fork. Other signs of talent are sometimes present, such as a long Apollo finger, a long Mercury finger, whorl fingerprints, or a strong, well-shaped thumb.

Over the years, I have read the hands of many successful people working in advertising, and I have rarely found a sensitive, "mental" heart line on any of them. This may be due to the fact that this competitive field involves a lot of rough-and-tumble negotiation that would not be attractive to a person who is overly sensitive or prone to emotional extremes. People involved in advertising tend to have a thrust-out Jupiter finger, which reveals self-assertion, independence, and the desire to stand out in a crowd. They also tend to have a prominent mount (or mounts) of Mars.

# ENTERTAINING HANDS

chapter
# 28

The life and work of famous entertainers fascinate many of us. The excitement of fame and the money and romance of being a famous actor, singer, or musician have led many to pursue a career in the entertainment industry. Whether one dreams of becoming a leading character in a soap opera or fantasizes about being an internationally known rock star, the desire to work in the public eye as a successful entertainer is, for many, a life-long dream.

Is there anything special in the hand that reveals the potential to become a famous actor? Does the gravel-voiced, Grammy-winning singer have hands similar to those of an operatic tenor? Is there something in the hand that whispers "Fame!" even from early childhood?

Actually, there *are* lines to look for and patterns to recognize in the hands of entertainers. If you have these signs in your own hands, you may be destined for center stage yourself. In addition to artistic ability, an entertainer's hand must show persistence, dedication, adaptability, and the capacity for hard work. We also cannot ignore the element of luck, which often plays a decisive role in the careers of many successful entertainers. One such example is Richard Gere, who skyrocketed to fame for playing a sex worker in the film *American Gigolo* (1980). Gere accepted the lead role after both John Travolta and Christopher Reeve turned it down.

## THE FATE LINE

The first place to look for potential success in the entertainment field is the fate line, the vertical line that (in most hands) runs up the middle of the palm. In its purest form, the line begins near the wrist and moves straight toward the middle, or Saturn, finger without breaks or islands.

However, the majority of fate lines are not as clear-cut as this. They often start higher on the palm and usually have various minor breaks and irregularities along the way. Most end near the mount of Saturn, although they can also stop short and veer to either side of the mount. All these variations have a story to tell.

Fate lines beginning near the wrist and joined to the life line reveal an unadventurous personality. This usually—but not always—implies a career that's quiet and stable. Some palmists believe that fate lines tied to life lines indicate a person who follows the profession of a parent or a person whose parent has had a strong influence on his or her career.

By contrast, fate lines that begin nearer to the center of the wrist and thus are separated from the life line are found on people who follow almost any career. If the line starts low, down at the bottom of the palm, however, its owner is likely to enter a career early in life, even during the teenage years. Fate lines that start farther over, on the mount of Luna, take a slanted path in order to make their way up to the Saturn finger. While some palmists believe that this is an indicator of a variety of careers, I've also found it on individuals who enjoy a career in the public eye. The farther over it gets, the more of a performer the person will be. While people with this pattern may or may not aspire to be famous (to verify, see if there is a wide space between the Jupiter and Saturn fingers), they need to interact with people. Any job that puts them in the spotlight will suit them admirably. To conclude that entertainers have this sort of fate line is correct. They often do.

Remember that there are many public jobs outside the entertainment field, such as politics, public relations, and sales. While the performing arts are always a magnet for anyone with this type of fate line, other people-oriented careers attract people with this destiny line as well.

Helen Hayes was a two-time Academy Award–winning actress whose career spanned more than seventy years. Like many who lived and worked in the public eye, her hand (shown in Figure 28.1) reveals two strong Saturn lines originating in the mount of Luna.

Actors who begin as child stars often have fate lines that begin very low on the mount, although the more common position is a little higher up on the hand. Some entertainers have two fate lines on their hands. When this happens, the first line rises only halfway up the palm, at which point the second line sweeps in from the side of the hand. This indicates a change from one career path to another. The date can be estimated fairly accurately from the place on the hand where the change takes place. It always indicates a shift from a sedate occupation to one that is more public. If the two fate lines run parallel to each other, it indicates that a person will follow two careers simultaneously, an increasingly common occurrence these days.

We should also examine the top of the fate line. Most lines stop just above the heart line. As long as the fate line ends more or less below the Saturn finger, however, the exact spot is unimportant. Cheiro, the famous Irish palmist of Edwardian days, wrote that a fate line ending at the heart line was indicative of a career thwarted by emotional upheaval. Although a great many fate lines end this way, I haven't found that they are necessarily related to emotional trauma.

There's also a traditional belief among palmists that a career line running up into the Saturn finger indicates someone whose life is predestined, or who is a "child of fate." My experience is that such a line

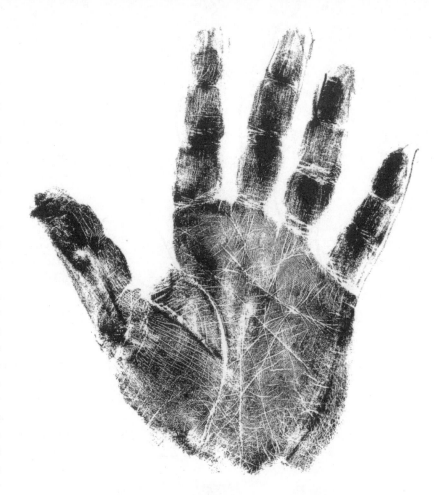

FIGURE 28.1. The hand of the legendary actress Helen Hayes. From *Lions Paws* by Nellie Simmons Meier (New York: Barrows Mussey, 1937)

reveals a career that continues far past normal retirement age. In the case of entertainers like George Burns, Eddie Albert, or Helen Hayes, a fate line of this type can be expected.

## THE LADDER OF SUCCESS AND THE TRIDENT

Two special markings often occur on the hands of entertainers. The first is especially common among people involved in radio or television broadcasting; it consists of a patch of lines running parallel to the fate line near its upper end. It has been called the ladder of success (Figure 28.2), and it is found on people who work their way to the top of a profession over the years. Its presence indicates a self-

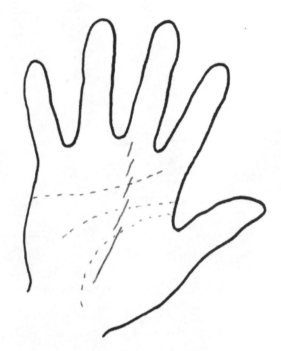

FIGURE 28.2. The ladder of success.

FIGURE 28.3. The trident.

made man or woman who has triumphed in his or her career through perseverance. The other is a trident at the top of the fate line (Figure 28.3), which is traditionally considered a sign of success and is often found on the hands of well-known entertainers.

## THE SUN LINE

Another interesting mark found on successful entertainers is a strong Apollo, or sun, line. This line indicates the potential for fame, money, and artistic success, depending on the other features of the hand. Fame and money often go together, so it isn't surprising that famous performers often have a deep and long sun line. The most favorable kind of sun line rises out of the fate line, which indicates that a person has the potential to achieve fame from his or her career.

One example of a strong sun line can be found in the hand of the film legend Marlene Dietrich, reproduced in Figure 28.4. In addition to a superb Apollo line, she has a long fate line that originates in the mount of Luna and a clear and imaginative head line. Her Jupiter finger is long and strong, as is her thumb. Both are indicative of a strong personality. The multitude of deep lines in her hand shows a great deal of nervous energy. The Mercury finger is very straight and long, though set somewhat low. Some palmists believe that a low-set Mercury finger indicates unresolved emotional difficulties from childhood.

Another strong Apollo line can be found in the hand of the Tony and Emmy Award–winning American actor Howard Da Silva (1909–86), seen in Figure 28.5. After finding early employment as a steelworker, Da Silva began his acting career when he was in his late twenties. Even though he was black-listed from Hollywood during the anticommunist scare of the 1950s, Da Silva eventually starred in more than a dozen Broadway plays and in more than sixty motion pictures, including *The Lost Weekend* and *1776*.

Whorls on most of his fingers, as well as a strong and sloping head line, confirm Da Silva's creative originality as a performer. The Mercury finger is especially long and strong. Like that of Dietrich, it is also set low on the hand. His hand has both a strong loop of seriousness and a loop of humor, revealing a balance between ambition and enjoyment. The large Venus mount reveals abundant energy: Da Silva fathered several children while in his sixties and was working well into his

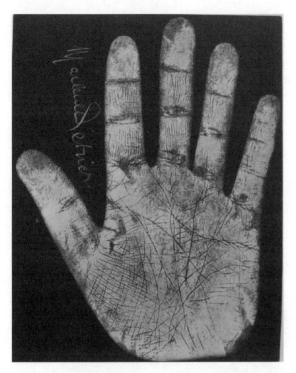

FIGURE 28.4. The hand of Marlene Dietrich. From *Hand und Personlichkeit* by Marianne Raschig (Hamburg: Gebruder Enoch Verlag, 1931)

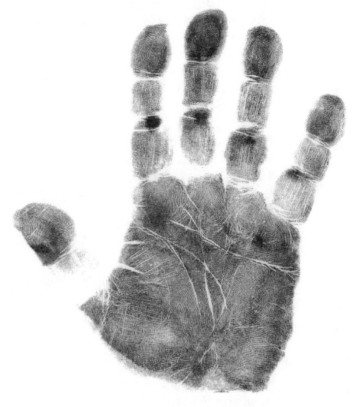

FIGURE 28.5. The hand of the renowned actor Howard Da Silva.

seventies. The Apollo line appears to break and then continues to the top of the palm, revealing professional success late in life.

A strong Apollo line can also be found on the hand of Heywood "Woody" McGriff, Jr. (1958–94), a choreographer and modern dancer who performed nationally with the Frank Holder Dance Company, the Bill Evans Dance Company, and the Bill T. Jones/Arnie Zane Dance Company, among others (Figure 28.6). At the time of his death, he was an associate professor of dance at the University of Texas, Austin, where he also served as resident choreographer.

The deep and clear lines in his hand reveal abundant energy. The long humanitarian heart line reveals a passionate individual: the *New York Times* described him as "a long, lean dancer of special intensity, who brought an equal passion to teaching dance."[1] His long, clear, and drooping head line betrays a strong creative imagination, while his long and straight Mercury finger is a sign of good communication skills and personal honesty.

Born in humble circumstances, Woody McGriff overcame tremendous odds to become a success: his clear and strong fate line begins at an early age and splits when he left professional dancing to become a professor at thirty years of age. Although Woody wasn't a household name, his long and clear Apollo line is indicative of a highly accomplished performer and teacher who gained fame and respect from his colleagues in the dance world.

Is it possible to attain fame as an entertainer without having a strong Apollo line? Yes, but it is still remarkable how many popular actors and singers have good Apollo lines on their hands. Many famous artists, writers, and millionaires do also. Remember that the sun line is especially prone to changes over time and can appear to grow stronger when a person begins to achieve success in life.

## THE RAJA LOOP

First noted by Beryl Hutchinson in her book *Your Life in Your Hands*, the Raja loop, or loop of charisma, is found between the Jupiter and Saturn fingers.[2] For an entertainer, or anyone who works in the public eye, it is a very favorable marking to have.

The Raja loop reveals charisma, that rare ability to attract and command attention. Those who have it naturally come to the public's attention and are prominent in whatever field they enter. Everyone takes notice of a person with the charisma loop. Although charismatic people seldom have any special quality one can put a finger on (such as extraordinary good looks), they tend to stand out in a crowd. Although rare, a high proportion of Raja loops occurs among entertainers who command a loyal following.

## LINES OF INFLUENCE

Virtually all famous people have a large number of small lines, or influence lines, on the mount of Venus, inside the life line. Lines on this mount often relate to important events and are a favorite of those who practice the fortune-telling side of palmistry, in which the palmist looks for specific details of a person's destiny.

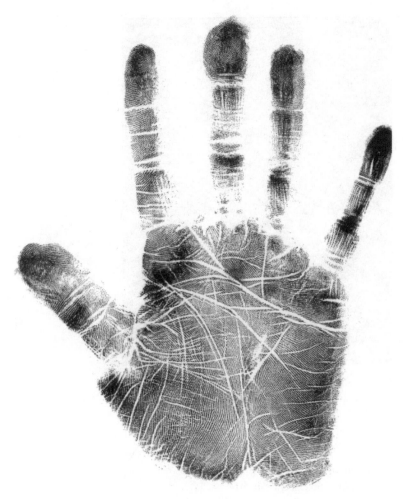

FIGURE 28.6. The hand of the dancer and teacher Heywood "Woody" McGriff, Jr.

Most influence lines—especially those that run parallel to the life line—are said to relate to the important people in our lives. Since famous people are almost always surrounded by others, you would expect to find many such lines on a celebrity's Venus mount. Occasionally, you will even be able to date the time when a performer first appears before the public (as well as the time of his or her retirement from show business) simply by looking for a clustering of these lines on a section of the life line. Look for several long lines running parallel to the life line rather than for lines crossing over it.

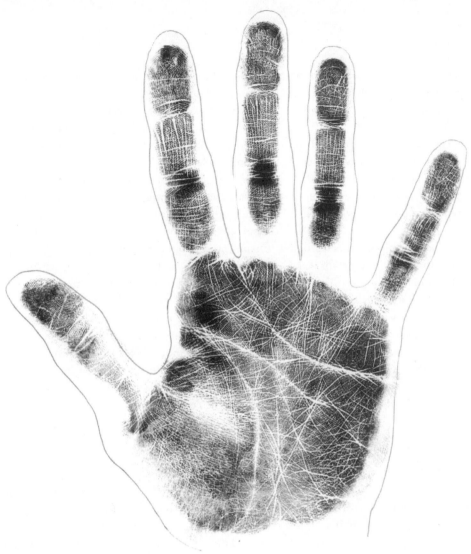

FIGURE 28.7. The hand of Rosanne Cash.

## THE ANGLES

Musicians, singers, and dancers tend to have one important feature of the hand in common—the angles, found on the bottom joints of the thumb. The first angle occurs where the joint rises from the wrist, and the second occurs where it parts from the thumb.

In most hands, the angles are barely noticeable, and a pencil outline of the hand will reveal almost no bump at these points. However, when we look at the hands of a born musician, we can often see a prominent angle at each joint. Any photograph of John Lennon or Elvis Presley that shows their hands will illustrate the angles nicely.

Acrobats and dancers often have well-developed angles in their hands. Professional golfers can have the lower angle developed without the upper angle. Beryl Hutchinson observed that comedians often have the upper angle, which she called "the angle of order in Time," well developed.[3]

A prominent angle can be seen on the hand of Rosanne Cash, the Grammy-winning singer, songwriter, and author (Figure 28.7). Her strong yet sensitive hand features a practical head line with a writer's fork, and a sensitive heart line ending between the middle and index fingers, a sign of balance between the heart and the head in relationships. The palm also contains several rings of Solomon and a grouping of Samaritan lines, revealing healing ability and a strong interest in metaphysics. Several fine diagonal lines on the mount of Luna reveal strong intuition, while high loops on the fingertips are a sign of intelligence and imagination and the ability to be inspired and to inspire others. Her hand contains two fate lines: one moves up the middle of her hand, while another begins in the mount of Luna, a marking often found on people who work in the public eye.

All the fingers have well-developed knots, a sign of an analytical person who focuses on details. Like those of other good communicators, Cash's Mercury finger is long as well as straight, showing that she has an honest and direct way of dealing with others. There is also a moderate space between her somewhat long Jupiter finger and her Saturn finger, showing that Cash is comfortable being before the public. The space between the ring and little fingers reveals an independent person who does not follow the crowd.

## THE MOUNTS OF VENUS AND MARS

In addition to the angles, musicians have other features on their hands specific to their profession, including many found on the mount of Venus. Remember that the Venus mount can vary from fairly flat to very plump, but on a small number of hands, the mount is not rounded at all but rather shaped like a sharp ridge running toward the life line. Andrew Fitzherbert considers this a sign of perfect pitch: the ability to hit a note exactly and to discern whether anyone else is even slightly off-key. The formation is rare, yet when it does occur, it is more likely to be found on the hands of an opera singer than a rock star. Of course, it is possible to have a good sense of pitch without this formation, but its presence is seen as an infallible sign that a person's sense of pitch is perfect.

The British palmist John Lindsay put forward a theory that singers may have strong mounts of Luna and Mars negative joined together.[4] When this occurs, they form a sort of long, kidney-shaped pad from the wrist to the heart line. Beryl Hutchinson noted that dancers also tend to have the Luna mount well padded just where it leaves the wrist, forming a sort of step from the wrist to the mount itself.[5]

Skin ridge patterns on the mount of Venus are associated with the love of music in its various forms. Loops that run onto the mount from the edge of the thumb are said to be associated with a love of brass instruments and big-band music.

A small oval patch of ridges cutting across the mount of Venus, known as the bee (refer to Figure 8.16), is considered an infallible sign of love for the music of stringed instruments. Although a great many guitarists and violinists may have this mark, remember that it indicates primarily a love of music rather than a talent for making it. You are as likely to see this formation in the audience at a string recital as among the performers.

## THE FINGERS

Musicians who specialize in piano or organ music usually possess squarish fingertips. Playing the harp tends to flatten out the fingertips and gives them a spatulate appearance. This is a purely physical effect and should not be interpreted psychologically. Drummers often possess very broad hands with the lines deeply etched: these appear similar to the hands of a professional wrestler or massage therapist. In addition, professional drummers usually have well-developed angles of the thumb.

## OTHER "ENTERTAINING" CHARACTERISTICS

The personalities of actors, musicians, and other entertainers are of course tremendously varied. However, as a group, entertainers tend to be psychologically complex and often reveal many conflicting strengths and weaknesses in their hands. In an actor's hand, for example, you may see individual fingers that seem to be too long or too short. We discussed finger length and its psychological significance earlier. There may be various types of kinks or irregularities in the fingers as well. In all kinds of entertainers, air hands abound; also, fate lines originating in the mount of Luna turn up frequently. Apollo lines are usually found on the hands of successful entertainers, and their head lines are long (which is often associated with talkativeness and with a wide range of intellectual interests). Long Mercury fingers—often accompanied by a long top phalange—reveal a love for communication.

The Mercury finger is especially linked to the emotional side of the personality. Problems in this area can often be detected by a little finger that is held apart from the rest of the fingers. If the little finger is set low on the hand, it can also be an indicator of emotional difficulties. It may contribute to a person's creativity, but it may indicate a difficult personal life.

Look through any celebrity magazine and focus on the Mercury fingers of the stars—if the finger doesn't sport a ring, it will often be carried away from the other fingers. If this is the case, it shows that emotional anxiety may be a motivating force behind that person's drive to act out psychological problems on the stage or screen. Of course, there are plenty of actors to whom this does not apply, but it cannot be denied that in many cases, creative brilliance in an actor, artist, dancer, writer, or musician stems from the subconscious desire to explore and work through certain psychological difficulties.

# BUSINESS HANDS

Executive ability and business skill show up clearly in the hands—as does the lack of them. Two or three good signs recorded in the hands bode very well for business and financial success. Two or three problematic signs can indicate that a person may have a difficult time succeeding in a business or executive career.

## SERIOUS OR HUMOROUS?

The primary indicators pointing to business ability are found in the skin ridge patterns of the palm. The loop of seriousness (found between the middle and ring fingers) is a good business indicator, while the loop of humor (located between the ring and little fingers) is not.

Approximately 35 percent of us are said to have one loop or another, and some people have both loops together on the same hand. The loop of seriousness occurs about twice as frequently as the loop of humor.

These loops mean much more than merely the ability to make money. They indicate one's basic attitude toward life. A loop of seriousness reveals a person who is serious, dependable, and pragmatic; a loop of humor reveals an essentially optimistic, good-humored, and fun-loving personality.

The loop of seriousness can vary in size from very small to quite large. The bigger and clearer it is, the more serious the owner is likely to be. Loops vary according to their length and width and the thickness of the ridges that comprise them. Ridge thickness, in fact, can vary throughout the palm.

Strictly speaking, the loop of seriousness isn't primarily a business sign but rather a reflection of a serious and sober attitude toward life. In practice, this attitude correlates very strongly with business success. Good loops of seriousness are found on highly reliable and ambitious people. I've seen them on CEOs of many big companies, including those involved in advertising, banking, and telecommunications. They always arrive at work on time, avoid taking sick days unless they are truly ill, carry out their duties well, and pay their debts. They believe in the work ethic and dislike being unemployed. The loop of seriousness is even more common among female executives than among their male counterparts. This may be due to the fact that female executives are still in the minority and those who pursue a career as an executive or in business administration tend to have strong personalities.

As students, people with strong loops of seriousness work hard, accept responsibility, take their duties seriously, and do their homework. As parents, they tend to be very involved in the lives of their children. Yet don't make the mistake of thinking that a person with a loop of seriousness is a paragon of virtue, because whenever we examine a hand, other factors need to be taken into account. Criminals have exactly the same percentage of loops of seriousness as the general population. Contract killers probably have it in the same proportion as well. After all, they are serious, disciplined people!

Among the 60 percent of the population that has some sort of a loop of seriousness, those with other aspects of strength in their hands are more likely to succeed in business. Although people with weak loops and soft hand features may share the same responsible attitudes, they tend to be content with jobs involving less pressure.

The loop of humor has exactly the opposite meaning. A person with this mark tends to be good-humored. He or she may enjoy working but has no problems with unemployment if it should occur. People with loops of humor feel that pleasure can be found in everything, so why should they pursue a difficult or stressful career?

A person with a loop of humor is often content with earning just enough to meet basic expenses and is rarely consumed by the desire to earn vast sums of money. For those with a loop of humor, spare time is very attractive. A good company is more important than a large salary. A pleasant working environment is worth more than being famous or receiving large financial rewards. People with loops of humor know how to enjoy themselves.

While reading hands at a party sponsored by Martha Stewart Omnimedia years ago, I was surprised to see that Stewart, the well-known media mogul, television personality, and homemaking guru, has a loop of humor on her hands. Aware that she's known for her intense work ethic and remarkable business acumen, I mentioned the meaning of this loop to her. She responded that enjoying her work was paramount and the challenges of running her various enterprises were fun and exciting. In addition, Stewart is known for her quick wit and self-deprecating sense of humor, qualities often found in owners of this loop.

Ironically, Stewart's loop of humor may have played a role in her 2004 insider-trading scandal and subsequent conviction and imprisonment. A person with a loop of seriousness would have taken a long, hard look at the consequences of the impulsive stock transaction that landed Stewart in trouble (which, in her case, enabled the billionaire to avoid a mere $45,673 loss) and would have decided against it.

Another famous media person with a loop of humor was Walt Disney (1901–66), the film producer, director, screenwriter, voice actor, animator, entrepreneur, and philanthropist. Disney's hand is as expressive as his famous signature (Figure 29.1).

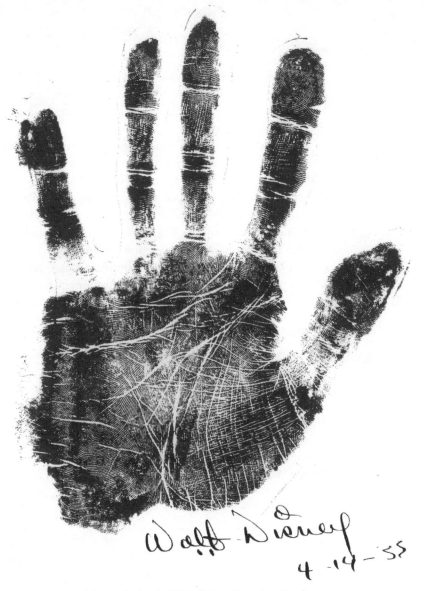

FIGURE 29.1. The hand of Walt Disney. From *Lions Paws* by Nellie Simmons Meier (New York: Barrows Mussey, 1937)

In addition to a loop of humor, his hand shows a memory loop just under the top branch of his forked head line, which appears to be connected to an influence line. The original head line plunges toward Luna, the seat of the imagination and the subconscious mind. Disney's heart line is long and deep and is accompanied by a long and fragmented girdle of Venus, revealing an emotionally sensitive person who was guided more by his heart than by his head. He was a very people-oriented individual and by all accounts enjoyed visiting with Disneyland employees and visitors. Interestingly, Disney's fate line is weak and fragmented, and his Apollo line consists of two weak parallel lines, a rarity among people as wealthy, famous, and successful as he was.

Disney also had several archlike fingerprints, revealing the ability to create with his hands, along with a very straight and long Mercury finger; both the Mercury and Jupiter fingers stand out from the others, showing independence.

It is difficult to evaluate Walt Disney's business acumen from his hand. Many considered him the creative force behind the myriad cartoon characters, films, amusement park rides, and other attractions in the Disney empire, while his brother, Roy, was said to be more involved with the business side. Some of Disney's projects were financial failures, while others were enormously successful. He reportedly said that one of his biggest mistakes was not to have bought enough inexpensive land to accommodate Disneyland's eventual expansion. When Disney built his "Florida Project" years later, he created dozens of shadow companies to quietly assemble the thousands of acres needed for what was to become Disney World.

## THE SATURN FINGER: SERIOUSNESS AND RESPONSIBILITY

Business and executive ability often make themselves known in the characteristics of the middle, or Saturn, finger. This digit varies little from hand to hand and is so stable that palmists use it to measure the relative lengths of the Jupiter and Apollo fingers. The two emotional qualities linked to the Saturn finger are seriousness and responsibility.

On rare occasions, the Saturn finger may appear abnormally long or short. When this happens, business ability can fluctuate accordingly. In addition, this finger tends to be well developed on many successful businesspeople. In them, it will tend to be thicker and stronger than the other fingers in the hand.

Long, strong Saturn fingers reveal a love for money and other material things. Their owners work hard for whatever it will bring them. Work and material possessions are their primary interests, and they often become workaholics. By the same token, they tend to be far more interested in pursuing a profitable occupation than an enjoyable one and will accept a high-paying job irrespective of what it entails, especially if a loop of seriousness is present. We can be almost certain that for those with long Saturn fingers, material gain will be a driving force in life.

Short Saturn fingers are even rarer than long ones and almost never turn up among members of the business community. A man or woman with a short middle finger lacks a basic work instinct. He or she has little interest in employment, dislikes responsibility, and is often careless about his or her material environment.

In spite of being associated with chronic unemployment, this feature is not linked to criminal behavior. People with short Saturn fingers can be law-abiding, but they refuse to take life too seriously. Although they are not necessarily amusing (unless they have a loop of humor), they often make pleasant company. Their carefree nature makes them easy to get along with.

While doing a publicity tour in Australia to promote the first edition of my book *Sexual Palmistry* in 1986, I met a man whose Saturn finger was actually shorter than his Jupiter and Apollo fingers. The man was a publisher of several erotic magazines, including a guide to local strip clubs, escort services, and massage parlors. Although his magazines made him a lot of money, the publisher considered his business more of a hobby than serious work. He found it amusing that he could earn a good living while enjoying himself in the process.

A well-developed or poorly developed Saturn finger may sometimes be accompanied by other signs of business skill often overlooked by hand readers. For example, Andrew Fitzherbert teaches that anyone wearing a ring on this finger is likely to be very involved in his or her work. This is especially true if no other rings are worn on the hand.

While many believe that wearing a ring is purely a matter of individual choice, experience shows that our choice of rings is often determined by our unconscious psychological preoccupations. It's not uncommon to find that rings worn on the Saturn finger are usually large and ostentatious. It's almost as though a person obsessed with money needs to hang a large, heavy sign proclaiming that fact on his Saturn finger!

## THE FATE LINE

The longer and straighter the Saturn, or fate, line, the greater the likelihood that a person will be grounded in a stable career path. Business- and other career-oriented individuals are more than likely to have strong and clearly marked fate lines because they know what they want out of life and strive to achieve it.

However, remember that a long, unbroken Saturn line does not indicate that a person will have only one career. Someone with such a line may actually change jobs several times. What he or she will not do is to change career focus continually. Ten years or more in each job is the normal pattern among businesspeople, although some executives may spend only a couple of years with each employer. Among those with long, unbroken Saturn lines, chances are good that each job will be related in some way to the previous one and not involve a totally different field of work.

It is common to learn that a person with a long and unbroken Saturn line has indeed followed a single line of work throughout his or her entire life. Remember that the Saturn line is primarily an index of psychological stability. It reveals steadiness, a capacity to deal with difficulties, and the ability to adhere to goals. The stronger the line, the stronger these qualities. In practice, this nearly always works out as a stable attitude toward employment. Only on rare occasions will you meet someone with a strong, unbroken fate line who has held many jobs in different fields.

Short fate lines may be deficient at either the top or the bottom. Even if they are of a respectable length, they are considered faulty if they are composed of three or more overlapping sections. Either of these formations indicates a varied career.

Fate lines that stop short of the head line do not necessarily mean that a person's career path will end at midlife. However, it is very common to find a person with such a line who has lost interest in work at about forty years of age, which is a time some psychologists refer to as the midlife crisis. Others with this type of fate line may change careers at about this time.

Fate lines that are short because they begin halfway up the palm may indicate several years of restlessness before a person settles into a definite career path. Late-starting fate lines are often found among late bloomers, who discover their career path late in life. Islands, branches, and overlapping breaks in this line often correspond to precise dates of career change.

Fate lines that begin joined to the life line indicate inhibition in the early years of life. This pattern is similar to having the head and life lines strongly joined together at their commencement. People who have these signs tend to be careful and cautious. They are generally conservative and dislike major changes. I've seen this type of hand on bankers and other executives who tend to be very careful with their or another person's money.

Many who have the tied fate line are likely to enter a career that is suggested by their parents rather than choose one for which they have a natural aptitude or interest. These people often enter the family business or take up the same career as a parent, uncle, aunt, or grandparent. In the former case, the fate line may actually begin inside the life line, which it crosses on the way up toward the middle finger.

## THE BUSINESS HEAD LINE

Traditional palmistry teaches that the head line on a business hand should not dip down very much toward the mount of Luna—after all, a horizontal head line indicates a practical and levelheaded approach to life, while a drooping head line is associated with a fertile imagination. Nowadays, however, many successful

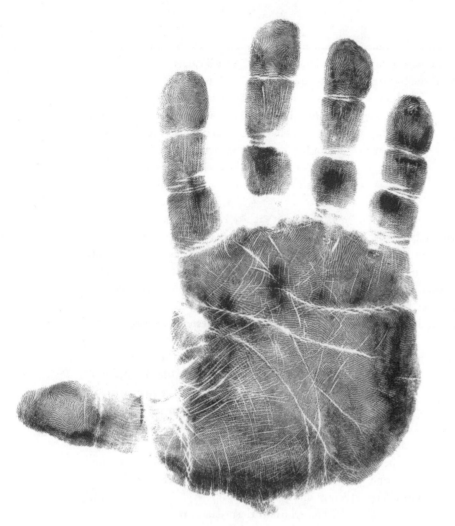

A good business head line is found on the hand shown in Figure 29.2, which belongs to a U.S. government employee with an MBA. This man put together an innovative federal and state partnership program that has saved hundreds of millions of dollars by identifying "double dippers," or people who claim government benefits in more than one state.

His fleshy hand, thick fingers, and loop of seriousness are common among successful businesspeople. While the closely held Jupiter and Mercury fingers show that he's a team player and the composite fingerprint on the Jupiter finger reveals his tendency to perform a thorough analysis of available material, the separation between the life and head lines and low-set thumb are signs of an independent person who has no difficulty making decisions for himself.

FIGURE 29.2. The hand of a government employee who is saving American taxpayers tens of millions of dollars a year.

## BUSINESS FINGERTIPS

executives and businesspeople possess imaginative head lines, especially if their work is entrepreneurial in nature or involves a great deal of creative problem solving.

For the most part, the classic business head line indicates a rather standard, plodding manner of dealing with business matters. A person with this type of line tends to approach everything from a utilitarian point of view. He or she would ask questions like "Does this work?" "How much is it worth?" and "What use is it?" A person with a straight head line is unlikely to be poor but also is not likely to become wealthy.

Most fingertips on business hands tend to be squarish, and those that aren't are usually rounded. Spatulate or pointed fingertips are rare, although spatulate fingertips are sometimes found on the hands of entrepreneurs and others who like taking risks in a rough-and-tumble business environment. Pointed fingertips can sometimes be found on women who design or develop a product and later go on to become head of the company. I've also seen pointed fingertips on other successful businesswomen in art- or beauty-related corporations, including the chair and CEO of one of the world's largest cosmetics companies.

Squarish fingertips indicate a love of order and structure. Those who have them tend to like physical tidiness and are tidy with their thinking as well. They work by method and are rarely happy unless they know exactly how something is supposed to be done. People with squarish fingertips delight in rules. They are punctual. They are accurate. They are very good with figures and measurements. Accounting is high on the list of professions for a square-tipped person. Bookkeeping attracts people with square-tipped fingers as well.

Contrary to popular belief, most accountants do not have boring hands. From my experience, I've found their hands varied and interesting. Their fingers can be either smooth or knotted, their head lines are often imaginative, and their hands can reveal either a cautious or spontaneous personality. Although detail is certainly part of their work, many accountants use intuition to understand their clients' financial situations (and often their life stories) in order to provide reliable financial advice.

The handprint of my own accountant is reproduced in Figure 29.3. His hand is fleshy and the fingers are thick, which is common among people working in the world of finance. Although his fingers are knotted, revealing attention to detail, there is a marked space between the life and head lines, a sign of a person who is impulsive, impatient, and self-reliant. He also has a strong and independent Saturn line, plus a good line of Apollo, two indicators of success. The head line reveals high intelligence and a good imagination, both of which can often be found in accountants.

Of special note are the double ring of Solomon, indicating a strong interest in what makes people

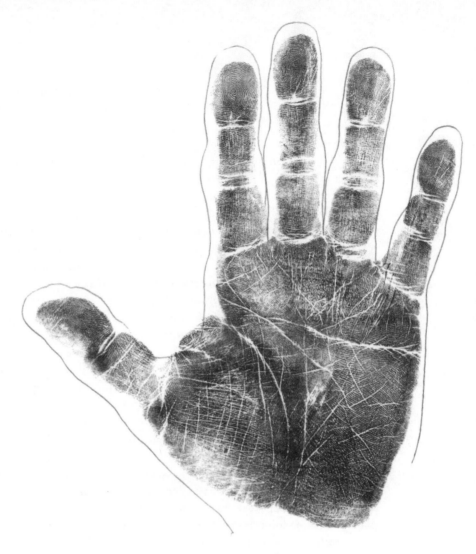

FIGURE 29.3. The hand of my accountant.

tick, and the several good Samaritan lines, a sign of healing ability. In addition to having this man do their taxes, many seek his advice on personal matters. The narrow space between the head and heart lines reveals a person whom others can safely confide in.

I've often found that successful accountants have unusual outside interests. In the case of the accountant mentioned here, his big passion is Chinese opera: he is both a noted performer and a set designer. The whorl fingerprint on the Apollo finger indicates strong artistic skills, and a long Mercury finger shows good communication ability. There is also a clear loop of humor on his hand, a sign of a fun-loving, laid-back personality.

## OTHER FINGER CHARACTERISTICS

In my experience, unusually long middle phalanges are commonly found on people who buy and sell things. Shopkeepers, salespeople, and Internet merchants are most likely to have them. The bottom phalange represents earthy qualities, and I've often found thick bottom phalanges (especially on the Jupiter finger) among successful real estate investors, restaurant owners, and businesspeople in general.

Many businesspeople are conservative by nature, which is usually shown in the hand by fingers that are held closely together. A few businesspeople show more open-minded mental attitudes, which is reflected by a wider space between the fingers. However, you will rarely find very wide gaps on the hands of businesspeople. Unusually wide gaps between fingers indicate a completely open, independent, and even radical approach to life. These qualities are usually incompatible with nearly all accepted business practices today.

The thumb of a successful businessperson or executive can be of almost any type, but when you examine the thumb, pay special attention to the flexibility of the top joint. It should have only a small degree of flexibility or, failing that, none at all. If the joint bends back easily, it is a sign of a happy-go-lucky person who finds it difficult to stand up to challenges, troublesome people, and problems at work. People with flexible thumbs are often full of great plans but are unlikely to do well in business unless they enlist the help of a stubborn-thumbed associate who can help them achieve their goals.

## THE JUPITER FINGER

Once you've determined that a hand shows characteristics related to success in business, the next thing to look for is signs of leadership. Is your client able to lead and inspire others? Will he or she rise to the top or remain low on or in the middle of the corporate ladder? These questions can usually be answered by observing the Jupiter, or index, finger.

The Jupiter finger is a symbol of self. It shows how we see ourselves, how self-assured we are, and how much we project ourselves into the world. Long index fingers are a sign of self-confidence, while short ones indicate a lack of it. The normal length of this finger is two-thirds of the way up the top joint of the Saturn, or middle, finger. People with an index finger of average length tend to see themselves as no better and no worse than anybody else.

A Jupiter finger that's longer than normal reveals a basically egotistical personality. Egotists are ambitious people who live to rule over others. They strive to reach the top in whatever they are doing, and many people with long Jupiter fingers can be found in executive positions or are on their way to achieving them. Anyone with a long Jupiter finger dislikes being in a subservient position at work. Young people with these fingers stay in junior positions for only as long as it takes to climb the corporate ladder. Failing that, they leave the company to set up a business of their own.

Perhaps the most noticeable aspect of a leader's Jupiter finger is not its length but the way it is held on the hand—markedly separated from the middle finger. Sometimes it is so far apart that it seems to operate from a different part of the hand. Managers, department heads, and others in high corporate positions tend to have this pattern.

The way we hold our fingers is not innate but develops at whatever point in life we establish a sense of self. A widely separated Jupiter finger is a sign of independence and decision-making ability. You will sometimes see a teenager with this feature, but it is more likely to appear when a person reaches his or her early twenties. Many self-employed people have a Jupiter finger that is markedly separated from Saturn. If you find this with a loop of humor as well, you can be almost certain that the person you are examining is (or hopes to be) self-employed.

A separated Jupiter finger shouldn't be confused with one that is actually stuck out, as though it were a flag. This abnormal jutting out is a sign of the constant desire to attract attention. Chances are that many celebrities who crave the spotlight have this type of Jupiter finger. In contrast, the "manager's sign" is simply a distinct gap between the middle and index fingers, as seen in the hand of Walt Disney (Figure 29.1). It is primarily an indicator of initiative and independence. Common among self-starters, it reveals the talent to see what needs to be done and the ability to do it.

Short index fingers are occasionally seen on business leaders as well. When this occurs, the index finger is almost always held firmly away from the other fingers. This is a sign that a fundamentally shy person has made strenuous efforts to overcome his or her shyness. In some cases, that person may have begun life with a genuine inferiority complex but masked it with the determination to succeed.

People with a short and separated index finger are driven by a need to prove their worth to themselves and others. For that reason, they are not always the easiest people to get along with on the job. The two most common fields in which one might find such people are politics and sales. Even dictators are known to have this feature in their hands. Idi Amin of Uganda and Saddam Hussein of Iraq (Figure 29.4) both had short index fingers.

Salespeople in general carry their (usually short) index fingers sticking out in the "notice me" position. Some salespeople even wear a ring on their

FIGURE 29.4. Saddam Hussein, in a pose that shows off his short index finger.

index fingers, calling more attention to the finger's meaning.

Successful salespeople often have other noticeable features on their hands as well, such as a long Mercury finger (revealing a facility with words) and a slightly curved Mercury finger (indicating astuteness). Loop fingerprints, an indicator of good social skills and the ability to fit in with a wide range of people, are also favorable for salespeople, as are a fate line originating in the mount of Luna (indicating work in the public eye) and a loop of charisma. The size and positioning of the index finger are perhaps the palmist's best guides to a person's choice of sales as a career, however.

# HEALING HANDS

*chapter*

## 30

I‍T IS TRULY SAID THAT WEALTH, fame, and success are worthless without the health to enjoy them. Although nearly everyone is interested in health and healing to some extent—because we all want to remain healthy—only a few of us choose health care as a profession.

As in other careers, the hands can reveal whether or not a person is suited for this particular field. Healers of all types—including medical doctors, nurses, massage therapists, herbalists, as well as naturopaths—have obvious signs in their hands that reflect an interest in and aptitude for healing the body. Those who help heal the mind, such as psychologists, counselors, and social workers, have these signs as well. A large percentage of spiritual healers also possess marks of healing in their hands.

It is very rare to find people working in these careers whose hands do not proclaim their vocation. It is equally rare to find someone with these "healer" markings who has never worked (or who has never wanted to work) in some kind of healing capacity, whether professionally or as a volunteer.

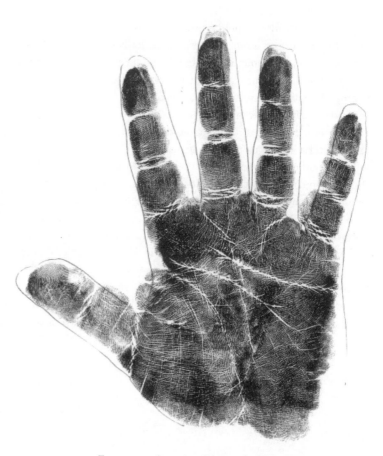

FIGURE 30.I. Samaritan lines on the Mercury mount.

### THE MEDICAL STIGMATA

The most common of these signs is called the medical stigmata, also known as the Samaritan lines. They comprise a group of short vertical parallel lines located in the mount of Mercury under the little finger (Figure 30.I). Just about everyone who works in the health-care field—physicians, chiropractors, nurses, physical therapists, psychologists, paramedics, and social workers—is likely to have these lines.

Samaritan lines are not rare; they are found on perhaps 20 to 30 percent of all hands and are relatively easy to locate and identify. They should be composed of at least three lines and no more than ten. They should be clearly marked; don't look at one or two scraggly lines and decide that they make up an embryonic form of the stigmata. Similarly, if there is a dense collection of dozens of small lines, don't take it as the medical stigmata, either. The true pattern is always composed of a small, neat patch of vertical lines.

If the entire area under all the fingers is covered with small vertical lines, do not focus on those on the mount of Mercury and declare them to be the stigmata. They are composed of a distinct and separate cluster of strokes.

Several palmistry books have suggested that true medical stigmata must feature a crossbar joining all the vertical lines. This isn't true. There is also no need for all the lines to be the same length. As long as they are fairly similar and appear as a set, they can be called Samaritan lines.

Usually, adults with medical stigmata have dreamed of becoming doctors or nurses since childhood, and many do indeed decide to pursue a medical career. Others are drawn to some other kind of medically oriented work. Several years ago I was asked to read hands at a staff party sponsored by a company that designs and manufactures medical devices. I discovered that virtually everyone I met there possessed Samaritan lines!

For nonprofessionals, healing work may be as simple as taking a course in first aid or cardiopulmonary resuscitation (CPR). In other people, the aptitude for healing may manifest itself as a willingness to care for sick relatives, even in the absence of any formal medical training. Those with Samaritan lines may also be the ones whom friends and relatives automatically consult when they need advice concerning health-related issues or psychological problems. Nine times out of ten, those who possess Samaritan lines become engaged in healing at some point in their lives.

## THE HANDS OF NURSES

While the majority of professional healers have a grouping of Samaritan lines on their hands,

the marking's presence is by no means universal. Among nurses, however, the percentage of hands with the medical stigmata approaches one hundred. Why is this?

Practically no one becomes a nurse without a strong interest in the healing arts, because nursing is a difficult and demanding career. The responsibilities of the job are immense and the pressures are often unrelenting. In many parts of the world, nurses are still grossly underpaid, although the situation is gradually changing, especially in the United States.

All types of people are attracted to nursing, and that's why you'll find all sorts of hands among them. Conic, or "watery," hands—an essentially feminine shape—are perhaps the most common, simply because the vast majority of nurses (approximately 93 percent) are female. However, I've found that strong hands occur more frequently among female nurses than among women in the general population. Nursing is hard work and is far from glamorous. It often calls for a tremendous amount of physical effort. People with able hands are generally well suited for such things. The nurse with delicate, feminine hands who does not shirk from performing these tasks deserves a lot of credit.

In a nurse's hand, the medical stigmata is often the most striking feature. The rest of the hand reflects individual character and personal interests, which can be quite varied. The fate line is usually strong, the Mercury finger is long, and the fingers are often held closely together, revealing a conservative and responsible individual. As a group, nurses are invariably very competent people, and you are not likely to find any specific weaknesses in their hands. In the absence of any strong counterindications, the medical stigmata point to nursing as an excellent career choice.

## THE HANDS OF PHYSICIANS

Among medical doctors, the stigmata aren't quite as common as they are on nurses, chiropractors, and naturopaths. The main reason is that many people choose to become doctors for reasons that have little or nothing to do with healing. Although the majority of physicians are dedicated and selfless individuals, a sizable minority choose a career in medicine primarily for the prestige, financial rewards, and power it provides.

Other doctors may come from families in which being a physician is part of an accepted tradition. These people may well become skilled and efficient healers, but they rarely possess a longing to help and serve others. The desire to heal is what so often distinguishes those who have the medical stigmata on their hands.

Nearly all the doctors I've met have strong Mercury fingers and often a prominent Apollo finger as well. This dual feature is a sign of strong intelligence. Many physicians are good communicators as well, especially those who are also teachers or who appear frequently on television and radio.

Unfortunately, many medical doctors are disturbingly narrow in their thinking, and those physicians who pioneer new techniques are forever complaining about the conservatism of their colleagues. The medical profession has a long history of opposing new ideas in the prevention and treatment of disease, and this narrow-mindedness can often be seen in the hands. Indications of conservatism include a head line that is tied to the life line, a lack of space between the fingers, and a slight narrowness between the heart and head lines.

Noel Jaquin, the great English palmist, called

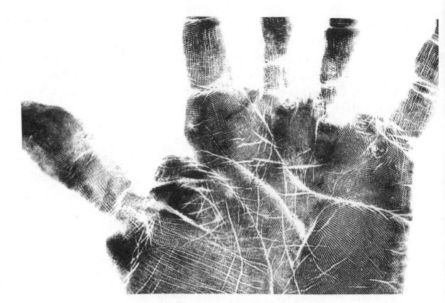

FIGURE 30.2. The vision meter, or the space between the head and the heart lines. A narrow space is shown at the top, and a broad space is shown below it.

the space between the heart and head lines—as measured between the middle and ring fingers—the vision meter. The wider the space, the more broadminded the person, as seen by the handprints compared in Figure 30.2. Broad spaces are not very common among medical doctors, except among those involved in innovative fields of medicine or the latest cutting-edge techniques.

## THE MOUNT OF VENUS

Over the years, I have observed the hands of hundreds of healers. Those involved primarily in physical healing—such as physicians, massage therapists, chiropractors, physical therapists, and therapeutic touch and Reiki practitioners—tend to have larger than average mounts of Venus.

Such individuals tend to have an abundance of physical and sexual energy, known as *ch'i* among the Chinese. It is almost as though they can jump-start the healing process through their hands. When used to help others, *ch'i* can produce amazing results. Very often people with Samaritan lines and a large mount of Venus visit a sick friend and give that person a hug or a backrub, and the friend feels better immediately. I believe that Samaritan lines in conjunction with a large mount of Venus can be a sign of a powerful healing presence.

## THE HEALING HEART LINE

Another formation to look for in a healer is a long, straight heart line. The heart line is an index of one's emotional and sexual nature, so it normally has little to do with career choice. However, a long, straight, "mental" heart line—known as a humanitarian heart line—is often associated with careers in healing and counseling. A heart line of this type ends under the mount of Jupiter at least halfway under the index finger. It may curve up slightly or droop downward a bit, but never enough to detract from its basically straight path. It will typically run so straight that it looks as though it's been drawn with a ruler.

A humanitarian heart line is a sign of selfless idealism. Those who have it care about others and often take up a profession involving service. It is found not only on professional healers but also on teachers and others who like to help people.

In their romantic affairs, those with a humanitarian heart line tend to look after their loved ones. They delight in offering care and attention and make devoted spouses and parents. Who's going to look after Grandma when she is bedridden? Probably the grandchild with the humanitarian heart line. Those with humanitarian heart lines never tire of supporting anyone they are fond of and often fall in love with someone in need of special care. People with this line may choose a mate with physical handicaps or other medical problems. They may also get involved with someone who is emotionally unstable and who needs a lot of attention. Friends may wonder why such people remain with spouses whom anyone else would have left long before. They need only look to the humanitarian heart line for the answer.

Humanitarian heart lines abound among practitioners of natural therapies such as homeopathy, herbal medicine, Reiki, and massage therapy, who tend to be very different in character from conventional physicians. They are drawn to the use of techniques that emphasize a more gentle, natural form of healing. The attitude of a naturopath or homeopath is fundamentally softer than that of most medical doctors or surgeons.

Social workers also share this "soft" approach to their profession. If you examine the hands of the staff at your local crisis center, or the hands of those who operate shelters for the sick or the homeless, you will find quite a few people with this type of heart line. When I lived in India, I looked at the hands of missionaries working with extremely poor people, and in most cases, they had prominent humanitarian heart lines. Many of these missionaries were offering medical care as well as spiritual counseling.

Psychologists who practice social work or other similar endeavors (such as psychotherapy, which many U.S. states allow social workers to practice as well) are also likely to have this type of heart line. Industrial psychologists, business psychologists, and others in less caring professions are less likely to have it.

## THE RING OF SOLOMON

The hands of psychotherapists usually feature a seal of Solomon, also known as a ring of Solomon, which is a diagonal line running either straight or curved across the mount of Jupiter. It reaches from about the start of the head line to a point between the first and second fingers. The ring of Solomon can sometimes be composed of two parallel lines. Strong forms of this line are always long and clear, while weaker lines may be short and cover perhaps only half the mount. Some trace of this line is found on one hand in three, but good, strong specimens occur in perhaps 10 to 15 percent of all hands.

People with this mark tend to be fascinated by human nature. They take an interest in the lives of their friends and enjoy discussing their friends' problems. Because they offer helpful advice, many seek them out when they need help. People with the seal of Solomon read books and articles about the mind. They are natural psychologists.

It is certainly an advantage for the professional psychotherapist to have a ring of Solomon, and, indeed, many do. Lawyers frequently possess this feature, and I've also seen it on accountants who take a personal interest in the lives and welfare of their clients (see Figure 29.3). The teacher's square (Figure 24.7) is often partially attached to a ring of Solomon.

Astrologers, card readers, graphologists, and palmists also tend to have this marking. In fact, some palmistry books have suggested that the seal of Solomon indicates mastery in the occult sciences. Although I would question this assertion, remember that in days gone by, astrologers and palmists were the equivalent of today's psychologists. The seal of Solomon should be considered an indicator of psychological insight rather than of occult power.

## THE VIA LASCIVIA

A well developed via lascivia is simply a bar or line that moves across the mount of Luna. In its strongest form, the end curves upward from the bottom of the

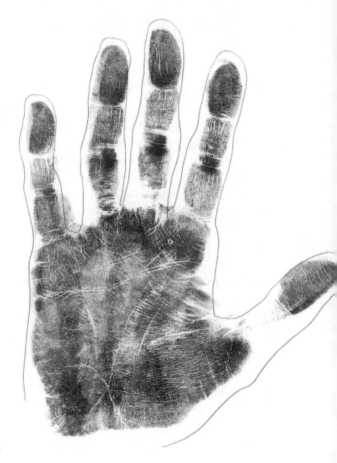

FIGURE 30.3. The via lascivia.

life line, as seen in the handprint shown in Figure 30.3. A more common form—which I've found on the hands of increasing numbers of people over the years—consists of a broken line running diagonally from the life line toward the lower mount of Mars, as seen in Figure 20.12.

Old palmistry books describe the via lascivia as "ye sister line to ye hepatica." The hepatic line is known in modern palmistry as the health line, which runs up the palm toward the mount of Mercury under the little finger. Several early French palmists concluded that the via lascivia must run parallel to the health line, although this is not always the case.

Members of the London Cheirological Society (which functioned between 1889 and 1940) were the first to notice how frequently a cross line on the mount of Luna appeared. They began to associate the mark with a craving for addictive drugs and therefore called it the line of drugs. A generation later, the German palmist Julius Spier independently discovered the meaning of this line, calling it the poison line. The word *lascivia* has nothing to do with the modern word *lascivious*. It refers to a far older meaning associated with the lust for stimulants and intoxicants rather than sexual lust and lewd behavior.

The via lascivia has two basic meanings regarding health. Its presence indicates either a sensitivity to irritants such as chemicals, alcohol, dust, pet dander, and certain foods or an addiction to substances such as caffeine, sugar, prescription medication, and legal or illegal drugs. The second meaning can also encompass an addiction to activities such as overeating, gambling, and sex.

Yet from a career perspective, the presence of this line can indicate that a person is employed in the production or sale of drugs, either legally or illegally. A high-level drug lord or local drug dealer will likely have this line, as will many of his or her customers. Chemists and pharmacists will probably have this line as well. I heard that the London Cheirological Society once found a nun with this mark and it turned out that her religious order had placed her in charge of the convent's medicine cabinet.

As mentioned earlier, I've found that many naturopaths and other natural healers also possess this line. The reason is probably because they discovered early in life that their bodies react badly to allopathic medications and food additives, such as artificial colorings, flavorings, and preservatives. Medicines administered during childhood may have made them seriously ill, and their parents turned away from conventional medicine and sought help through herbal remedies, balneotherapy, oxygen therapy, homeopathy, acupuncture, or other drug-free measures. Inevitably, some of these people take up a career in natural medicine when they are adults.

## THE HANDS OF CHIROPRACTORS

The hands of chiropractors are similar to those of most natural healers, except that chiropractors usually display signs of strength in their hands. The fingertips may be rounded or slightly spatulate, the mount of Venus may be larger than normal, and the life line will usually swing out into the palm in a nice curve. I've also found many chiropractors with arch fingerprint patterns, revealing a practical ability to fix things.

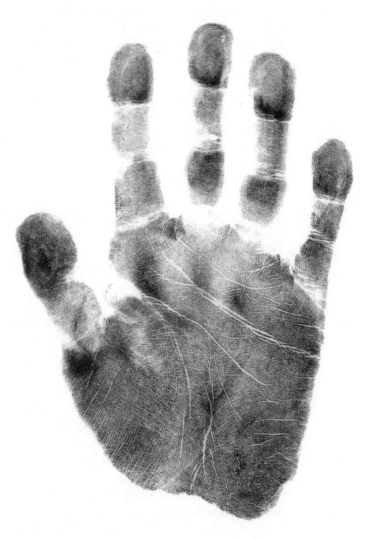

FIGURE 30.4. The hand of a practitioner of Network Spinal Analysis.

Over the years I have had extensive contact with practitioners of Network Spinal Analysis, a chiropractic-related healing technique that involves administering gentle precise touch to the spine. Often guided by the practitioner's intuition, these subtle applications are believed to cue the brain to create new wellness-promoting strategies. Intuition lines, revealing powerful psychic ability, are common in the hands of Network Spinal Analysis practitioners, such as the one whose hand is depicted in Figure 30.4. Like many natural healers, this person has hands that show a series of Samaritan lines and a humanitarian heart line. There is also a girdle of Venus, which is a sign of emotional sensitivity and depth. Both the Jupiter and Saturn fingers reveal an arch fingerprint, found on people with good manual skills. In addition to a via lascivia and several intuition lines moving up the mount of Luna, there is an unusual skin ridge pattern, revealing strong instinctual creativity.

## THE HANDS OF MASSAGE THERAPISTS

In addition to maintaining a practice devoted to people (especially patients suffering from severe illnesses), the massage therapist whose hand is shown in Figure 30.5 is also one of the handful of massage therapists in the United States who perform therapeutic massage on show and race-horses. Typical of a person involved with massage, his hand contains a number of the traits of a healer (including the medical stigmata, a sensitive heart line, the via lascivia, and long Apollo and Mercury fingers). His hands have good general strength and breadth, and the clear pattern on the Luna mount reveals a powerful instinct, which plays a major role in his healing work.

This man's work as an equine sports therapist has brought him to competitive horse events around the world. A highlight of his career involved working with the U.S. Equestrian Team at the 1992 Olympic Games in Barcelona, where he performed massage therapy on the horses and their riders.

## THE HANDS OF SPIRITUAL HEALERS

I have no doubt that there are people who genuinely possess a healing gift. But some professional psychic, or energy, healers achieve their results simply through the power of suggestion and the soothing effect of their ministrations. This does not in any way diminish the importance of what they're doing, because old-fashioned tender loving care may be just what a sick body or broken spirit needs to initiate the healing process. A strong dose of faith can work miracles as well. The fact that no special ability on the healer's part is involved has no bearing if it helps a sick person get well.

The few people who do have the ability to heal others through physical means alone (especially through what is known as magnetic healing) tend to share similar traits. In my experience, these people tend to be solidly built and have strong, earthy hands. Their hands may have a somewhat rough appearance, including coarse lines and skin texture. Their hands also reveal a strong energy level and a large mount of Venus, an indication of a powerful sex drive.

By contrast, a minority of healers—those who believe that their healing power comes from a higher source—tend to have hands that are thin, sensitive, and spiritual looking. Such were the hands of Blanche Meyerson, an outstanding spiritual healer who worked in New York City. She treated several dozen people a day in her small apartment, working almost nonstop, with amazing results. Her hands were small and delicate, with very fine skin and conic fingers.

Some spiritual healers have fine vertical lines running up the inside of their fingers. These lines cluster thickly on the two lower phalanges and somewhat more thinly on the uppermost phalange. They are called energy lines in palmistry, and they reveal that a person is pouring out energy in some way.

Energy lines are most commonly found on people who are constantly overworked and always tired. They are like leaky batteries, from which vital energy is being lost. These people need to relax

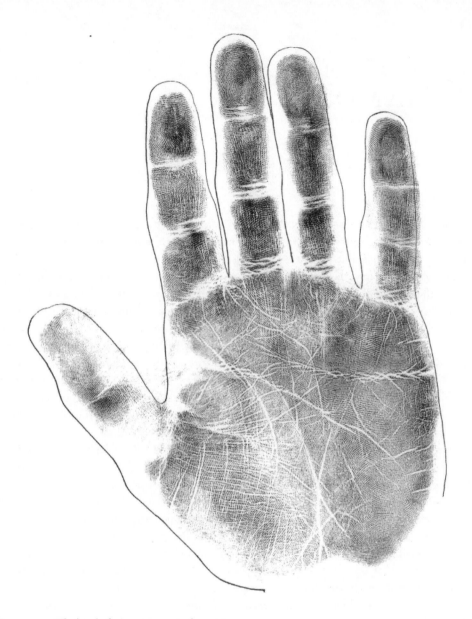

Figure 30.5. The hand of an equine sports therapist.

and do something to recharge themselves, such as bathing in the ocean or sitting quietly under some trees. By contrast, psychic healers who have these marks on their hands have them not because they are tired but because they are continually giving energy to others.

Remember that most people with narrow, delicate hands do not have much, if any, ability to heal others with energy, so if you run across a person with this type of hand it doesn't mean that he or she is a spiritual healer. Like many other sensitive and often empathic individuals, these people may be better suited for a career in counseling or psychotherapy than in spiritual healing.

Finally, don't forget that just because you may lack certain healing features in your hands, it doesn't mean that you should avoid working in a healing profession. Before he began to study massage therapy, for example, the person whose hand is shown in Figure 30.5 had no Samaritan lines whatsoever, but he didn't let that stop him from pursuing his chosen line of work!

# OTHER HANDS

We saw in the previous chapters that many careers are related to specific hand traits. Most of these jobs can be grouped together, but there are others that do not fit conveniently into the previous chapters. We'll cover these hands in this chapter about "other" hands.

## THE HANDS OF SCIENTISTS

Probably the most common feature of scientific hands is knotty fingers, which—when not caused by arthritis or another kind of joint inflammation—indicate a love for detail and analysis. Some scientists, such as astronomers and physicists, are more often knotty fingered than not, while others, including biologists and engineers, have this feature less frequently. The proportion of knotty fingers is probably higher among people in scientific fields than in any other professional group.

There are two basic types of knotty fingers. Some able hands, with their short fingers, have a knotty appearance. In some cases, the fingers appear to be strong. In able hands, the knotting is more pronounced at the lower joints. The fingers have a broad appearance due to the presence of these joints.

Conic hands, with their long fingers, can also possess knots. The fingers appear to be thin, since the phalanges themselves are usually slender. This exaggerates the bulge of the joints. Knots have the same meaning irrespective of which type of hand they are found on.

Knotted fingers reveal an analytical, detailed mind. People who have them love to argue, reason, and investigate. People with knotty fingers often ask, "How does it work?" "What is it for?" "Why is it done this way?" "Is there another way to do this?" "What does it mean?" "Is it true?" People with knotty fingers love to examine, investigate, and discuss.

Obviously, people with these personality traits are well suited to jobs that require an analytical mind. They also enjoy leisure activities that demand the same mental processes. Many of them play games like chess. Many belong to the school debating team. They tend to find a few special friends with whom they can sit all night arguing things out. They enjoy activities that challenge their intellects and spatial abilities, like crossword puzzles and sudoku. They enjoy research and investigation.

Knotty fingers are often found on the hands of astronomers and others who deal with the physical sciences, such as meteorologists, geologists, and physical anthropologists. Physicists who work in such fields as atomic energy and aerospace also tend to have knotty fingers.

There are a number of nonscientific fields that attract people with knotty fingers, including library science. Clerks who specialize in information gathering or investigation are likely to have them as well. Knotty fingers tend to predominate among people involved in any kind of research.

## THE HANDS OF ENGINEERS

Short fingers are more common among engineers than among other types of scientists. Engineers tend to think and act quickly and tend to see things as a whole.

Engineers also tend to have hands of a solid, earthy type. The skin ridges are inclined to be broad and there are likely to be arch fingerprints as well. Lines on the hand tend to be thick. A person with a "high elementary" or earth hand who also happens to be highly intelligent is likely to pursue a career in engineering or a related technical field.

Some engineers also possess a special mark on the palm. Like the teacher's square and medical stigmata, it is almost a trademark. The mark of an engineer is a head line that is short and straight and possesses a gentle downward slope. The shortness is accentuated by the fact that the line does not taper toward its end. While most head lines tend to thin out, the engineer's head line looks as though it has been abruptly cut off two-thirds of the way across the hand. If you see one of these lines on a fire hand, you can be fairly certain that the owner is an engineer of some kind.

A handprint of an electronics engineer—my father—is shown in Figure 31.1. Though the head line is slightly longer than most, it is clear and does not taper at the end. Note especially the high loop on the Saturn finger and the strong arch-and-loop combination on the index finger. Until his death at the age of fifty-two, his career as an engineer was very successful, with more than two hundred patents to his credit.

If an engineer's field is very narrow, you may find a single whorl fingerprint on the middle finger, indicating that its owner is indeed a specialist. A hydraulic engineer can have this pattern, for example, as can an engineer who works exclusively on the design and installation of nuclear power stations. Remember, however, that this whorl pattern can be found on the hand of any specialist and isn't limited to engineers.

## THE HANDS OF COMPUTER SCIENTISTS

The largest of all scientific fields today is computer technology. Nearly everybody nowadays has at least

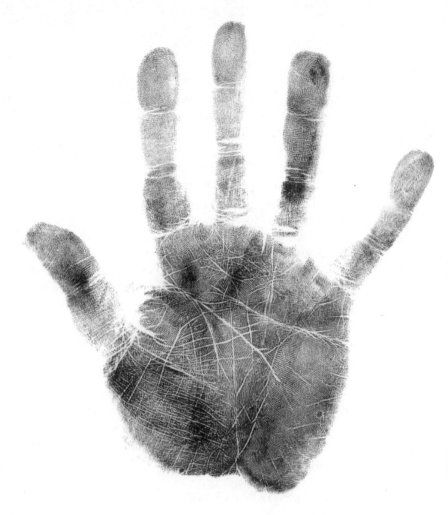

FIGURE 31.1. The hand of an electronics engineer.

some contact with these machines, whereas when the modern computer was first developed after the Second World War, only a few top scientists were involved in it.

Unfortunately, because computers are ubiquitous, it is impossible to lay down any rules about the hands of people who work with them. However, some people, such as programmers and those working in software design and development, have certain identifiable features in their hands that reflect their abilities and interests.

For the most part, they are the same characteristics that distinguished the original computer enthusiasts when the UNIVAC I (Universal Automatic Computer I) was commercially introduced in 1951. The majority are long-fingered folk, and nearly all the remainder possess hands with a long palm, short fingers, and a predominance of whorl fingerprints. (Whorls are common among long-fingered computer people as well.)

A good set of whorl fingerprints reveals the ability to focus. The intense concentration necessary for computer programming definitely suits the "whorl mentality." Long fingers—with or without whorls—reveal the capacity to work in a thorough, patient, and detailed manner.

Long fingers are often accompanied in computer scientists by a long head line with a pronounced downward curve. Traditionally, a line of this type is associated with imagination and not scientific thinking, so palmists of that era may have associated it with the stereotype of the computer nerd who had long hair, read science fiction, and may have believed in flying saucers. Nevertheless, the work of computer design and programming involves a lot of imagination and creative thinking, which may explain the presence of a downward-sloping head line in so many computer scientists today.

## THE HANDS OF LAWYERS

The practice of law, which is considered a prestigious career, attracts some very interesting hand types. A number of years ago, I was asked to read hands at the Christmas party of one of New York City's most reputable white-shoe law firms. Based on my observations of more than a hundred lawyers at that event, I would say that plain, ordinary hands are rarely found among members of the legal profession.

Generally speaking, the lines on lawyers' hands tend to be long and strong, their hand consistency is neither plump nor muscular, and their fingerprint patterns are nearly always noteworthy. There are few specific rules to follow regarding legal hands, but three features occur fairly regularly—the ring of Solomon, a fork at the end of the head line, and a long Mercury finger. The ring of Solomon is a sign of psychological insight; it's found on many people who are curious about what make others tick. The fork in the head line, or writer's fork, indicates the ability to look at all sides of a question. People with this type of line can consider more than one point of view. It is an invaluable gift in a writer, and I've found it with marked frequency in legal hands.

Nearly all lawyers have prominent Mercury fingers. In lawyers, this finger is usually long and strong and is often slightly curved. This reveals an astute, calculating turn of mind. When there is a distinct bend to this finger, there is a devious side to the personality, indicating a knack for turning situations to the owner's personal advantage. I've found this trait more frequently on trial lawyers than on corporate lawyers, who specialize in law specifically relating to the ownership and structure of companies, such as mergers and acquisitions, corporate finance, corporate recovery, and private equity acquisitions.

Marked straightness in the little finger is likely to indicate scrupulous honesty. I've found some corporate lawyers with such a finger, as well as some judges. Judges also tend to have a long, powerful thumb and other typical features of a legal hand.

The hand reproduced in Figure 31.2 belongs to a lawyer known for his honesty and compassionate nature. The head line is clear and realistic, while the humanitarian heart line is long and chained; there is also an abundance of lines on the hand in general, signifying a person with a nervous and sensitive nature. The long Mercury finger is typical of lawyers, while the grouping of Samaritan lines is common among healers. Such a lawyer would probably be happiest helping those who are in trouble— for example, defending an abused wife, restoring medical insurance for a sick child, or representing a community in a lawsuit against a corporate polluter. However, it would not be surprising to find the presence of stress lines on such a hand.

## MILITARY HANDS

Generally speaking, the hands of people in the military tend to be strong, with square-tipped fingers. Loops are more common than any other fingerprint pattern, though the proportion of other types will

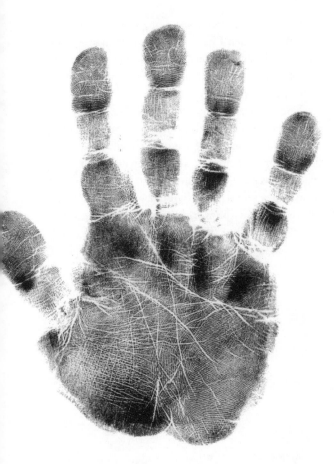

FIGURE 31.2. The hand of a lawyer.

join the military, particularly those who want to make it a career.

Military life is totally ordered. There is a time to wake up, a time to go to bed, and a way to cut your hair, tie your shoelaces, and lay out your belongings. Who but a square-fingertipped man or woman could enjoy this way of life?

Another interesting feature found in the hands of military professionals is a well-developed mount of Mars positive. This mount is located in the area below where the life line begins, just above the top of the mount of Venus. Most people have no distinct pad here, and the area is simply a web of skin. The few people on whom this mount is well developed are known for their courage. They never back away from conflict and are always ready to fight for a worthy cause.

Soldiers who have this mount are usually men and women who volunteered for service as soon as they were old enough to do so. They dreamed of warfare when they were young and hoped to go into active service as soon as possible. Soldiers with this feature but with no prospects of going into battle may take up boxing, wrestling, martial arts, or target practice in their spare time. In their personal lives, they are likely to challenge others. This doesn't mean that they are actively seeking trouble; they are merely letting everyone know that they will stand up for what they believe in and that they shouldn't be "messed with." Of course, in these cases it is important to examine the entire hand for features that either strengthen or modify this personality trait.

As with other aspects of the hand, a family may pass the developed mount of Mars positive down through several generations. It is often found on people whose ancestors were prominent in the military.

## THE HANDS OF LAW ENFORCEMENT PROFESSIONALS

Law enforcement also attracts people with square-tipped fingers. There is no obvious way to distinguish them from members of other square-tipped

rise among officers and those who pursue specialized jobs. Women who enlist in the armed forces or the police force tend to have more varied hands, although their hands are often strong and feature well-defined lines. At the bottom of the military hierarchy, in those who never get beyond "footslogger duties," there is normally a high incidence of defective head lines and other poor features in the hands.

There is a difference between the military hands found during peacetime and those of soldiers going to war. In times of war, men and women of all types either enlist or get drafted. Many of them are poor and uneducated and feel that a stint in the military will provide them with educational opportunities and greater job possibilities. By contrast, in times of peace, mainly men and women with square fingertips professions (including accountants and mathematicians) except that their hands tend to be strong and masculine, like the hands of those who are attracted to a military career.

Like many military people, those involved in law enforcement often have a prominent mount of Mars positive. Police officers, firefighters, professional bodyguards, security specialists, and others who exhibit conspicuous bravery tend to have this trait, as do boxers, wrestlers, and others who are proficient in the martial arts. This doesn't mean that a person is aggressive in the sense of being a troublemaker. Rather, a strong mount of Mars positive is a sign of a crusader and a warrior.

It is at least as common among women as among men. The women I have met with this mount have strong and dynamic personalities. They are protective of their friends and family members, not unlike a mother lion protecting her cubs.

The handprint shown in Figure 31.3 belongs to a policeman. The small number of lines reveals a strong and uncomplicated individual who has a well-defined sense of himself and his environment. The space between the head and heart lines is narrow, revealing a secretive individual with a somewhat limited view of the world around him. The short and clear heart line indicates that compassion is not his strong point; he would likely be very tough in

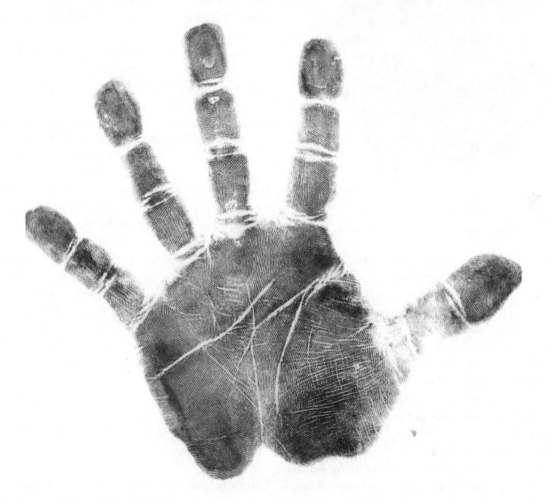

FIGURE 31.3. The hand of a police officer.

his dealings with criminals. However, his long and straight Mercury finger reveals a good communicator who is honest in his dealings with others.

## THE HANDS OF PILOTS AND FLIGHT ATTENDANTS

Andrew Fitzherbert wrote that the index fingers on professional pilots are invariably straight and well formed. He cited the theory of the German palmist Julius Spier, who believed that good eyesight and straight Jupiter fingers go together.

Certain professions appear to attract people with good eyesight. Driving is one of them. Truck drivers and long-distance bus drivers are, on the whole, spectacle free. Pilots, particularly in the air force, are inclined to have perfect vision and straight index fingers. Professional athletes often have a straight index finger as well.

Pilots must be detail oriented, and so, not surprisingly, knotted fingers are common among them. Their jobs also demand good organizing skills, and they need to be counted on for clear thinking and leadership in an emergency. Strong Jupiter fingers indicate these qualities.

Airline flight attendants are also inclined to have long and well-formed Jupiter fingers. Like their colleagues in the front of the plane, they must be well organized, clear thinking, and decisive in the event of an emergency. A long index finger is a symbol of self-assurance and self-awareness and reveals that its owner has the capacity to make the most of him- or herself in every possible way.

Because they don't work a traditional five-day week, many flight attendants pursue other interests, such as a part-time career in business or modeling. While many female flight attendants possess the long-fingered feminine hands of a model or actress, others have good business hands. Many flight attendants (both female and male) use their airline experience as a stepping-stone toward a career in business or the hospitality industry. I have also met many flight attendants with Samaritan lines (an indication of healing ability) and loop fingerprint

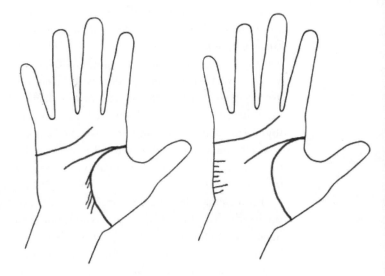

FIGURE 31.4. Travel lines.

patterns, which reveal an ability to get along with a wide variety of people.

Since flight attendants work in the public eye, they often have fate lines that rise from the mount of Luna. Ancient tradition links this mount to travel. I've occasionally seen frequent travelers with this type of fate line.

Some palmists claim that short lines leaving the life line, pointing in the general direction of Luna (Figure 31.4), indicate individual journeys. These lines are called travel lines and appear at a point corresponding to a person's age at the time the trip occurs.

However, I believe that more accurate travel lines are found on the side of the palm—the small horizontal lines moving up the mount of Luna. Each line represents a major journey. The later in life the travel occurs, the higher it will be found along the side of the hand.

## THE HANDS OF FOOD SERVICE PROFESSIONALS

Many waiters and waitresses have fate lines starting in the mount of Luna, which is to be expected for people who are in the public eye. However, you would probably not find many with strong index fingers or signs of major talent, unless they are waiting tables while pursuing another career like acting or writing, as many do. Because they need to get along well with a wide variety of people, they often have hands that are loop predominant, like flight attendants. Some waiters have the "angles" of the thumb, as musicians do. This may be due to the fact that many waiters are also interested in musical careers.

Professional chefs have no specific features on the hands that point to their profession, but their hands are inclined to be fleshy (even when their bodies are not fat). You will find very few chefs with thin, bony hands! The traditional fleshiness often found in the hands of chefs usually includes a full mount of Venus accompanied by a well-curved life line.

Over the years, I've found that many excellent cooks, whether professional or not, have an arch print on at least one of their fingers. This is a sign of an ability to work well with one's hands.

Yet for many modern chefs, cooking is not just about preparing food, but about art. This is why many professional chefs have a whorl on the tip of the Apollo, or ring, finger. Such people have an ability to present food in a beautiful and appetizing way. I would imagine that many of the winners of *Iron Chef* competitions on TV—in which food appearance and presentation are paramount—have whorls on their Apollo fingers.

Among chefs, the bottom phalanges of the fingers deserve special attention. Broad, plump lower phalanges indicate self-indulgence and a love of sensate pleasures, such as eating. However, if the flesh of this phalange is not broad but instead forms a high pad that is not particularly wide, the owner is said to have a highly developed sense of taste. Andrew Fitzherbert met several professional wine tasters with this formation; it can be found on hands of the finest chefs as well.

## THE HANDS OF INTUITIVE CONSULTANTS

What about the hands of people who provide intuitive services to others, such as palmists, astrologers, and professional clairvoyants?

It's not uncommon to find palmists whose hands resemble those of a psychologist or social worker. After all, most hand readers emphasize advice and counseling in their readings.

Many people believe that palm readers are clairvoyant or that they possess some special type of psychic skill. This legend has gained credence because many gypsy fortune-tellers claim to practice palmistry. Although intuition indeed plays a role, hand analysis is basically a science that has no connection whatever with psychic powers. Although some hand readers may indeed be psychic, sound knowledge (as you can see from this book, there are literally hundreds of things to remember about the features of the hand), a compassionate heart, and a good mind are the major requirements necessary to become a competent hand reader. The gypsies actually have no tradition of studying the hand.

The handprint reproduced in Figure 31.5 belongs to the late John Lindsay, one of Britain's most respected palmists. His widely separated fingers reveal an open and expansive nature, and the long and straight Mercury finger betrays his essential honesty and strong communication skills. Like the hands of many psychologists, his hand features a ring of Solomon. His hand also features a modified simian line with a heart line moving up to the mount of Jupiter; segments of a girdle of Venus, indicators of an emotional and sensitive nature, can be seen above this line. There are also a variety of interesting skin ridge patterns, including a prominent memory loop and a large vanity loop. Several lines of intuition can be seen moving up diagonally from the mount of Luna.

In the hands of true clairvoyants, such as genuine psychic readers or mediums, the most striking sign of psychic ability is the line of Uranus (also known as the line of clairvoyance), a diagonal line that begins in the mount of Luna, moves toward the center of the palm,

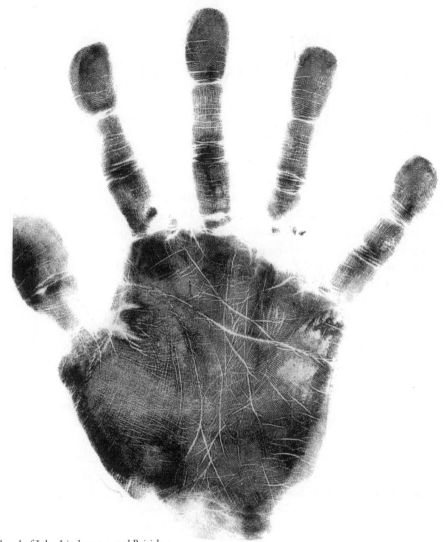

FIGURE 31.5. The hand of John Lindsay, a noted British palmist.

and then gracefully curves around toward the lower mount of Mars, or Mars negative (see Figure 22.3). Lines of Uranus are quite rare, yet most highly intuitive people feature at least one diagonal line moving up from the mount of Luna.

Dermatoglyphic patterns make up another important indicator of psychic ability. The most common is a loop on the mount of Luna. Among the good psychics I have known over the years, at least half have this pattern. In fact, any dermatoglyphic pattern on this mount emphasizes creative or intuitive powers in some way or another. Whorls on the mount of Luna reveal an ability to

visualize strongly. Any other type of pattern may suggest some type of psychic talent, although it may not necessarily have to do with telling fortunes or counseling.

Andrew Fitzherbert has written that skin ridge patterns on the fingers also offer clues to psychic ability. He claims that if the ring finger and little finger both have whorl prints—provided there is an absence of whorls on the other fingers—the owner of the hand will be prone to experiencing precognitive dreams. Anyone who experiences this may also be inclined to receive impressions in their waking state as hunches and premonitions.

# YOUR HAND AND THE SPIRITUAL LIFE

# chapter 32

Throughout human history, sages have taught that we possess a spiritual center, or core. This core can be loosely defined as the conscious life that animates our being, and it has been referred to as the Christ Within, the higher self, and the atman. Dr. John C. Pierrakos, cofounder of a spiritual movement known as the Pathwork, wrote:

> Core consciousness is universal consciousness. Our core is the wellspring of awareness, our font of communion with outer reality, and our nucleus for self-expression. . . . Moving from the core, from the higher self, means moving towards fulfillment of our greatest potential.[1]

The goal of spiritual evolution, according to Pierrakos, is to become conscious of this inner core and allow it to manifest itself in our lives.

Learning how to connect with and express the universal self, the higher self, or the "spark of God within" is a major part of our life task. Our core is the part of our being that possesses superior wisdom, love, and strength. It is inclusive, compassionate, and ageless.

Sometimes we are lucky enough to know a person older and wiser than ourselves who is a source of common sense, practical wisdom, and infinite patience. This person accepts us the way we are without judgment and is happy to offer counsel, which is always helpful. Such a person is a source of calm and reassurance in an often crazy and chaotic world.

The higher self is not unlike that special person. No matter what time of the day or night, or wherever we happen to be, we can go there for comfort and wisdom. Whether we believe in a higher power, an organizing wisdom, universal intelligence, Gaia, Allah, or God, one of our most important tasks in life is to access this source of wisdom and power. I believe that everyone can access this spiritual source, although the path may be different for each individual.

When considering the human hand from a spiritual point of view, bear in mind that living a spiritual life does not necessarily involve escaping from the world, nor does it call for the repression of our feelings. Rather, it is grounded in the conscious awareness of *what is* and the integration of our physical body, thoughts, and emotions with our spiritual center, or core. The goal of spirituality is essentially to establish right human relations, promote goodwill, and do our part toward establishing peace on Earth, including peace with the environment. In addition, spirituality also implies deepening our connection with our higher self, with Mother Earth, and with the universal consciousness some people call God. It is a challenging process, but it can bring about incredible joy and a zest for adventure.

## THE SPIRITUAL HAND

Over the years, serious teachers of palmistry have used hand analysis to help guide us toward developing our spiritual potential. Unfortunately, however, several myths persist regarding what constitutes a spiritual hand.

In most books, long, tapered fingers are seen as a good indication of spiritual potential, along with the presence of mystic crosses, lines of intuition, rings of Solomon, and other signs. In some cases, the existence of these markings in the hand has become a status symbol among students of occultism ("Hey, take a look at my mystic cross!"). There has also been a tendency among hand readers to stress the importance of psychic ability over developing intuition and spiritual consciousness through meditation, opening the heart, and selfless (and often anonymous) service.

Still, understanding the human hand can help us and those we counsel to achieve our spiritual potential. Because the hand is the mirror of our spiritual essence as expressed through our personality, talents, and mental abilities, it helps us expand our awareness, develop our intuition, and come into deeper contact with our spiritual core. By understanding the clues it provides, we can discover new avenues of spiritual fulfillment and service according to our energies, talents, and aspirations.

## LOOK TO THE COMPLEMENT

All types of hands—be they elementary, square, spatulate, or conic—express essential qualities that enable us to achieve spiritual revelation and the expansion of consciousness. While these goals are important by themselves, the hand may also indicate what is needed to achieve a deeper level of personal integration and harmony in life.

In many cases, especially where there is dissatisfaction and frustration, the existence of a particular personality trait may indicate the need to develop a *complementary* quality so that a person may become a fully integrated human being. For example, those who are primarily intellectual might strive to develop their emotional natures, while a person who is primarily sensate might need to develop self-discipline.

## ELEMENTARY HANDS

People with elementary or earthy hands are often grounded in three-dimensional reality and function well in the material world. These people are usually physically strong and are also reliable, stable, and practical. They think before they act and prefer to see things in a simple, uncomplicated way. They are naturally attracted to the outdoors and often work in agriculture, forestry, and the building trades. Many like to work with animals.

From a spiritual point of view, the earthy quality of these individuals helps keep them grounded, which is an important part of spiritual development. They are often instinctual and can be in tune with the earth's energy. They can be suspicious of spiritual teachings unless they have practical value. To quote the American Indian medicine man Sun Bear, whose earthy hands were strong and fleshy: "I don't care what your philosophy is unless it can grow corn." People with elementary hands tend to lack pretense and want to see how an idea can work on an everyday level.

However, a negative aspect of such a personality is the tendency to see life in the simplest terms and not consider other points of view. People with elementary hands can easily become close-minded and prejudiced as a result. In addition, they can be overly cautious and not want to take risks, especially if they have rigid hands. This can keep them stuck in old patterns that need to be relinquished.

From a spiritual perspective, people with elementary hands need to expand their range of interests. Beginning a new hobby, taking adult education classes, going to a museum, reading, and other activities are useful in helping them appreciate new ideas and other approaches to life. They are often good healers and have a tremendous capacity to share. They also show great potential for service, an important practical manifestation of spirituality.

## SPATULATE HANDS

People with spatulate hands are high-energy people. They are enthusiastic, emotional, and excitable. They are not resistant to new ideas, nor are they afraid of moving forward into unfamiliar areas of activity and study. They are risk takers. These characteristics are often found in leaders of religious groups and organizers of spiritual events. In spiritual matters, as with all areas of life, people with spatulate hands show an innate enthusiasm for discovery, learning, overcoming obstacles, and moving ahead.

The fingers of people with spatulate hands tend to be short when compared to the length of the palm, which means that their owners tend to see issues on a large scale. Unless the fingers are knotted, they don't like to pay attention to details and may scorn careful study and analysis. Receptivity may need to be developed, along with the ability to sit quietly and develop mindful awareness. If the first phalange of the thumb is thin, there may be a need to reduce stress through exercise, diet, and meditation. The goal of any spiritual activity for the owners of spatulate hands is to increase receptivity while acknowledging the dynamic, outgoing qualities that their hands represent.

## SQUARISH HANDS

The squarish hand reflects primarily an intellectual character. Common sense, order, method, and determination are several of the essential qualities the squarish hand represents. Administrators, researchers, and teachers often reflect the characteristics shown in square hands, as do those who are drawn to traditional religious teachings. They love order, rules, and stability and can express their ideas in a clear, well-organized manner. While the spatulate hand may express the principle of spirituality in action, the squarish hand might reflect the principle of divine order and authority.

However, there is a tendency to be afraid of change and closed to new ideas in people with squarish hands, especially if the hand is rigid. While healthy skepticism is useful when dealing with metaphysical matters, people with squarish fingertips (especially if the nails are naturally short) are often skeptical and demand that an idea be proven rationally beyond any shadow of a doubt before they will accept it. In cases where the hand and thumb are rigid, the ability to share—which might apply to feelings, ideas, or possessions—is an important spiritual lesson to learn in life.

Another major goal for people with squarish hands involves the development of the sensate and emotional aspects of the personality, especially if their fingers are thin and knotted. Generally speaking, people with squarish hands need to be more spontaneous and learn how to let go. Whereas the owner of the spatulate hand may need to take up meditation and organize his or her life, the square-handed individual might consider hatha yoga (to develop flexibility), active sports (to mobilize physical energy), and aerobic dancing to help them get out of their own heads and become more in tune with their body rhythms.

## CONIC HANDS

People with conic hands are very sensitive to their environment. They also have little trouble getting in touch with their feelings. They are governed by their emotions and are drawn to things spiritual. Their conic fingers reveal a keen appreciation of nature, while a pointed Jupiter finger in particular (especially if it is long and accompanied by a well-developed mount) reflects a strong interest in inspirational and devotional matters. Meditation, prayer, chanting, and drugs are often used by conic-handed people to achieve their spiritual ideals.

Conic-handed people are also drawn to psychic phenomena, especially if there is a pronounced mount of Luna with strong lines of intuition. Their capacity to express spiritual ideals through beauty and art is especially notable, as is their innate ability to support others in their spiritual endeavors.

However, people with conic hands (especially if the thumb and hand are flexible) have difficulty being consistent and have a tendency to move quickly from one spiritual group or teaching to another without developing a deep understanding or commitment. They can also be capricious and are easily swayed by moods. If the hands are thick and soft, there can be an inordinate love for material things and the tendency to focus on sensate aspects of life at the expense of spirituality.

People with a conic Jupiter finger are especially easily inspired. Inspiration can come from many sources: listening to a piece of beautiful music, attending an uplifting sermon or speech, walking in the forest, or watching a sunset. At the same time, these people often have the ability to inspire others and get them motivated. It should be no surprise that this type of finger is often found on the hands of ministers, teachers, healers, and mentors.

Generally speaking, the owners of conic hands need to develop their intellects. They need to analyze and question more and not be swayed by sentiment and impulse. If the fingers are knotted, intellectual tendencies are already an important part of the personality, but when the fingers are smooth, there is a need to focus on details. The development of order, tact, responsibility, and consistency are also major keys to their spiritual integration. For that reason, spirituality through service is an important goal for those with conic hands.

## PSYCHIC HANDS

Although psychic hands are extremely rare in their pure form, their occurrence reveals a person who has a natural affinity for spirituality and religion. This type of hand reflects all the positive aspects of the conic hand, including a love of beauty, harmony, and religious inspiration. Meditation, prayer, and philosophy (especially when the fingers are knotted) are enjoyed by people with this type of hand.

However, people with psychic hands need to be more grounded in the nuts and bolts of daily living. Because they are highly sensitive, they require pure food and a minimum of alcohol, tobacco, caffeine, and other toxins. Drug abuse can also be a problem for those with psychic hands.

Because they have a tendency to get lost in dreams and separate themselves from day-to-day reality, contact with the earth, through activities such as gardening and taking long walks in the country, is useful for people with psychic hands. Exercise is also important, especially those forms that strengthen the legs and ankles. The need for strong and stable friendships—especially those that provide a "grounding" influence—is essential for these people.

## PHILOSOPHICAL HANDS

Philosophical hands—hands with knotty joints—are typical of religious thinkers and scholars. Like the owners of square hands, people with knotty fingers are logical, reasonable, and studious. Such hands are often found in India among yogis, ascetics, and philosophers.

People with these hands are not seduced by appearances and have the ability to penetrate deeply into the nature of truth and reality. Being inherently patient, they are careful and thorough in their undertakings. As teachers and writers, they can examine all sides of a question and analyze concepts often passed over by others, especially if their fingers are long and one or more composite fingerprints are present.

However, such individuals can get lost in details and lack the ability to perceive the totality of an issue, especially if their fingers are both knotted and long. They may also have a tendency to lose themselves in metaphysical concepts and avoid contact with everyday reality. A classic example is the scholar who is well versed in Hermetic or kabbalistic philosophy but forgets to eat her dinner and has a habit of losing her keys.

In some cases, an analytical understanding of spiritual matters is pursued at the expense of intuitional perception. As part of the process of spiritual integration, people with philosophical hands should work on developing qualities like playfulness, emotionality, and body awareness.

## MIXED HANDS

The mixed hand is by far the most common you will see, and by definition it reflects many of the traits discussed in the preceding pages. These hands reveal a complexity of tendencies, talents, and abilities, including ease in adapting to new situations and openness to unfamiliar teachings and spiritual practices. While such hands reveal a strong mystical tendency (especially if the Jupiter finger is long and tapered and a mystic cross or ring of Solomon is in evidence), they also indicate an ability to express spiritual understanding in practical terms.

When analyzing the mixed hand in a spiritual context, try to be aware of the hand type or types that seem to predominate. Is the hand basically square, conic, or spatulate? Which finger or fingers are the strongest? What are the outstanding mounts? What do the lines reveal? Is the hand receptive, or is the energy more assertive? Is the hand fleshy or thin? Is it rigid or does it bend? What do the skin ridge patterns on the fingers and palm reveal? By developing an analytical technique based on sensitivity and careful attention to detail, we can help people become aware of their inner qualities and offer insights that can help them connect with their higher selves and achieve their deepest spiritual potential.

## THE LINES

The lines on the hand can offer additional insights into spiritual direction and unfoldment. The heart line, for example, indicates the depth and quality of the emotions. In a spiritual context, these emotions, when properly channeled, are essential in helping us attain our spiritual goals.

Generally speaking, a long, deep, straight, or otherwise predominant heart line reveals a person who is oriented toward universal brotherhood and service to humanity. Such a person enjoys contact with other people, whether as a spiritual teacher, healer, administrator, or volunteer in a hospital. Shorter or more "physical" heart lines can indicate that a person experiences devotion on a more intimate scale, such as with a particular religious figure or group.

The large fleshy hand and the strong physical heart line of John B. S. Coats, the sixth international

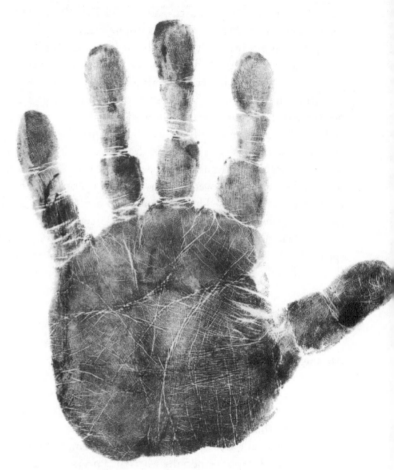

FIGURE 32.1. The hand of John B. S. Coats, the sixth international president of the Theosophical Society.

president of the Theosophical Society (Figure 32.1), reflects a balance of these attributes. Though known as an inspiring teacher and articulate lecturer, he is primarily remembered for his warm, sympathetic heart and wonderful sense of humor. Committed to the ideal of universal brotherhood—a basic goal of the Theosophical Society—he was known to thousands of people around the world, many of whom considered him a personal friend. Note the large loop of humor and the clear, strong memory loop (revealing a memory for names and faces plus a strong intuition) that dips far down into the mount of Luna.

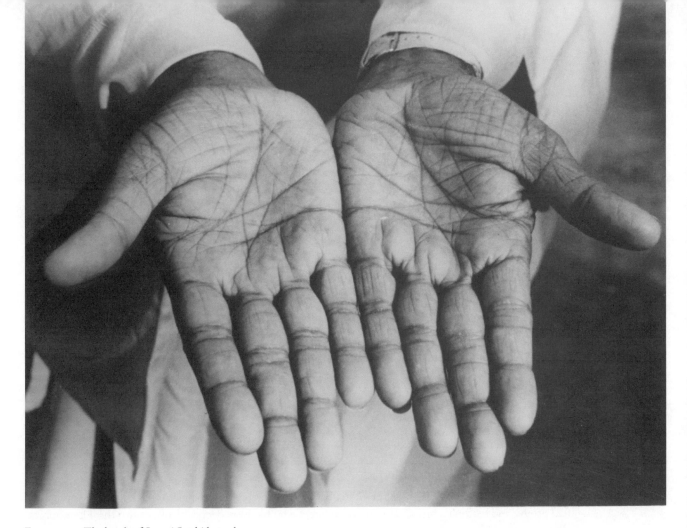

FIGURE 32.2. The hands of Swami Satchidananda.

The head line is another good indicator of spiritual direction. When the head line predominates over the heart line, an individual will be drawn more to study, thinking, and meditation than to devotional practices like prayer and singing.

If the line moves straight across the palm, a realistic and practical approach to spirituality is evident. A prominent downward slope of the head line (as seen in the hand of Coats) reveals that dreams, visions, and instincts play an important role in that person's spiritual life. The positive aspects of such a line include an ability to easily grasp abstract or esoteric subjects, while the negative aspects include a tendency to be disorganized and have difficulty translating spiritual understanding into daily practice. If the head line is islanded as well, there can be a tendency toward poor concentration and an inability to focus.

Slightly sloping head lines reveal a balance between the realistic and imaginative aspects of spirituality. This quality is evident in the beautiful hands of Swami Satchidananda, the founder of the Integral Yoga Society, shown in Figure 32.2. His strong, clear lines indicate abundant physical energy and sharp mental focus, while the prominent mount of Luna reveals a powerfully nurturing and instinctual nature.

Lines of intuition begin in the mount of Luna and move toward the center of the palm. They indicate strong intuitive powers and the ability to follow one's own instincts rather than rely on analysis.

On a tiny minority of individuals, a single line of intuition moves from the mount of Luna and forms a gentle arc toward the mount of Mercury, indicating that strong psychic ability may be present. Known also as the line of Uranus, this line is found on the hands of

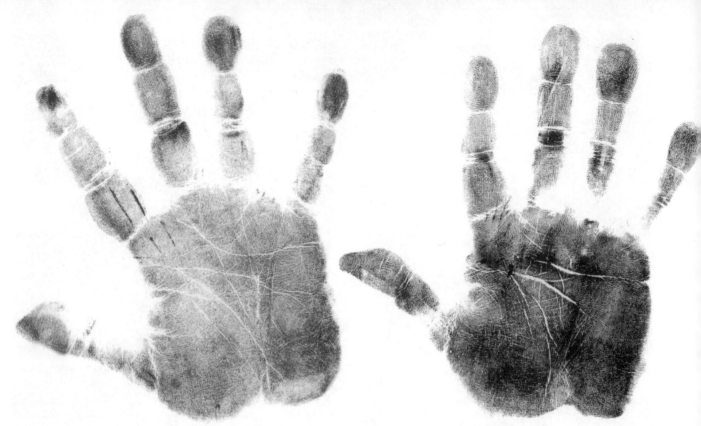

FIGURE 32.3. The hand of a gifted clairvoyant.

FIGURE 32.4. A hand with a mystic cross.

mediums and clairvoyants, such as that of Gloria B., a gifted psychic and healer (Figure 32.3). Gloria also has an interesting series of skin ridge patterns on her mount of Luna, which accentuates her instinctual nature.

Gloria's hand also features a ring of Solomon, a diagonal line (often in the form of an arc) that passes through the mount of Jupiter. This marking, which may also comprise two parallel lines, shows a strong interest in metaphysics, occultism, and unorthodox religion. It also is found on people who are fascinated by human nature and are called on by others to offer advice and counsel. People with this line are frequently drawn to careers as psychologists and take up study in fields such as astrology, yoga, and mysticism.

The mystic cross is considered a sign of strong interest in spiritual development. Appearing as a cross between the lines of heart and head, it is not the result of two long lines (such as the Saturn line and an influence line from the mount of Venus) coming together but rather is formed by two short lines that cross each other, as seen in Figure 32.4.

The hand in the picture belongs to a young man who has been deeply involved with the Theosophical Society since early childhood. His hand also features a rare charisma loop between the Jupiter and Saturn fingers, a loop of seriousness between the Saturn and Apollo fingers, and a strong memory loop located under the end of his head line. His hand also features strong whorls on three of the fingertips, a sign of originality and specialization. While they do not reveal spiritual tendencies by themselves, these skin ridge patterns do reveal an independent, creative, and charismatic person who is serious about his spiritual development.

Remember that the absence of these markings does not indicate any lack of spiritual development or capacity for devotion, nor should their existence be interpreted as a sign of special spiritual advancement. Rather, these signs, whether read individually or collectively, are merely guideposts that indicate certain interests and abilities. They merely help the hand consultant provide a detailed reading.

PART VI | PRACTICAL HAND ANALYSIS

# chapter
# 33

# HOW TO READ HANDS

Reading someone's hand is a very serious matter, involving tremendous responsibility. Simply stated, hand analysis involves one person letting another person study a part of his or her body and then make pronouncements on highly sensitive and personal issues. In a sense, hand analysis can be compared to reading someone's private letters or journals. For this reason, a hand reader must bear responsibility for both what is said and how it is expressed during a consultation.

The underlying intent of the hand reader is of paramount importance. Hand analysis must never be used to impress or seduce (sexually or otherwise) or to gain power or control. Efforts must be made to be as objective as possible, while maintaining close physical contact during the reading. Honesty is an essential component of each hand analysis, yet we must phrase every observation and suggestion in a way that is truthful, kind, and helpful. If what we have to say does not satisfy these three requirements, it is better to say nothing.

At the same time, we need to avoid the tendency to focus only on the positive aspects of the hand. While we should help our clients become aware of their talents and abilities, we do them no favor by glossing over difficult aspects or areas of conflict in their lives.

Closely related to honesty is timing. In certain situations, it is not appropriate to reveal information, especially if we feel that it would cause unnecessary pain or that a person would not be able to deal with a particular issue or problem. This can often be dealt with by stressing the fact that the hands show tendencies, and that the lines in the hand can change over time.

## THERAPY, COUNSELING, OR EDUCATION?

It is important to realize that, as hand readers, we are not practicing therapy. Therapy involves a regular, ongoing process of deep psychological change that should be overseen only by a qualified psychotherapist. Counseling, on the other hand, is relatively brief and is usually intended to address specific areas of concern, such as health, career, or relationships. Although the hand reader's task often involves some level of counseling, it is not our major goal. Rather, our primary task is that of education—the simple sharing of information. A person receiving a reading wants to be told about him- or herself with the goal of expanding self-knowledge and personal well-being.

While it is possible that a consultation may lead an individual to seek counseling or therapy, this is not the hand reader's main concern. In fact, many professional chirologists discourage frequent consultations (usually limiting them to one or two a year) and refer particularly troubled clients to an appropriate counselor, therapist, or health professional as needed.

Some hand consultants take courses in psychology or counseling and may even obtain certificates or degrees in these fields. A deep grounding in the science of palmistry in conjunction with the knowledge and training needed to be a good therapist can be a very important combination that can be of enormous benefit to those who seek our help.

Perhaps one of the most difficult tasks for the hand reader is to be able to take a personal interest in a client while remembering that each client is responsible for his or her own life. Nevertheless, when major issues are exposed and discussed, we should never leave a client hanging but should try to lead him or her to the next step whenever possible. According to the noted astrologer Stephen Arroyo, author of the classic *Astrology, Psychology, and the Four Elements*:

> One should realize that merely giving advice without also giving a means for deeper understanding is of little value, for each person must do his or her own work and must, through his or her own experience, arrive at the higher awareness that enables the person to outgrow or transcend the difficulty.[1]

Such a process may involve eliciting reactions and questions so that a client takes an active role in the reading rather than remaining a passive listener. This participation often leads a person to seek solutions on his or her own. Very often, human beings know the solutions to their problems on a deep level but are accustomed to avoiding them or having someone else provide the answers. A hand analysis can help a person bring these deep answers to the surface.

Unfortunately, some hand readers overlook respect for privacy. In my own work, I prefer to read an individual's hands alone, in a quiet setting, without a third party looking on or asking questions. Although the presence of a tape recorder tends to encourage the client to pay less attention to the reading when it is being given, I do not object to its use. I never discuss a reading with others. At the time I read a person's hands, it is *our* business, but after the consultation is over, the information discussed is no longer my affair.

## A NOTE ABOUT CHILDREN

In my experience, I've found that kids are very curious about palmistry. Whenever I am invited to read hands at a party where children are present, they are invariably the first to come up and demand, "Read my hand!"

It's important to be extremely careful when reading a child's hands because kids are very impressionable and will likely remember everything you tell them, especially if it resonates with what they already feel is true. For this reason, it's important to be positive in a hand reading and focus on a young person's gifts, such as intelligence, creativity, and capacity for friendship.

Whenever a negative trait is found, it's good to try to present it in a balanced light. For example, a chained heart line can indicate a very sensitive person who easily feels compassion for others. At the same time, that person can be easily hurt. A reader can say, for example, "Wow. You really care about your friends. You have a big heart. But sometimes they hurt your feelings and you feel bad."

It's also a good idea not to be too specific with young children and to use humor whenever possible. If a preteen asks when she will marry, one can reply with a smile, "I see a good marriage, but don't get married right away. Wait until you're out of college."

## TECHNIQUE

There is no single method or technique to reading a hand. However, it's always useful to be thoroughly prepared. Whenever you are about to read a person's hand, try to become aware of the privilege and the responsibility involved. Meditation and prayer can help you become grounded in your core, or higher self, and come into close contact with your intuition.

Before you look at a person's hands, ask whether he or she has ever had a reading before. Point out that the hands show tendencies and not always definite facts and that the hands can change, even within a matter of weeks. I sometimes mention as an aside that I know of some very old people with short life lines, as well as young people with long life lines who have been killed in accidents.

Ask your client's age and find out if he or she is right- or left-handed. Explain that the passive hand is the storehouse of our potential, while the active hand expresses what we are doing with it.

Sitting directly across from the client, take both hands in yours and look at them. Close your eyes for a moment and say a silent prayer to help you focus and do your best. I ask simply, "Thy will be done," while a friend prefers "I pray that all I may now tell him/her will be for his/her highest good and the highest good of all concerned." This momentary spiritual focusing need not be so obvious as to be noticed by the person who has come to you for a consultation but can appear as though you are merely collecting your thoughts before proceeding with the reading.

Look carefully at both hands. Take note of the size, shape, skin texture, and flexibility. Note the positions and length of the fingers, taking account of the basic hand types. Don't be afraid to touch, bend, and squeeze the hands gently as you examine them.

Observe the fingers carefully, taking special note of their size, flexibility, shape, and contour. Are any of the fingers bent? Which are prominent and which are weak? How are they "held" or positioned on the hand? In addition, take note of the skin ridge patterns on each of the fingertips. Use a magnifying glass if you need to.

Turn the hands over and observe the nails, and ask your client to open his or her hands wide. Check out the knuckles as well as the position of the fingers relative to each other and to the hand as a whole.

Turn the hand over again and examine the mounts. Run your finger over each mount and judge its relative strength. Note any markings on the mounts, such as squares, crosses, and grilles. Be aware of any specific skin ridge patterns between the fingers or on the mounts of Luna, Venus, or Mars.

Look at the lines, taking careful note of their strength, clarity, and length. Where do they begin and where do they end? Are there breaks, dots, or islands on the lines? Are there branches or color changes? How do the lines differ on each hand?

After examining the hands for a few minutes, you will get a feel for the hand and a basic understanding of who your client is. At this point, take the active hand and begin reading, being ready to look at the passive hand for confirming or contrasting traits. Begin the reading at a point that feels most appropriate. With some people, you may decide immediately to discuss health issues, while with others you might begin with some observations about character or career. You may also prefer to simply go over the hand features one by one. Use your judgment.

Continue your reading, being sure to cover all areas of interest, including health, life history, emotional characteristics, career, travel, relationships, and other aspects such as creativity and spirituality. Proceed slowly, always being open to intuitive messages from your subconscious. Make frequent eye contact with the client. You may prefer to answer questions during the reading itself, or ask for questions when you are done.

Throughout the reading, try to keep the following issues in the back of your mind and ask yourself whether you are dealing with them:

- What is my client really looking for?

- What is she or he ready to hear?

- Is what I am saying appropriate for this person at this time?

- What is the best approach to help this person develop his or her sense of initiative, responsibility, and participation in life?

- Does the reading touch on sensitive issues of my own that may affect my objectivity?

- Am I making myself clear and am I being understood?

At the conclusion of the reading, people often ask questions like "Will I get married [or divorced]?" "How many children will I have?" and the classic "When am I going to die?" If you encounter any of these questions, make it clear that any specific prediction along those lines would be pure guesswork. *Never* predict a time of death.

When practiced with care, sensitivity, and humility, hand analysis can be an endless source of adventure, learning, and inspiration. By helping others increase their self-knowledge, we invariably deepen our own. By helping others "remove the stones from the path," we open our own channel for compassion and service.

# HOW TO TAKE HANDPRINTS

$O$NE OF THE BEST WAYS TO DEEPEN OUR UNDER-standing of the hand is to maintain a record of the hands we analyze. Although plaster casts faithfully show hand shapes and lines, they are complicated to make and extremely difficult to store. In the past, photographs of the hands were simple to take and store but were not always clear and often involved considerable expense.

Thanks to advances in digital technology, it is now easy to take photographs or use a scanner to obtain very detailed images of the hands that can clearly show even the smallest lines and the most subtle skin ridge patterns. Because they don't have to be repro-duced on photographic paper, the images can easily be saved on a computer hard drive or on a CD-ROM and displayed on a computer screen virtually for free.

I find this method especially useful when I do long-distance readings. Clients send me images of their hands on a CD-ROM or by e-mail and I can do a detailed analysis based on the digital images. Yet when it comes to doing readings in person, I still prefer the tried-and-true method of taking prints on the spot with paper, roller, and block-printing ink.

## TAKING PALM PRINTS WITH INK

Although prints taken with a roller and block-printing ink do not always reveal the exact shape of a person's hands, lines and skin ridge patterns can be faithfully reproduced, especially after some practice. When used in conjunction with the Hand Analysis Worksheet (page 274), an inked handprint can be very useful. In addition to providing a permanent record of the hand itself, it can be compared with subsequent follow-up prints to reveal changes in the hands over the years.

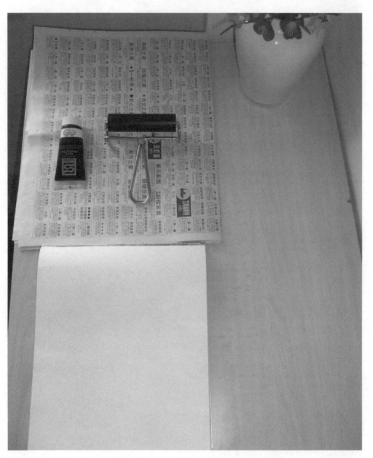

FIGURE 34.1. Art paper, roller, and ink.

*Materials*

The materials needed for taking handprints (Figure 34.1) are not only inexpensive but also easy to obtain at most art stores:

1. A rubber roller approximately four inches (ten centimeters) wide

FIGURE 34.2. Rolling out the ink.

2. A tube of black water-based block-printing (lino) ink; in my opinion, the best ink available is manufactured by Daler-Rowney in England, although Speedball brand ink is suitable for North American palmists

3. Good-quality drawing paper; you may prefer single sheets, or a spiral-bound sketchbook for easier storage.

4. A thin pad of foam rubber to provide a suitable cushion for the paper

5. A sheet of glass, linoleum, or newspaper for applying the ink

*Procedure*

1. First, lay the paper over the foam rubber, which helps the paper conform to the contours of the hand. Using the roller, roll out the ink on the glass, linoleum, or newspaper (Figure 34.2).

2. Carefully ink the subject's hand by passing the roller over it, using just enough ink to lightly cover the entire palmar surface (Figure 34.3).

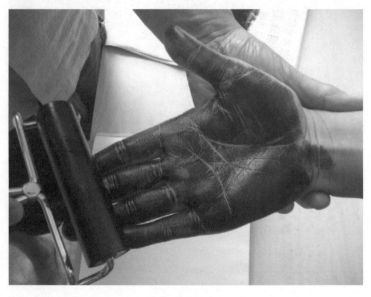

FIGURE 34.3. Inking the hand.

3. Have the subject place his or her hand on the paper in a natural way, without intentionally opening or closing the fingers. Apply pressure to the entire hand (paying special attention to the center of the palm and the space between the finger mounts) in order to obtain a complete impression (Figure 34.4). You may also want to carefully outline the hand in pencil to record its approximate shape (Figure 34.5).

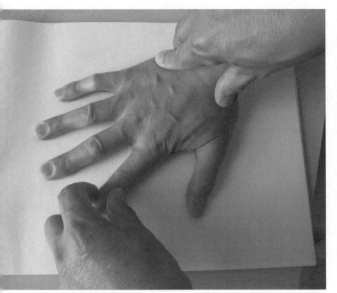

FIGURE 34.4. Placing the hand on the paper.

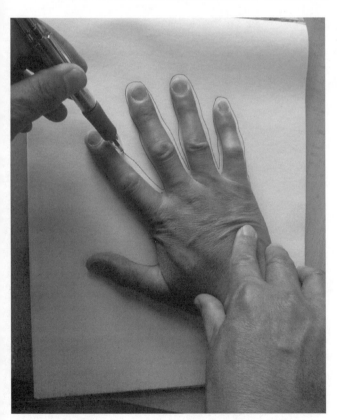

FIGURE 34.5. Drawing the outline of the hand.

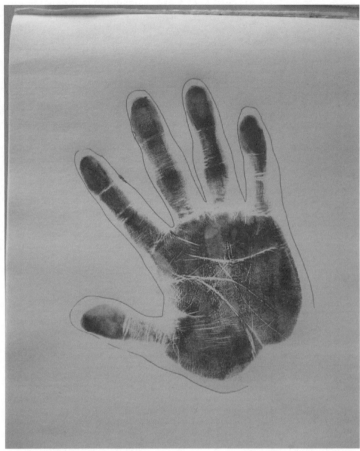

FIGURE 34.6. The finished print.

4. Hold the paper to the table as the hand is slowly withdrawn. This will prevent the print from blurring.

In addition to the print itself, you should include a record of the major features of the hand, such as the shape and dominant fingers and mounts, as well as personal information concerning the individual whose print you are including in your collection. A Hand Analysis Worksheet is included here for your convenience in recording this data.

# Hand Analysis Worksheet

NAME: _____

DATE OF BIRTH: _____

TODAY'S DATE: _____

PREDOMINANT HAND TYPE: _____

STRONGEST MOUNTS: _____

WEAKEST MOUNTS: _____

SKIN TEXTURE: _____

SKIN COLOR: _____

FLEXIBILITY: _____

CONSISTENCY: _____

FINGERS: _____

Jupiter:

Saturn:

Apollo:

Mercury:

Predominant:

Longer or shorter than palm?

Straight?

Bent?

THUMB: _____

Size:

Flexibility:

How set (high, medium, low)?

Will phalange (describe):

Logic phalange (describe):

SKIN RIDGE PATTERNS: _____

Thumb:

Jupiter:

Saturn:

Apollo:

Mercury:

On the palm itself:

NAILS: _____

Size:

Shape:

Color:

OVERALL: _____

Unusual features:

Additional comments/personal data:

# NOTES

## Chapter 1. The Hand as Hologram

1. John Napier, *Hands* (New York: Pantheon Books, 1980), 68.

2. Julius Spier, *The Hands of Children* (London: Routledge & Kegan Paul, 1955), xv.

## Chapter 4. Consistency, Size, and Skin Texture

1. William G. Benham, *The Laws of Scientific Hand Reading* (New York: Hawthorne Books, 1974), 43.

## Chapter 8. Skin Ridge Patterns

1. Julian Verbov, "Dermatoglyphics," *International Journal of Dermatology* (December 1985): 640–42.

## Chapter 10. Will: From Inertia to Action

1. H. P. Blavatsky, *Theosophical Glossary* (Los Angeles: Theosophy Company, 1971), 111.

## Chapter 11. Hand Gestures, Postures, and Movements

1. Sandor Ferenczi, "Stages in the Development of the Sense of Reality," *Sex in Psychoanalysis* (Boston: Richard C. Badger, 1916).

2. H. M. Halverson, "Studies of the Grasping Responses in Patients with Neurosis, Epilepsy, and Migraine," *Archives of Neurology and Psychiatry* 56 (1946): 631.

3. Charlotte Wolff, *The Hand in Psychological Diagnosis* (London: Methuen, 1951; repr., New Delhi, India: Sagar Publications).

4. Stefan Zweig, *Twenty-Four Hours in the Life of a Woman*, in *Stories and Legends* (London: Cassell, 1955).

5. Eugene Scheimann, MD, and Nathaniel Altman, *Medical Palmistry* (Wellingborough, UK: Aquarian Press, 1999), 21–22.

6. Walter Sorell, *The Story of the Human Hand* (Indianapolis, IN: Bobbs-Merrill, 1967), 145–62.

7. Bruno Munari, *Speak Italian: The Fine Art of the Gesture* (San Francisco: Chronicle Books, 2005).

## Chapter 14. Sexual Varieties, Sexual Choices

1. Edward B. Foote, *Dr. Foote's New Book on Health and Disease, with Recipes* (New York: Murray Hill Publishing, 1903).

2. Cathy Winks and Anne Semans, *The New Good Vibrations Guide to Sex* (San Francisco: Cleis Press, 1977).

3. J. G. Bennett, *Sex* (York Beach, ME: Samuel Weiser, 1981).

4. S. M. Breedlove et al., "Finger-Length Ratios and Sexual Orientation," *Nature* 404 (March 30, 2000): 455.

5. Caleb Crain, "Did a Germ Make You Gay?" *Out* (August 1999): 46–49.

6. D. J. West, *Homosexuality* (London: Gerald Duckworth, 1955).

7. Sam Janus et al., *A Sexual Profile of Men in Power* (Englewood Cliffs, NJ: Prentice-Hall, 1977).

8. Jack Lee Rosenberg et al., *Body, Self, and Soul: Sustaining Integration* (Atlanta: Humanics, 1987).

## Chapter 15. Compatibility in Relationships

1. Julia A. Bondi with Nathaniel Altman, *Lovelight: Unveiling the Mysteries of Sex and Romance* (New York: Pocket Books, 1989), 13.

2. John L. Hoff, "Practical Friendship," *In Context* 10 (Summer 1985): 15.

3. Omraam Mikhael Aivanhov, *Love and Sexuality* (Frejus, France: Editions Prosveta, 1976).

4. H. J. Eysenck and Glenn Wilson, *The Psychology of Sex* (London: New England Library, 1979).

## Chapter 16. Elements of Medical Palmistry

1. *Stedman's Medical Dictionary*, 26th ed. (Baltimore: Williams and Wilkins, 1995), 764.

2. Charlotte Wolff, *The Human Hand* (New York: Alfred A. Knopf, 1943; repr., New Delhi, India: Sagar Publications), 84.

3. Editors of the *Journal of the American Medical Association*, "The Hand and Cardiovascular Disease," *Journal of the American Medical Association* (February 6, 1954): 508.

4. Theodore J. Berry, MD, *The Hand as a Mirror of Systemic Disease* (Philadelphia: F. A. Davis, 1963).

5. S. Polovina et al., "Qualitative Dermatoglyphic Traits in Brachial Plexus Palsy," *Collegium antropologicum* 4 (December 31, 2007): 1077–81; Chintamani et al., "Qualitative and Quantitative Dermatoglyphic Traits in Patients with Breast Cancer: A Prospective Clinical Study," *BMC Cancer* 7 (March 13, 2007): 44; A. Rosa et al., "Dermatoglyphic Anomalies and Neurocognitive Deficits in Sibling Pairs Discordant for Schizophrenia Spectrum Disorders," *Psychiatry Research* 137 (December 15, 2005): 215–21; J. H. Weinreb, "Dermatoglyphic Patterns in Alzheimer's Disease," *Journal of Neurogenetics* 3 (July 3, 1986): 233–46.

6. Condict W. Cutler, *The Hand: Its Disabilities and Diseases* (Philadelphia: W. B. Saunders, 1942).

7. Eugene Scheimann, *A Doctor's Guide to Better Health through Palmistry* (West Nyack, NY: Parker Publishing, 1968), 11.

## Chapter 17. The Basics of Medical Palmistry

1. William G. Benham, *The Laws of Scientific Hand Reading* (New York: Hawthorne Books, 1974), 36.

2. Eugene Scheimann, "The Comparison of the Psychodiagnostic Findings of Graphology and Hand Psychology," *Journal of Nervous and Mental Disease* 107, no. 3 (March 1948).

## Chapter 18. The Nails in Medical Diagnosis

1. A. Hauptmann, "Capillaries in Finger Nail Fold in Patients with Neurosis, Epilepsy, and Migraine," *Archives of Neurology and Physiology* 56 (1946): 631.

2. Peter D. Sammon, *The Nails in Disease* (London: William Heinemann Medical Books, 1972).

3. Charlotte Wolff, *The Human Hand* (New York: Alfred A. Knopf, 1943; repr., New Delhi, India: Sagar Publications), 84.

4. Maurice Pierre, ed., *The Nail* (Edinburgh: Churchill Livingstone, 1981).

## Chapter 19: Dermatoglyphics: Their Medical Significance

1. H. Cummins and C. Midlo, *Fingerprints, Palms and Soles* (New York: Dover Publications, 1961), 280.

2. Eugene Scheimann, *A Doctor's Guide to Better Health through Palmistry* (West Nyack, NY: Parker Publishing 1968), 59.

3. Ibid., 60.

4. Editors of *New England Journal of Medicine*, "Dermatoglyphics in clinical medicine," *New England Journal of Medicine* (December 8, 1966):1314.

5. Charlotte Wolff, *The Human Hand* (New York: Alfred A. Knopf, 1943; repr. 1972, New Delhi, India: Sagar Publications), 93–95.

6. David Brandon-Jones and Veronica Bennett, *Your Palm – Barometer of Health* (London: Rider and Company, 1985), 87.

7. B. Schaumann and S. B. Barden, "Medical Applications of Dermatoglyphics," in *Progress in Dermatoglyphic Research*, ed. C.S. Bartsocas, vol. 84, *Progress in Clinical and Biological Research* (New York: Alan R. Liss, 1982).

8. C. Basso, C. Frescura. D. Corrado, M. Muriago, A. Angelini, L. Daliento and G. Thiene, "Congenital heart disease and sudden death in the young," *Human Pathology* 10 (October 26, 1995): 1065-72.

9. *Indian Journal of Medical Research* (January 1986): 56–67.

10. T. Takashina and S. Yorifuji, "Palmar Dermatoglyphics in Heart Disease," *Journal of the American Medical Association* 197 (August 29, 1966): 689.

11. Milton Alter and Robert Schulenberg, "Dermatoglyphics in Congenital Heart Disease," *Circulation* 41 (1970): 49–54.

12. J. Milicic et al., "Dermatoglyphics of the Digito-Palmar Complex in Autistic Disorder: Family Analysis," *Croatian Medical Journal* 4 (August 2003): 469–76.

13. M. Arrieta et al., "Dermatoglyphic Analysis of Autistic Basque Children," *American Journal of Medical Genetics* 35, no. 1 (January 1990): 1–9.

14. S. H. Gottleib and M. M. Schuster, "Dermatoglyphic (Fingerprint) Evidence for a Congenital Syndrome of Early Onset Constipation and Abdominal Pain," *Gastroenterology* 91, no. 2 (August 1986): 428–32.

15. Dr. Chintamani et al., "Qualitative and Quantitative Dermatoglyphic Traits in Patients with Breast Cancer: A Prospective Clinical Study," *BMC Cancer* 7 (March 13, 2007).

16. M. H. Seltzer et al., "Dermatoglyphics in the Identification of Women Either with or at Risk for Breast Cancer," *Journal of Medical Genetics* 37, no. 4 (December 1990): 482–86.

17. M. Ciovirnache et al., "Dermatoglyphics in Thyroid Cancer," *Endocrinologie* 24 (July–September 1986): 171–83.

18. Herman J. Weinreb, "Fingerprint Patterns in Alzheimer's Disease," *Archives of Neurology* 42 (January 1985): 50–53.

19. Benjamin Seltzer and Ira Sherwin, "Fingerprint Pattern Differences in Early- and Late-Onset Primary Degenerative Dementia," *Archives of Neurology* 43 (July 1986): 665–67.

20. Emilio Cuadrado and Maria José Barrena, "Immune Dysfunction in Down's Syndrome: Primary Immune Deficiency or Early Senescence of the Immune System?" *Clinical Immunology and Immunopathology* 78, no. 3 (March 1996): 209–14.

21. A.P. FORBES, "Fingerprints and Palm Prints (Dermatoglyphics) and Palmar-Flexion Creases in Gonadal Dysgenesis, Pseudohypoparathyroidism and Klinefelter's Syndrome," *New England Journal of Medicine* 270 (June 11, 1964): 1268–77.

## CHAPTER 20. PALM LINES AND MARKINGS

1. J. S. Thompson, *Genetics in Medicine* (Philadelphia: W. B. Saunders, 1966).

2. P. A. Davies and V. Smallpiece, "The Single Transverse Palmar Crease in Infants and Children," *Developmental Medicine and Child Neurology* 25 (October 1963): 491–96.

3. *Indian Journal of Medical Research* (January 1986): 56–67.

4. Eugene Scheimann and Nathaniel Altman, *Medical Palmistry* (Wellingborough, UK: Aquarian Press, 1989), 81–82.

5. Walter Sorell, *The Story of the Human Hand* (Indianapolis, IN: Bobbs-Merrill, 1967), 205.

6. Charlotte Wolff, *The Hand in Psychological Diagnosis* (London: Methuen, 1951; repr. 1972, New Delhi, India: Sagar Publications), 95–100.

7. William G. Benham, *The Laws of Scientific Hand Reading* (New York: Hawthorne Books, 1974), 408–9.

8. Ibid.

9. Scheimann and Altman, *Medical Palmistry*, 86.

## CHAPTER 21. ALTERATIONS IN THE HAND

1. Mark E. Silverman and J. Willis Hurst, "The Hand and the Heart," *American Journal of Cardiology* 22 (November 1968): 718–19.

2. Eugene Scheimann, *A Doctor's Guide to Better Health through Palmistry* (West Nyack, NY: Parker Publishing, 1969), 49.

3. Max Ellenberg, "Diabetic Neuropathy of the Upper Extremities," *Journal of Mount Sinai Hospital* (March–April 1968).

4. "Diabetes: Disabling Disease to Double by 2050. At a Glance 2008," Chronic Disease Prevention and Health Promotion, Centers for Disease Control and Prevention, Department of Health and Human Services, 2008.

5. Editors of the *Journal of the American Medical Association*, *Journal of the American Medical Association* (December 20, 1965).

6. R. L. Dobson et al., "Palmar Keratosis and Cancer," *Archives of Dermatology* 92, no. 5 (November 1965): 553–56.

7. J. Cuzick et al., "Palmar Keratosis of the Bladder and Lung," *Lancet* (March 10, 1984): 530–33.

8. Eugene Scheimann, *A Doctor's Guide to Better Health through Palmistry* (West Nyack, NY: Parker Publishing, 1969), 57.

9. Eugene Scheimann and Nathaniel Altman, *Medical Palmistry* (Wellingborough, UK: Aquarian Press, 1989), 29.

10. Ibid., p. 30

## Chapter 22. Diseases of Anxiety Traced through Palmistry

1. "Emotions and Disease: Stress and Deprivation," History of Medicine Division, National Library of Medicine, National Institutes of Health, Washington, DC. http://www.nlm.nih.gov/hmd/emotions/stress.html [Site was accessed on April 26, 2009]

2. William H. Sheldon, *Atlas of Men* (New York: Macmillan, 1970).

3. M. Koleva et al., "Somatotype and Disease Prevalence in Adults," *Reviews on Environmental Health* 17, no. 1 (January–March 2002): 65–82.

4. Leland E. Hinsie, MD, *Understandable Psychiatry* (New York: Macmillan, 1948), 12.

5. David Henderson et al., *Henderson and Gillespie's Text Book of Psychiatry* (London: Oxford University Press, 1962).

6. Charlotte Wolff, *The Human Hand* (New York: Alfred A. Knopf, 1943; repr. 1972, New Delhi, India: Sagar Publications), 124.

7. Ibid., 140.

8. S. D. Anisman and J. M. Joelson, "Left Main Coronary Artery Dissection Associated with Emotional Stress," *Disease-a-Month* 52, no. 6 (June 2006): 227–53; M. Egred et al., "Myocardial Infarction in Young Adults," *Postgraduate Medical Journal* 81 (2005): 741–45; "Emotional Stress and Coronary Disease," *British Medical Journal* (March 19, 1960): 866–68.

9. Eugene Scheimann and Nathaniel Altman, *Medical Palmistry* (Wellingborough, UK: Aquarian Press, 1989), 160–61.

10. Ibid., 161–62.

11. Eugene Scheimann, *Sex Can Save Your Heart and Life* (New York: Crown Publishers, 1961), 160–61.

## Chapter 24. Lines, Mounts, and Career Choice

1. Nathaniel Altman and Andrew Fitzherbert, *Career, Success and Self-Fulfilment: How Scientific Hand Analysis Can Change Your Life* (Wellingborough, UK: Aquarian Press, 1988), 44.

2. Katherine St. Hill, *The Book of the Hand: A Scientific Guide to Palmistry* (New York: Freeway Press, 1974).

## Chapter 26. Creative Hands

1. "David Manzur Paints a Picture," Facets Multimedia, 1965, http://www.facets.org. [Site was accessed on April 26, 2009]

## Chapter 27. Communicating Hands

1. Julius Spier, *The Hands of Children* (London: Routledge and Kegan Paul, 1955), 26.

2. Nathaniel Altman and Andrew Fitzherbert, *Career, Success and Self-Fulfilment: How Scientific Hand Analysis Can Change Your Life* (Wellingborough, UK: Aquarian Press, 1988), 118.

## Chapter 28. Entertaining Hands

1. "Heywood McGriff, a Dancer," *New York Times*, online edition, May 14, 1994. http://www.nytimes.com/1994/05/14/obituaries/heywood-mcgriff-a-dancer-36.html [Site was accessed on April 26, 2009]

2. Beryl B. Hutchinson, *Your Life in Your Hands* (London: Neville Spearman, 1967), 117.

3. Ibid., p. 26.

4. John Lindsay, personal communication.

5. Hutchinson, *Your Life in Your Hands*, 27.

## Chapter 32. Your Hand and the Spiritual Life

1. John C. Pierrakos, *Creative Aspects of the Ego* (New York: Institute for the New Age of Man, 1977), 11.

## Chapter 33. How to Read Hands

1. Stephen Arroyo, *Astrology, Psychology, and the Four Elements* (Davis, CA: CRCS Publications, 1975), 52.

# ANNOTATED BIBLIOGRAPHY

Following are a number of books I personally recommend for the serious student of palmistry. Some have been mentioned in the text.

Benham, William G. *The Laws of Scientific Hand Reading*. New York: Putnam, 1958. First published in 1900, this book remains one of the all-time palmistry classics. It has frequently been reprinted by various publishers in the United States and India.

Brandon-Jones, David. *Practical Palmistry*. London: Rider, 1981. An excellent book on the fundamentals of hand analysis.

Fitzherbert, Andrew. *Hand Psychology*. New York: Avery, 1988. A fine book about how palmistry can help in solving life's everyday problems.

Gale, Marion. *Read His Hands, Know His Heart: Use the Secrets of Hand Reading for a Better Relationship with Your Man*. Philadelphia: Running Press, 2005. A well-written book with accompanying cards that allow users to "diagnose" their hands (and those of their partners) and read about the corresponding personality traits.

Gettings, Fred. *The Book of the Hand*. London: Paul Hamlyn, 1965. This comprehensive book has excellent graphics and accurate information.

Hipskind, Judith. *Palmistry: The Whole View*. MN: St. Paul: Llewellyn, 1977. One of several excellent palmistry books by a highly competent hand analyst.

Hutchinson, Beryl. *Your Life in Your Hands*. London: Neville Spearman, 1967. An excellent book by a pioneer researcher in skin ridges.

Jaquin, Noel. *The Hand of Man*. London: Faber and Faber, 1933. A classic text on the psychological aspects of hand analysis written by one of the world's foremost authorities of palmistry. Reprinted by Sagar Publications in India.

McCue, Donna. *Your Fate Is in Your Hands: Using the Principles of Palmistry to Change Your Life*. New York: Pocket Books, 2000. An entertaining yet practical book about how palmistry can change one's life.

Sen, K. C. *Hast samudrika shastra*. Bombay: D. B. Taraporevala, 1960. An excellent book about the Indian approach to palmistry.

Unger, Richard, *Lifeprints: Deciphering Your Life Purpose from Your Fingerprints* (Berkeley: Crossing Press, 2007). A fascinating book about how understanding fingerprint patterns can help us discover what we are meant to do in life.

For the more advanced researcher, I recommend the two books by the late Dr. Charlotte Wolff:

*The Human Hand* (New York: Alfred A. Knopf, 1943) and *The Hand in Psychological Diagnosis* (London: Metheun, 1951). Both of these books have been reprinted in India by Sagar Publications.

Of course, I also recommend the other books I have written or coauthored on palmistry. Some include:

*The Little Giant Encyclopedia of Palmistry*. New York: Sterling Publishing, 1999. In addition to an introduction to Western palmistry, this book includes sections on both Chinese and Indian palmistry traditions.

*Medical Palmistry* (with Eugene Scheimann, MD). Wellingborough, UK: Aquarian Press, 1989. This is a revised and updated edition of Dr. Scheimann's classic work, *A Doctor's Guide to Better Health through Palmistry*. West Nyack, NY: Parker Publishing, 1969.

*Palmistry: Your Career in Your Hands* (with Andrew Fitzherbert). Wellingborough, UK: Aquarian Press, 1988.

*Sexual Palmistry*. Avon, MA: Adams Media, 2003. The most recent edition of this title, originally published by Aquarian Press in 1986.

Other books used in my research for this volume include:

Aristotle. *Chiromantia*. Ulm: Johann Reger, 1490.

Arroyo, Stephen. *Astrology, Psychology and the Four Elements*. Davis, CA: CRCS Publications, 1975.

Bacher, Elman. *Studies in Astrology*. Oceanside, CA: Rosicrucian Fellowship, 1962.

Benham, William G. *How to Choose Vocations from the Hand*. New Delhi: Sagar Publications, 1967.

Colomar, Orencia. *Quirología*. Barcelona: Plaza y Janés, 1973.

Federal Bureau of Investigation. *The Science of Fingerprints*. Washington, DC: U.S. Department of Justice, 1984.

Gaafar, M. M. *Ilm-ul-Kaff*. Bombay: D. B. Taraporevala, 1964.

Heron-Allen, Edward. *The Science of the Hand*. London: Ward, Lock, 1886.

Issberner-Haldane, Ernest. *El diagnóstico por la mano y el diagnóstico por la uña*. Buenos Aires: Editorial Kier, 1966.

Issberner-Haldane, Ernest. *Tratado de quirosofía*. Buenos Aires: Editorial Kier, 1966.

Jaquin, Noel. *The Signature of Time*. London: Faber and Faber, 1950.

MacKensie, Nancy. *Palmistry for Women*. New York: Warner Books, 1973.

Meier, Nellie Simmons. *Lion's Paws*. New York: Barrows Mussey, 1937.

Napier, John. *Hands*. New York: Pantheon Books, 1980.

Raschig, Marianne. *Hand und Persönlichkeit*. Hamburg: Gebrüder Enoch Verlag, 1931.

Révész, Gesa. *The Human Hand*. London: Routledge and Kegan Paul, 1958.

Robinson, Mrs. [A.] *The Graven Palm*. London: Herbert Jenkins, 1924.

Rosenblum, Bernard. *The Astrologer's Guide to Counseling*. Reno, NV: CRCS Publications, 1983.

Sorell, Walter. *The Story of the Human Hand*. Indianapolis, IN: Bobbs Merrill, 1967.

Spier, Julius. *The Hands of Children*. London: Routledge and Kegan Paul, 1955.

# INDEX